France's Overseas Frontier

To Marie-Aline de Lavau
RA

To Kathryn
JC

Other books by Robert Aldrich
Economy and Society in Burgundy since 1850 (1984)
The French Presence in the South Pacific, 1842–1940 (1990)

With Frank B. Tipton
An Economic and Social History of Europe, 1890–1939 (1987)
An Economic and Social History of Europe since 1940 (1987)

Other books by John Connell
The End of Tradition (1978)
Taim Bilong Mani: the Evolution of Agriculture in a Solomon Island Society (1978)
New Caledonia or Kanaky? The Political History of a French Colony (1987)

Edited by Robert Aldrich and John Connell
France in World Politics (1989)

FRANCE'S OVERSEAS FRONTIER

DÉPARTEMENTS ET TERRITOIRES D'OUTRE-MER

Robert Aldrich

Associate Professor of Economic History
University of Sydney

John Connell

Associate Professor of Geography
University of Sydney

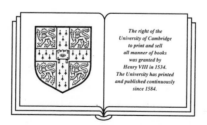

The right of the
University of Cambridge
to print and sell
all manner of books
was granted by
Henry VIII in 1534.
The University has printed
and published continuously
since 1584.

CAMBRIDGE UNIVERSITY PRESS
Cambridge   New York   Port Chester
Melbourne   Sydney

Published by the Press Syndicate of the University of Cambridge
The Pitt Building, Trumpington Street, Cambridge CB2 1RP, UK
40 West 20th Street, New York, NY 10011-4211, USA
10 Stamford Road, Oakleigh, Victoria 3166, Australia

Printed in Hong Kong by Colorcraft

National Library of Australia cataloguing-in-publication data:
Aldrich, Robert, 1954–
France's overseas frontier.
Bibliography.
Includes index.
ISBN 0 521 39061 3.
1. France — Colonies. I. Connell, John,
1946–   . II. Title.
325.344

British Library cataloguing-in-publication data:
Aldrich, Robert 1954–
France's overseas frontier.
1. France. Colonial administration, history
I. Title
325.3144
ISBN 0 521 39061 3

Library of Congress cataloging-in-publication data:
Aldrich, Robert, 1954–
France's overseas frontier: Départements et territoires
d'outre-mer / Robert Aldrich, John Connell.
Includes bibliographical references and index.
ISBN 0-521-39061-3
1. France — Territories and possessions — Economic conditions.
2. France — Territories and possessions — Social conditions.
3. France — Territories and possessions — Politics and government.
I. Connell, John. II. Title. III. Title: Départements et
territoires d'outre-mer.
HC276.3.A64   1991
909'.0971244 — dc20

Contents

Maps

Tables

Preface

THERE IS no single study of the history, politics and contemporary socioeconomic structure of what remains of France's overseas empire — the *départements et territoires d'outre-mer*, or DOM-TOMs. Material on the DOM-TOMs is rare in English (although several recent books have looked at French Polynesia and New Caledonia). In French, coverage is dispersed among various theses, highly specialised journals and official publications which are not easily accessible even within France. This book therefore represents the first full-scale academic treatment of the DOM-TOMs. Without claiming to be an in-depth study of each of the DOM-TOMs, it examines the historical evolution and socioeconomic structure of the DOM-TOMs and assesses their contemporary political and economic importance to France, the genesis of nationalist movements and the impact of France on the evolution of its distant territories. It also explores the phenomenon of the DOM-TOMs in a theoretical sense, to examine whether the DOM-TOMs represent the 'failure' or the 'end' of French decolonisation or quite different paths of decolonisation from the more usual one towards independence. The results of this analysis suggest that existing ideas on the theory and practice of decolonisation must be modified to take account of the particular situation of these remnants of empire.

One or both of us has completed work on the DOM-TOMs in Martinique, Guadeloupe, Réunion, French Polynesia, Wallis and Futuna and New Caledonia, and we have also done substantial research in Paris. Various research institutes, government offices and individual scholars in the *métropole*, the DOM-TOMs and elsewhere have kindly helped us in our study. We have benefited as well from the research assistance of Olivia de Bergerac and Ayling Rubin, funded by a grant from the Australian Research Council to Robert Aldrich. John Raven-hill read and commented on the work before its publication. Julie Manley and Kay Foster typed the manuscript, John Roberts and Peter Johnson prepared the maps, and Sharon Davidson assisted with the index. Thank you to all of them.

Robert Aldrich
John Connell

1

Overseas France

THE TROUBLES which wracked New Caledonia in the late 1980s, the controversy about French nuclear testing on the atoll of Mururoa in the Pacific, the periodic launching of satellites from French Guiana (Guyane) and even the 'cod war' between France and Canada over fishing rights near Saint-Pierre and Miquelon have intermittently brought the existence of the French *départements et territoires d'outre-mer* (DOM-TOMs), France's overseas outposts, into a wider focus. The ten DOM-TOMs are strategically scattered around the world in the Atlantic, Caribbean, Pacific and Indian Oceans and in Antarctica. Despite their distance from France, the metropolitan 'hexagon', the *départements d'outre-mer* (DOMs), are legally as much a part of France as Paris or Marseille. The DOMs, at least in theory, have institutions and legal systems that replicate those of the *métropole*; the *territoires d'outre-mer* (TOMs), although enjoying greater autonomy and particularistic institutions, are also legally part of the French Republic. Many of the DOM-TOMs have been part of France much longer than Nice and Corsica. The remnants of France's once vast overseas empires, they account for a population of one and a half million French citizens and cover a land area of over 120,000 square kilometres, even excluding the French region of Antarctica. With the recognition of exclusive economic zones in the Law of the Sea agreements, the DOM-TOMs give France the third-largest maritime area in the world.[1]

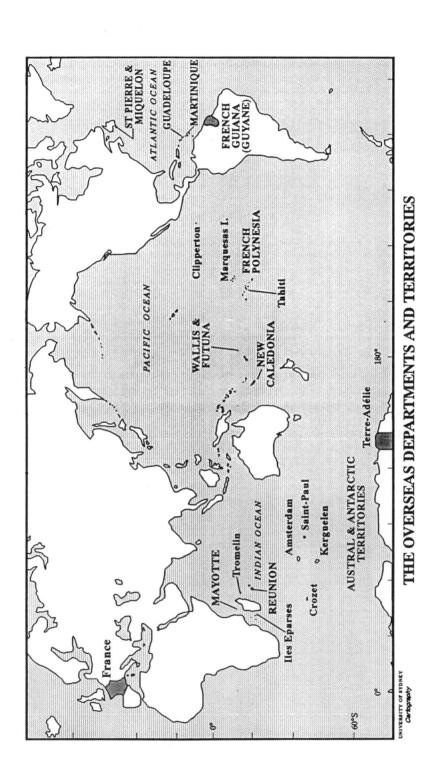

THE OVERSEAS DEPARTMENTS AND TERRITORIES

UNIVERSITY OF SYDNEY
Cartography

Table 1. French Overseas Territories

Territory	Population 1988	Area (sq. kms)	Date of first establishment of French control
Départements			
French Guiana (Guyane)	90,200	91,000	1630s
Guadeloupe and Dependencies[a]	337,500	1,780	1630s
Martinique	335,100	1,100	1630s
Réunion[b]	569,600	2,510	1630s
Territoires			
French Polynesia[c]	188,814	4,000	1842
New Caledonia and Dependencies[d]	164,173 (1989)	19,000	1853
Wallis and Futuna	14,500	274	1887
TAAF[e]	—		late 1800s
Collectivités Territoriales			
Saint-Pierre and Miquelon	6,041 (1982)	242	1763
Mayotte	about 72,000	375	1843

a. Includes Marie-Galante, La Désirade, Les Saintes, Saint-Barthélémy and the French part of Saint-Martin.

b. The Iles Eparses in the Mozambique Channel (the Glorieuses group, Juan de Nova, Europa, Bassas da India) and also the contested Tromelin reef east of Madagascar are administered by the prefect of Réunion.

c. The unoccupied island of Clipperton is administered by the High Commissioner of French Polynesia.

d. The major dependencies of New Caledonia are the Loyalty Islands and the Isle of Pines.

e. The TAAF, the Terres Australes et Antarctiques Françaises, include Terre Adélie, the French part of Antarctica, and the islands of Crozet, Kerguelen, Saint-Paul and Amsterdam in the southern Indian Ocean.

The smallest of the DOM-TOMs in area and population (Table 1) is Saint-Pierre and Miquelon, off the coast of Newfoundland, two small islands which France retained in the 1700s when it lost its formidable North American empire to Britain. In the Caribbean lie the relatively large islands of Martinique and Guadeloupe, as well as much smaller Saint-Barthélémy further north and half of Saint-Martin, the smallest island in the world to be divided between colonial powers, France and the Netherlands. Martinique and Guadeloupe were plantation colonies of the 1600s, and France bought Saint-Barthélémy from Sweden in the 1800s.[2] Guyane is an enormous but sparsely populated part of the northeastern coast of South America, which only officially became a French possession in 1816.[3] Two French islands lie in the western Indian Ocean: Réunion, also an old sugar colony, like the *vieilles colonies* of the Caribbean, and Mayotte in the Comoros archipelago.

The three French overseas territories are all in the South Pacific: the five archipelagos dominated by Tahiti, which make up French Polynesia; New Caledonia and its outlying islands; and the small territory of Wallis and Futuna, the last of the three to be claimed, in virtually the final phases of global colonialism in the nineteenth century. The French Austral and Antarctic Territories (TAAF) are composed of several intermittently populated islands off the coast of Antarctica, as well as the French zone of the Antarctic continent. Finally, France also possesses several other uninhabited islands in the Mozambique channel between Madagascar and the African coast, and Clipperton, an island lying off the Pacific coast of Mexico, which, after disputes with Mexico, international arbitration awarded to France in 1931.

Most of the French population take little notice of the DOM-TOMs, except when a dramatic or controversial development, such as the political discord in New Caledonia in the 1980s, brings them to the front pages of daily newspapers, and most textbooks on French history, geography and politics wholly ignore them. Wallis and Futuna, Saint-Pierre and Miquelon, Mayotte and the TAAF, in particular, are little known to the French public. Guyane is known only for the space station, its vast jungle, the history of the penal colony, popularly if erroneously known as 'Devil's Island', gold-mining and Cayenne pepper. Martinique, Guadeloupe and Réunion are better known because of the presence of numerous migrants from these islands in metropolitan France and because Martinique and Guadeloupe, along with Tahiti, enjoy a reputation as pleasant vacation spots.

In fact, the most common image of the French tropical islands is that of sun and sea, exoticism and holidays. Tourist brochures promote the image, such as the one which says of the Antilles:

Martinique and Guadeloupe welcome you to an exotic world with a magical name: the Caribbean. They are a tropical carnival. The scenery: majestic volcanoes, tropical forests, shimmering lagoons and grand plantations. The participants: the people and the infectious *joie de vivre*, dances and music. And you, come to the carnival . . . Let us show you paradise . . . Be tempted. Each island is an adventure.[4]

Such advertising promotes the idea of the DOM-TOMs as places for play and relaxation, with warm climates and pretty beaches, exotic foods and music, but familiar French language and customs.

Other observers create different images for the DOM-TOMs. Political activists in France, and beyond, consider them either the vestiges of an outdated and rapacious colonialism or, conversely, trump cards which France can play to maintain its diverse political, economic, strategic and cultural influence in world affairs. For legal scholars the DOM-TOMs provide interesting cases of sometimes contested overseas sovereignty. For other researchers they provide domains for study of such topics as economic development and dependency, the mix of ethnic and racial groups, and international relations. Above all the mere presence of the DOM-TOMs seems an extraordinary anomaly after decades of decolonisation which have seen most colonial powers rid themselves of their overseas possessions.

A fundamental question which the existence of the DOM-TOMs poses for most observers is why France has held on to these small, scattered and expensive possessions while other colonial powers have granted similar colonies independence. Of all France's colonies, the four *vieilles colonies* of Guadeloupe, Martinique, Guyane and Réunion are the oldest, the possessions through which France demonstrated its early imperial powers. For centuries they were almost indistinguishable from other nearby colonies, all of which have now become independent. The later acquisitions are also surrounded by other states which gained independence from their colonial masters, and in some of the DOM-TOMs pro-independence groups unsuccessfully campaign for a similar status. The answer to continued dependent status lies in a complicated set of constitutional, socioeconomic, political and strategic considerations which are often part of more general questions about France's history and politics. Analysis of these issues points the way towards understanding whether the DOM-TOMs represent the failure of French decolonisation, a refusal to decolonise, or a different sort of decolonisation, centred on integration with the *métropole*. Are the DOM-TOMs unique, are they similar to the overseas territories of other colonial powers which have retained their links with the centre, or are they like the independent island micro-states?

Traditional analysts have usually interpreted events in the DOM-TOMs largely in terms of their relations with France, often either to condemn or to justify the continuation of that relationship. But there also exists an internal dynamic in each of the DOM-TOMs, a particular structure of politics, economics and society which is influenced by the duration of attachment to France, the mix of different populations, cultures and resources, and disparities between the standard of living in the French islands and neighbouring states. The diversity of the DOM-TOMs hinders simple explanations of the relationships between colonialism and development, or the lack of development. Beyond their particular histories, and the international issues which they illuminate, the DOM-TOMs are also relevant to contemporary French politics. In the past few years they have episodically become a topic of animated debate in French public life, an electoral stake, a platform for the espousal of various theories and programmes. The use (and abuse) of the DOM-TOMs by French politicians is suggestive of political currents in France and forms another of the ties that bind the overseas frontier to the mother country.

Despite their diversity, several general characteristics link the DOM-TOMs. The first is their constitutional attachment to France. The *départements d'outre-mer*, Martinique, Guadeloupe, Réunion and Guyane, have the same status as the *départements*, the principal administrative divisions, of metropolitan France. The *territoires d'outre-mer*, French Polynesia, New Caledonia, Wallis and Futuna and the TAAF, are not so totally assimilated into the metropolitan administrative structure; each has a separate legal statute and a certain degree of autonomy. (The TAAF, without a permanent population, and recently New Caledonia, which Paris briefly ruled directly, are special cases.) The third group, the *collectivités territoriales*, composed of Saint-Pierre and Miquelon and Mayotte, are intermediate between a *département* and a *territoire*, with Saint-Pierre resembling the former and Mayotte the latter. But in the case of both DOMs and TOMs, the parliament in Paris is the ultimate source of legislation: Paris controls many areas of policy and appoints a representative to carry out its orders (a prefect in the DOMs, a High Commissioner or other administrator in the TOMs). The French law code and administrative structure in the DOMs is almost identical to that of the *métropole* and very similar in the TOMs. The DOMs, Saint-Pierre and Mayotte all use French currency, and the French Pacific franc used in the Pacific territories is freely convertible at a fixed exchange rate with the metropolitan franc. The systems of education are likewise generally identical for DOMs, TOMs and the *métropole*. France provides lavish financial support for the infrastructure and bureaucracy of each of the DOM-TOMs. All areas of political and commercial life in France and the overseas regions are closely linked. Obvious disparities do occur, as popular images suggest; the majority of the population of Mayotte is Muslim and enjoys the right to polygamy, the three customary chiefs (or 'kings') of Wallis and Futuna retain an important role and the Catholic religion is a key element in primary school education there — but overseas France otherwise provides a mirror, albeit sometimes grossly distorted, of the mother country.

Insularity is a second characteristic of the DOM-TOMs. All are archipelagos or islands, except for the French section of Antarctica and Guyane. Guyane, however, composed of a long coastal band of settlement on the edge of the vast Amazonian forest, displays a marked insularity of its own. So too does French Antarctica and the nearby islands. Insularity implies a degree of isolation, distance from the *métropole*, and sometimes inhospitable landscapes. The coral atolls and volcanic islands of the Pacific, the wind-swept Austral Islands, semi-arid Mayotte and Saint-Pierre are unpropitious for most forms of contemporary economic development. The Pacific territories are literally on the other side of the world from France, 18,000 kilometres distant. The archipelagos of French Polynesia cover a sea area as large as Europe, and even communications within the country are sometimes difficult. Futuna is often isolated from Wallis. Saint-Pierre can be reached from France only by changing planes in Canada, Mayotte only by going via Réunion or the Comoros — and it costs as much to fly from Réunion to Mayotte, or from Papeete to the Marquesas, as from Paris to New York. Jet travel, international communications systems and other advances of technology have diminished the isolation of the French DOM-TOMs, but insularity — perhaps psychological and cultural, as much as physical — has posed its own problems.

Insularity and small size especially have contributed to the economic dependency which also characterises the DOM-TOMs. In most of the DOM-TOMs, exports cover only about 15 per cent of imports. The DOM-TOMs consume French and foreign goods yet produce very little. The nickel of New Caledonia, the rum and exotic fruits of the tropical islands, timber from Guyane and the cod of Saint-Pierre make up a limited range of exportable commodities, and several DOM-TOMs sell their sun and sea to eager tourists, but all are economically dependent on the metropole. They have become transfer economies or consumer colonies. This situation is, in some respects, little different from that of a number of recently independent states which rely over-whelmingly on aid payments from international organisations or national donors. However, the links between the DOM-TOMs and France make possible the high standard of living which the residents of the DOM-TOMs enjoy by comparison with their neighbours and re-inforce a perceived need to maintain those links, notwithstanding their 'colonial' nature.

Another general characteristic of the DOM-TOMs, with the minor exception of such small islands as Saint-Pierre, Saint-Barthélémy, and to some extent, Mayotte and Wallis and Futuna, is their multicultural nature. In the Antilles, Réunion and French Polynesia, intermarriage between different ethnic groups has produced a large group of residents with a mixed racial background, groups which now hold the reins of political power in those regions. In most of the DOM-TOMs there are long-established European settlers. The most obvious settler colony, and the only one in the island Pacific, is New Caledonia, where some settler families have lived for as long as six or more generations. In the West Indies and Réunion, the co-called *Békés* formed a powerful white caste from as early as the 1600s. Other contemporary French residents are a mixture of descendants of the penal colonies in Guyane and New Caledonia and long-established metropolitan public servants. In the Pacific, the indigenous Melanesians and Polynesians remain dominant ethnic groups, though there has been a large immigration of Indonesians, Vietnamese and Chinese. In Guyane the indigenous population, like the Melanesians of New Caledonia, have become a minority in their own land. The Caribbean islands and Réunion were unpopulated when France annexed them, except for a population of Indians in the Antilles (who were quickly eliminated), so they have a non-native population based largely on African stock. The various racial and cultural groups of the DOM-TOMs do not always cohabit harmoniously and, in New Caledonia at least, racial questions have marked political debates.

Discontent with the structure of administrative control from Paris, economic dependence on France and ethnic conflict have fuelled political movements in each of the DOM-TOMs (with the partial exceptions of Saint-Pierre and Wallis and Futuna) calling for a change in status. Groups ranging across the political and ideological spectrum have demanded redress of various grievances and recognition of cultural identity, producing variants of 'nationalism' from the Caribbean to Polynesia. In most of the DOM-TOMs, politicians have claimed greater autonomy, administrative decentralisation and sometimes outright independence. For both advocates and opponents, the possibility of independence provides a challenge for the DOM-TOMs, and this has inflamed passions and served as a constant debating point in political campaigns. Nowhere is this more true than New Caledonia, where the demand for an independent Kanaky has been particularly strident and has fostered episodes of violence. Elsewhere the 'Caledonian contagion' has been generally feared or less frequently welcomed. Defusing, accommodating or opposing autonomist and pro-independence groups has been a central aim in Paris' policy in the DOM-TOMs. Yet independence is certainly not inevitable and, indeed, is probably unlikely for any of the DOM-TOMs, at least in the foreseeable future.

For their promoters, the importance of the DOM-TOMs is almost unbounded. For Jean Maran, a centrist *député* from Martinique, the DOM-TOMs

represent a not insignificant market of more than a million people. France exports its primary produce and manufactured goods according to local needs, and this is not without implications for French commerce and industry. Furthermore, France imports raw materials and agricultural and manufac-

tured products . . . Finally, the expanses of seas and oceans surrounding the
DOM-TOMs present considerable economic prospects.

Maran also sees a political significance in the DOM-TOMs:

The DOM-TOMs not only . . . provide an appreciable number of votes for
various elected governments. France has begun a new experiment that is an
example for many other countries; France is the only global power to have
granted full citizenship in these former colonies, by giving them the status of
départements and *territoires* and according full constitutional rights there.

Furthermore, the DOM-TOMs have a great value in spreading French
cultural influence:

These *départements* and *territoires* at the gates of America, Africa and the
Pacific provide France with bases from which it can certainly spread its political influence, but also demonstrate its economic, artistic, intellectual and
technological achievements.

The DOM-TOMs are also important militarily:

The location of the DOM-TOMs gives France a great strategic advantage.
They enable it to be present on the great world trade and communication
routes. They provide a much envied space centre in Guyane, a nuclear testing
site in French Polynesia, and commercial and naval ports in Martinique,
Guadeloupe and Réunion.[5]

Many of Maran's colleagues in the French parliament agree. Senator
Albert Ramassamy of Réunion sees the basic force of the DOM-TOMs
as 'centres for the diffusion of French culture', while for Senator Paul
Moreau of Réunion, the DOM-TOMs 'assure the nation a more than
symbolic presence in all of the world's regions and particularly in the
most strategic ocean areas.' For Senator Marcel Henry of Mayotte the
DOM-TOMs 'show France's real face as a multi-racial society, frater-
nal and generous', while 'the ability of our country to maintain and
reinforce its ties with the most distant populations demonstrates the
power of the French idea of nationality'.[6]

By contrast those who favour independence view attachment to
France as no more than an unfortunate accident of history, a brief
colonial era that must be left behind to enable genuine aspirations to
surface and national development to be achieved. Nationalist movements in the DOM-TOMs have been constructed around the need to

rediscover and enact traditions and culture, restore land rights (especially in New Caledonia) and combine the virtues of the old ways with the best of modern developments to forge new nations. Jean-Marie Tjibaou, the late leader of the New Caledonian independence movement, the Front de Libération Nationale Kanake et Socialiste (FLNKS), for example, sought to restructure colonial society completely:

When we speak of Kanak Socialist independence we want institutions which reflect the Melanesian approach to their heritage, their property and their resources. Equally there is a Melanesian approach to the management of their patrimony, to small or medium-sized enterprises, and there is a Melanesian way of viewing the distribution of work, welfare, social services and the environment so that the country may have a soul which comes from itself and not elsewhere.[7]

Yet even there the FLNKS has not sought to break off all ties with France; language and religion are culturally entrenched and economic autarky is impossible. In the *vieilles colonies* especially, ties to the *métropole* have become so pervasive that nationalist movements have taken quite different forms.

The statements of politicians such as Ramassamy and Maran, convinced of the virtues of continued ties with France, provide some answers to the question of why France has maintained its sovereignty in the DOM-TOMs. By contrast critics such as Jean-Marie Tjibaou charge that these characterisations represent the structure of absolute colonialism, not merely a more gentle, benevolent colonialism in new clothes. The commitment with which both advocates and opponents of the continued status of the DOM-TOMs voice their sentiments indicates how the French *départements et territoires d'outre-mer* provide extraordinarily rich case studies of the manner in which decolonisation and dependency remain crucial issues in large parts of the world. In some respects the DOM-TOMs are 'little Frances' across the seas, microcosms of the post-industrial, multiracial society that is emerging in France itself. In other respects they are quite different worlds, each unique, with a sense of identity and interest that often challenges the ties that bind France to these remote corners of the world. From being forgotten corners of the empire, the DOM-TOMs have emerged onto centre stage. The tumult in New Caledonia, the dreams of vast oceanic mineral resources, the increasing importance of such regions as the South Pacific and the Indian Ocean, in the eyes of advocates and opponents of French control, point to the significance of the DOM-TOMs. Such events have shaken them out of a tropical torpor, away from the *joie de vivre* and relaxation of the tourist brochures. The complexity of the issues that confront DOM-TOM politicians and those in France challenge simplistic rhetoric about 'colonialism' or 'national liberation'. These far-flung relics of French expansionism now pose important questions about the future of France itself.

2

The Colonial Heritage

FRANCE'S TEN overseas departments and territories are the remains of more than four centuries of imperial expansion and contraction which, at various times, gave France sovereignty over large
areas of North America, Africa and Asia, as well as, more briefly, much
of the European continent and the East Indies. Since at least the time of
the Crusades, French voyagers have moved outwards to explore, trade,
proselytise, settle and sometimes to conquer. In the 1500s and 1600s
France put together its first empire, centred in the Antilles but including parts of eastern Canada and the Mississippi basin and outposts in
Africa and India. Most of this empire was lost to England in the 1700s.
Then, from the early 1800s, after the defeat of Napoleon's ambitions
for a Levantine or a Continental empire, France created a second overseas empire embracing islands in the Pacific and vast domains in Africa
and Asia. At its height in the 1930s, this French empire counted some
12 million square kilometres of territory and almost 68 million subjects
alongside 1.5 million French settlers. Later in the twentieth century,
France relinquished almost all its vast second empire through decolonisation, sometimes easily, sometimes very painfully.

The ten DOM-TOMs are the legacy that history has left to France
far beyond its European shores. Though they are certainly not the only
regions where France maintains a political, economic and cultural
presence, they are now the only territories outside Europe over which
Paris exercises legal sovereignty. Their importance to France, and the

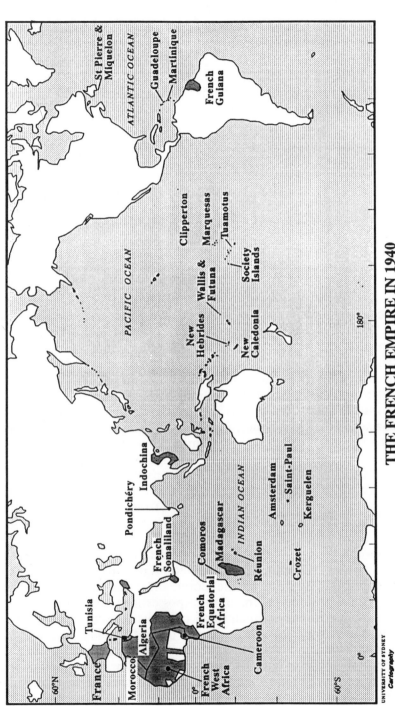

THE FRENCH EMPIRE IN 1940

particular socioeconomic structures which each displays must be understood, therefore, in the context of four hundred years of French expansion overseas and the contraction of those overseas empires. This chapter recapitulates the colonial history of France, the acquisition of the domains that are now the DOM-TOMs and the French experience of decolonisation.

THE FIRST OVERSEAS EMPIRE

The acquisition of the *vieilles colonies* — Martinique, Guadeloupe, Guyane and Réunion — dates from the period of the first French overseas empire.[1] From the 1500s onwards, French navigators travelled across the Atlantic to the New World and sailed southwards around the African continent. Exploration combined with commercial interests, hopes for an El Dorado and access to the markets and spices of Asia accessible through a maritime passage. The state-building of the absolutist monarchs and the theories of mercantilist economists inspired the voyages of men like Jacques Cartier, Samuel Champlain and de la Salle. They discovered, and France claimed in the 1500s, areas around the St Lawrence and Hudson Bay, and French colonists settled in what would become Nova Scotia, Newfoundland and Quebec in Canada, and Louisiana and the Mississippi basin further south. In the next century, the French advanced into the Caribbean, taking nominal possession of Saint-Christophe (St Kitts), Martinique and Guadeloupe, Grenada and the Grenadines, Sainte-Lucie (St Lucia), Tobago, Montserrat and various other islands, culminating in the takeover of Saint-Domingue (Haiti), the western half of the island of Hispaniola, in 1665. France's claim on Guyane, on the north coast of South America, also dates from this century. Meanwhile, the French acquired trading stations, forts or outposts in other parts of the world, although they could hardly yet be called colonies: the Bastion de France in North Africa, Saint-Louis, the island of Gorée and the town of Rufisque in Senegal and posts on the Guinea coast, Fort-Dauphin in Madagascar, the Ile Bourbon (Réunion) and the Ile Rodrigues in the Indian Ocean, and several trading posts on the Coromandel and Malabar coasts of India. The most important of all these possessions were the Caribbean islands, whose tropical climates and potential for settlement seemed far more promising than the expanses of cold Canada, that Voltaire dismissed as 'quelques arpents de neige' ('a few acres of snow'), or the tropical jungles of Guyane. And among the Caribbean possessions, the real jewel was Saint-Domingue, the prototype of the plantation colony.

In this outward movement, France competed against its European rivals, particularly Spain and Portugal, which, through a papal bull and the late 1400s Treaty of Tordesillas, claimed a monopoly on the new worlds. One of François I's motivations in expansion was to challenge this Iberian birthright; the French king remarked that the sun shone on him just as on other monarchs, and he would like to see the will in which Adam had divided the overseas world between only two maritime powers. France also had to rival the Dutch, the English, the Danes and the Swedes, all of whom wanted their share of the New World and who jostled over islands in the Caribbean and sometimes over toe-holds on the American continents. The Dutch tried to set up a colony in Brazil and managed a longer-lasting settlement in Manhattan; the other powers picked up various small Caribbean islands. Tiny Saint-Barthélémy became Sweden's only overseas colony. By the late 1600s Britain had established an uneasy coexistence with France in North America, and Spain and Portugal had indeed divided Central and South America except for an English colony in Honduras (Belize) and English, French and Dutch enclaves in the Guyanas.

In the 1700s, France's rapidly assembled empire began to shrink. By the Treaty of Utrecht in 1713, France lost to the British Newfoundland, Acadia and its claims around the Hudson Bay and, at the conclusion of the Seven Years War and the Treaty of Paris in 1763, ceded Quebec and other territories of Canada to England; Spain occupied Louisiana. The treaty also confined the French in India to five unfortified outposts and stifled French hopes for a division of the subcontinent with England. In an effort to compensate for those losses, France acquired several islands in the Indian Ocean, notably the Ile de France (Mauritius) and the Seychelles archipelago.

The empire was further reduced at the end of the eighteenth century with the Revolutionary Wars, during which the English occupied a number of French territories. The Treaty of Amiens in 1802 restored some of them to France, but the continuing Napoleonic Wars resulted in renewed French losses. At the end of the Napoleonic period, France had lost several of its islands in the Caribbean, as well as Mauritius and the Seychelles. Napoleon, in 1803, had already sold the Louisiana territory — which had been given back to France — to the United States. A revolution and the declaration of the world's first black republic and the first independent state in the Caribbean deprived France of Saint-Domingue. At the time of the Restoration, therefore, the French were left with their *vieilles colonies* in the Antilles and the Indian Ocean, the islands of Saint-Pierre and Miquelon off the coast of Canada — which the English had abandoned to the French — and also Guyane, as well as the old outposts in Africa and India. The French empire already seemed reduced to 'confetti', having a somewhat residual character by contrast to the expanses of land over which France had held sovereignty in the 1750s.

The first empire, considered part of the king's domain, enjoyed an ambiguous relationship with France. Initially, colonial enterprises were the endeavours of royally chartered companies, although the crown maintained the right to certain appointments and gradually usurped the companies' rights and annexed the territories. Appointed governors (sometimes called *intendants*), responsible to the king and ministers, then ruled the colonies; as yet there was no Ministry of Colonies, and the coordination of colonial activities was the brief of the Ministry of the Navy. Given the distance from the *métropole* and the specificities of the colonies, governors often ruled in virtual autonomy, but they also clashed with French settlers. In the *ancien régime*, the governor generally was a noble or a military officer, more concerned with national prerogatives than settlers' demands. A small group of public servants assisted him, notably an *ordonnateur* who was second-in-command and held special responsibility for financial matters. Consultative councils of *colons* or municipal governments were not established in the colonies until the 1700s, and then only in selected regions, and colonists continually baulked at Paris' imposition of regulations which they considered disadvantageous to their interests.

Economically, the early colonies were intended for the sole benefit of the mother country. The accepted economic theory of the 1600s and 1700s, mercantilism, put a premium on trade, approved of state intervention to stimulate the economy and argued that each nation must carve out its own sphere of economic domination and exclusive profit. Since possibilities for profit were limited, overseas expansion, and a consequent internationalisation of the economy, were necessary, and each nation had to hold tight to the domains it had conquered. The colonies, therefore, had to be complementary to the mother country, producing only those commodities not available in Europe (and which were generally therefore exotic products, such as sugar and furs). All trade took place with the mother country and national flagships carried all goods. These ideas were embodied in the Edict of Fontainebleau of 1727, which formally inaugurated the *Exclusif*, the economic policy whereby France retained monopoly rights on colonial production, import and export. So strong were these restrictions that some *colons*, such as the Antillais traders, objected, and in 1763, the system was slightly loosened to allow for greater trade between the colonies and foreign countries; this *Exclusif mitigé* endured until the Revolution. Even afterwards, the so-called *pacte colonial* maintained the monopolistic rights of France in the empire until the era of free trade in the 1860s.

When the fiscal bonds loosened, France still maintained strong administrative control of the overseas domains.

PLANTATION ECONOMY AND SOCIETY FROM 1635 TO 1848

The Antilles

The islands of the Antilles were discovered by Christopher Columbus in his westward search for the spice islands.[2] On his first voyage in 1492, Columbus became the first European to visit Madinina, the future Martinique, and on his second trip, the following year, he landed on Karukera, which he renamed Guadeloupe. These lands, as well as the others in the eastern Caribbean, impressed the Spanish sailors with their volcanic mountains and valleys, luxuriant vegetation, good harbours and sparse populations. The chain of islands stretching between North and South America was occupied by Indians, the Arawaks and the Caribs who had migrated from South America. The Arawaks were the first inhabitants; the Caribs, later arrivals who subdued and intermixed with the Arawak population. European settlement of the islands led almost to the extinction of these Indians, who were massacred, died from the diseases brought by the Europeans or fled from the islands of European settlement. Small groups of native Indians from the region survive in Dominica and in Central America, but elsewhere their traces have virtually vanished from anything other than the archaeological record.

The Spanish settled in the east of Hispaniola, in Cuba and in Puerto Rico, and other European nations defied theoretical Spanish sovereignty and established settlements in the Caribbean. The English took Jamaica, Barbados and a host of smaller islands, as well as Bermuda in the western Atlantic. The Dutch established themselves in six islands — Aruba, Bonaire and Curaçao off the coast of South America, Sint-Maarten, Sint-Eustatius and Saba further north, all of which still remain part of the Dutch kingdom. Sweden occupied Saint-Barthélémy, until it sold the island to France in the 1800s; the Danish took over St Thomas, St John and St Croix in the Virgin Islands and kept them until 1917, when they were sold to the United States. Every contemporary colonial power, except Portugal, possessed at least a foothold in the Caribbean.

The first French settlement in the Antilles was in Saint-Christophe, an island which the French shared with the English. From this settlement in the 1620s the first Frenchmen moved to Martinique and

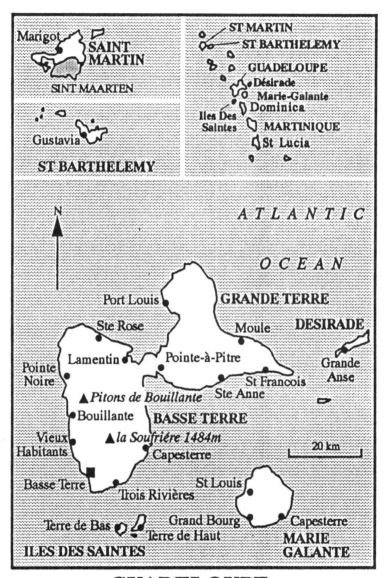

GUADELOUPE

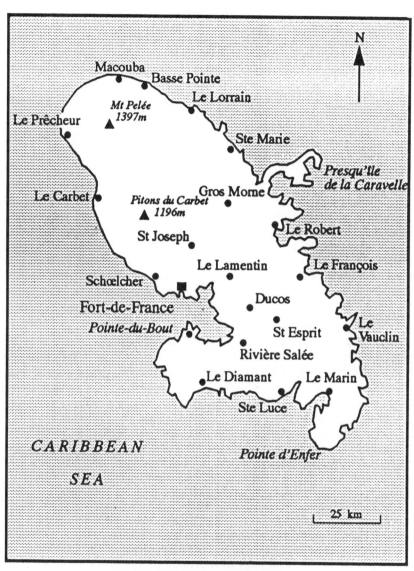

MARTINIQUE

Guadeloupe in 1635. These two islands, and Saint-Domingue, became the centrepiece of France's Caribbean enterprise. Various islands changed hands during the early centuries of colonisation, occupations were often more nominal than real, and divisions of territory sometimes arbitrary; the tiny island of Saint-Martin is the prime example. Both the French and Dutch were interested in the 52-square-kilometre island and, to resolve the dispute, a French and Dutch officer supposedly set off from a common point to walk in opposite directions around the island in order to divide it, as it remains, between the two European powers.

Each of the powers created its colonies in its own image. The Spanish imported Catholicism and constructed baroque buildings in Santo Domingo and Havana; the English set up the western hemisphere's oldest parliament in Bermuda. What tied (and ties) the Caribbean (and Bermuda) together, in addition to a similar geography and climate, was the import of African slaves and the setting up of plantation economies for the growth of tropical products, predominantly, sugar cane.

The first tropical product tried in the Caribbean had been tobacco, in order to satisfy the growing nicotine habit introduced into Europe from the New World. However, the tobacco boom receded as higher-quality and larger crops of tobacco from Virginia and elsewhere in mainland North America created competition. Cotton was also tried, but North America proved more favourably situated for that as well; coffee enjoyed a certain success in such islands as Martinique, and indigo was grown in Saint-Domingue. However, it was sugar that was to make the fortune of the Antilles. Sugar was a luxury food in Europe and, before the development of the process by which sugar could be extracted from beets, supplies depended on vast plantations of cane. The principal by-product, rum, was of great importance as an alcoholic beverage and other by-products, such as molasses, were also in demand.

From the 1660s and 1670s onwards the French Antilles colonies really began to develop, based on direct political stimulation and the expansion of the sugar economy. Much of the credit went to the French finance minister, Colbert. Colbert was an economic genius: he reformed France's financial system, set up royal factories, acquired a navy, and perhaps above all, he saw in the colonies a way to challenge the power of France's rivals, increase the prestige of the Sun King and develop a profitable and exclusive source of coveted products for the nation. Previously, the West Indian economies had attracted little interest in Paris, but Colbert, through a new Compagnie des Indes Occidentales charted in 1664, took over the islands which had largely been the possessions of private individuals. Colbert also encouraged the production of cane, introduced into the French islands (and elsewhere in the Caribbean, especially Barbados) in the 1650s. Holland was then the major European sugar producer, and Colbert, fighting the Franco-Dutch War, saw an opportunity for France to surpass its competitor. By the 1680s, his ambition fulfilled, France was Europe's largest producer of sugar.

The West Indies was perfect for sugar production; the soil was fertile and despite mountain ranges in most of the islands, enough land was available.[3] The warm, wet climate allowed cane to be grown through-out the year. Growing cane did not involve much equipment or technical prowess, but did demand a large and cheap labour force to do the back-breaking work of cutting the cane in torrid tropical weather and then processing it. The heat, it was thought, was a bar to Euro-peans' working the cane fields; such work was considered degrading and dangerous, since cane-cutters could easily be injured by knives, bruised by the stalks of cane, or have limbs amputated in the machines which crushed the cane to extract the juice. After the extermination of the local Indian populations a new source of labour had to be found; black Africa provided that manpower.

From the 1500s Europeans had explored the coasts of Africa by ship and taken the first hostages back to Europe, a contact which began the infamous slave trade. The slave trade came into its own in the 1600s, focused on the Caribbean and such South American regions as Brazil and the southern colonies of English North America. Until the out-lawing of the trade in the 1800s, millions of Africans were forcibly shipped to the western hemisphere, including 1.6 million to the French West Indies and 1.7 million to the British Caribbean. Slaving ships from European nations procured slaves from the various tribes of western Africa as far south as Angola; some were taken hostage, others were acquired from local chieftains willing to sell off prisoners from wars with rival tribes. The Isle of Gorée, off the coast of present-day Senegal, became the great entrepôt for this trade in human flesh. In the 1600s was created a 'triangular trade' of slaves from Africa, tropical products from the New World and manufactured goods from Europe. Great profits were made, and few worried about the moral questions implied in slaving. The gruesome story of this slave trade is familiar — the capturing and loading of the human cargo into the ships, the pain-ful crossing of the Atlantic, during which as many as one-third of the Africans perished, the acclimatisation to the work of the New World, the auctioning of slaves on the block, and the frequent mistreatment and overwork of the Africans on the plantations.

Production of sugar was a relatively simple process. Vast estates (*habitations*) were planted in cane harvested by the slaves. The stalks of cane were then fed into crushers, which pressed out the juice (*vesou*).

Some of the juice (and the foam skimmed off) went to make molasses
and rum; initially a by-product, rum became increasingly important
(especially in Martinique, where it ultimately dominated the economy). The process of sugar refinement became more technologically
sophisticated over time; at the beginning of the colonial period, refinement took place largely on the *habitations*, but later the process was
concentrated in larger refining-plants. Costs for sugar production were
low, profits high, and demand elastic: sugar was the right crop in the
right place at the right time. The pre-eminence of sugar in the Antilles
had a detrimental effect on economic diversification. Auxiliary export
crops were produced, and so were some foodstuffs, but almost all manufactured goods were imported from Europe, as well as such essentials of
French life as wine. The Antilles represented an early and almost perfect example of the classic structure of production of primary products
for export in return for commodities from factories and services provided by the *métropole*.

Slaves and sugar, therefore, became the bases of the French colonies
in the Caribbean, a combination pointed out by the Martiniquais abolitionist Victor Schoelcher: 'If you want an apt symbol for the colonies,
take a stalk of sugar cane crossed with a foreman's whip.' Sugar production and slave-holding developed with a rapid tempo. In 1674, the
French islands produced 5400 tons of sugar; a decade later 9300 tons.
Over a long period, the number of sugar refineries in Guadeloupe
increased from 122 in 1671 to 530 by 1847 and in Martinique, from 111
to 498; the number of slaves grew, during the same period, from 4267 to
87,087 in Guadeloupe and from under 16,731 (in 1701) to 72,859 in
Martinique.

The Antilles existed as an odd permutation of French society with a
certain institutional separation from Paris. Many of the characteristics
of the French *ancien régime* were absent from the colonies: such taxes
as the church tithe were not collected; the aristocracy, with its panoply
of rights and privileges, was less visible; the role of the church was
reduced in a society that was increasingly secularised (or, for the blacks,
not entirely converted).

For obvious reasons, Antillais society developed a structure of its
own. The early colonial period saw a great articulation and stratifi-
cation of West Indian society. Colour was the primary arbiter of status,
but the increasing number of mixed-blood men and women and the
larger number of freed slaves created new nuances in the social spectrum. At the top came the white plantation owners, set apart by their
wealth and acquired pretensions. Most had been of rather modest background when they arrived in the Antilles, contrary to popular notions
about expatriate noblemen. However, they had the capital to buy land

and slaves and become the pillars of the plantation economy. They constructed large manor-houses, retained strong connections with the mother country and sometimes married their wealthy daughters to the penurious scions of aristocratic families. As time passed, more and more of these white West Indians were born in the Caribbean — *Békés* became the term applied to powerful whites native to the islands — and created a culture particular to them and removed from that of France. Accompanying cultural differentiation came a desire for some political and financial autonomy. Contesting such notions, but living alongside the *Békés* in status, were the administrators and other whites sent from France, whose loyalties lay with Europe rather than with the Caribbean.

Below the *notables* were the *petits blancs*, the poorer whites, some of whom migrated to the Antilles as contract labourers (*engagés*), others of whom were demobilised soldiers, still others soldiers of fortune in the New World. Such men and their families lived in a precarious position in the colonies: they lacked education, capital and political power and relied on their skin colour as a source of prestige. Many were small farmers or tradesmen, but in these domains they were challenged by the *métis* and freed slaves. Consequently, they were in the forefront of opposition to the liberation of the slaves.

At the top of non-white society in the two centuries before 1848 were the mixed-blood residents of the Antilles, generally the children of European men and African women. They were free, according to the law, but that freedom was circumscribed with various restrictions on their personal and professional activities and was often honoured only in the breach. There were also freed slaves, those who had been granted their freedom by their masters or who were required to be given freedom under certain conditions (for instance, if the slave became the legal guardian for the master's children). Masters, less philanthropically, also liberated slaves when they became handicapped or too old to work, a strategy to avoid paying for the upkeep of useless labour, and such freed slaves often lived in misery. Slaves could also purchase their freedom, although the difficulty in collecting their own purchase-price meant that such an occurrence was rare.

Much the greatest proportion of the West Indian population before 1848 lived in slavery. The *Code noir* of 1685 was an attempt to regulate slave-holding and to ameliorate some of the earlier excesses. It maintained the right of slave-holders to buy and sell slaves, although families were not to be separated. Masters were supposed to provide adequate clothing and food for their slaves, although in practice, both were often sub-standard and masters sometimes gave slaves a small plot of land to grow their own food (and thereby acquitted themselves of the requirement to feed them). Slaves were given a day of rest each week, but otherwise worked from sun-up until dusk. Corporal punishment was allowed, and masters punished slaves by whipping, attaching heavy iron balls to their feet or painful iron collars to their necks. Masters could search for and punish escaped slaves by having a *fleur de lys* burned on a runaway's shoulder or an ear cut off. Because of overwork and bad living conditions, slaves fell prey to a variety of diseases, and medical care was generally inadequate. Despite their sufferings, the slaves did construct a society of their own, complete with traditions and customs. Antillais cuisine (also enjoyed by the whites) combined local products with hot spices, and the music and dances of the French West Indies (notably *zouk* and the more Europeanised *biguine*) drew heavily on African rhythms. The African slaves were evangelised by Catholic priests and most were converted, although sometimes still practising a syncretic mixture of Catholicism and traditional African religions or, especially in Haiti, voodoo. Very few slaves married with the formalities of civil or religious authorities, but they did establish families, and the birth rate was particularly high among the African populations. A special language also emerged, based on the simplified French which slave-owners used to talk to the slaves, but which, as Creole, combined various foreign influences and became the colourful *lingua franca* of the French Caribbean. Whites denigrated such cultural manifestations, but they remained important elements of cultural identity and community among the black population.

In the islands there were also a small number of escaped slaves, *marrons* (maroons), who managed to hide in the mountains and scratch out a living; they remained marginal to the social structure. In Guyane, however, they were fairly numerous; these *marrons* (such as the *Bonis*) disappeared into the Amazonian jungle and recreated an African style of existence. In the colonial period, as afterwards, they lived separately from both the white and the black societies of the settled areas. Also marginal were the Indian tribes of Guyane, who lived in the forests and had little contact with other elements of Guyanais society (except during the gold rushes).

The economic, political and social structures which emerged in the Antilles from the 1630s to the 1840s provided a model of many contradictions in colonial society: dependence on the mother-country, yet demands for fiscal and political autonomy; prosperity for a white elite and misery for the non-white masses, a successful export economy but lack of diversification; a society removed from the *métropole* yet subject to the changes in ideology, political problems and military engagements of the capital, an orderly society beset with grievances among both the whites and the blacks.

Guyane

Guyane during the early colonial period displayed marked particularities.[4] Compared with the small Caribbean islands, the territory — one-sixth the size of France — was enormous; dense tropical rainforest, most of it unexplored and unknown to the colonists, covered most of the land. The climate and environment of the Guianas were universally considered inhospitable; only the littoral was thought suitable for European habitation, and even on that strip the soil was infertile. Furthermore, the lack of navigable waterways and distance from other European colonies hindered transportation. Yet several European countries established settlements in the Guianas; ownership of land and rights to colonise were unclear — the borders between French Guiana and Brazil were not entirely mapped out until the twentieth century and in the earlier period, groups settled almost indiscriminately. All hoped to find the legendary El Dorado, or at least an equally mythic chain of mountains, the Tumuc-Humac. The ventures of early propagandists for the Guianas, including Walter Raleigh, came to nothing. The first long-lasting colonies, set up by the British and Dutch, dated from the first decades of the seventeenth century. The French, coming from Saint-Christophe, followed and set up small sugar colonies in Sinnamary and Cayenne Island in the 1600s. The European wars caused the French and Dutch to tussle over the jungle, but the French finally extended their claims to the territory lying between the Maroni and Oyapock rivers.

Yet the private companies responsible for the efforts, the Compagnie de la France Equinoxiale and the Compagnie des Indes Occidentales, suffered reverses, and in 1672 the crown annexed the territory. Three years later, fewer than two thousand Frenchmen and women and slaves had been lured to Guyane; sixty years later there were 4297 African slaves, 475 whites (including soldiers) and twenty-seven sugar plantations. A new presence in Guyane in the early 1700s was that of the Jesuit priests who came both to evangelise the Indians and set up a model plantation. The priests and other settlers eked out an existence planting sugar or raising rocou for dye. In 1763, the French government tried a massive migration to Kourou in Guyane. Some 12,000 Europeans were sent to the colony in a matter of months; because of malaria and yellow fever, 7000 of them died, and the rest had to be repatriated. This effort ended as a total failure and reinforced the region's deadly image in France. Later in the century, another chartered company became interested in the colony but only for the shipment of slaves; at the time of the Revolution, a minuscule colony of Europeans and a growing workforce of slaves exported some sugar, cocoa and coffee.

GUYANE

At the end of the eighteenth century, the first convoy of prisoners, the start of a series which lasted until the middle of the twentieth century, was shipped to 'Devil's Island', adding another negative trait to the colony's image. Only one other serious effort was made at development, when, in 1828, Mère Javouhey, founder of a religious order, grouped together liberated slaves in Mana in an agricultural settlement; yet when the mother superior left Guyane in 1842 the effort faltered.

Slow development did take place; the population of whites grew from 969 and of free blacks from 1040 in 1807 to a total, for the two groups, of 6432 in 1847, while the number of slaves rose from 13,474 in 1807 to a maximum of 19,102 in 1831, then fell back to 12,943 by 1847. The Guyanais enjoyed a modest prosperity thanks to the sugar plantations, although Guyane had only a quarter of the area under cane of tiny Martinique, as well as small quantities of spices (such as cloves), cacao, coffee, rocou and cotton. Guyane remained, however, the least reputable and least developed region of the French empire.

Wars and Revolutions in the New World

The colonial world in the Americas was troubled in the late 1700s, first, by the Seven Years War which pitted France and England against each other in the New World, then by the American War of Independence, in which France took the part of the American colonies against their mother country. Naval battles between the French and English ensued in the Caribbean, and each nation temporarily conquered islands belonging to the other. Several years after the American War ended in 1783, however, came a bigger shock, the French Revolution.[5] The Declaration of the Rights of Man proclaimed the equality of Frenchmen, but that precept did not apply to either women or slaves. Some revolutionaries thought that it should, and campaigns for the abolition of slavery were led by the Société des Amis des Noirs, which counted among its members Condorcet, Brissot, Siéyès and Robespierre. Plantation owners in the Antilles, not surprisingly, opposed emancipation, which they feared would bring ruin to the islands; lobbyists mobilised and organised the Club Massiac to put their cause to the new Assembly; they also mustered support among the *petits blancs*. On the other hand, the *colons* saw in the Revolution a chance to secure greater political and financial autonomy from the *métropole*, as the National Assembly had authorised the colonies to elect local assemblies. The colonists in Saint-Domingue jumped ahead and elected a council (subsequently dissolved) and agitation troubled the Antilles and Guyane. Slaves, getting wind of the changes in Paris, became restive and in 1791 broke out in open revolt in the north of Saint-Domingue. In Paris, in the same year, the National Assembly proclaimed equality of non-whites born to free parents and, in the following year, 1792, accorded equality to all free black males. In 1794, the legislature, now the Jacobin Convention, abolished slavery; responding to planters' opposition came Robespierre's famous 'Périssent les colonies plutôt qu'un principe' ('Let the colonies disappear rather than a principle'). By now, however, the Antilles were in turmoil. Pro-revolutionary revolts had occurred in Martinique and Guadeloupe, and in Saint-Domingue, local authorities had not waited for Paris' decision but had already proclaimed the end of slavery in 1793.

Martinique and Guadeloupe in 1794 fell prey to the English, who were fighting the French in both hemispheres. The French soon retook Guadeloupe, and Victor Hugues, the Jacobin commissioner, instituted the Terror on the island and executed 865 people charged with 'collaboration' with the English. Most of the planters and many other whites subsequently fled the island. This marked the end of the Guadeloupe *Békés* and meant that the island's population was subsequently 'blacker' than that of Martinique. The English occupied Martinique until 1802, the abolition law was never applied in that colony and the *Békés* retained their authority. Meanwhile, in 1797, Toussaint Louverture, a black revolutionary, took control of Saint-Domingue, chasing out the French administrator and establishing a separate state — which he still, however, considered part of France — and began a dictatorial government which lasted until 1802. By now, Napoleon was First Consul, and the radical days of the Revolution had come to an end. Napoleon asserted French authority in Guadeloupe and Martinique, which England returned to France by the Treaty of Amiens in 1802. Perhaps influenced by his Martiniquaise Creole wife Joséphine, Napoleon agreed to re-establish slavery in the French colonies in 1802. In Guadeloupe, a group of former slaves, led by Delgrès, preferred to jump to their deaths from a peak rather than submit to the re-establishment of servitude. But Bonaparte was unable to regain control of Saint-Domingue. The rebel Toussaint Louverture was deported to France, but insurrection continued in 1803 and General Dessalines proclaimed the independence of Haiti in 1804, one of a long line of dictators in this Francophone state. Troubles continued in the remaining French colonies; the English retook Martinique in 1809 and Guadeloupe the following year and held them until 1814 (as well as during the Hundred Days of 1815) and the Portuguese occupied Guyane from 1808 to 1817.

Napoleon was uninterested in the colonies, as his ambitions were directed to Continental Europe and to the Middle East. After all,

Napoleon had briefly ruled Egypt under the Directory, nourishing his dream of an Oriental empire, and even encouraging rumours that he was ready to convert to Islam. Some thought that Napoleon wanted to use Egypt, or, alternatively, the eastern Mediterranean coast and Persia, as a stepping-stone to India. Bonaparte did not become a new Alexander, although his interests foreshadowed later French activities in the Arab world. The emperor's strategies resulted in the total disappearance of France's overseas empire at the end of his reign, and it was only through the various treaties which followed Waterloo that France's sovereignty over the three Caribbean colonies — Guadeloupe, Martinique and Guyane — was restored, as was French control over Réunion.[6]

The Revolution and Napoleonic rule brought few lasting benefits to the colonies but did sow the seeds for several later developments. In the headier days of the Revolution, *colons* had elected delegates to the French Constituent Assembly; this short-lived representation (temporarily renewed under the Convention) continued to fuel hopes among settlers for greater political influence. The *Exclusif* was maintained, but the English occupation, Continental blockade and European turmoil had forcibly taught the colonies greater self-sufficiency and broadened trade contacts. Conversely, the troubles threatened the basis of the Antillais plantation economy. Cut off from sources of sugarcane, farmers in France had developed production of beet sugar, and from this period onwards there was a continuing dispute between European beet sugar and Caribbean cane sugar producers; some West Indian planters demanded that the beet refineries be destroyed and sales of sugar be reserved for them. Never again would planters in the islands enjoy the monopoly they had in the *ancien régime*. New ideas also threatened the other pillar of their fortunes, slavery. The emancipation of slaves had lasted only eight years, but support remained for permanent liberation. During Napoleon's return during the Hundred Days of 1815, he had abolished the slave trade under pressure from the British, and England, in 1833, was to outlaw slavery in its empire. The example of neighbouring Haiti served as a reminder, too, that the old order was not immutable.[7]

Réunion

In the 1600s, at the same time that the French began to be seriously interested in the Caribbean, they also looked towards the Indian Ocean.[8] The great Indian subcontinent had attracted explorers and traders from Europe who wanted trading posts and stopping points on the route east. But Madagascar, the 'Grande Ile' of the Indian Ocean,

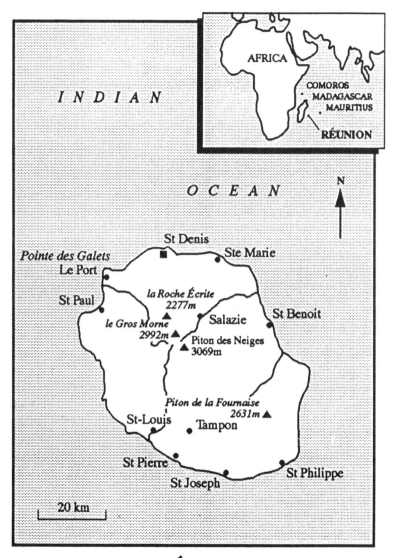

RÉUNION

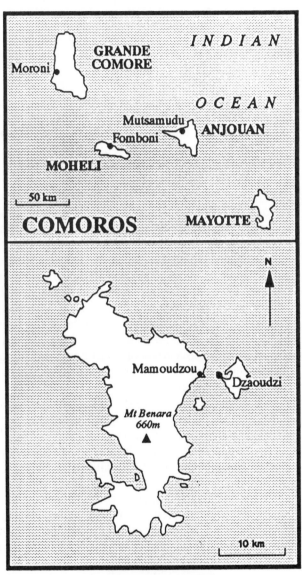

MAYOTTE

also attracted interest, and the Dutch established a colony at the Cape of Good Hope on the African mainland. The French explored the Mascareignes, a fragmented archipelago which included the Ile Bourbon (Réunion), Rodrigues and the Ile de France (Mauritius), uninhabited but blessed with a fine climate and, in the case of the Ile de France, a superb harbour. The Compagnie Française de l'Orient reconnoitred the region in the 1640s, and a handful of French settlers moved to Madagascar; a formal French act of possession was declared over the Ile Bourbon in 1642. In the coming years, once in 1646 and again in 1654, small groups of prisoners were deported from Madagascar to Réunion, where they flourished but were more or less forgotten by the authorities. Later in the century, the Compagnie des Indes Orientales began a small-scale colonisation of the Ile Bourbon. However, by 1713, only 538 whites and 633 slaves lived a largely self-sufficient life on the island and produced some coffee for export. Pirates, meanwhile, used Réunion as a base for their activities — giving rise to the legends of fabulous treasures buried in the Mascareignes. Such was the largely inauspicious start to the new colony's development.

The Dutch, who had claimed Mauritius in the late 1500s, evacuated their minuscule colony there in 1710, and five years later the French claimed the island. French attention was now devoted to Bourbon's sister island, which was considered more promising. The two, however, were administered jointly. The Governor-General of the islands in the 1730s and 1740s, Mahé de la Bourdonnais, saw in his domain a base for French expansion in India; as a naval officer he was more interested in the strategic value of the islands than in their worth as places for settlement. After the Treaty of Paris of 1763, which reduced France's hold in India to five *comptoirs*, some of Mahé's successors treasured the never-realised hope of using the Mascareignes as the base for a French reconquest of greater territories in India.

It was as a plantation colony rather than as a base for conquests that Bourbon struggled along in the late 1700s and early 1800s. The end of the trading privileges of the Compagnie des Indes Orientales created a crisis in the coffee economy, and new sources of farming were sought, including nutmeg and cloves, spice production being developed by the aptly named Pierre Poivre. Manioc and cotton were unable to provide prosperity. During the 1700s lack of development meant that many of the white settlers were reduced to poverty on tiny upland parcels of land (*les Hauts*), which were particularly unprofitable. By the 1830s such indigents made up two-thirds of the local white population. Several families had carved out large estates, and they began to reproduce a

Réunion-born elite (like the Antillais plantocracy also called *Békés*) who dominated the *métis* and the slaves.

The end of the 1700s promised great changes for Bourbon. The Revolution meant that the island elite had greater control of its own affairs, and, more than their compatriots in the Antilles, they resisted the abolition of slavery. The newly organised colonial assemblies in the Ile de France and Réunion, as Bourbon was now renamed, simply defied Paris and did not apply the decrees abolishing slavery. The Directory sent two *commissaires* and two thousand troops to the Mascareignes in 1796 to put the refractory islands in order; the emissaries were greeted by such steadfast refusal to accept emancipation that they were forced to leave, their mission unaccomplished. The English then invaded and occupied Bourbon for five years.

The English defeat of the French in the Napoleonic wars caused the permanent loss of Mauritius, but France was allowed to keep Réunion. The independence of Haiti and the loss of other tropical colonies emphasised that new potential existed for sugar producers, and so Réunion from the early nineteenth century onwards became in its turn a sugar colony. Planters enlarged their estates, set up refineries, and imported large numbers of slaves from Africa. Much of the old land used for coffee was now converted to sugar and new lands were cleared; production of sugar grew from only 21 tonnes in 1815 to 73,000 in 1860, when some 68 per cent of all cultivated land was under sugar. The population also grew, from 36,000 inhabitants in 1778 to 110,000 in 1848, both because of the use of slave labour and because of a substantial immigration of Europeans in the first half of the nineteenth century. In the years before the abolition of slavery in 1848, Réunion flourished.

Saint-Pierre and Miquelon

The islands of Saint-Pierre and Miquelon, the last of the present DOM-TOMs acquired in the first overseas empire, were — and are — an anomaly in the general pattern of French tropical colonies.[9] Lying off the southern coast of Newfoundland, they were France's consolation prize for the loss of the Canadian empire of the early modern period. The islands were discovered in 1520 but remained unoccupied, except for episodic visits by Micmac Indians, for a century and a half. In 1670, a French officer annexed the islands when he found a dozen French fishermen camped there. English ships soon began to pester the French, pillaging their camps and ships. By the early 1700s, the islands were again uninhabited, and were ceded to the English by the Treaty of

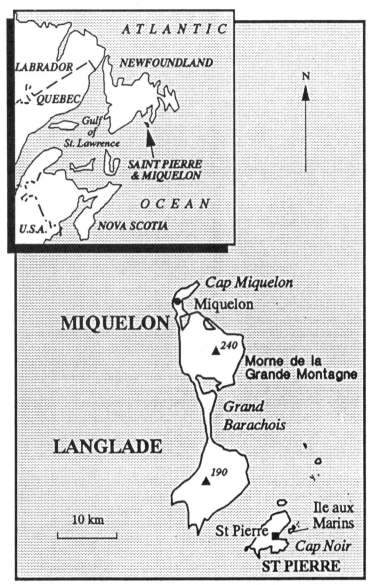

ST PIERRE AND MIQUELON

Utrecht in 1713. French fishermen occasionally still visited the region, although they preferred the 'French Shore' of Newfoundland, richer in fish and with greater possibilities for provisioning and repairs than the barren and forlorn smaller islands. Most of the fishermen, who came from Normandy and the Basque country, were particularly interested in cod, which could be dried on ship or on shore and sold in France or, as food for the slaves, in the Antilles. In 1763, a treaty between France and England returned Saint-Pierre and Miquelon to Paris and gave the French legal rights to fish the 'French Shore'. France dispatched a governor, and the church sent priests. By the 1780s, about 1000 or 1500 people lived in the islands, and their numbers doubled during the fishing season. Exports of dried cod rose from 15,153 quintals in 1766 to 91,582 in 1790.

The Revolution sent shock waves towards France's sole remaining possession in North America. A Jacobin club formed, and the *curé* (priest), refusing to take the new civil oath of the clergy, fled the islands. In 1793, the English landed in Saint-Pierre and, the following year, expelled the French population (most of whom returned to Bordeaux or Le Havre) and tried to install English settlers. In turn their colony was sacked by French troops in 1796. The Treaty of Amiens of 1802 gave the islands back to France, but England reoccupied them when hostilities recommenced the next year. The Treaty of Paris in 1814 returned them to France, though England occupied them yet again during the Hundred Days. France then recovered deserted islands on which all the buildings and other facilities had been destroyed or fallen into disrepair. During the first decades of the nineteenth century, a sedentary population drifted back into the archipelago, but only around the middle of the century did increased fishing bring a certain prosperity to the little colony.

THE NEW OVERSEAS EMPIRE

In 1830 France began to acquire a second overseas empire, and over the next century gained a vast colonial empire, second only to the domains of Britain.[10] The new empire, in addition to the old colonies, eventually included Algeria, plus the protectorates of Tunisia and Morocco, in North Africa; areas of west Africa that encompass present-day Senegal, Mauritania, Niger, Guinea, the Ivory Coast, Burkina Faso and Benin, at the time organised as Afrique Occidentale Française (AOF); Afrique Equatoriale Française (AEF), consisting of present-day Gabon, Congo, Chad and the Central African Republic; the Côte Française des Somalis (now Djibouti); Madagascar and the Comoros Islands in the

Table 2.　French Colonies and Independent States, 1830–1980

Territory	Date French control established	Date of independence
Middle East Mandates		
Lebanon[a]	1919	1946
Syria[a]	1919	1946
Asia		
Vietnam[b]	1860s–1880s	1946/1954
Cambodia[c]	1903	1954
Laos[c]	1893	1953
French India[d]	1759	1954
Africa		
North Africa		
Morocco[c]	1912	1956
Algeria	1830	1962
Tunisia[c]	1881	1956
Afrique Occidentale Française		
Senegal[e]	1854–98	1960
Mauritania	1876–98	1960
Mali	1880–95	1960
Burkina Faso (Upper Volta)	1899	1960
Niger	1891	1960
Guinea[e]	1854–98	1958
Ivory Coast	1842–83	1960
Benin (Dahomey)	1880–95	1960
Afrique Equatoriale Française		
Congo	1880	1960
Gabon	1883–84	1960
Central African Republic	1876–98	1960
Chad	1887–1912	1960
Mandates in Africa		
Cameroon[a]	1919	1960
Togo[a]	1919	1960
Djibouti[f]	1888	1977
Indian Ocean		
Madagascar[g]	1895–96	1960
Comoros[h]	1886	1975
Pacific Ocean		
Vanuatu (New Hebrides)[i]	1906	1980

Page: 2　　OP: HAKR　　DATE: 8.10.1991　　FM: 1388　　SU: 06

N.B:　This table does not include territories which France possessed temporarily or lost to the British at the end of the Napoleonic Wars, e.g. Dominica, St Lucia, St Kitts and Trinidad in the Caribbean, and Mauritius and the Seychelles in the Indian Ocean. Nor does it include the DOM-TOMs.

Indian Ocean. In Asia, France took over Tonkin, Annam and Cochin-china, grouped together as French Indo-China, and controlled Laos and Cambodia as protectorates. In the Pacific, France annexed the five archipelagos that made up the Etablissements Français de l'Océanie (EFO), New Caledonia and the Loyalty Islands, and Wallis and Futuna. In addition, France jointly governed the New Hebrides ar-chipelago as a condominium with Great Britain, administered Syria and Lebanon, Cameroon and Togo under a League of Nations man-date after the First World War, and claimed a tract of Antarctica and several uninhabited islands in the Indian and Pacific Oceans. Of the new colonies acquired in the 1800s, all became independent by 1980, with the exception of the three Pacific territories, Mayotte and the Austral and Antarctic lands, which make up the present-day *territoires d'outre-mer*.

Few topics have caused so much historical debate as this round of 'new imperialism' in the nineteenth century. The reasons for Euro-pean expansion, and, more particularly, whether economics provided the 'taproots' (in Hobson's famous phrase) for the enterprise have been hotly debated. Scholars have even questioned whether there was a 'new' imperialism which marked a break from earlier conquests, and if

---

Notes to Table 2

a. France administered these territories under mandates from the League of Nations. Syria and Lebanon had been part of the Ottoman Empire before the First World War, while Cameroon and Togo were former German colonies. Cameroon was, in fact, divided between British and French control by the League.

b. The French conquered Cochinchina from 1862 to 1867 and acquired Tonkin and Annam in 1885. These were then grouped as French Indo-China. The war of independence waged against the French from 1945 to 1954 led to the emergence of two states of Vietnam, which were reunified in 1975.

c. Protectorates.

d. From the mid-1600s, France traded in India; the five outposts — Pondichéry, Chandernagor, Karikal, Yanaon and Mahé — were granted to France, after a conflict with Britain in India, in the mid-1700s. They were ceded to independent India from 1951 to 1954; a formal treaty between France and India was signed in 1958, but not ratified by the French until 1962.

e. The French had maintained posts in Senegal and Guinea from the mid-1600s, but did not establish sovereignty until the 1800s.

f. Under French rule, Djibouti was known as the Côte Française des Somalis (French Somaliland), then the Territoire Français des Afars et Issas.

g. The French had carried out various activities in Madagascar since the 1600s but did not establish formal control until 1896.

h. The French took over Mayotte in 1843 and the remaining three islands of the Comoros came under a French protectorate in 1886; annexation followed in 1904.

i. Britain and France governed the New Hebrides as a condominium from 1906 to 1980.

so, what the timing for it was. The roles of various metropolitan concerns — missionary groups, the military, commercial interests, settlers and politicians — have been assessed, and the activities of the explorers and soldiers who put together the empire — Savorgnan de Brazza, Galliéni, Lyautey, Bugeaud — have been examined. Responses to imperialism, the collaboration and resistance of indigenous populations, have lately received much attention. Comparisons have been made between the various colonial experiences of France and Britain, Belgium and Germany, the Netherlands and Italy, and later imperial powers like Japan and the United States. The effects of imperialism on both the *métropoles* and the conquered territories have been calculated and recalculated. At the time the new empire was being amassed, controversy was already raging, and the dispersal of the colonies has neither cooled the rhetoric nor resolved all the questions. Generalisations remain hazardous.[11]

The construction of the new empire was not a consciously worked out design: no one in Paris drew lines on maps to indicate areas that must be taken over. Acquisitions were haphazard, and *prises de possession* were sometimes the acts of generals or admirals, for their own glory or to thwart opponents, without precise directions from their superiors. Some parcels were relinquished, others traded away. A number of attempts, such as the French takeover of Mexico, were unsuccessful. Local circumstances generally created the possibility, or at least provided the occasion, for conquests. Expansion on continents usually proceeded from coastal outposts to control of the interior, followed by efforts to tie together the various reaches of these domains, such as the AEF and AOF. 'Pacification' of the 'natives' was seldom total, as the various rebellions which occurred in almost all areas of the new empire — the intransigence of Abd el-Kader and the Kabyle mutiny of 1870 in North Africa, the Druse rebellion of the 1920s — amply showed. Development of local resources was not always adequate, even for the French interests, and almost never aimed at the betterment of the indigenous populations.

Behind this unplanned and even illogical empire-building, however, lay a certain theory of imperialism. Jules Ferry, the architect of the new empire and spokesman for imperial groups, in a key speech to the Chamber of Deputies in 1885, outlined the economic reasons for expansion. 'Colonial policy is the daughter of industrial policy', argued Ferry:

For the rich states, where capital abounds and accumulates rapidly, where the manufacturing system is in continual expansion. . . — where the cultivation of the soil is itself subsumed to support industry — export is an essential factor of public prosperity, and the domain of capital, like the demand for labour, is measured by the extent of the foreign market.

The great nations, Ferry continued, were locked in an economic rivalry to produce and export, and France must take part. His second argument for expansion was humanitarian: 'superior' races had the right and duty to take over the 'inferior' ones and bring them the fruits of their civilisation, religion and justice, science and technology. Thirdly came political questions; if France was to maintain its international prestige and compete with Britain, Germany and the other powers, it must expand overseas. To do otherwise would be to abdicate France's status and sink to the level of a third- or fourth-rate power.

Ferry's arguments did not win unanimous support. Opponents argued that France's efforts should be directed to the reconquest of Alsace and Lorraine, or that money and effort should be devoted to domestic matters or the social question rather than foreign adventures. Others thought Ferry's expansionism overambitious, and indeed his ministry fell because of dissatisfaction with his policy in Tonkin. Not until the last decades of the nineteenth century did the French, even in the political elite, develop real enthusiasm for empire. The change was due largely to the *parti colonial*, a dedicated group of pro-imperial lobbyists both inside and outside the Chamber and Senate which included academics, traders, military officers, colonists and politicians. The *parti colonial* worked ceaselessly, through publications, meetings and specific projects aimed at colonial development, to convince the public of the benefits, indeed the necessity, of empire. By the 1890s, the hesitant Radicals had been converted to empire, and after the First World War, the Socialists too were convinced of its virtues; only the Communist Party remained anti-colonial. By the early twentieth century, widely disseminated images of empire — heroic explorers, kindly priests and doctors, pioneering settlers, brave colonial soldiers who had served in the First World War — had won the hearts and minds of Frenchmen. The great Colonial Exhibition of 1931, organised by Marshal Lyautey in the Bois de Vincennes, brought the empire home with exotic displays and live entertainment. This was the apogee of expansionism, the time when the empire reached its greatest extent, the golden age of colonialism.[12]

Not coincidentally, in the 1930s, partly as a result of the Depression, the empire became more important to France as a source of raw materials, a market for manufactured exports, a placement for capital, and a venue for settlement. In the nineteenth century the empire was not profitable in an aggregate sense, but a number of different individuals and companies indeed made a profit. By the early 1900s, as French economic activity had dwindled in other areas, notably the Russian empire, the colonies assumed greater importance and by this time the empire played host to various vested interests, including close to a million *pieds-noirs* in Algeria. Such entrenched interests made subsequent decolonisation difficult.

The running of the colonies was based on the institutional and administrative centralisation of decision-making in Paris. In the capital, however, authority over the colonies was divided. The Ministry of the Interior administered Algeria, and the North African protectorates were the concern of the Ministry of Foreign Affairs. The other colonies came under the control of the Ministry of Colonies, itself a creation of the 1890s; previously, they had been under the purview of the colonial section of the Ministry of the Navy. Paris appointed governors (and, for the AOF, AEF, Indo-China and Madagascar, governors-general); generally navy officers in the early years, governors after the 1880s were increasingly civilians. A new Ecole Coloniale was established to train the administrators for the empire; they came from all walks of French life, though Corsicans and Antillais (including blacks) were over-represented in the colonial service. Those posted overseas received increased salaries and various other emoluments, but imperial assignments were never the plums of the French public service. Native appointees assisted administrators, both in the European institutions and as customary chieftains. In addition to the civilian *fonctionnaires*, Paris stationed soldiers and sailors in the colonies and (until the first decade of the twentieth century, when most were disbanded) in the colonial fleets. The Foreign Legion, formed in 1831, was based in Algeria and sent contingents to other colonies.

The colonies also had local consultative councils, the exact names and powers of which varied over the years. Local municipalities were organised, but they too had restricted powers. Some of the colonies elected deputies to the Chamber in Paris, at least during the Second and Third Republics, and the colonies also sent representatives to the consultative *Conseil supérieur des colonies*. Yet in the nineteenth and twentieth centuries, there was little thought of decentralisation or autonomy, let alone the responsible government and dominion status already implemented by Britain in several of its colonies.

Only the European French enjoyed full political rights in the colonies, and some regions (particularly Algeria) had a large number of non-French white settlers who were in an ambiguous legal position. The status of the indigenous population differed, but few were French citizens, although ways existed for them to become so. Generally, potential citizens had to be male, demonstrate knowledge of French, hold a job and renounce any customary legal rights (such as the right to be judged by Islamic courts). By the twentieth century, others could gain French nationality by having served in the First World War or worked in the administration. In some parts of the empire, such as the *communes* of Saint-Louis, Dakar, Gorée and Rufisque in Senegal, native residents enjoyed particular rights which Africans outside these enclaves did not.

The idea behind attitudes to and treatment of natives in the nineteenth century was *assimilation*, at least in the African and Asian colonies. The aim, in theory, was eventually to turn non-Europeans into Frenchmen and to make the colonies as much like France as possible. Education, administration, military service and fiscal policy aimed at this goal. The policy was manifestly unworkable, and simultaneously both naively utopian, sexist and racist; it was replaced at the turn of the century by a theory of *association*, separate but equal treatment which favoured the development of male native elites but kept women and the masses at arm's length from legal equality or political power. Under this system prominent politicians such as Habib Bourguiba, Léopold Sedar Senghor and Ferhat Abbas eventually emerged to become leaders of independence movements in their countries. The French administration provided for some medical care and schooling, and private organisations, especially Catholic and Protestant church groups, supplemented government efforts. However, in many parts of the empire, indigenes continued to live according to their age-old customs and traditional subsistence and trading economies. Their contacts with white society were episodic and incidental.[13]

The French also kept a tight financial rein on their empire. Paris fixed monetary and taxation policy. A period of free trade between the colonies and the empire lasted for several decades after 1860, but generally there existed a variety of duties on colonial products exported to France and metropolitan commodities shipped to the empire. By the early 1900s, the colonies were divided into two groups, those assimilated to the French customs structure and those outside it. Various sorts of taxes were collected, including, in many regions, a head-tax (*capitation*) on indigenes payable in money or labour. The colonies themselves had sources of revenue, such as the *octroi de mer* tax collected on all imported products, irrespective of their origin. The various colonial banks composed of both government and private banking interests held monopolies on note-issuing and credit in the colonies.

Economically, the empire produced many tropical products of interest to the French market. Minerals, such as phosphate from Morocco and Makatea (French Polynesia) and nickel from New Caledonia, were extremely important to the French. Much of France's coffee, cocoa and sugar came from the colonies, and rice was a major product of French Indo-China. Other tropical products such as rubber were also produced, although in smaller quantities. Algeria grew large quantities of grain and also manufactured wine. Luxury products, for example, pearls from the Pacific, were sold on the Paris market. Some of the firms handling these commodities were major concerns, and the shipping companies active in the colonial trade — especially the Compagnie Générale Transatlantique and Messageries maritimes — helped to make Bordeaux and Marseille great entrepôts for trade. Furthermore, the infrastructure built in the colonies — buildings, roads, ports and especially railways — became giant economic concerns of their own.

Not all the French colonies were equal. Algeria took pride of place; officially it formed part of the 'national territory', counted the largest number of French settlers and was the oldest of the new colonies, Algiers having been taken over in 1830. A close attachment also bound the French to Tunisia and Morocco, although they remained only protectorates. Second in importance came the great African domains, the AEF and AOF, and, perhaps to a lesser degree, Indo-China and Madagascar. Finally, came the remote and thinly populated Pacific island territories. The *vieilles colonies* retained a special, almost familial, status in the imperial group. Ironically, these *anciennes colonies* and the Pacific archipelagos remained under French control when the larger domains had been decolonised.

The Origin and Development of the TOMs

France's three present-day *territoires d'outre-mer* date from the new empire of the nineteenth century. All lie in the southern Pacific Ocean, which French explorers such as Bougainville and La Pérouse had sailed at the end of the 1700s.[14] Their voyages did not lack commercial and political motives, but no efforts were made to establish French settlements. In 1788, the English narrowly beat the French in taking possession of and establishing a settlement in Australia, when Captain Arthur Phillip arrived at Botany Bay a few days before La Pérouse. A similar sequence was repeated in 1840, when British ships took over the islands of New Zealand, although the French, arriving soon afterwards, installed a small group of settlers — under British sovereignty — on the Akaroa peninsula. Yet neither the British nor the French were particularly interested in the southern seas in the early 1800s; their economic utility seemed uncertain, despite sandalwood trade and whaling, and the primary interest of the British was to establish a penal settlement after the loss of their North American colonies.

France, however, did pick up several archipelagos in the Pacific. French missionaries had arrived in the Polynesian islands in the early 1800s and prepared the way for other visitors. In 1842, Admiral Dupetit-Thouars took possession of the Marquesas archipelago in eastern Polynesia, then sailed to Tahiti. The French and British had already clashed in Tahiti, when French priests had been expelled by the Tahitian queen under the influence of an English missionary; to right this wrong, Dupetit-Thouars established a protectorate over Tahiti and the remainder of the realm of Queen Pomare, which included Moorea and other smaller Society Islands. Later in the century the protectorate was extended to the Gambier, Tuamotu and Austral archipelagos, and the five island groups were organised as the Etablissements Français de l'Océanie (EFO). In the 1880s, formal annexation replaced the protectorate. In that decade France also set up a protectorate over the islands of Wallis, Futuna and Alofi in central Polynesia. In the Melanesian region of the western Pacific, New Caledonia and the Loyalty Islands attracted French interests, and in 1853 Admiral Febvrier-Despointes annexed all these islands. The French were also interested in the New Hebrides archipelago, north of New Caledonia, but never succeeded in gaining complete sovereignty over the island group; French, British and Australian interests collided there, and London and Paris finally arranged, in 1906, to rule the islands jointly as a condominium, complete with two official representatives, two flags and two administrations. France's Pacific possessions were completed with the tiny island of Clipperton, far off the coast of Mexico, which France had claimed in 1858. The island was uninhabited — except, for a brief period, by a group of Mexican settlers who almost starved but were finally rescued by a passing American ship. Mexico continued to contest France's control, and the issue was only resolved in 1931, to the benefit of France, through the arbitration of the king of Italy.

The Pacific ventures had given France in New Caledonia one of the largest islands of the South Pacific and, in Tahiti, the most legendary. Despite the seductiveness of the Pacific islands, they remained small and distant parcels of the French empire. In the first century of French administration, the EFO developed as an agricultural and trading centre. A profitable pork trade began in the early years of the century, supplying a variety of visiting ships, and reaching its zenith with the expansion of whaling in the 1830s. In the second half of the century the main export product was copra, the dried meat of coconuts, collected by indigenous labour, and useful in the production of oil for foodstuffs and soap, but there was now a diversity of exports, including oranges and vanilla. Efforts to grow cotton, coffee and other tropical crops in

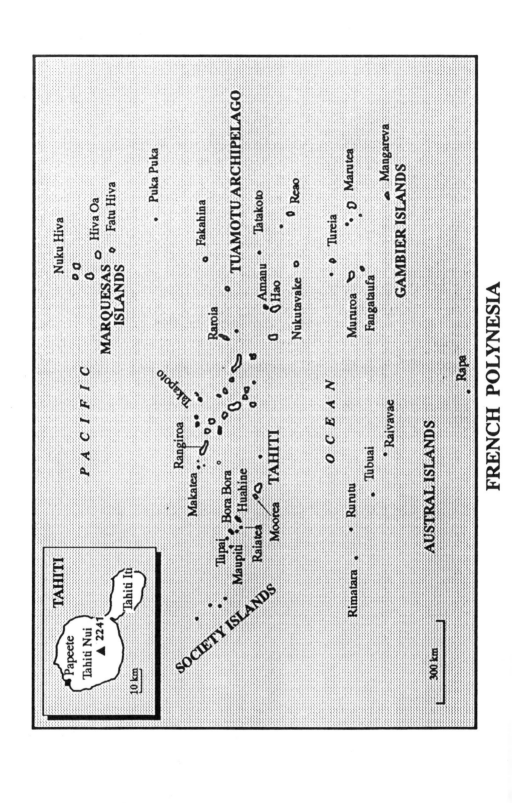

FRENCH POLYNESIA

the EFO were largely unsuccessful. The Tuamotu islands supplied pearls, and the island of Makatea became a significant source of phosphate from 1908 onwards. Papeete was a major entrepôt of the Pacific, although, ironically, no French shipping line regularly served the port until the 1920s.

The French had a demographic as well as commercial impact on the EFO. The indigenous Polynesian population was much affected by European diseases and tribal warfare; in the Marquesas archipelago, population may have dropped by half during the first fifty years of French control, one of the most dramatic declines ever recorded. The few French settlers who moved to the EFO included traders and demobilised soldiers given grants of land, and refugees from the gold rushes of Australia and California; gradually a small French settlement developed on Tahiti, and the other islands hosted a handful of foreigners. The notables of Tahiti, even after French takeover, remained largely an Anglo-Polynesian elite, resulting from the intermarriage of English settlers and Polynesian nobles. The presence of Protestant English missionaries in the islands since 1797 limited the potential for Catholic conversions and French displacement of the influential Protestant community. Increasingly important in the EFO was the growing number of Chinese migrants, who had arrived in the 1860s to work on the cotton plantations, but the failure of cotton led most to become shopkeepers. With these diverse groups, society in the EFO became stratified: French *métropolitain* administrators and an Anglo-Polynesian (gradually becoming a Franco-Polynesian) *métis* class, termed the *demis*, at the top, then a commercial class of largely Chinese traders, and, at the bottom, the full-blood Polynesians living mostly outside the European economy and society except in Tahiti itself. On the other islands, only occasional contacts with missionaries, traders and officials measured Polynesian fraternisation with Europeans.

Tahiti kept its mythical image as either paradise or paradise lost, the image which caused Rousseau to dream and attracted Loti, Segalen and Gauguin to the South Seas. Policy-makers were interested in the strategic value of Tahiti, particularly with the incursions of other powers into Oceania in the late 1800s — Germany, the United States and Britain also took over islands and archipelagos, and rivalry between the great powers, a constant feature of the scramble for Africa and Asia, was played out in miniature in the Pacific. But there was also commercial potential for Tahiti with the possibility of opening a canal through the isthmus of Panama; some observers predicted that this would revolutionise the world's economy and argued that France would be in a fine position to benefit from this development because of its Polynesian territories.

New Caledonia's main interest to the French was initially as a penitentiary, particularly since Guyane had such a dismal reputation. Not until ten years after French takeover were the first convoys of prisoners transported to New Caledonia but, from the 1860s until, as one governor put it, the 'dirty tap' of transportation was turned off in 1897, about 22,000 criminals and political prisoners were sent to New Caledonia. Best-known among these were the rebels of the Paris Commune of 1871, including such personalities as Henri de Rochefort and Louise Michel. A longer-lasting attraction of New Caledonia was its deposits of minerals, and at the time of French colonisation the sandalwood trade was still flourishing and bêche-de-mer, copra and pearlshell were also traded. Small-scale booms in gold, cobalt and chrome took place soon after the French arrival, and in 1863 nickel was discovered on the mainland, the Grande Terre. New Caledonia contains one of the globe's largest reserves of nickel, increasingly important in the nineteenth century as an additive to steel and for use in armaments manufacturing. Companies set up to exploit the mineral, especially the giant Société le Nickel (SLN), made New Caledonia the world's largest exporter of nickel by the end of the century.

To work the nickel mines, the French imported labourers, first from neighbouring islands, then from Japan, the Dutch East Indies (through an agreement with the government of the Netherlands) and French Indo-China. These contract labourers worked under conditions which seemed close to servility. Yet after their terms expired, many elected to remain in the French colony, continuing to work in the mines or setting themselves up as shopkeepers; in the 1920s, Asians briefly outnumbered Europeans. The French government meanwhile made several efforts to attract free European migrants, but programmes to encourage settlement by dispossessed Alsatians and Lorrainers in the 1870s, by French peasants in the 1890s and by refugees from the war-torn north of France in the 1920s did not produce the hoped-for results. New Caledonia, like Guyane, suffered from its reputation, in this case the unlovely picture of convicts, nickel mines and supposedly cannibalistic indigenes.

The local Melanesian population was almost totally excluded by French control. Few entered the French economy, even as workers in the mines, and no plantation economy was established. Intermarriage was not uncommon in the early years of French administration, but later became rarer and no *métis* class emerged as in Tahiti or the Antilles. Demands for land by European farmers and pastoralists who settled in New Caledonia led to the gradual dispossession of the Melanesian landowners. Ultimately, they were confined to reservations, through a policy of *cantonnement*, which totalled only one-tenth of the

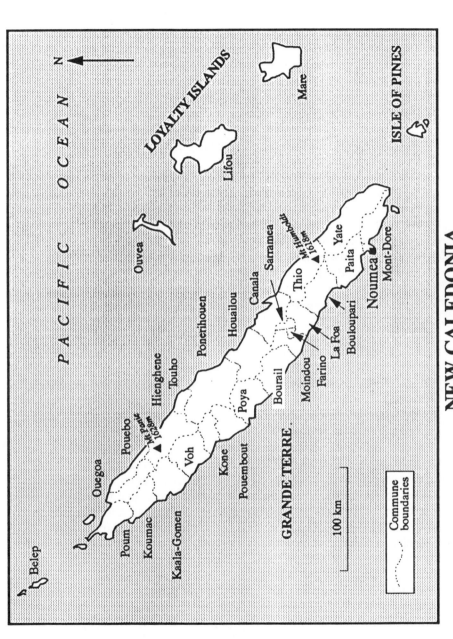

NEW CALEDONIA

land area of the territory (excluding the Loyalty Islands, which were not settled by Europeans). Yet Melanesians were obliged to provide labour for the Europeans and pay tax; their movements about the country were severely restricted and they were granted no political rights; under the *code de l'indigénat* they could be fined or otherwise punished, without benefit of a trial, for a large variety of infractions. European diseases, alcoholism, and outright massacre worked their effects on the indigenous population. Loss of their land, encroachment on their fields and cemeteries by European cattle, forced labour and attitudes ranging from paternalism to racism fuelled Melanesian dissatisfaction against the French, which erupted in a large-scale rebellion in 1878 and a smaller revolt in 1917.

New Caledonia and the EFO were administered, like the other colonies, by a governor; demands by some colonists for the creation of a government-general of the Pacific went unheeded. Chief executives changed so frequently, however, that contemporaries spoke of the *valse des gouverneurs* (waltz of the governors). As elsewhere in the empire, consultative councils, entirely composed of appointed *colons*, were set up, as were municipal governments. The form of colonial administration, well established by the late 1800s, changed little until after the Second World War. As in the other colonies, policies were decided in Paris and implemented by colonial officials. Colonists alternately supported the French administrators and baulked at their efforts to dominate colonial development. Colonists, missionaries, administrators and others often clashed on a variety of issues — notably, in New Caledonia, on the Saint-Simonian and anti-clerical theory and practice of Governor Guillain in the 1860s. All called for a greater development of the colonies, but Paris' attention was generally diverted to the larger colonies of Africa and Asia.

Wallis and Futuna, for their part, remained the province of the Catholic priests who had established a virtual theocracy in the islands together with the three local chiefs (or kings, as they came to be called). A French Resident, who did not always see eye to eye with either the priests or the chiefs, administered the colony as a deputy of the governor of New Caledonia. The legal code of the islands, based on Catholic precepts, banned many Polynesian customs as heathen, and the indigenous population remained submissive to the priests' control. European ships visited infrequently to collect the small amount of copra which formed the only export of the islands. European settlers were notable by their absence, and the Polynesians of Wallis and Futuna remained largely unincorporated into the European economy.

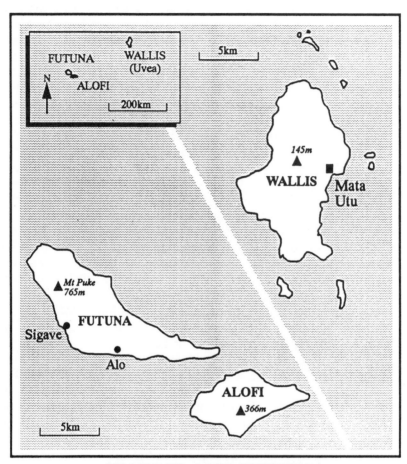

WALLIS AND FUTUNA

Mayotte

From their base in Réunion, the French in the 1800s began to be interested in other islands in the Indian Ocean, in particular, Madagascar. The Grande Ile, as it was called, did not become a French colony until 1896, but France had by then already acquired several islands off the coast of Madagascar and Africa, starting with the Ile Sainte-Marie, northeast of Madagascar, in 1821, and including the island of Mayotte in the Comoros archipelago.[15] In 1840, a French admiral sailing from Réunion negotiated a treaty with the queen of Nossi-Bé, off the northwestern Malagasy coast, to cede Nossi-Bé to France in return for a pension. The next year, France took over Mayotte. Mayotte was the easternmost of the four main islands of the Comoros, and the most fertile and least populated of that impoverished chain. The Islamic population was a melding of Africans, Arabs and Sakalave and Merina stock from Madagascar. Mayotte had been the victim of attacks from Madagascar and designs by the sultans of the other Comoros islands. The rulers of Mohéli invaded the island, then were chased out by the sultan of Anjouan, whose representative lived in the shadow of Andriantsouli, a Sakalave king who had taken over the island in the years before the French arrival. In 1841, Andriantsouli signed a treaty which gave full sovereignty over the island to the French, in return for a pension and the education of two of his sons in Réunion. The French promised to accept the inviolability of native lands and to respect the practices of Islam.

However, French presence in Mayotte was slight and few Europeans settled there. The island remained a subsistence economy, although it produced a certain number of spices for export, such as ylang-ylang (which was used for perfume), vanilla and cloves. What had once been a significant sugar industry, with more than a dozen processing plants and a workforce of more than 2000 men imported from Africa, had been reduced by economic problems in the 1880s and completely annihilated in an 1898 cyclone. Paris maintained an administrator in Mayotte, who also gained authority over Mohéli, Anjouan and Grande Comore when the other islands of the Comoros came under a French protectorate in 1886. The entire chain then passed under the control of the governor-general of Madagascar in the early twentieth century. Because of its long-standing attachment to France, and the local population's fears of domination by the other Comoros islands, Mayotte retained a special position which was affirmed when it refused to accept the independence of the Comoros in 1975.

The TAAF

In the great imperial division of the world, the great powers were anxious to pick up even uninhabited islands, such as Clipperton and the Iles Eparses (the Glorieuses, Juan-de-Nova, Europa, Bassas de India) in the Mozambique channel, which France obtained at the same time as Madagascar. Also included in the French domain were several unpopulated islands in the Southern Indian Ocean: Saint-Paul and Amsterdam, Kerguelen, and Crozet. French ships had reconnoitred these islands in the 1700s, and formal *prises de possession* took place in 1843 because of the interests of Réunionnais fishermen in working the waters surrounding the islands. No permanent occupation of the islands resulted, and the major visitors were American and British whalers and sealers. In 1840, the French captain Dumont d'Urville discovered and claimed French sovereignty over that section of the Antarctic continent which bears the name Queen Adélie Land. In 1924, the southern islands and French Antarctica were placed under the control of the governor-general of Madagascar. No endeavours were made to exploit them or to establish a real French presence in the Austral and Antarctic possessions, though whaling and sealing lasted for most of the nineteenth century until over-exploitation severely depleted stocks. Yet they were retained by France, just as several other powers also claimed other small and empty islands in the expanses of the world's oceans.

THE *VIEILLES COLONIES* AFTER 1848

The Antilles

As France's empire extended from the Antarctic to the Sahara, the old colonies underwent dramatic change, none more important than the abolition of slavery. Abolitionist ideas had been circulating since the late 1700s, and the short-lived and ineffective emancipation of slaves under the Convention had provided a precedent. In 1815, Napoleon, in an attempt to mollify the English during his brief return to power, forbade slave-trading, although shipments of Africans continued to arrive clandestinely in the Antilles, Guyane and Réunion. The British forced the French into signing a covenant in 1831 which gave the British the right to inspect ships suspected of slave-trading. Two years later the British abolished slavery in their empire. By the end of the decade the Pope had become openly critical of the institution, and such

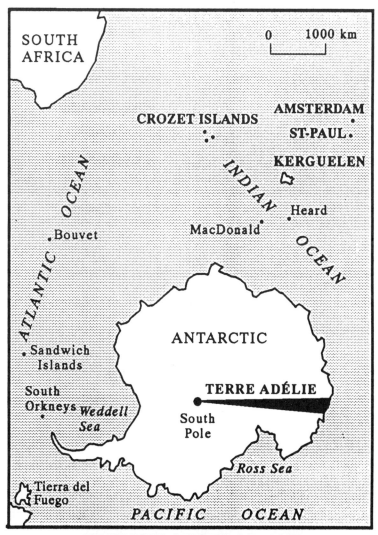

FRENCH AUSTRAL AND
ANTARCTIC TERRITORIES

prominent French intellectuals as Lamartine demanded the end of slavery in the French empire, either immediately or (as a plan drawn up by Tocqueville projected) over several years. The most ardent of the abolitionists was Victor Schoelcher, whose visits to the Caribbean had convinced him of the evil of slavery, and his books and political lobbying helped turn the tide. Meanwhile, greater rights were granted to freed slaves and *métis*, the small number of slaves owned by the French state were freed (as were several thousand slaves in Mayotte) and the number of private emancipations of slaves had reached more than 40,000 by 1842. Ultimately, the economic value of slavery also came into question; the high mortality rate among slaves meant that the number of slaves in the colonies was dropping and declined still further without new but now illegal infusions from Africa. And the crisis in sugar production, created by the competition from sugar beet, reduced both the need for slaves and the means for plantation-owners to buy and support them.

The Revolution and overthrow of the July Monarchy in 1848 sped up the process, and on 17 April of that year the National Assembly passed a law emancipating slaves throughout the French empire. Before the decree could reach the Antilles, a major revolt broke out in Martinique on 22 May (accompanied by a smaller rebellion in Guadeloupe), which demonstrated that the institution of slavery could not last and the blacks might gain their freedom themselves. For some observers, the abolition of slavery, therefore, represented a humanitarian gesture granted by an egalitarian France; for others it was an inevitable occurrence based on lessening profitability; and for still others, including some Antillais nationalist historians, an emancipation that blacks were in the process of winning for themselves.[16]

The end of slavery and the freeing of some quarter of a million slaves in the French plantation colonies, however, did not solve many problems for either the slaves or their former masters. Provisions were made for slave-owners to receive indemnities: although the planters claimed they were ruined by abolition, and inadequately compensated with treasury bonds, they probably exaggerated their plight. Nevertheless, they did lack some of their old capital and labour. The emancipation laws mandated a registration of former slaves and granted them political rights, but it also allowed various regulations to curb their freedom of movement and the full enjoyment of those rights. The forced labour required for several years after 1848, in some cases even from blacks who had not been slaves, perpetuated servile conditions but calmed planters. Most slaves, without capital or training, found it difficult to make their way in the new world. Many fled the *habitations*, and the blacks and *métis* in the colonies thereafter exhibited a horror of plantation employment. They crowded into cities, searched for alternative jobs, or tried to support themselves on small plots of land. For many there was no escape from work on the sugar fields. If they could not buy land — which was sometimes possible as some of the old *habitations* broke up — they could sign on as contract day labourers on the plantations, agree to piecework payment for their duties, or enter into a system resembling share-cropping in which they would receive a share of the production for their own use and sale.

Given the opposition of former slaves to plantation work, however, the *Békés* and other landowners sought new sources of labour. Several possibilities, including the import of more Africans as contract labourers, were rejected. Some migrants were recruited in Japan and China, but the most feasible solution was the import of labourers from India, both from the French *comptoirs* and, by arrangements with the British or more secretly, from the British Indian empire. (This was similar to the approach the British themselves employed, as they were then in the process of moving such large numbers of Indians to work the cane fields of Mauritius and Fiji that Indians eventually formed the majority of the population in both those countries.) From 1850 to 1914, some 25,000 Indians arrived in Martinique, 37,000 in Guadeloupe and 8000 in Guyane. Not all stayed or survived; of those migrating to Martinique, almost 15,000 died within a few years after their arrival, and 4500 were repatriated. Nevertheless, they added a new component to the Antillais, Guyanais and Réunionnais population.

Emancipation broke down the differences between free men and slaves in the West Indies but could not equalise the social structure. The *Békés* still ruled in Martinique, and metropolitan companies became increasingly important in Guadeloupe. The Indians had become a new agrarian proletariat. The blacks lived as peasant farmers, plantation workers and small-scale artisans and traders. Of rising importance, from 1848 through to the present, were the mixed-blood Antillais. They had benefited from education and freedom, and now they moved into a position of greater commercial importance as traders and merchants; they increased their numbers in the administration, both in the Caribbean colonies and elsewhere in the French empire. They also began to gain political clout. Whites, after the declaration of universal male suffrage — another great gain of 1848 — felt that they had lost political power in the colonies and sometimes abandoned local politics, content to maintain economic domination in the islands. This opened the way for the *métis* and blacks to gain substantial political control in municipal government and, somewhat later, win election as representatives to the National Assembly and colonial councils. The black and *métissé* bourgeoisie, therefore, became the key element in

Antillais society. Furthermore, this group, rather than demanding the autonomy which the plantation owners and *Békés* had sought in the *ancien régime* and before 1848, wanted France to put into practice the *assimilation* which it preached. Their full political and economic liberation, in short, should come from the utmost integration of the *vieilles colonies* into the French state.

The road to that *assimilation*, institutionally achieved with the *départementalisation* of the *vieilles colonies* in 1946, was long. The heady days of 1848 and the Second Republic were followed by the reaction of the Second Empire of Napoleon III; in opposition, Victor Schoelcher, the hero of emancipation who had been elected a *député* from Martinique, Guadeloupe and Guyane, went into exile. In the late 1800s, France diverted its major international efforts to the Crimea, Italy, Lebanon and Mexico and to the emperor's vain attempt to create an Arabic kingdom in Algeria. In the meantime, the economy of the Antilles began to stagnate.

The 'war of the two sugars' affected French production in the Antilles, but competition also came from other cane producers, such as Cuba, particularly for the North American market. Yet sugarcane retained its dominance of the Antillais economy. In Martinique, 55 per cent of cultivated land was planted in cane in 1856, 49 per cent in 1895 and 66.7 per cent in 1939; the corresponding figures for Guadeloupe were 59, 45 and 55 per cent. In both colonies, the largest proportion of workers (42 per cent) worked in the sugarcane fields at the end of the nineteenth century. Almost the entire value of exports in Guadeloupe and Martinique during the nineteenth century was provided by sugar and its derivatives, such as rum and molasses and, by 1934, cane products still amounted to 71 per cent of the value of Guadeloupe's exports and 81 per cent of the value of those of Martinique.

These figures do suggest some diversification. In the case of Guadeloupe, this was due to the planting of other tropical products, primarily bananas, in the early twentieth century; the island also produced some coffee, indigo, spices and pineapples. For Martinique, rum assumed increased importance; in fact, rum overtook raw sugar as Martinique's main export, and by the first years of the 1920s, represented 60 per cent of the island's sales, compared with 36 per cent for sugar itself, and at the end of the nineteenth century Martinique was the world's leading rum exporter. Overall exports increased as farming and refining techniques improved yet many crops experienced difficulties. In Guadeloupe, coffee production, widespread in the early nineteenth century, had disappeared from most regions by the end of the century, remaining only in the uplands around Basse-Terre. Consequently in Guadeloupe in 1934, sugar represented 40 per cent of exports, rum

31 per cent and bananas 21 per cent. France remained the major
trading partner of the Caribbean colonies, accounting for about three-
quarters of their imports and exports. The free trade system which
lasted for two decades after 1860, replacing the *Exclusif*, only margin-
ally cut into France's trade superiority, and protectionist tariffs were
subsequently reintroduced and continually increased.

Just as the economy changed little, there were few surprising political metamorphoses in the French Caribbean in the century after
1848. Little institutional change occurred, except for efforts by local
councils to win greater influence in political affairs. The major political
movements came from contestation by the working-class population: a
riot in Martinique in 1870, led by blacks, then strikes by workers in both
Martinique and Guadeloupe in the 1890s and after the turn of the
century. By this time, socialist groups had organised in the colonies and
confronted the representatives of the older political parties. Other developments common to France also had an impact on the Caribbean:
increased urbanisation and the setting up of public schools (although
much of the population remained illiterate).

The most dramatic event in the Antilles was the eruption of the Mont
Pélée volcano in northern Martinique in 1902. In less than a minute,
the major city of the island, Saint-Pierre, was totally destroyed. The loss
of 30,000 lives and the destruction of the city deprived the colony of
the centre of its social life and much of its infrastructure. The eruption
was a vivid reminder of the natural dangers faced in the Caribbean,
where islands were prey to hurricanes, tidal waves and various other
disasters.

Réunion

The history of Réunion after the abolition of slavery resembles that of
the Antilles, including the same flight of freed slaves from the plantations. The Réunionnais planters also then recruited new workers,
68,000 of whom arrived within fifteen years; the largest numbers were
Indians, but some came from China, Madagascar and the African coast
(the 'Cafres'), adding still further to the ethnic diversity of the island's
population. Because of this available labour force, the next decades
marked the apogee of Réunion's plantation economy as production of
sugar increased from 30,000 tons in 1846 to 73,000 tons by 1860. The
government carried out significant public works projects, even constructing a small railway, and the economy boomed. Réunion also
began to engage in a form of 'sub-imperialism' in the Indian Ocean
with the takeover of the Ile Sante-Marie, Nossi-Bé and Mayotte, and
the greater designs on the Grande Ile. At the end of the century, these

efforts showed success, but, ironically, the conquest of Madagascar eclipsed Réunion in the French empire.

From 1863 the colony entered a period of decline caused by a dramatic fall in sugar prices on the world market. Réunion was also affected by the ravages of a cane disease and outbreaks of cholera and malaria. In the decade after 1860, production of sugar fell from 73,000 tons to only 23,500. The major proprietors struggled through, but many of the smallholders were ruined and joined the penurious farmers of the Hauts. The opening of the Suez Canal in 1869 also played a role, as it turned ships away from the maritime route around southern Africa and the Indian Ocean islands.

The economy of Réunion, like that of the Antilles, responded by a slow diversification in the late 1800s — production of vanilla, introduced into the island in 1848, peaked at the end of the century; vetyver (a plant producing an aromatic oil) was brought from India and ylang-ylang from the Philippines. Yet another new crop was geraniums, and Réunion became the world's largest producer after 1900. Such new plants, and especially geraniums, helped ease the effect of the crisis in sugar production and export in the late 1800s, and Réunion alongside the other *vieilles colonies* had become one of the world's principal rum exporters by the end of the century. Nevertheless, recovery from the sugar crisis did not really occur until after 1920. Then production of both sugar and geraniums reached unparalleled levels, and a balance of trade was achieved.

Guyane

Guyane experienced many of the effects of the 1848 emancipation that had so comprehensively influenced the plantation islands. Sugar had never been so important in Guyane as in the Antilles or Réunion, but it was a major export crop and was also produced on large plantations worked by slaves. Emancipation led to a great shortage of labour; slaves left the plantations even more quickly than in the islands because of easy access to unclaimed and vacant land for subsistence farming. The need for new immigrants was filled by recruits from the Indian subcontinent. Farmers continued to grow some export crops, but agriculture was overshadowed by the two dramatic changes which occurred in Guyane: the establishment of the penitentiary and the gold rush.[17]

The prison colony in Guyane was created in 1851, and prisoners continued to be sent until 1932; only in 1945 was the prison establishment officially closed. Saint-Laurent on the Maroni River became the centre, and the seat of the penal administration, but Devil's Island (in the Iles du Salut) had the most notorious reputation for receiving such famous prisoners as Alfred Dreyfus and 'Papillon'. As many as 70,000 prisoners, some convicted of common crimes and some of political activities, were transported to Guyane. The prison further tarnished the image of Guyane and did little for the development of the colony. Many prisoners died, including 7600 of the 18,000 deported in the first fifteen years. Those who remained had little possibility for rehabilitation outside the penal system. Prisoners resident in the colony from 1906 to 1936 numbered around 7000, which generally represented about 20 per cent of the total population of Guyane. Since 400 to 500 public servants were employed in the penal administration, the penitentiary represented a colossal enterprise in the colony. Indeed the penal administration was the primary purchaser of both agricultural and industrial goods produced in the colony and was the single largest importer. Colonists (and lobbyists in Paris) denounced the penal settlement, but feared the deleterious effects on the Guyanais economy if it were disestablished without an alternative activity to sustain the colony.

Gold was discovered in Guyane in 1855. Two years later, Guyane had already produced 11 kilograms of gold, and gold production totalled 81 kilograms by 1861. But the real gold rush came in the period from 1880 to 1916. Gold-diggers moved deeper and deeper into the jungle, setting up camps and mining towns, such as Maripasoula on the Maroni River, some finding their fortunes, others disappointed, even dying of tropical diseases. Thousands of miners poured into Guyane from the Antilles, Brazil, English and Dutch Guiana and Venezuela; some were salaried labourers of the mining companies, others independent searchers. Some miners (the *bricoleurs*) had official permission to prospect and work concessions; others (*maraudeurs*) were illegal. In 1906, the government officially listed 7000 gold-diggers, and in 1911 some 12,000; the number then dwindled to around 5000 by 1936. Although local Guyanais companies had started mineral exploitation, metropolitan interests gradually took over. Prospecting remained more practical than scientific. The government approved concessions which were gradually concentrated in the hands of about sixty or seventy major proprietors. The owners did well from the gold rush, but the hard-worked and badly paid employees did less well.

From 1864 to 1874, the annual average of gold exports attained 425 kilograms, then soared to 3179 in the period from 1894 to 1904 only to drop in the following decade. On a world level, Guyane was a minor producer of gold — its output was only 0.47 per cent of the world's production in 1915. But in a region with a population of fewer than 30,000 inhabitants at the end of the nineteenth century, gold mining employed most of the working population and covered almost all imports. Not surprisingly, gold made up well over nine-tenths of the colony's total exports. Gold also led to the growth of Cayenne as a centre of trade and finance, and brought in its wake the development of various service activities — trade in mining equipment, cafés, brothels and money-lending — that were common to gold rushes around the world.

The gold rush also had a devastating effect on other sectors of Guyane's economy, as farmers and pastoralists, already few enough, abandoned their holdings to seek their fortunes in gold. The colony continued to export skins, cocoa, gum and a little rum, but gold was king. Then, after 1916, the gold boom declined as deposits were exhausted and prices dropped. Guyane plunged into crisis. The old diggers drifted away from the mines and back onto the farms, a return to the soil that even included a revival of sugar plantations that had been abandoned for thirty years and the setting up of rum distilleries. The new agricultural efforts produced some results, exports of rum increasing from only 8 hectolitres in 1904 to 1145 in 1928, and new sources of income, such as balata gum, were developed for short periods at the beginning of the century. However, by the 1930s, the prices of the primary commodities which Guyane could export had all declined. Guyane, after the gold boom, became what it had been before, a small and underdeveloped settlement, the gold of the mining boom tarnished by the prison colony.

Another unsuccessful development in Guyane was the attempt to develop the territory of the Inini, the vast southern jungle set apart as a particular administrative entity in 1930. Forestry, mining and agriculture presented the mirage of potential development in this region, and ideas were mooted for sending a thousand Indo-Chinese prisoners to the Inini to provide labour. Yet nothing came of these plans, and the Inini remained a largely remote and uninhabited reach of the French empire. It could not release the elusive and ambiguous potential of this enormous colony.

Saint-Pierre and Miquelon

France's North American colony slumbered on in the century before 1945. Gradually an infrastructure was put in place — a cable link with Canada in 1867, a savings bank in 1874, a Banque des Iles in 1889. A civilian governor replaced the military commander as the representative of Paris in the islands, and a handful of troops were stationed in the islands. The economy still centred on fishing, both that done by local men and the metropolitan fishermen who came to the area each year; ship-building and maintenance activities associated with the profession complemented fishing. The 1880s marked the most successful period of Saint-Pierrais fishing, typically marked by the value of imports doubling between 1882 and 1887, but the archipelago suffered a great crisis in 1903–4 — several years of shipwrecks, increasing use by competitors of steam power for fishing, bad harvests, a decline in ship-building, a drop in population and clashes with the administration of Newfoundland. The British authorities in Newfoundland in 1887 had forbidden the shipment of fishing bait to Saint-Pierre, which created a problem for the fishermen. Then in 1904, after numerous debates and quarrels, the French ceded their fishing rights to the 'French Shore' of Newfoundland (which had also allowed some shore rights) to the British.

A brief return to prosperity occurred after the First World War. The United States, in 1920, had instituted a ban on the manufacture and sale of alcoholic beverages, and Prohibition lasted until 1933. From 1922, Saint-Pierre turned this to its profit by becoming a giant entrepôt for the smuggling of liquor to the United States. Bottles of alcohol were legally imported from Europe or Canada, stocked on shore, then loaded onto ships at sea for an 'unknown' destination. The tax revenues on the imported alcohol were large enough to finance the sealing of island roads and the renovation of the port. This activity also provided profits for local entrepreneurs and work for colonists. The end of Prohibition, coming during the Depression years, plunged Saint-Pierre and Miquelon into renewed economic troubles and made the archipelago once again dependent on its historic mainstay of cod fishing.

THE *VIEILLES COLONIES* AND THE FUTURE TOMs IN THE MID-1900s

A century after the emancipation of slaves in the *vieilles colonies*, the discovery of gold in Guyane, and the takeover of the EFO, New Caledonia and Mayotte, these colonies remained small pieces of a French empire that had grown to embrace major chunks of Africa and Southeast Asia. Madagascar alone was larger than France itself. Yet the small colonies had served a variety of purposes for France. The *vieilles colonies* provided the cod from Saint-Pierre, most of France's sugar, and supplies of such tropical products as copra, coffee, cocoa, perfume essence and pearls, as well as the phosphate of the EFO, the nickel of New Caledonia and — though apparently all but mined out — the gold of Guyane. New Caledonia, for thirty-five years, and Guyane, for a hundred, had provided a place for France to send its unwanted convicts and political agitators; Martinique provided a home in exile for King Béhanzin of Dahomey when France took over his realm, and both Wallis and the EFO provided places of detention for rebels from the New Caledonian insurrection of 1878. These colonies gave France a strategic presence in the Atlantic and Caribbean, the Pacific and the Indian Oceans, at a time when France was wary of its old imperial rivals like Britain, and more and more alarmed by the expansion of Germany and Japan. The colonies had sent soldiers to fight in the First World War: 30,000 soldiers from the French Antilles and Guyane served in the war, and Réunion sent 20,000. Of the 51,618 men who fought for France from the *vieilles colonies*, 32,918 were lost in action. The Pacific colonies sent some 2300 men to the front, most of them Melanesians and Polynesians. On the eve of the Second World War, about 850,000 French citizens or subjects lived in the *vieilles colonies* and Pacific colonies, including the white *Caldoche* settlers of New Caledonia, the *Békés* of Martinique and Réunion, and the Europeans of the EFO. But there were also the *demis* of Tahiti and the *mulâtres* of the West Indies, many of whom regarded themselves as French, migrants brought in from Asia, the descendants of African slaves, and the diverse Melanesians and Polynesians of the Pacific, the Amerindians of Guyane and the Mahorais of Mayotte. Though small, distant and seemingly peripheral to the new French colonial adventure, these little colonies had a particularly complex social structure, decided economic and strategic interests and a long future of evolution within the French Republic. They were never inconsequential.

3

Decolonisation and Institutional Change since 1940

T HE 1930s was the golden age of colonialism, and France and its empire, despite the effects of the Depression, seemed secure. However, the expansionism of Nazi Germany and the invasion of France endangered the very survival of the nation and its colonies. The war years brought dramatic upheaval to France and its overseas domains, and the political and economic reconstruction of the late 1940s set in place new institutions under the Fourth Republic. Little more than a decade later, in the midst of the Algerian war of independence, another change of regimes, and the foundation of the Fifth Republic, meant that the relationship between the *métropole* and its DOM-TOMs was again recast. The constitutional and institutional history of France and its colonies since the Second World War shows the changes of attitude and policy that occurred during a phase of decolonisation and explains provisions of the constitution of the Fifth Republic, still in force, which are the legal framework for the links between France and its overseas outposts.

THE SECOND WORLD WAR

The Second World War cut off metropolitan France from its overseas empire. After only six weeks of fighting, France capitulated to the

German invaders and was subsequently divided into a German-occupied sector and the Vichy zone, under the rule of the collaborationist Marshal Pétain. Charles de Gaulle, then a young officer, issued a call from London for continued French struggle and refusal to collaborate; he subsequently organised the Free French forces overseas and the Resistance inside France. The rapidity of these events, and the bitter division between the *collaborateurs* and *résistants*, took the empire by surprise. Governors and political elites had to decide where to place their loyalties, a difficult task considering the token legality of the Vichy regime and the initial weakness of de Gaulle's movement. Only two colonies initially rallied to de Gaulle. In Chad, the governor, Félix Eboué, a black Guyanais, threw in his lot with the Free French, although his action was not followed elsewhere in the AOF and AEF. In the Franco-British condominium of the New Hebrides, the French Resident, Henri Sautot, also rallied to de Gaulle. With encouragement from the British and Australians, Sautot then sailed to New Caledonia and overthrew the pro-Vichy governor in that colony. Meanwhile, in the EFO, pro- and anti-Vichy factions fought for control, which the pro-Gaullist group eventually won. By late 1940, only Wallis and Futuna, of the three territories of French Oceania, maintained loyalty to Vichy, but elsewhere in the empire the Vichy government ruled. French Indo-China proved especially loyal to Pétain, and the *vieilles colonies* and much of the nineteenth-century empire refused to recognise de Gaulle or participate in his struggle. The Allied invasion of North Africa in 1942 began the emancipation of the French Maghreb and allowed de Gaulle to set up in Algeria a year later the national liberation committee that became the provisional government of France. Elsewhere, *résistants* worked against the pro-Nazi régimes and gradually the other colonies came around, first the AOF and Guyane, then Martinique and Guadeloupe. By the end of 1943, practically all the empire had rallied to the Free French.[1]

The war years created great changes in the colonies. Separated from the *métropole* which had supplied many of their imports and taken the lion's share of their exports, they had to subsist as best they could; in fact, with great efforts, most of the colonies attained self-sufficiency in basic supplies. Administrative autonomy also resulted, as the war removed the centralised direction from Paris that had existed before 1940. The stationing of some half-million Allied soldiers (mostly Americans) in New Caledonia, on Wallis and on the EFO island of Bora Bora, and the presence of the Allied armies in North Africa, injected large sums of money into some of the colonies. The presence of foreign troops also tore some colonies, especially those of the South Pacific, out of their isolation, exposing both *colons* and natives to different customs, social relations, dislocation and new ideas. The impact of the Americans in New Caledonia was so strong that a group of Caldoches even hoped that the colony would become part of the United States when the war was over. After the war years a new political elite emerged: men who had first rallied to de Gaulle, members of the Communist party who achieved a new respectability for opposition to the Axis and the Vichyites and native leaders whose political sensitivities were awakened during the war.[2]

The war also provided the crucible for a heating-up of nationalist passions among the indigenous population of the empire. Already in the 1930s, cultural and political movements had demanded improvement in native rights and welfare; the intellectual movement of *négritude* championed the black race of Africa and the Antilles, while in Tunisia, Morocco and Algeria nationalist political groups organised. Their aims varied; most called for constitutional changes, citizenship for the non-French populations, betterment of working conditions and more self-government, but few demanded outright independence. During the war such demands matured, notably in North Africa, where nationalist leaders were accused (sometimes wrongly) of having collaborated with the Germans in order to fight French colonialism. In Vietnam, the pro-Vichy Hanoi government agreed to Japanese influence over the colony, and Ho Chi Minh, in response, set up the Viet Minh; just before the end of the war in Asia, Japanese troops invaded Indo-China and proclaimed Vietnam independent. In the Middle East, British and French troops invaded the French mandated territories of Syria and Lebanon; in 1941 de Gaulle recognised the sovereignty of the Syrian and Lebanese republics, accessions to independence which became effective with the evacuation of French troops in 1946.[3]

In the midst of the war, de Gaulle called a conference of French African colonies in Brazzaville to discuss the fate of the empire. The conference put forward a large number of social and economic measures to be carried out after the war, including efforts to improve indigenous employment and bring about greater equality between Europeans and other inhabitants of the colonies and plans to modernise agriculture and encourage industrialisation. The conference documents also foreshadowed administrative changes and greater colonial representation in Paris. However, the general tone of the Brazzaville declarations remained conservative, despite acquiescence to greater economic and political liberty. A principle printed in capital letters in the conference's papers left no doubt:

The objectives of the civilising endeavours carried out by France in its colonies exclude any idea of autonomy, or the possibility of political evolution outside the French empire; even the distant possibility of self-government in the colonies is to be excluded.[4]

The conference therefore argued explicitly for a continuation of direct and centralised rule and denied the possibility of autonomy, let alone independence. Various changes could take place, but a severing of the imperial bond could not. Whether that position could be maintained in the face of rising nationalism, the anti-colonial position of France's American and Soviet allies and the charter of the United Nations, which recognised the rights of all peoples to self-determination, necessarily remained uncertain.

DECOLONISATION, 1946-62

The fifteen years after the end of the Second World War saw the dismantling of most of the French empire. France was not alone in decolonisation, as Britain, the Netherlands, Italy and Belgium also gave up all or most of their colonies by the early 1960s; Portugal held out but, after the mid-1970s, it too withdrew. The speed and the relative completeness of decolonisation were remarkable. Critics charged that Britain carried out the process rather better than France, more rapidly and with less loss of life and internecine quarrelling; the British willingness to allow self-government and a gradual transition to independence, and unwillingness to fight to the end, have been given credit for this success.[5] However, Britain retains a significant colonial empire and the United States increased its presence in the northern Pacific; the disparities are not so clear-cut, and are even less so when other imperial countries enter into the comparison. The particular regions of French colonisation, French ideology, the political constellation in post-war France and different aims in international relations were all components in the specific French structure and process of decolonisation, and it would have been surprising if any two nations had followed the same path.

The new post-war constitution which established the Fourth Republic in 1946 recast France's relations with the empire. The constitution founded the Union Française which, according to Article 60 of the constitution, 'is formed on the one hand of the French Republic which consists of metropolitan France, and the overseas *départements* and *territoires*, and on the other, of the associated territories and states'. The Union, therefore, included metropolitan France, the *vieilles colonies* which were now transformed into *départements* and the overseas territories (for the most part, the nineteenth-century colonies). But the constitution did make allowances for changes in status and for the association of other entities (including independent states) with the Union Française. The aim, according to the constitution's preamble, was to bring together nations and peoples 'which may combine or coordinate their resources and their efforts in order to develop their respective civilisations, improve their well-being and maintain their security'. The constitution defined the overseas role of France:

Faithful to its traditional mission, France intends to enable the people of which it has taken charge to achieve the freedom to govern themselves and to manage their own affairs democratically; excluding any system of colonisation based on arbitrariness, it guarantees to all equal access to public office and the individual or collective exercise of the rights and liberties proclaimed and confirmed above.

The constitution thus made all residents of the colonies French citizens.

The Union was a form of federalism, but one in which France kept the upper hand. The President of France was head of the Union, Paris retained constitutional control of matters relating to defence and the assembly could debate only legislation referred to it by the French National Assembly. Half the members of the assembly of the Union Française came from metropolitan France and half were deputies from the overseas *départements* and *territoires* and associated governments and states. Governors and other administrators were appointed by Paris and local assemblies only had consultative powers. In short, Paris maintained firm control, and the spirit of Brazzaville endured.

Even before the new constitution was promulgated, troubles began. The first round of decolonisation took place in the large colonies of Asia. Immediately the Second World War ended, as Britain faced insurrection in India, and the Netherlands in Indonesia, France experienced new problems in Indo-China. The year 1945 saw chaos in Vietnam with the Japanese invasion, Ho Chi Minh's opposition to both the Japanese and the French, and American concern leading to the parachuting of a group of soldiers into Vietnam to train Ho's troops to fight the Japanese. With the defeat of the Japanese, China occupied the northern part of Vietnam, the British the southern region. Ho called a convention which elected him head of a provisional government; he then captured Hanoi. The French sent in forces to re-establish French sovereignty and subsequently divided Indo-China into a federation composed of northern Vietnam (under Ho, who was now recognised by Paris), Cambodia and Laos, all of which became part of the Union

Française; France retained direct control over Cochinchina. In 1946, the French bombarded Haiphong, controlled by Ho, which led the Viet Minh leader to campaign for outright and total independence. Fighting continued until 1954, when the French suffered a substantial defeat at Dienbienphu. Vietnam was then divided between Ho's communist regime in the north, and the French-supported emperor Bao Dai in the south. Elections, supposed to take place within a year, were never held, and Bao Dai was soon deposed. With the withdrawal from Vietnam, and the earlier independence of Cambodia and Laos in 1953, France had lost its empire in Indo-China.[6] In 1954, Paris also ceded Pondichéry, the most important of the *comptoirs français de l'Inde*, to the Republic of India, finally winding up the French empire in Asia.[7]

Over the same period nationalist movements in Tunisia and Morocco had gained strength. France acknowledged in the early 1950s that Tunisia had a 'vocation' for independence but repressed dissent and tried to design a plan for Franco-Tunisian co-sovereignty. This proved impossible, and France recognised an autonomous government in 1954. That government, however, was short-lived, and Tunisia gained complete independence in 1956. In Morocco, too, France at first opposed independence, going so far as to depose the sultan in 1953; that action merely made him a focus for nationalist campaigns and generated a wave of terrorism. In 1956 independence was granted to Morocco, and the deposed sultan returned as king.[8]

Algeria, however, remained France's most important overseas possession, one of the first of the new French territories conquered in the nineteenth-century. Incorporated into the French national territory and divided into *départements* in 1848, it was not strictly a colony. The other distinguishing fact about Algeria was the settlement there of close to a million Europeans, the *pieds-noirs*, though a large proportion of them (about half at the end of the 1800s) were not of French ancestry. They were far outnumbered by eight million non-Europeans, almost all Muslim. Algerian nationalism had developed steadily since the 1930s and become increasingly radical. In 1954, the same year as Dienbienphu, a rebellion broke out in Algiers; the French quickly put it down and pronounced secession inconceivable. A rebellion in Constantine followed in 1955, which led to the death of some 150 Europeans; in reprisal, as many as 15,000 Arab Algerians were killed. Confrontation continued throughout 1956, the year of the Suez War, pitting the French army against the militant Front de Libération Nationale (FLN), and in 1957 the insurrection and strikes in the capital of French Algeria were so dramatic that observers spoke of the 'battle of Algiers'. The struggle became vicious as the FLN practised violent guerrilla warfare, and the French troops responded with summary arrest and torture. By 1958, the situation had dissolved into chaos and the government of the Fourth Republic fell in Paris.

Charles de Gaulle then returned to power as prime minister and soon devised a new constitution, inaugurating the Fifth Republic with himself as the new president. Coming out of retirement to serve, de Gaulle was considered by his supporters to be a non-partisan figure, popular with the electorate and the army and able to solve the Algerian crisis; for his opponents, the new constitution and de Gaulle's heavy-handed rule represented little less than a *coup d'état*. Soon after returning to power, de Gaulle visited Algeria and his famous cries of 'Vive l'Algérie française' ('Long live French Algeria') and 'Je vous ai compris' ('I have understood you') convinced the *pieds-noirs* that the new government would suppress the FLN and ensure that Algeria remained French. Yet violence continued and the FLN's guerilla tactics were quickly matched by the terrorism of the pro-French Organisation de l'Armée Secrète (OAS). At a certain unknown point in this struggle de Gaulle became convinced of the necessity to decolonise Algeria. This unexpected conviction provoked great hostility, including an attempted coup by generals in Algeria, terrorism in France and plots to assassinate de Gaulle. However, negotiations with the FLN worked out an arrangement for Algerian independence with, in theory, the safeguarding of the interests of the *pieds-noirs*. The Evian accords, ratified by the French and the Algerian electorates, brought independence to Algeria in 1962, but most Europeans left Algeria for France or for other French overseas possessions. The protracted and bloody war in Algeria left bitter memories on both sides.[9]

The constitution of 1958, promulgated in the midst of the Algerian crisis, renamed the Union Française the Communauté (Community) (with the adjective 'Française' removed) and offered 'to those overseas territoires which express the desire to join it, new institutions based on the common ideal of liberty, equality and fraternity and conceived with a view to their democratic evolution'. Acceptance of the new arrangements, therefore, depended on votes taken in each of the former colonies (although not the *départements* of Algeria or the other overseas *départements*); each could retain its status as a *territoire d'outre-mer*, opt for *départementalisation*, become an autonomous member of the Community or obtain total independence. If a territory accepted membership, it would accede to self-government but give France certain responsibilities, namely in foreign policy, defence, currency, economic and financial policy and control of strategic raw materials, as well as, unless a separate arrangement was made, justice, higher education, transport and telecommunications. The French president would remain as president of the Community, and there would also be a *Conseil exécutif* made up of the heads of government of the member states, a Senate and a Community court.[10]

Most of the political leaders of the overseas territories rallied to de Gaulle's proposals. Notable among those who argued against the new constitution were the leader of Guinea, Sékou Touré, and a major political figure in Tahiti, Pouvana'a a Oopa. De Gaulle made it clear that any territory which rejected the Community would become independent with France's blessing but would no longer be eligible for French aid, since it would have judged itself mature enough to manage its own affairs. In the event, apart from Guinea, all the overseas territories (including French Polynesia) voted in favour of membership, and then gained independence. The result was celebrated in Paris and in many of the former colonies, but the Community did not last, and some of the Community institutions, such as the court, never met. In Africa, leaders were uncertain whether to establish separate states based on more traditional divisions or to combine old colonies into new federations; there was also dissatisfaction with the extent of powers reserved to the Community (effectively to France itself).

New legislation in 1960 made it possible for a member state to become fully independent without leaving the Community and, without much fuss or opposition, the states of Africa quickly separated from France and the Community. In that one year Senegal, Mali, the Ivory Coast, Dahomey (Benin), Upper Volta (Burkina Faso), Niger, Mauritania, the Central African Republic, Congo, Gabon, Chad and Madagascar all became independent. Soon afterwards, France signed agreements to provide aid and technical assistance (*accords de coopération*) with these states, and the old Ministère de la France d'Outre-Mer became the Ministère de la Coopération. (The overseas *départements*, attached to the Ministère de l'Intérieur, were unaffected by the constitution or the independence of the African territories.) The Community withered away almost immediately although references to it remain in the French constitution.

DECOLONISATION: THE FINAL PHASE?

The independence of the African territories in 1960 and of Algeria in 1962 left France with its four *départements d'outre-mer* and the territories of Saint-Pierre and Miquelon, French Polynesia, New Caledonia, Wallis and Futuna in the Pacific, the TAAF (organised as a territory in 1955), the Comoros (including Mayotte) in the Indian Ocean, French Somaliland (Djibouti) on the horn of Africa, and the condominium of the New Hebrides. In all except the TAAF and the New Hebrides, territorial assemblies were set up, some degree of autonomy was recognised and most observers assumed that the era of French decolonisation had come to an end.

Three of these fragments of empire eventually became independent, almost as an afterthought, during the presidency of Valéry Giscard d'Estaing (1974–81). In many respects it was scarcely surprising that this was belated since all three, the Comoros, Djibouti and the New Hebrides, were quite different from the colonies that had preceded them to independence. Above all, each of the three was much smaller than most other independent states. The New Hebrides (Vanuatu) had a population of no more than about 120,000 when it became independent, and Djibouti and the Comoros each had around 300,000. They were relatively poor, isolated and seemingly without the political institutions to guarantee a successful transition to independence.

The Comoros, after 1958, enjoyed self-government under a local sheikh, who moved the capital from Dzaoudzi in Mayotte to Moroni on Grande Comore island. This aggravated discontent in Mayotte, where the local Mahorais population had always felt themselves different from the other islands in the group. In the 1960s, a pro-independence party, based overseas, won support inside the Comoros and also from the Organisation of African Unity and the Soviet Union, whilst the Socialist Party in the Comoros also called for independence. The rebel movement gained ground, public discontent erupted in 1968, and in 1973, a pro-independence political leader, Ahmed Abdallah — a rich importer and the leading businessman of the territory — gained power. He won concessions from Paris, including promises for a referendum on the future of the island within five years. Opinion in the Comoros divided on the question of independence, but voting in December 1974 showed an overwhelming 95 per cent in favour of independence in three of the islands. However, in Mayotte voters opposed independence by 8783 to 5110. France had not stated whether the vote totals would be counted globally or island by island in order to determine the outcome, and the French now procrastinated. Abdallah's opponents called for consultations between the Comorians and the French, but Abdallah unilaterally proclaimed the independence of the Islamic Republic of the Comoros in July 1975. He claimed sovereignty over Mayotte as well as the other three major islands, but the Mahorais leaders and Paris held out. Mayotte remained attached to France, although its constitutional status was most unclear.[11]

Discontent with the 1958 provisions also grew in French Somaliland. A visit by de Gaulle in 1966 provoked violent demonstrations in the capital, Djibouti, and the following year the administrative structure was modified after a referendum in which 60 per cent of the population voted for continued association with France, rather than independence. The territory, now renamed the Territoire Français des Afars et des Issas (TFAI), was given a Chamber of Deputies and autonomous local government. By the early 1970s, independence groups existed in the territory and, in 1975, they captured the French ambassador in Somalia, releasing him only when a pro-independence dissident was also freed. Violent demonstrations continued and in the following year further kidnappings occurred. In 1977 Paris held a round-table conference of all political parties to work out a plan for independence, which was granted, after a successful referendum, in June of that year. A pro-French politician, Hassan Gouled Aptidon, became president. France promised aid and worked out an agreement to station a large number of soldiers in Djibouti, as the new state was called.[12]

Institutional change in the New Hebrides was awkward because of the dual administration, strong local loyalties on more than sixty populated islands, and other divisions of the population (for example, over religion and custom, and between the one-third who were Francophone and the two-thirds Anglophone majority). Nevertheless, in 1957 a consultative council was set up, and more wide-ranging reforms occurred in 1975. By that time, a nationalist political party, subsequently named the Vanua'aku Party, had formed and moved towards a pro-independence position. This party won the 1975 elections but the results were annulled because of fraud. In 1977, the Vanua'aku Party boycotted new elections and set up a provisional government, leaving the largely Francophone Union des Partis Modérés to take all the seats in the legislature. The next year, with the establishment of an autonomous government, the two parties cooperated to form a united government. This government, led by an Anglican priest, Walter Lini, worked out a plan for the independence of the archipelago. The British were eager to leave this distant, unprofitable colony, but the French hesitated, conscious of settler interests, and the impact of independence in the New Hebrides on nearby New Caledonia. French authorities did nothing to discourage secession movements based in the islands of Espiritu Santo and Tanna. When the independence of the New Hebrides, under the name of Vanuatu, was declared in 1980, the two renegade islands refused to accept the decision and attempted to form separate governments with the support of many Francophone residents and French settlers. Paris, embarrassed at these developments, nevertheless recognised the independence of Vanuatu and sent in a token force of troops who joined a British contingent to restore order. They soon withdrew, however, and it was with troops from Papua New Guinea that Lini finally overcame the secessionists in the dissident islands. In 1981 the new government expelled the French

ambassador in Vanuatu. He subsequently returned, but relations
between France and Vanuatu have remained stormy, aggravated on the
Melanesian side by a feeling that the French had opposed independence and fostered divisions by supporting the rebels, and on the
French side by the view that the Vanuatu government has interfered in
New Caledonia with its support for the pro-independence parties
there.[13]

THE AFTERMATH OF DECOLONISATION

The troubled relations between France and Vanuatu are similar to the
cloudy links between many newly independent countries and their former colonial masters. The rhetoric of the immediate post-colonial age
simultaneously blamed the imperial powers for most of the evils of
underdevelopment and for new forms of neo-colonialist exploitation,
yet pleaded for increasing levels of aid, concessional trade and technical assistance from the developed countries. In black Africa, France has
been remarkably successful in retaining close ties with its former colonies; it provides the largest share of economic assistance, forms the
major trade partner, works to preserve French language and culture
and, in some states, maintains French military establishments. The
zone franc links France and fourteen African countries in a single currency zone, where the African currency (the CFA franc) is fixed to the
French franc, a tie closer than any other post-colonial power has negotiated with former colonies. Links with Morocco and Tunisia have also
remained. In the successor states to Indo-China, France has had less
success as that part of southeast Asia remained embroiled in political
turmoil and war. Time has effaced many of the remains of the French
presence, but in recent years France has once again begun to build a
political, economic and cultural presence in Vietnam, Cambodia and
Laos.

Relations with the Comoros, Madagascar, and Algeria have been
particularly troubled since independence. The Comoros broke off relations with France; within several years of independence, President
Abdallah was defeated by a candidate considered anti-French, Ali
Soilih, who was later assassinated by a band of mercenaries led by a
French expatriate, which reinstalled Abdallah in power. In Madagascar, a new government in the early 1970s carried out a programme of
nationalisation, reduced French interests, and pursued policies which
led to the repatriation of many French citizens still resident in the
island; more recently, however, a rapprochement with France has occurred. Problems between France and Algeria were fuelled by the
recriminations of the pieds-noirs who had lost their 'homeland' and

properties in North Africa (and felt inadequately compensated by Paris), the militant stance (including nationalisation and a neutralist foreign policy) of President Houari Boumedienne, and the migration of thousands of Algerian workers to France. Under Boumedienne's successor, Chadli Benjedid, relations have become warmer, and the president of France in 1975 paid a state visit to Algeria for the first time since independence. However, frustrations linger, now fuelled by rising racism in France directed against Maghrebin migrants and a variety of severe political and social problems in Algeria.

In general, however, with the *zone franc* in Africa, the Francophone movement and French technical assistance (*coopération*), as well as bilateral agreements, the phenomenon of migration from both the Maghreb and black Africa to France, and cultural and personal links, decolonisation has not meant a total withdrawal of France from its former empire.[14] Indeed, in many respects, the French presence is as pervasive and vital as it has ever been, merely falling short of formal political power. French aid in various forms, including military assistance, remains vital almost everywhere, but especially in the smaller, recently independent states of Djibouti and the Comoros; in Vanuatu French aid is less substantial and was briefly withdrawn in 1987 when diplomatic relations were also temporarily broken off. The threat of withdrawal of aid elsewhere has enabled France to pull into line what it has regarded as potentially dissident Francophone states: when the United Nations voted on the issue of the decolonisation of New Caledonia, France was supported by most of its former colonies; only Algeria, Syria, Laos, Vietnam and Vanuatu voted to reclassify New Caledonia as a colonial territory. The sub-Saharan African states (and also Tunisia and Morocco) either voted with France, abstained or made themselves absent. The Francophone states are also linked to France in other ways: through substantial French foreign investment; in cultural terms through Francophonie, where there has been increasing politicisation; through bilateral aid (which France prefers to multilateral aid); and through a substantial military presence in sub-Saharan Africa, which has enabled France to play a very direct role (especially in Chad). All this is marked, especially in Africa, the region to which France attaches greatest priority, by an exclusivity that guarantees French privilege and authority. In many respects this represents a neo-colonialism little different from the preceding colonial era.

The *Départements d'Outre-Mer*

Integration of the *vieilles colonies* and the *métropole* had long been a demand of certain groups in those colonies. Already in the nineteenth-century, local councils sought the *départementalisation* of the French

Antilles, and such requests were renewed in the 1920s. Both the Comité Martiniquais de Libération Nationale, which rallied to de Gaulle in 1940, and the *Conseil général* of the colony in 1946 asked for the 'complete assimilation' of Martinique to France. The spearhead for assimilation came from the Communist parties in the colonies, benefiting from their status as fighters against Nazism and opponents of collaboration during the war years and now, at the end of the fighting, supported by their Socialist and Radical coalition partners who, with the Communists, formed a majority in the French National Assembly. In Réunion, for example, Raymond Vergès, a Communist Party *député* in the French parliament, argued: 'This colony considers that only its integration in the French fatherland could resolve numerous problems it must face.' The principal spokesman for *départementalisation* was Aimé Césaire, poet, mayor of Fort-de-France and *député* to the Assembly, where he was sponsor for the proposed law. Césaire argued that the law would mean that, first, 'Martinique, Guadeloupe, Guyane and Réunion now join the French family and participate in the destiny of France on an equal footing with the metropolitan *départements*' and, secondly, that

these *départements*, recognising the necessity there may be to adapt certain general measures to specific geographical or economic conditions, no longer leave such an adaptation to the ministers, but give it to Parliament and thus wish to have accepted the principle that assimilation should be the rule and derogation the exception.[15]

The change had multiple goals. It would end the second-class status which the *vieilles colonies* had suffered, even though they had been attached to France longer than Corsica, Nice, Savoy and Franche-Comté and all of their residents had been citizens since 1848. Furthermore, it would recognise the significant *francisation* of the local populations and acknowledge the sacrifices they had made on behalf of France in two world wars. Secondly, *départementalisation* would end the arbitrary rule of Paris over the colonies. Since the *sénatus-consulte* of 1854, the colonies had come under the direct control of the French head of state (at that time the emperor and, since 1870, the president), who ruled by decree rather than by legislation: the constitution of the Third Republic had designated the chief of state to be the 'législateur colonial' (the lawmaker for the colonies) and left an uneasy division between executive and parliamentary authority. The President, the Minister of Colonies, and the governors had almost unchallenged control over the colonies. The National Assembly could and did intervene, but such parliamentary intervention was exceptional. *Départemental-isation* would therefore mean a democratisation of politics and make legislation rather than decree the normal administrative process. A third benefit was that *départementalisation*, in theory at least, would bring to the *vieilles colonies* the various benefits of the French social security system then in the process of being established, including health care, education, and government services, as well as the effects of greater government efforts to stimulate the economy.

Underlying these stated aims were additional motivations. *Départe-mentalisation* gained support from 'leftist' politicians, such as the Communists, and Césaire in 1946 was a member of the French Communist Party. But the *métis* of the Antilles also advocated the change. The white planters, the *Békés*, had repeatedly demanded greater political and financial autonomy for Martinique, Guadeloupe, Guyane and Réunion: in the *ancien régime*; during the Revolution (the Convention's emancipation decree was not enforced in Réunion because of the planters' opposition); and then in the nineteenth-century. The freed blacks, and the *métis* elite, however, had a different view. The *métis* had become the intellectual elite of the Antilles, and formed a major political force, even when economic power remained in the hands of the *Békés*. *Départementalisation*, therefore, seemed a means of escaping from the yoke of the white planter class. It was the logical extension of the liberation of slaves in 1848 and the way for the blacks and *métis* to secure greater participation, against the arbitrariness of both Paris and the white elite, in the running of the colonies. *Départementalisation*, somewhat optimistically, was seen as decolonisation. Not surprisingly the plantocracy opposed *départementalisation*; in Réunion it was seen as 'a criminal heresy that would lead to a spiritual failure and to ruin.'

Départementalisation was also viewed (not necessarily by the same groups) as a way to anchor French interests in the Caribbean and, more generally, in the western hemisphere. In particular, it represented a stand against perceived American designs on the Antilles. At the end of the Second World War, much as in 1918, rumours circulated that the United States would like to acquire (by purchase or donation) the French islands of the Caribbean. On the other hand the new American advocacy of decolonisation threatened to spread to the West Indies. Many feared either of these new possibilities.

Césaire's proposals therefore met with a favourable response in the National Assembly, helped by his own considerable oratorical skills and personal prestige. The assembly unamimously voted for *départemen-talisation* on 19 March 1946. The law meant that the *départements d'outre-mer* now had the same institutions as those in the *métropole*: a *préfet* (instead of a governor), a *conseil général* elected by adult suffrage (now including women voters), representation in the French Senate, Chamber of Deputies and *Conseil économique et social*, the same law code and system of justice as in the *métropole*.

Article 73 of the constitution of the Fourth Republic, promulgated in October 1946, enshrined the *départementalisation* law; according to the constitution the legal structure in the DOMs 'is the same as that of metropolitan *départements*, other than for exceptions determined by law'.[16] The conditional clause was extremely important, for it meant that exceptions to legislation could be made: certain laws might not apply to one or all of the DOMs or could be specifically adapted. This fine legal point recognised that *départements* located thousands of kilometres from France and exhibiting a different economic, demographic and cultural structure could not be treated in exactly the same way as metropolitan *départements*. However, a recognition of their specificity was not explicitly offered, nor were the limits to absolute assimilation spelled out. What the law did provide was that all legislation passed after 1946 would automatically be applicable in the DOMs, unless the exception or adaptation was specified in the laws themselves.[17] Laws passed before 1946, however, had to be specially promulgated by the government (through the person of the new *préfet*) to be applicable; some legislation was never promulgated in this way, thus disparities between metropolitan and overseas *départements* were never legally erased.[18] The nature of the legal exceptions or adaptations of metropolitan law were unclear. Two subsequent judgements tried to clarify the matter. In December 1946, the Conseil d'Etat ruled that adaptation must be 'limited in extent and [carried out] in order to take account of the very different situations between the *métropole* and the new *départements* without there being any check on the general principle of assimilation' and the following year the Conseil said that measures of adaptation 'should not harm the general spirit of the basic intentions'.[19]

The disparities between the DOMs and the metropolitan *départements* were not inconsequential. For instance, the *préfet* in the DOMs held greater powers than his metropolitan counterpart, making him resemble the old colonial governor. He served as chief executive of the DOM, presiding over all the state's bureaucracy and services. Significantly, he was responsible for the defence of the DOM against outsiders and for the maintenance of domestic law and order. Unlike a metropolitan *préfet*, he could declare a state of siege, could call out the army, navy and air forces stationed in the DOM (and the military forces could not carry out any operation, except in emergencies, without his authorisation), and could expel foreigners, whereas in the *métropole* these powers were reserved for Paris. The DOM *préfet* could modify certain tariffs and taxes and fix certain prices. Given the insularity of the DOMs, the *préfet* had implicit diplomatic attributions concerning accreditation of foreign consuls, relations with neighbouring states and general questions of protocol.

Financially, the DOMs had a different tariff system from that of the *métropole* which disallowed the import or export of different articles or charged different duties. The DOMs retained the *octroi de mer* tax, established in the colonies in the 1890s, which was imposed on all articles entering the *département* and which formed the basis for communes' income. Finally, the social security system was adapted to the DOMs, which generally meant lower levels of coverage and smaller payments. The minimum wage in the DOM-TOMs was also lower than in the *métropole*. However, public servants in the DOMs, from 1953 onwards, benefited from increments in their salaries; the old *prime coloniale*, renamed an *indemnité d'éloignement* (compensation for distance), usually increased their salaries by 40 per cent. These discrepancies, not all of which were specifically intended though some were unavoidable, continued through the life of the 1946 constitution.

The Constitution of 1958, still in force today, confirmed the legal assimilation of the *départements*, but elaborated some subtle nuances. Article 72, 'Des collectivités territoriales', made no reference to the DOMs: 'the territorial entities of the Republic are the communes, the *départements* and the territories overseas'. The DOMs, therefore, were regarded simply as *départements* located overseas and not constitutionally separate entities; the principle of assimilation was reinforced. Article 73 stated: 'The legislative structure and the administrative organisation of the overseas *départements* may be modified by measures necessitated by their particular situations.' This represents stronger wording than in the 1946 constitution with disparities now treated as 'adaptations' rather than 'exceptions'. But the idea that legislation passed by parliament and promulgated by the president was applicable immediately and in its totality to the DOMs, unless otherwise indicated, was retained. Once again, the extent of this adaptation remained undefined.

Also unclear was whether *départements* could change their status. The constitution made provisions for territories either to secede or to become *départements*, but it was silent on any possible evolution of the *départements* themselves. Adaptation of laws was possible, and Article 72 said that 'other territorial entities may be created by law', providing latitude for new entities. Most legal authorities believe that the constitution did not allow for the accession to independence of a *département* or even any change to an entirely different status (for instance, as a *territoire d'outre-mer*). Reinforcing this interpretation is Article 5 of the 1958 constitution, which charges the president with guaranteeing the 'integrité du territoire' ('territorial integrity'), and Article 2, which defines France as a 'république indivisible' ('indivisible republic'), but exactly what this indivisibility means has also provoked debate among legal scholars.[20]

Several institutional changes have occurred in the DOMs since the 1958 constitution. In the late 1950s, DOM politicians became increasingly dissatisfied that they had no share in deciding policies concerning their *départements*. For some, this amounted to a challenge to the notion of *départementalisation* and a demand for autonomy (at least in administration). Paris did not satisfy all the grievances of the critics, but it did pass a new law, in 1960, which required that

all proposals for laws and decrees that might adapt the legislation or the administrative organisation of the *départements d'outre-mer* to their particular situations shall first be submitted, for advice, to the *conseils généraux* of these *départements*.

Furthermore, the *conseils généraux* 'may address the Government concerning all measures relating to the particular situation of their *départements*'. (Another law in the same year gave certain Chambers of Commerce and Chambers of Industry in the DOMs a non-obligatory right to be consulted 'on questions related to their areas of concern'.) Thus, the *conseils généraux* were granted the rights to supplicate and to give a non-binding opinion on legislation that would affect the DOMs *before* it was submitted to parliamentary vote. This right of advice led some observers to speak of a *départementalisation adaptée* (adapted departmentalisation).[21]

Another development was the creation of the *régions*. President de Gaulle put forward a project for regionalisation, but it was defeated in a referendum in 1969, a defeat which provided the occasion for de Gaulle's resignation. However his successor, Georges Pompidou, established the *régions* in 1972; in metropolitan France such *régions* were formed by grouping together several *départements*, which generally corresponded to traditional regional and cultural areas similar to the provinces of the *ancien régime*. The *régions*, however, were not separate *collectivités territoriales* of the sort envisaged by Article 72 of the constitution. Each *région* had a *préfet de region* and a *conseil régional* given responsibility for, among other duties, long-term planning for local development. The *conseils régionaux* were elected on a basis of proportional representation (while the *conseils généraux* were elected by two rounds of first-past-the-post voting). In the case of the DOMs, the regions coincided with the departmental boundaries.[22]

In 1982, the government of François Mitterrand, as part of its new policy on decentralisation, passed a law combining the *conseil général* and the *conseil régional* in each of the single-*département* DOMs, the new *assemblée unique* to be elected by proportional representation and exercising jointly the powers of the two antecedent bodies. However, the *Conseil constitutionnel* ruled that this creation was unconstitutional since it would thereby create a different local government system from the one existing in the *métropole* (and, because of the proportional method of election, would not assure representation for the various geographical areas of the *départements*), a situation which contravened Article 73 of the constitution of 1958. The government consequently had to allow the persistence of both the *conseil général* and *conseil régional* in the DOMs, though they were given new powers in the decentralisation acts.

For the DOMs, the new *conseils régionaux* were mandated in a law of 1982, but their powers were not specified until legislation was passed in 1984, a delay which came under criticism. The division of power between the two types of councils in the DOMs was not initially clear, and many *conseillers généraux* strongly objected to the creation of another elected body which they thought would take away some of their powers. Paris worked out an arrangement whereby the *conseil régional* powers were devolved from the state, and the areas of competence of the two bodies were carefully delimited. The *conseils régionaux* were charged with giving an opinion to the prime minister on any international agreements France proposed to sign with neighbouring states, to make propositions to the prime minister on economic, social and cultural development of their respective DOMs, and to take part in long-term planning for these *départements d'outre-mer*. The *conseils généraux* continued to manage day-to-day administration, allocation of financial resources, public works and local services. In practice, the two councils initially squabbled over the division of duties, but after several years of the new system, settled down to a mutually satisfying, and largely complementary, power-sharing arrangement.

With this new structure of *décentralisation*, the *préfet* in French *départements* was given the auxiliary title of Commissaire de la République; some of his functions, notably the requirement that he approve the *département* budget and sign measures passed by the *conseil général*, were handed over to the president of the *conseil général*, who became the new elected chief executive of the *département*. Certain fiscal and administrative powers were also devolved onto the *conseils généraux* and *conseils régionaux*. Supporters of the Mitterrand government judged this a satisfactory move towards a degree of autonomy, and many opponents of *décentralisation* were ultimately won over.

In 1982 a new organisation was also set up in the DOMs (similar to one established for Corsica), a *Comité de la culture, de l'éducation et de l'environnement*, to advise the government on matters pertaining to issues indicated by its title. This was represented as a recognition of the cultural specificities of the DOMs, including the Creole language, local art and literature, as well as the environmental needs of the islands.

The *Territoires d'Outre-Mer*

The 1946 constitution, in addition to the *départementalisation* of the *vieilles colonies*, recognised the existence within the Union Française of *territoires d'outre-mer*, considered part of the Republic, and both *territoires* and *États associés* (associated states). The last categories were little used: the *territoires associés* consisted of the old mandates of Togo and the Cameroon, and the *États associés* were the protectorates of Morocco and Tunisia and, for a time, Vietnam, all of which eventually gained independence. The *territoires d'outre-mer*, therefore, were the former colonies under a new name, set up as individual territories (*territoires unitaires*) or grouped together (the AOF and AEF). The underlying principle held that these territories, unlike the *départements d'outre-mer*, were not assimilated into French law. They continued to be administered by a governor (or governor-general), who exercised broad powers much as in the years before the new constitution. The constitution reserved to the French parliament direct control of 'criminal law and political and administrative organisation'. Otherwise, legislation passed in Paris was applicable in the *territoires d'outre-mer* only 'by special mention or if subsequently decreed'. The constitution further allowed that 'arrangements particular to each territory may be decreed by the President of the Republic'. In short, direct and particularistic rule was to be the norm, and no constitutional demand existed for harmonising legislation between the various TOMs or between the TOMs and the *métropole*. The *code de l'indigénat* was abolished, but Article 75 allowed individuals to retain their 'statut civil de droit commun' ('civil status in customary law') if they so desired and, therefore, to be judged outside French civil law. The *territoires d'outre-mer* elected members of the French parliament but, through a complicated system of electoral colleges rather than on the basis of universal suffrage; the bulk of the non-Europeans lacked the vote. Territorial assemblies existed, but they were restricted to deliberative functions and had no legislative power.

A major change occurred with the 1956 *loi-cadre* Defferre, named after Gaston Defferre, then Ministre de la France d'Outre-Mer. The *loi* Defferre introduced universal suffrage to the overseas territories and abolished the different electoral colleges for Europeans and non-Europeans. The law increased the powers of the territorial assemblies and also created *conseils de gouvernement*, territorial executives elected by each local assembly. The governor served as president of the *conseils de gouvernement*, but with an elected vice-president. The members had responsibility for designated domains, divided by ministerial portfolios. France therefore moved towards decentralisation of the *territoires d'outre-mer*, although with neither a British-style self-government nor the recognition of outright administrative autonomy.

The constitutional referendum of 1958 gave the territories the possibility of choosing immediate and total independence from France, entering the Community as *Etats-membres* (member states), or remaining *territoires d'outre-mer*, as indeed the Comoros, French Somaliland, New Caledonia, French Polynesia and Saint-Pierre and Miquelon decided to do. The TAAF, with no permanent inhabitants, retained its status as a *territoire d'outre-mer* which had been decreed in 1955. Wallis and Futuna remained a protectorate until it formally became a *territoire d'outre-mer* in 1961. The *territoires d'outre-mer* were given a legal personality as 'collectivités territoriales' in Article 72 of the new constitution. Article 74 stated:

the *Territoires d'Outre-Mer* of the Republic have a particular organisation which takes account of their specific interests in the context of the interests of the Republic. This organisation is defined and modified by law after consultation with the appropriate territorial assembly.

This article thus emphasised that French metropolitan law would not be applicable in the TOMs unless it was specifically stated to be so in the law itself (quite unlike the DOMs, where legislation was automatically applicable unless it was stated that it was not so). The territorial assemblies also had to be consulted on laws affecting their territories, the same right extended to the *conseils généraux* of the DOMs in 1960. Underlying this article was the principle that legislation for the TOMs must take account of their own particular interests within the context of national interests; in the case of any conflict, it was, however, unclear which should take precedence.

Article 76 allowed for significant institutional change among the TOMs: 'the *Territoires d'Outre-Mer* may retain their current status within the Republic', but

if they express their desire through deliberation in their territorial assembly within the allowed time [four months] . . . they may become either *départements d'Outre-Mer* of the Republic or, whether or not grouped among themselves, member-states of the Community.

The principle of potential *départementalisation* was therefore admitted, although it was not stated whether this could occur after the four-month period specified. Article 86 of the constitution added that

the transformation of the status of a member-state of the Community may be sought either by the Republic, or by resolution of the legislative assembly of the state concerned, confirmed by a local referendum . . . By the same process, a member-state of the community may become independent.

Whether this provision also applied to the *territoires d'outre-mer* was not specifically stated either, although subsequent interpretation judged that the constitution did allow for such a development. Even so, the constitution did not set out the exact means for such a decision to be made, including, for example, the question of the composition of the electorate. Article 53 of the Constitution limited itself only to the statement: 'No cession, no exchange and no acquisition of territory is valid without the consent of the population concerned.' In effect, wide latitude was left for future legislation and a number of points remained unclear. Nevertheless, on the basis of these articles Djibouti and the Comoros gained independence, and the statutes of the other TOMs have been substantially modified since 1958.[23]

In the Fifth Republic, the TOMs (with the exception of the TAAF) have many of the same institutions as the *départements*. All elect representatives to the Senate and the Chamber of Deputies, and such 'collectivités territoriales' as *communes* also exist (although with slightly different powers).[24] Much of the law applicable in the *départements* (including the DOMs) has been extended to the TOMs with little modification. However, in many respects, the TOMs are different not only from the DOMs but from each other (and Saint-Pierre and Miquelon and Mayotte have particular structures of their own).

A common denominator, however, is that in each of the TOMs, areas of competence are divided between the state and local authorities (*conseil de gouvernement, assemblée territoriale, communes*, etc.). In general, the state retains control over defence and security, the enforcement of laws and decrees, foreign relations, higher levels of education, the public service (that is, the state bureaucracy), customs, currency issues, administrative and financial systems and the administration of justice. However, since the TOMs are so dependent on funding from Paris, the power of the French parliament and actual state control can be much greater. An *Haut-Commissaire de la République Française* represents the state in French Polynesia and New Caledonia. The resident chief executive in Wallis and Futuna is called an *Administrateur supérieur*; in practice, he exercises the duties carried out by the High Commissioner in the other Pacific territories although, in theory, the Ministry of the DOM-TOMs retains a tutelary power over him.

In addition to this distinction, Wallis and Futuna's councils differ from those of other TOMs. There exists a *conseil territorial*, a consultative body formed of the three traditional 'kings' of Wallis and Futuna and three other members named by the *Administrateur supérieur* with the accord of the Territorial Assembly. This second body, an elected assembly of twenty members, is also consultative. Local divisions (*circonscriptions*) each have their own council and a government *délégué*, but Wallis and Futuna does not have communes and mayors.

The TAAF is headed by an *Administrateur supérieur*, charged with the powers of the Republic. The official administrative centre of the territory is Port-aux-Français, Kerguelen, but the administrator and his staff are resident in Paris. A *Conseil consultatif territorial* of seven members, representing certain ministries and scientific organisations, and a *Conseil scientifique* of seventeen members named by the *Administrateur supérieur*, discuss TAAF affairs. Unlike the other TOMs, the TAAF does not have representation in the French parliament or the *Conseil économique et social*.

In French Polynesia, soon after the promulgation of the Constitution of 1958, a new law specific to French Polynesia limited the effects of decentralisation. It maintained the powers of the territorial assembly but limited the quasi-ministerial powers of the members of the *Conseil du gouvernement*, who were no longer assigned specific portfolios. This marked a move away from the autonomy of the 1956 *loi-cadre*, but responded to a request from the Polynesian Territorial Assembly itself. In 1977, new legislation restored the office of an elected vice-president (abolished in 1958) but not the 'ministerial' portfolios of the other *conseillers de gouvernement*. The council's powers increased, but the official French representative of Paris, whose title was changed from *gouverneur* to *haut-commissaire*, retained most of his powers.

In 1980, Gaston Flosse, a *député* for Tahiti, proposed a new statute for French Polynesia to the National Asembly. Negotiations lasted for

four years, and in August 1984 the statute adopted for French Polynesia was heralded by Flosse as a grant of 'internal autonomy'.[25] Some
of the changes in the 1984 legislation were primarily yet powerfully
symbolic. Alone of all regions of France, French Polynesia was allowed
its own flag — a horizontal tricolour of red, white and red (recalling the
flag of King Pomare) with a central medallion featuring a Polynesian
canoe (decorated with five stars to represent the five island groups of
the territory) against sun rays and ocean waves. The flag always flies
alongside the French Tricolour. Tahitian was confirmed as an official
language of the territory, to be used with French in assembly debates
and publications.

Institutional changes in French Polynesia were based on the principle enunciated in Article 1 of the new legislation: French Polynesia is
'a *territoire d'outre-mer* with internal autonomy in the framework of the
Republic' with a 'specific and changing organisation' determined by
legislation; furthermore, 'the territory of French Polynesia is freely
governed by its elected representatives'. Article 2 stated that the territorial authorities 'are responsible for all matters that are not reserved to
the State', and the following article enumerated the state's responsibilities: foreign relations, control of immigration, foreign transport and
communications, currency, financial relations with foreign countries,
defence, import and sale of military and strategic goods, maintenance
of order and security, questions of citizenship, civil and labour law,
justice, the state bureaucracy, communal government, higher education, audio-visual policy. Though the list remained long it left much
of the day-to-day running of French Polynesia, and great latitude for
interpretation of law, to the territorial authorities.

The law maintained the Territorial Assembly (of thirty *conseillers*),
but made its President, rather than the High Commissioner, responsible for opening, closing and summoning the body and removed the
High Commissioner's right to suspend execution of Assembly decrees.
The President of the Government, elected by the Assembly, chooses six
to ten ministers (formerly elected by the Assembly), who form the territory's government. The President of the Government is the chief
executive of the territory and, from 1984, took over functions previously belonging to the High Commissioner: notably, the President is
the comptroller of the territorial budget, he represents the territory in
legal matters (or in conventions between the state and the territory),
and he heads the local administration. He also has a right to be consulted on international discussions concerning French Polynesia. The
President is responsible to the Territorial Assembly, which can vote on
censure motions and thereby force the resignation of the President and

ministers. The acts of the Assembly have the force of law. The ministers have responsibility for special areas and direct the administrative services in their domains. For example, the 1984 government of Gaston Flosse included ministers of economics; education; agriculture; finance and the interior; development, energy and mines; social affairs; health, scientific research and the environment; youth, sports and artisanal activity; transport and communications; and labour, professional training and housing. Thus the government structure established in 1984, and amended in 1990, in many ways replicated the governmental organisation of independent states and, according to its supporters, gave French Polynesia self-government. The degree of decentralisation was unparalleled elsewhere in the French *outre-mer*.

The institutional and administrative structure of New Caledonia since 1945 has been particularly volatile, especially in the 1980s. The 1956 *loi-cadre* and the Constitution of 1958 were applied in New Caledonia as elsewhere in France. The 1956 law also gave the vote to the Melanesian population of the territory. A 1963 law, the *loi* Jacquinot, however, restricted the powers of the New Caledonian territorial assembly, much as the 1958 statute had done in French Polynesia. The *loi* Billotte of 1969 further reinforced the powers of Paris and the High Commissioner, especially concerning economic and fiscal affairs and mining, by far the most important economic sector in the territory. Another bill, in 1976, essentially confirmed this organisation of the territory, reserving to the High Commissioner the right to promulgate laws and decrees, have control over foreign relations and defence and take charge of a range of services similar to those of French Polynesia. New Caledonia maintained a territorial assembly, government and president. By the 1970s, therefore, New Caledonia enjoyed a significant degree of autonomy, comparable to that of French Polynesia, although it had restricted authority on such essential services as mining. The European settler population (the Caldoches) in New Caledonia had long dominated the territorial government, but a Melanesian, Jean-Marie Tjibaou, the leader of the independence movement, served as president of the government at the beginning of the 1980s.[26]

The rise of Melanesian nationalism in the late 1970s and 1980s, culminating in calls for an immediate and total 'Kanak and socialist independence', and the strong reaction of opponents determined to retain ties with France, inflamed passions in the territory. The polarisation and radicalisation of politics, accompanied by mounting tension and violence, made some institutional change necessary. The government of François Mitterrand, elected in 1981, brought together the major competing factions, but it proved impossible to establish an institutional framework acceptable to all parties. In 1984, the Melanesian pro-independence coalition (the Front de Libération Nationale Kanake et Socialiste) boycotted elections to the Territorial Assembly, leaving the Assembly in the hands of anti-independence parties. The French High Commissioner in New Caledonia, Edgard Pisani, announced a plan which would quickly have brought New Caledonia 'independence in association' with France, with Paris keeping control of defence and foreign relations. This proposal was not satisfactory to pro-independence groups, who continued to demand total independence, or to the anti-independence groups who viewed it as capitulation to terrorism and little short of a treasonous dismemberment of French territory. The Pisani plan was never implemented.

Instead, the Socialist prime minister Laurent Fabius formulated a new plan for New Caledonia in 1985. The territory was divided into four regions and elections were held in which pro-independence groups gained control of three of the regions. Under the Fabius plan the High Commissioner retained substantial governmental powers and could work directly with the four regional assemblies (*assemblées régionales*) and New Caledonia's *communes*. A territorial congress, composed of the members of the regional assemblies and presided over by a president, had diminished powers. This arrangement worked relatively well for a brief period, although extremists on either side felt they had been cheated of a victory, and all thought that the ultimate fate of New Caledonia remained to be decided.

New legislative elections in France brought to power a conservative government in 1986, with Jacques Chirac as prime minister in uneasy *cohabitation* with President Mitterrand. Chirac announced that he would hold a referendum in New Caledonia on whether the territory should become independent and then promulgate new statutes reflecting the outcome. In the referendum, held in September 1987, pro-independence groups staged a boycott, and the 59 per cent of the electorate which did vote decided overwhelmingly in favour of the maintenance of New Caledonia in the French Republic. The Chirac government in December of that year successfully introduced into the National Assembly new legislation which would have granted considerable autonomy to the territory, but by redrawing the regions (and reducing their number to three) would have assured a greater degree of Caldoche control. In any case, the Melanesian pro-independence front stated that it intended to boycott all institutions set up in the new Pons plan, so called after Chirac's Minister for the DOM-TOMs. Before the legislation could come into effect, violence increased to the point that New Caledonia seemed on the verge of civil war; hostage-taking and killings by Melanesian nationalists and French military forces occurred in April and May 1988, just before the French presidential elections. Those elections renewed Mitterrand's mandate, but the subsequent legislative elections failed to give the Socialists a parliamentary majority, and the new Prime Minister, Michel Rocard, formed a minority government.

Rocard summoned the pro- and anti-independence parties to Paris for consultation. The Matignon Accord, approved by the competing parties in June 1988, ratified by the French National Assembly and confirmed in a nationwide referendum, provided for direct rule by the High Commissioner for a one-year period from July 1988. The old regional assemblies and the territorial assemblies were suspended, and the High Commissioner exercised almost total power over the territory. The old law codes remained in place, as well as most state and territorial services and the structure of commune administration. At the end of this transition period, in July 1989, territorial elections in New Caledonia for three redrawn 'provinces' took place. The local assemblies have substantial powers to manage day-to-day administration, and there is also a territorial assembly. However, the High Commissioner retains more discretionary power than in the other TOMs. In the long-range, the Matignon Accord foreshadows another referendum on independence in 1998.[27]

The cases of French Polynesia and New Caledonia illustrate the constitutional flexibility for institutional arrangements in the TOMs, ranging from direct rule by the High Commissioner to a substantial degree of self-government. Underlying political and social tensions have encouraged administrative experimentation for these two TOMs, but the trend has been towards a cautious autonomy, despite backtracking in French Polynesia in 1958 and in New Caledonia in 1963 and 1988. What most legal scholars interpret as constitutional allowances for either independence or *départementalisation* have widened the options for the two territories, while in New Caledonia (and, to a certain degree, in French Polynesia) domestic difficulties have made it seemingly impossible to agree on a final statute. Nevertheless, through all the changes, the principle of non-assimilation and the possibility for decentralised self-government differentiated the TOMs from the DOMs, even after the decentralisation programmes for the latter in 1982.

The *Collectivités Territoriales*

Mayotte and Saint-Pierre and Miquelon both have the status of *collectivité territoriale* (territorial collectivity) of the French Republic, a status made possible by Article 72 of the Constitution of 1958. In the case of Mayotte, this followed the independence of the other islands of the Comoros after the referendum of December 1974, and the subsequent unilateral declaration of independence by the Comoros that was officially recognised by France late in 1975. Paris organised two referenda in Mayotte in 1976. In the first the Mahorais voted almost unanimously to remain part of France and, in the second, they expressed their desire for the *départementalisation* of Mayotte. This decision did not altogether please Paris, since many political figures there felt that an eventual integration of Mayotte into the new Islamic Republic of the Comoros would be preferable. The limited extent of economic development made the total assimilation implied by *départementalisation* impossible for the immediate future. Moreover the United Nations and the Organisation for African Unity (OAU) condemned continued French administration of Mayotte, the government of the Comoros claimed the island and a small group of Mahorais wanted to join the Comoros. France therefore decided on a temporary statute, making Mayotte a *collectivité territoriale*, and set 1979 as the date for a new vote on the definitive status for the island. However, in 1979 the government of President Giscard d'Estaing asked the National Assembly to put off the referendum for another five years; then, in 1984, the government of President Mitterrand asked parliament to postpone the decision on a final statute 'à durée indéterminée' (for an indefinite period). For advocates of *départementalisation*, these decisions provided proof of French lack of interest or worse, whilst the supporters of *départementalisation* charged French politicians with betraying a cause they had previously supported. For the OAU and other bodies, as well as the Comoros government, unwillingness to change the statute in the opposite sense was evidence of continued French colonialism.

Mayotte thus retains the statute of 1976; the island is neither a *département d'outre-mer* nor a *territoire d'outre-mer* in a constitutional sense. Its administration and legal system, in fact, have elements of both. A *préfet* is charged with the normal duties of safeguarding national interests, maintaining law and security and presiding over the bureaucracy; the Mayotte *préfet* also has some of the additional duties of the DOM *préfets*. In addition, there is an elected *conseil général*, although no *conseil régional*, since Mayotte is not a *région*. Mayotte elects a Senator and a *député* to the Assemblée Nationale but not a representative to the Comité économique et social. *Communes*, set up in 1977, are similar to those elsewhere in France. According to the 1976 statute, those laws previously in force in the old territory of the Comoros continue to be applicable in Mayotte, so long as they do not contravene other legislation. This means, for instance, that most of the Mahorais continue to have customary Islamic civil status. Provision was made for the adaptation of these laws by ordinance until 1979 and has continued since then. The statute also provided that 'new laws would be applicable to Mayotte only if specifically stated'; this is similar to the case of the TOMs. The French government furthermore has the power to use the legal method of decrees for administrative purposes, although they must conform to the constitution and legislative acts.[28]

Saint-Pierre and Miquelon remained a *territoire d'outre-mer* after the referendum of 1958 until 1976, when the National Assembly passed a law making it a *département d'outre-mer*, which was conceived in France as a form of 'symbolic promotion' and a remedy to economic decline. Some contested the validity of the act, particularly because the local electorate had not been officially consulted (and local sentiment did not favour *départementalisation*); an unofficial vote on *départementalisation* found very few in absolute favour. Canada also objected to this reassertion of French sovereignty and the effect it might have because, as a DOM, Saint-Pierre and Miquelon became fully part of the European Community and the number of European fishing boats was likely to increase. The application of metropolitan fiscal and administrative regulations to Saint-Pierre and Miquelon also provoked local discontent because of the rapid growth in the number of French public servants. The new *département* lost the right to produce its own postage stamps, a not inconsiderable loss of revenue, and the increased salaries of bureaucrats following *départementalisation* created dissatisfaction among those not on government pay-rolls.

The upshot was a new law of 1985 which removed the departmental status of Saint-Pierre and Miquelon and made it a *collectivité territoriale*. Much of the administrative structure, however, remained. There is a *préfet*, and the *conseil général* has the right to be consulted on legislation affecting the islands. Representatives sit in both houses of the French parliament. Metropolitan legislation is, in general, automatically applicable in Saint-Pierre and Miquelon just as in the DOMs. And, not insignificantly, Saint-Pierre regained the right to sell its own distinctive stamps.

Finally, there are other distant islands which have no constitutional status: Clipperton in the Pacific and the Iles Eparses in the Mozambique Channel. Like the DOMs and TOMs they are not enumerated in the constitution and have no defined status in French law. Since 1936, the island of Clipperton has fallen under the administration of the governor (then high commissioner) of French Polynesia. Since 1960 and the independence of Madagascar, the Iles Eparses have been administered by the minister responsible for the DOM-TOMs, who delegates his authority to the *préfet* of Réunion. Regulation is by decree, although the National Assembly can and does intervene (for example, on the designation of economic zones in waters surrounding the islands).

MÉTROPOLE AND *OUTRE-MER*

Certain anomalies exist inside the French Republic, both in the *métropole* and the *outre-mer*. For example, the three major cities, Paris, Marseille and Lyon, have special statutes not shared by other urban areas; Corsica also has a distinctive status. The fact that pre-1946 laws had to be specifically promulgated for the *outre-mer* meant that both intentional and accidental oversights have occurred; for instance, the 1905 law on the separation of church and state has never been enforced in Guyane. The *octroi de mer* continues to be collected in the DOMs and TOMs although not in the *métropole*. Such disparities are perhaps necessary in view of the very different social and economic situation in the *outre-mer*, and the division between financial and administrative particularities, on the one hand, and constitutional and institutional ones on the other has never been clear.

The phenomenon of the DOM-TOMs raises other matters of interest, such as the relationship between national and international law. This has particularly been the case with Mayotte (and, more recently, New Caledonia). France subscribes to the resolutions of the United Nations that the old colonial boundaries should be maintained and that nothing should be done that would seriously unbalance the population structure by migration of non-indigenous populations. Critics of French policy charge that separation of Mayotte from the other islands of the Comoros in the 1970s violated the first principle, and that large-scale migration of Europeans (and also Polynesians) to New Caledonia in the 1960s contravened the spirit of the second.

The DOM-TOMs also raise general questions about the function of law. Is law the result of social, economic, political and cultural changes or is it intended to engineer them? In the case of the *départementalisation* of the *vieilles colonies* in 1946, the answer seemed to be both. The process represented a recognition of the changes in Martinique, Guadeloupe, Guyane and Réunion that had occurred over three centuries of French presence and, at the same time, was an effort to secure greater economic development and political and social equality. The decentralisation of 1982 could be similarly interpreted. If Mayotte were departmentalised, however, weight would be placed on the law as a

cause rather than a result of change, given limited economic development and the relative lack of *francisation* of the population.

For the DOM-TOMs which have witnessed the emergence of pro-
independence movements, an even more general question is whether
economic and social transformation should be prefaced on a change of
statute (including both the exact relationship with the *métropole* and
the institutional structure) or whether such change can be accommodated within the existing framework. For those who favour independence, or at least a great distancing between a territory or *département*
and Paris, the change in statute takes priority. For others, however, the
close ties with France do not impede change (or 'progress') and, in fact,
may be necessary in order to safeguard already acquired human rights,
international security and high levels of financial and technical aid.

The variety of statutes and administrative structures in the French
outre-mer indicates the constitutional flexibility of the Fifth Republic.
It has caused some to question whether France is indeed the 'indivisible' Republic which the constitution proclaims and the centralising
tradition denotes.[29] The trend in the 1980s was towards greater decentralisation with the statute for French Polynesia, the special statute for
Corsica, and the law on the *régions*. Yet the interpretation of the *Conseil
constitutionnel*, rejecting an *assemblée unique* in the DOMs, shows the
limits to this trend.

Possibilities also exist for changes of status. The changes in the statutes of Mayotte and Saint-Pierre and Miquelon provide precedents.
Constitutional experts agree that *départementalisation* of a territory is
possible. The so-called Capitant Doctrine maintains that a territory can
secede from the Republic subject to both the approval of the local
population and a vote by the French Parliament. The 1985 statute for
Saint-Pierre and Miquelon also implies the possibility of ending
départementalisation, although the procedure is less clear in this case.
Finally, a constitutional law of 1960 (relating to Article 86, concerning
the Community) held that an independent state may associate itself
with the Community on the basis of accords worked out between the
two. This unused constitutional provision was invoked by Edgard
Pisani in 1984 in his programme for independence for New Caledonia
in association with France and could make possible a statute whereby a
state established ties of free association or other connections with
France.

In general, besides the great differences between DOMs, TOMs and
collectivités territoriales, the institutions of the *outre-mer* resemble those
of the *métropole*. All parts of the Republic are represented at a national
level in the French parliament, and there exist several levels of local
administration (*conseils généraux* and *conseils régionaux* for the DOMs,

assemblées territoriales for the TOMs, and — except for Wallis and
Futuna and the TAAF — *communes*). Underlying the various administrative arrangements, however, is a general assumption that power
emanates from Paris. Even in largely autonomous French Polynesia,
Paris reserves important powers and those held locally have been delegated to Papeete by the National Assembly. Ultimately they can also
be withdrawn.

Given the particularities of the DOMs and TOMs, French authorities agreed that some institution was needed to coordinate policy in
the *outre-mer* and to exercise responsibility for the special considerations created by distance, underdevelopment and other local problems. This central institution, from 1894 to 1946, was the *Ministère des
Colonies* (although some of the overseas regions did not fall into its
ambit). From 1946 to 1958, the ministry was renamed the *Ministère de
la France d'Outre-Mer* and since that date it has been the institution
dealing with the '*départements et territoires d'outre-mer*'. The exact title
of the person in charge, however, has variously been '*Ministre*', '*Ministre délégué*', '*Ministre chargé*' or '*Secrétaire d'Etat*'. The difference
concerns the power to propose legislation (since only a full Minister can
introduce legislation into the National Assembly), the ability to sign
ordinances alone or the necessity to obtain the counter-signature of a
full Minister, and also regular presence at meetings of the *Conseil des
Ministres* (as *Ministres délégués* and *Secrétaires d'Etat* are invited only
when subjects of concern to them are discussed). The exact title has also
been largely indicative of the priority attached to the DOM-TOMs at
various times; those governments with a greater interest, it is argued,
usually appointed a full minister, whereas those less concerned established only a *Secrétariat d'Etat*. In any case, the ministry or secretariat of
state responsible is known in French shorthand as the Rue Oudinot,
from the location of its offices in Paris.[30]

Currently at the head of the institution is a minister, named by the
president for an indefinite term of office. Several past ministers or secretaries of state have been well-known political figures, such as Jacques
Soustelle under de Gaulle and Bernard Stasi under Giscard d'Estaing;
one of these, Pierre Messmer, minister of the DOM-TOMs under
Georges Pompidou, subsequently became prime minister. Another has
served under two governments of different political orientation; Olivier
Stirn was Giscard's secretary of state for the DOM-TOMs in the 1970s
and then, briefly, François Mitterrand's minister for the DOM-TOMs
in 1988. Most ministers have held other portfolios, either before or after
their time at the Rue Oudinot. Two ministers, Stasi and Bernard Pons,
have been leading figures in their respective political parties, the
Republicans and the RPR. The DOM-TOM post, lacking the power

and prestige of such other ministries as Foreign Affairs, Defence and Finance, has been of junior rank in the *Conseil des Ministres*, but entrepreneurial and strong-willed politicians (such as Pons) have projected themselves and their portfolios into the limelight at critical times and have had considerable impact on the *outre-mer*.[31]

The minister has a separate budget, which in 1985 amounted to just under 1.4 million francs, and a staff of over 300 *fonctionnaires* at the Rue Oudinot.[32] The exact organisation of the ministry changes from government to government, sometimes with a division of duties by geographical region (or between DOMs and TOMs), sometimes by areas of political responsibility. Thus, there is at present under the minister a director of political, administrative and financial affairs and a director of economic, social and cultural affairs; further down are the various assistant directors (*sous-directeurs*) and their staffs.[33] Under the aegis of the ministry are a number of institutions and investment funds, notably the Fonds d'Investissement dans les Départements d'Outre-Mer (FIDOM) and the Fonds d'Investissement pour le Développement Economique et Social (FIDES). The ministry is represented on various other bodies, such as the bureau concerned with DOM-TOM migrants to France.

The powers of the Ministry of the DOM-TOMs remain circumscribed. Other ministries may intervene independently in the DOMs, although they are obliged to give notification to the Rue Oudinot of their actions. For the DOMs, the Ministry of the DOM-TOMs coordinates and supervises operations, and, often, formulates specific policies. In the case of the TOMs and the *collectivités territoriales*, the possibility for intervention is rather greater. For the TAAF it is near total, and in New Caledonia the Ministry of the DOM-TOMs has used extensive powers in response to political troubles. The Rue Oudinot occasionally must also share its powers. In 1985 and early 1986, for instance, President Mitterrand appointed Edgard Pisani — returned from his position as High Commissioner in New Caledonia — to the position of *Ministre pour la Nouvelle-Calédonie*. In the Chirac government of 1986–8, Gaston Flosse, as *Secrétaire d'Etat chargé du Pacifique-Sud*, and Lucette Michaux-Chevry, as *Secrétaire d'Etat à la Francophonie*, held portfolios which in practice, if not in legislative theory, impinged on the Ministry of the DOM-TOMs. The government of Michel Rocard also appointed a *Secrétaire d'Etat à la Francophonie*, Alain Decaux; it did not appoint a secretary for the South Pacific but revived a South Pacific Council which was created (but remained largely inactive) during the government of Laurent Fabius. Even more obviously, the powers of the minister are overshadowed by those of the president or prime minister.

The Ministry of the DOM-TOMs controls real budgetary and administrative powers and also has the function of enunciating and representing the government's policy on the *outre-mer*. The minister is often the government's spokesman on DOM-TOM matters and serves as an advocate or ambassador of the DOM-TOMs inside the government, to the French public and internationally. Ministers can and do clash with local and national politicians who often represent different political parties. Some critics have suggested that the ministry be dismantled, and such administrative changes as the decentralisation laws of 1982 redefined its areas of competence. But it plays an important symbolic and real role in bringing together a group of disparate regions governed in a complex network of varying institutional arrangements.

4

Population and Society

MIGRATION FLOWS have long characterised the DOM-TOMs and have contributed, in most places, to ethnically very diverse populations. Traditionally much of this migration has been towards the DOM-TOMs, but more recently it has become oriented to France. In the post-war years, migration has increased in volume and distance and become more complex in pattern and purpose, while economic change has stimulated a substantial redistribution of population within the DOM-TOMs; this is most marked in high rates of urbanisation. The mixing of populations has led to race and ethnicity assuming social and political significance, in terms of access to land and other resources, and migration itself has assumed political dimensions. In some places rapid population growth has led to considerable pressure on often limited resources, but more often it has hastened migration. Changes in population composition and distribution have thus played a substantial role in the evolution of the economy and society of the DOM-TOMs. These themes in the demographic history of the DOM-TOMs — immigration into and emigration from these regions, the cohabitation and, sometimes, the intermingling of the different ethnic groups, and the changes in population structures — reveal many of the specific characteristics of the DOM-TOMs, and also clarify the origins of a number of social tensions which exist in the French *outre-mer*.

In the Antilles drastic population changes were apparent in pre-European times. The Arawak Indians had been killed and driven out of

Guadeloupe and Martinique even before Columbus had reached the Caribbean, to be replaced by the Caribs who were there at the time of European contact. In Martinique the French initially cleared land on the Caribbean side of the island and were separated by mountains from the Caribs on the Atlantic side.[1] Despite initial proposals to educate and convert the Carib population, relations quickly deteriorated and, at the end of the 1650s, settlers organised a punitive expedition to rid the island entirely of its native population. Though some must have survived, there are now no identifiable Caribs in Martinique or Guadeloupe, as there are in Dominica, though many families claim Carib ancestry. In Guyane, the impact of small-scale coastal European settlement was relatively slight; only missionaries, numerous miners, and runaway slaves had penetrated the interior before the twentieth century, though penal settlement and plantations had reduced Indian population numbers, especially on the coast. Nevertheless, estimates of the coastal Indian population of Guyane at the time of contact suggest that there may have been 10,000; by the start of the eighteenth century, no more than 900 remained, the others victims of European diseases after only half a century of effective settlement.[2] The vast size of the thinly-populated colony, the minimal significance of the plantation economy and the deaths of so many convicts ensured that the major influences on changing population composition did not occur until well into the twentieth century.

In the Pacific territories Melanesians had been so long established in New Caledonia that there were some twenty-eight different language groups around the time of European contact. In Wallis and Futuna and French Polynesia, Polynesians had settled more recently; both Wallis and Futuna had their own languages and each of the archipelagos of French Polynesia had its own distinctive but related language. Diversity of language was often matched by diversity of cultural traditions, social organisation and leadership structures. European contact dramatically altered the content, pace and character of change, especially in New Caledonia with the establishment of a settler colony, the displacement of Melanesians from their land and an absolute decline in Melanesian population numbers. Though observers had little doubt that this was associated with European introduction of new diseases and weapons, the lack of documentation ensures that there remains considerable doubt over the extent of the decline, which continued into the second decade of the twentieth century.[3]

In French Polynesia there is no doubt about a population decline. Indeed, in the whole of the Pacific the Marquesas region was the most affected by what has otherwise been over-dramatically referred to as the 'fatal impact',[4] and in other archipelagos a similar situation prevailed.

In the Marquesas estimates suggest that the Polynesian population could have declined from perhaps 90,000 to around 6000 by the 1870s, a fall attributed to new diseases, alcohol and psychological stresses as Marquesans 'embarked on a course of suicidal violence'.[5] As in New Caledonia, the decline continued into the twentieth century. The same epidemic diseases had a similar effect in Tahiti itself where, by 1797, thirty years after the arrival of the first European ship, the population had fallen from a generously estimated 40,000 to 16,000.[6] Though, in reality, the decline was probably not so severe, it nonetheless continued until the middle of the nineteenth century when the population had fallen below 8000. This evolution was replicated on most of the Society Islands. In the more isolated islands, such as Rapa and Wallis and Futuna, declines were not recorded and colonial contact may have been less consequential for population change.

Neither in Réunion, Saint-Pierre and Miquelon (or the TAAF) was there an indigenous population before European contact; hence the contemporary populations are descendants of relatively recent migrants. In other respects their population histories could scarcely be more different. Saint-Pierre and Miquelon were populated entirely by migrants from France, principally from Brittany and Normandy.[7] By contrast Réunion was populated primarily by slaves and plantation labourers from various parts of Africa and the Indian sub-continent. At the start of the eighteenth century slaves had been brought in by the Compagnie des Indes, mainly from regions of India such as the Malabar coast, Bengal and Surat, but during that century the source of slaves shifted to Africa. The greatest numbers initially came from Madagascar and subsequently from the east coast of Africa, which dominated labour migration by the end of the century.[8] Diverse regional and ethnic origins paralleled different cultures and religions, giving Réunion one of the most complex population structures of any contemporary DOM-TOM.

DEMOGRAPHIC COLONISATION

The process of colonisation eventually led to substantial changes in the demographic structure of each of the DOM-TOMs. In every case but one, those changes resulted principally from immigration; only in Wallis and Futuna was there minimal immigration although, much later, massive emigration. In the *vieilles colonies*, where early immigration swamped indigenous populations, emigration also became a major demographic variable by the second half of the 1900s.

In the earliest years of European settlement in the Antilles, the

indentured labourers (*engagés*) were young Frenchmen, but as small
farms quickly gave way to plantations, so contract labourers were replaced by African slaves. Within fifty years after the landing of the first
settlers, the slave population was twice that of the European population, which had reached a peak around 1738,[9] and the imbalance
became more marked in succeeding centuries. Migration on this scale
necessarily transformed and reconstructed the social order:

Under the plantation system, Martiniquan society was doubly stratified: by
class and by colour. The great landowners, government officials, professionals
and clergymen were white; the agricultural labourers, servants and artisans
were negro and mostly slaves. Yet shortly after the introduction of slavery a
third group appeared, the freedmen, who were intermediate both in colour
and position. The illegitimate offspring of white masters and female slaves
provided the largest source of freedmen.[10]

Elsewhere in the *vieilles colonies*, similar contours took shape as plantation economy and society were consolidated.

After emancipation in 1848 the social order of the *vieilles colonies*
again metamorphosed as former slave-owners were forced to hire
labourers, while most of the slaves themselves abandoned the estates
and moved into peasant hamlets, mainly in the hills. The resultant
labour shortage led to the reintroduction of a system of contract labour
with workers imported primarily from India, although a few arrived
from Africa and China.[11] For three decades after emancipation there
was also some migration from the British Caribbean islands into
Guadeloupe and Martinique. More than 30,000 migrants went on five-
year contracts to Guadeloupe; only about one-sixth ever returned to
their home islands. Though 'the Indians' were regarded by planters as
'almost as good as Africans'[12], there was never enough migrant labour
adequately to replace the African slaves. Already in the Antilles, there
was a 'politique d'immigration' as the European oligarchy rejected the
possibility of further European immigration, arguing that it was too
costly, whilst preferring to retain absolute control of the labour force.[13]
A more jaundiced view of this situation was that France

scoured the overpopulated sections of the globe to obtain labour for the
Antilles and the similarly situated Réunion. Heedless of the social and political
problems she was thus laying up for the future . . . she made the islands a
dumping ground for unassimilable Africans and Asiatics.[14]

In conditions little different from slavery, migration continued to diversify the population of the *vieilles colonies* through the late 1800s.

In neither of the northern Antilles islands, Saint-Martin and Saint-Barthélémy, was the agricultural economy based on sugar, and in both islands the first settlers were 'poor whites' from St Christopher (St Kitts). Almost all the early settlers in Saint-Barthélémy came from Normandy; there has never been any significant migration of blacks[15] and the island is sometimes labelled by its occupants 'the white pearl of the Caribbean'. Other 'island refuges' of Guadeloupe such as Désirade and the Saintes are also primarily areas of white settlement.[16] Black migration to Saint-Martin was as substantial as in most other parts of the Caribbean. Africans dominated the island's demography by the end of the eighteenth century; many were freed slaves from Guadeloupe[17].

Throughout the early colonial era, Guyane was best known as a penal colony, and as a plantation economy it remained disappointing: thinly populated and unproductive. Slaves were introduced onto the plantations, but in much smaller numbers than in the Antilles; slave numbers reached a peak of just over 1900 in 1830. On a small scale, the social structure replicated that of the Antilles, but only along the Atlantic littoral of the colony. Penal settlement from 1792 onwards introduced a new European element to the population, though the number of penal settlers was tiny until the 1850s and many convicts eventually returned to France. Thus 'the recourse to immigration is a constant theme in Guyanais history' as 'workers were sought on all continents of the planet'.[18] The first immigrants in the post-slavery era came from Madeira, moving on from British Guiana or Brazil; others came from the Canary Islands, India, China or Vietnam. As sugar prices declined and tropical diseases took a heavy toll of new migrants, mortality rates were unusually high.[19] Gold miners diversified the 'creuset de races' ('melting pot')[20] even further but there was only slight overall population growth in the nineteenth century.

In Réunion immigration followed a similar course to that of the Antilles; the sugarcane growers imported Indian plantation workers from 1827 until 1851, when Britain prevented further recruitment from its Indian empire, and Réunion turned to Madagascar, the Comoros and the African coast.[21]After recruitment on parts of the African coast was made illegal in 1859, Réunion once again turned to India; for more than twenty years Indians arrived, initially at the annual rate of 5000, but declining to 1000 a year when the last convoy landed in 1885. Most were repatriated, but others, widely known as 'Malabars', remained on the east coast sugar plantations; they contributed to the massive growth of the Réunion population in the nineteenth century. After the end of Indian migration, several thousand other migrants were introduced from Mozambique, and smaller numbers from

Vietnam (Tonkin), Somalia and even Yemen. Chinese and Indian Moslems (mainly from Gujarat) arrived as voluntary migrants, the Chinese in large enough numbers to dominate commerce and the Moslems — 'Z'Arabes' — to become mainly tailors.[22] Both in Réunion and Guyane 'voluntary' migrants, largely sought in the more impoverished and densely populated parts of the world, effectively arrived in conditions much like slavery, and only at the end of the century was there genuine free migration from anywhere other than France.

In the Pacific territories European colonisation, especially in the settler colony of New Caledonia, was firmly in place by the end of the nineteenth century. Some of the earliest settlers in New Caledonia were Australians, followed by a handful of sugarcane planters from Réunion. Though the thirty-year period of penal settlement (1863–97) emphasised the French basis of the colony, the first wave of free French settlers did not come until the 1870s. Nonetheless, by the end of the century, European settlement had given New Caledonia the basis of its contemporary economic and social structure, as the grazing and mining industries were established, Noumea became a prosperous small town and Melanesians were slowly displaced into reserves, mainly in the mountains or on the east coast. European settlement of French Polynesia was relatively slight but early in the commercial history of the territory, labour shortages led to a search for Asian labour. Between 1862 and 1892 some 2600 Chinese 'coolies' from Hong Kong, alongside Melanesians from the New Hebrides, Polynesians from the Cook Islands and Gilbertese from Micronesia, were recruited.[23] Though some, notably the Melanesians and Micronesians, were later repatriated, many of the others remained; the Chinese moved into the commercial sector, which they eventually dominated. The Chinese, and particularly the Europeans, intermarried with the Polynesian population. In New Caledonia there was minimal intermarriage between Europeans and Melanesians, and thus a small *métis* (mixed-race) population, quite different from that of French Polynesia or the *vieilles colonies*. In both territories the native Melanesians and Polynesians were largely marginalised. The Polynesians were able to retain much of their land, but in New Caledonia, Melanesians were confined to reservations on only one-tenth of the land area on the main island.

The Grande Terre of New Caledonia saw violent Melanesian opposition to French colonialism. Conflict over land was inevitable in the clash of contrasting and mutually unintelligible cultures. Regular and widespread clashes culminated in an insurrection in 1878, the most substantial opposition to European colonisation in the island Pacific. For almost a year Melanesians throughout a wide area of the west coast fought against settlers, French soldiers and other Melanesians. Perhaps a thousand Melanesians died, including the supposed leader, Ataï, alongside two hundred Europeans. There was extensive damage to Melanesian agricultural systems and European cattle stations; Melanesian survivors were dispersed and resettled on remote reservations; divisions between Europeans and Melanesians became more apparent; and brutal reprisals, exile and further land occupations contributed to 'suicidal despondency'[24] amongst the Melanesian population. Intermittent violence continued and flared again in 1917 in the north, much discouraging the further migration of French settlers.

The early phase of European settlement in the Pacific territories was also accompanied by a widespread belief, common until well into the twentieth century, that Melanesians and Polynesians were dying races, and that it was only a matter of time before many islands would be depopulated. Indeed the indigenous populations did decline, victims of epidemics, alcoholism and inadequate sanitation, and there were general reactions of demoralisation and despair. A Protestant missionary, Maurice Leenhardt, was warned on his arrival in Noumea in 1903 that 'you've come for the Kanaks but in ten years' time there won't be a single Kanaka left'; he found one Melanesian reaction to colonialism in the Canala area to be 'just let me drink and die'. Even in the 1930s, when demographic revival had begun, he wrote of the people of the Grande Terre as 'submerged in a flood of alcohol'.[25] In French Polynesia the administration also believed that they ruled a dying race, and that the spectacular decline of the Marquesan population provided evidence: 'The main thing is to let them die in peace.'[26] Even as recently as 1954, seasoned observers of the South Pacific were able to write of the 'eastern Pacific region, where the population as a whole has declined to such an extent that Polynesian racial regeneration appears probable but remote'.[27] Yet it was not so distant; in most parts of the Pacific territories the indigenous populations had been growing since at least the 1920s and, in time, their growth rates accelerated beyond those of more recent migrants.[28]

Though the impact of migration into the DOM-TOMS was almost everywhere greatest during the first century of colonial history, migration in the twentieth century has also had a substantial impact on population change. In New Caledonia, European settlement declined or stagnated for the first half of the century; of the almost 16,000 Europeans recorded in the 1936 census, some 80 per cent were born in New Caledonia. The settler colony had implanted its roots. Slow European settlement, difficulties in obtaining Melanesian workers and the end of deportation from France led employers to seek Asians from other French colonies. The first Asian migrants were Indians to work in the sugarcane plantations; by the end of the nineteenth century there were Chinese, Vietnamese, Javanese and Japanese workers, as well as some Arabs released from the New Caledonia penal colony. In the 1920s Asian immigration increased to the extent that, at its peak, Asians briefly outnumbered Europeans. Asians inevitably concentrated in areas of European settlement. As early as 1891, Melanesians had become a minority in the southern third of the Grande Terre. By the 1920s they were a minority in New Caledonia and, despite the demographic revival, only briefly in the 1960s did they form a majority in their own land.

One more era of migration further changed the population composition of New Caledonia, just as Melanesians had become the majority. The nickel boom of the early 1970s attracted substantial migration from France and from France's two other Pacific territories. Even before that influx there had been a minor wave of *pieds-noirs*, French colonists displaced from Algeria. Requests from other Pacific island states for employment opportunities were rejected; France recruited its own citizens. As the French Prime Minister, Pierre Messmer, argued at the time:

New Caledonia, a settler colony . . . is probably the last non-independent tropical territory in the world where a developed country can encourage its nationals to migrate. It is necessary to seize this last chance to create another Francophone country so that the French presence in New Caledonia could only be threatened by a world war and not by nationalist claims from the indigenous people supported by allies from other Pacific communities. In the short or medium term the massive immigration of metropolitan French citizens or citizens from the Overseas Departments (Réunion) would enable this danger to be averted.[29]

Attempts to ensure that all migration to New Caledonia came from distant regions were not wholly successful, though the arrival of migrants from Wallis and Futuna and French Polynesia 'both as docile labour and "reliable" voters . . . tossed across the Pacific by the existence of the labour market or the vagaries of electoral politics'[30] had a similar effect to that Messmer had sought. Moreover, more than half of those who migrated to New Caledonia came from France and many others moved from Martinique and Guadeloupe. The nature of migration policy thus preserved political and economic interests.[31]

The impact of new migration, as Messmer perceived and intended, was enormous, principally in its relegation of the Melanesian population to the position of a minority group. Moreover almost 90 per cent of the nearly 10,000 French who migrated to New Caledonia between 1971 and 1976 lived in the Noumea area; hence there was a major 'Europeanisation' of the town as it passed through its period of most rapid growth. By the start of the nickel boom, wage-earners' local purchasing power represented about twice that in France;[32] consequently not only French migrants came, but also Italians, Spaniards and Australians. The character of the white settler colony changed as the migrants of the boom years, and the years that followed, were temporary expatriates rather than settlers, urban salary-earners rather than landowners.

The Melanesian population of New Caledonia had fallen by 1976 to only 42 per cent of the total, its smallest proportion in the post-war years. Polynesians from the other French Pacific territories made up about 10 per cent of the population, and Indonesians and Vietnamese constituted a further 5 per cent. Most of the Asians had been in New Caledonia since the pre-war years but a minority of Vietnamese had come after the fall of Saigon in 1975. The new Polynesian population, especially that from Wallis and Futuna, grew rapidly; by 1976 over 9500 Wallisians and Futunans lived in New Caledonia, a total already greater than that of the two home islands, and the fertility rate of the new population was extremely high. Wallis and Futuna became perceived as no more than 'holiday islands and homes for the retired' and return was an admission of failure.[33] Like many other recent migrants, the Polynesians lived on the fringes of Noumea, competed for and obtained jobs to which Melanesians aspired and were thus quickly resented by Melanesians who perceived a new 'black colonisation'[34] by migrants desperate for the jobs and salaries non-existent in their home islands. As the nickel boom turned to bust by the mid-1970s, some of the new migrants left New Caledonia, but more rapid Melanesian population growth has never redressed the shift in ethnic balance that the boom produced.[35] Even after the political disturbances of the 1980s, and further return migration (especially to French Polynesia), Melanesians in 1989 still accounted for only 45 per cent of the total population of the territory.

Of the other DOM-TOMs, only Guyane has experienced the same volume of immigration as New Caledonia, a migration of equally diverse origins. In many respects Guyane is the most recent settler colony in the world, though the particular pattern of settlement had not been anticipated by France, and official attempts to encourage the growth of a settler colony with Hmong (Laotian) refugees and French citizens have failed. 'Logical as it might seem to build up French Guiana by unburdening overcrowded Martinique and Guadeloupe, the French government is well aware that even this would be a "ticklish matter" involving complex social, political and economic problems.'[36] France preferred that migration tie Guyane more directly to the 'hexagon'. At times, the volume and structure of immigration has caused considerable resentment; in 1985 the Front National obtained proportionately the highest vote in Kourou that it has ever received in French elections, and a group of Hmongs who arrived in 1985 from elsewhere in South America were deported because of hostility to further immigration.[37] Formal settlement schemes, meanwhile, have given way to illegal migration.

Hmong migrants arrived as part of the Plan Vert (Green Plan) of Olivier Stirn, Secretary of State for the DOM-TOMs in the 1970s; the plan sought to 'develop this *département d'outre-mer* and to this end to favour the migration of French citizens to Guyane'. The Green Plan, primarily designed to boost agriculture and forestry, announced the intended migration of about 30,000 people to a *département* that then contained about 53,000 people. Since the Hmong refugees were the first group of migrants under this plan, and had virtually no French connections of any kind, their welcome in Cayenne was anything but warm. They were subsequently moved into rural areas, but many, especially the young, quickly migrated to towns; others left Guyane as soon as they had become naturalised and could afford the airfare for France. This last attempt to create new villages in Guyane, previously but unsuccessfully attempted with North Vietnamese (Annamites) at the start of the century and Indonesians in the 1950s, proved to be one more failure. In 1985 about 1300 Hmongs remained but poorly integrated into the socio-economic structure of Guyane; though they continue to provide about two-thirds of the market-garden produce of Guyane, that proportion is falling as they move out of agriculture.[38]

In contrast to official attempts to encourage the settlement of Guyane has been a substantial influx of illegal migrants, mainly from Surinam, Haiti and Brazil, to take advantage of high wage rates. The population has doubled in two decades (Table 3); in 1982, only 57 per cent of the population were born in Guyane, and a further 11 per cent in France. These proportions almost certainly fell further in the late 1980s. By 1985 about a quarter of the population (between 20,000 and 22,000) were Haitians, three-quarters of whom were illegal migrants, though Haitian migration only began around 1967. Most are unskilled labourers in agriculture and construction, principally in and around Cayenne,[39] as are Brazilian migrants. Illegal Brazilian migration is less substantial, though there were approximately 55–70,000 migrants in Guyane by the mid-1980s, about two-thirds of whom were illegal.[40] More recently there has also been substantial illegal migration from neighbouring Surinam; more than 9000 'Bush Negro' refugees have moved across the Maroni River into Guyane since the failure of a coup against the Surinam government and the destruction of many villages by the Surinamese army. About a quarter of these new migrants have sought employment, and some have been able to move into the urban areas rather than remaining in refugee camps close to the border.[41] The longer that political problems persist in Surinam the more likely these new migrants are to remain in Guyane, further diversifying an already complex population structure.

The superior wages and living standards of the DOM-TOMs have ensured that there has usually been some post-war migration, often quite illegal, from neighbouring states. This is particularly true in the West Indies, where distances are much smaller and the possibility of illegal migration much greater; the same holds true over Guyane's lengthy land borders. Guadeloupe, since its earliest colonial days, has 'acted as a magnet, pulling workers from the four corners of the globe';[42] the majority of sugarcane workers come from Haiti often to work for less than the legal minimum wage. The tiny French territory of Saint-Martin has also played a significant role in the clandestine movement of Haitians, via the Dutch zone, into Guadeloupe, and has itself a significant 'squatter' population of illegal migrants.[43] Haitians perceive Guadeloupe as an El Dorado where wages and welfare payments are both high; despite their low wages, they remit substantial sums to their home country.[44] In Martinique the situation is much the same, though numbers are smaller. In both *départements* there has also been substantial immigration from neighbouring independent states, especially Dominica and St Lucia, and violent opposition to migrants from Haiti and Dominica especially.[45] Haitian migrants work primarily in agriculture and in the construction industry, many in seasonal employment; most migrants take jobs that local people do not want, for example, as sugarcane cutters. In the Pacific and Indian Oceans, by contrast, migration during the 1980s from non-Francophone states has been slight, though there has been a history of migration from Vanuatu to New Caledonia. For a brief period after Mayotte's separation from the Comoros, many migrants from the other three islands, especially Anjouan, returned to their home islands, just as political problems later led French Polynesians to leave New Caledonia. In the 1980s, however, there occurred massive illegal immigration to Mayotte from the Comoros, leading to a very substantial growth in the population. More than 10,000 Comorians were attracted by wages three times the level of those in the Comoros, which provoked frequent disputes and demonstrations against migration and

Table 3. The Population of the DOM-TOMs, 1945–1989

Year	Guyane	Guadeloupe	Martinique	Saint-Pierre and Miquelon	French Polynesia	New Caledonia	Wallis and Futuna	Réunion	Mayotte
1945									
1946	28,506	278,464		4,354	55,734	62,700			
1947			261,595						
1948									
1949									
1950									
1951						66,400	8,771		
1952									
1953									
1954	27,864	229,120	239,130						
1955								242,067	
1956					76,327	68,480			
1957				4,822					
1958								274,400	
1959									23,364
1960									
1961	33,535	283,223	290,679						
1962				4,990	84,551		8,325		
1963						86,519		349,300	
1964									
1965									
1966									
1967	44,392	312,724	320,030	5,186	98,378		8,546	416,500	32,607
1968									
1969						100,579			

Year									
1970									
1971					119,168				
1972									
1973									
1974	55,125	324,530	324,832	5,840	137,882				47,246
1975									
1976						133,233	9,192		
1977								476,700	
1978									
1979									
1980								495,000	
1981									
1982	73,012	327,002	326,717	6,041	146,124		11,943		
1983					166,753	145,368			
1984									
1985									67,205
1986							14,160		
1987									
1988	c.90,200	c.337,500	c.335,100		188,814			c.569,500	
1989						164,173			

Source: Various censuses. All data, except for that for Mayotte (1985) and for 1988, are from censuses. Some census data is inaccurate, especially for New Caledonia.

led to new regulations to control and restrict migrant flow.[46] On balance, though not in the *vieilles colonies*, migration into the DOM-TOMs from countries other than France has been much greater than migration away from the DOM-TOMs.

Despite migration into some DOM-TOMs from neighbouring states, the most characteristic feature of immigration is otherwise its dominant European French origin.[47] Every DOM-TOM has witnessed steady immigration from France, so much so that it sometimes appears, as in the Caribbean, that

the recent influx of *métropolitains* looking for a place in the sun has only made a racially disturbed and unequal situation worse . . . Large numbers of white immigrants to the islands have entered the civil service, professions and businesses, even taking up menial jobs. The process is so serious that if the trend continues, black West Indians may well find themselves in a minority on their islands by the turn of the century.[48]

This prediction is, however, improbable. Yet migration has been serious enough to be denounced as 'genocide by substitution' by Aimé Césaire's Parti Progressiste Martiniquais. The immigrant '*métros*' are widely regarded in the Antilles as 'employment thieves'[49] and to a significant extent racial friction has increased between '*métros*', recent migrants from Dominica and Haiti and long-term residents. As in New Caledonia and most DOM-TOMs, migration has aggravated social problems and the structure of migration has become a political issue.

The smallest of the DOM-TOMs, Saint-Pierre and Miquelon was the only territory to be exclusively populated from France. The population of Saint-Pierre and Miquelon grew slowly in the nineteenth century, reaching a peak of 6842 at the 1902 census; decline followed in difficult economic circumstances, until the population had fallen to a low of 3918 in 1921. Slow population recovery in the Prohibition era increased further in the post-war years as *départementalisation* boosted wages and living standards, and the population once again passed 6000 in the 1980s. It was, however, a growth rate below that of natural increase, since there was constant emigration, mainly to Canada. Some 86 per cent of the contemporary population were born there, and a further 8 per cent were born in France. Finally, among the DOM-TOMs, the TAAF have only intermittently had a settler population. The nineteenth and early twentieth century saw tentative attempts at colonisation by agriculturalists and fishermen, but none of these all-male settlements were permanent. In the post-war years they have been replaced by at most several hundred equally transitory scientists.

EMIGRATION

Especially in the *départements d'outre-mer*, the 1950s and 1960s was a period of substantial employment growth, as the bureaucracy expanded rapidly and new services followed in its wake. Yet employment growth was more than matched by population growth, and hence the emergence of overt unemployment, accompanied by the expansion of education and more widespread aspirations towards the range of social and economic opportunities that France could offer. In the *vieilles colonies* of Martinique, Guadeloupe and Réunion, the 1960s marked the start of a wave of emigration to France. In the Caribbean lack of employment opportunities emphasised the standard West Indian response to limited development and, as occurred in the British Caribbean at the same time, France began to encourage emigration when the birth rate declined and economic growth in France produced new opportunities in a range of jobs not sought by the local population.[50]

An early phase of migration followed the institution of compulsory French national service in the DOMs in 1959, which initially led to young men from Réunion and the Antilles fighting for France in Algeria and subsequently to recruits going to France and often remaining there after demobilisation. Though there had been some early individual migration from the Antilles, the most powerful formal influence on emigration from the *vieilles colonies* was the establishment in 1963 of the Bureau pour le Développement des Migrations Intéressant les Départements d'Outre-Mer (BUMIDOM), specifically designed to encourage migration to France. The aim was to supply France with cheap labour at a time of declining population growth, as well as to reduce unemployment in the DOMs. Migration from the overseas *départements* seemed more appropriate than migration from either Africa or the Iberian peninsula, traditional sources of imported labour, because it solved employment problems both inside the *métropole* and in the *outre-mer*; furthermore it was rather easier to regulate and was wholly Francophone.[51] Emigration was thus widely seen as beneficial to the DOMs; Paul Dijoud, Secretary of State for the DOM-TOMs, claimed in the 1970s:

In ten or twenty years migration will be the only real option for many young people . . . there will be no economic miracle; many young Antillais will have to accept spending a part of their life in the *métropole*.[52]

By contrast, Aimé Cesaire denounced emigration, as he denounced immigration of metropolitan public servants to the Antilles, fearing that 'the Antilles-Guyane are without doubt best known as countries of emigration'.[53] Further local opposition to the plan focused on the argument that it was designed to be of benefit primarily to France,[54] rather than the overseas *départements*, where employment problems had been created by French policies and should be solved there by capital investment. Many groups favouring greater independence for Guadeloupe and Martinique saw this as effectively writing off the future of their *départements* as independently productive economies.[55] Radical Guadeloupeans argued simply that France's sole objective was 'to replace Guadeloupeans with French, and to obtain a "population equilibrium" in order to better entrench domination of our country';[56] they opposed the loss of a labour force which would be crucial to an independent Guadeloupe and rejected its replacement by metropolitan migrants. Emigration consequently stimulated some new organisations to press for greater autonomy, such as the Front Antillo-Guyanais (FAG), founded in 1961, and dissolved by government decree a year later. Radicals argued that emigration was one more means 'preventing our country from following the example of Algeria or Cuba'.[57] Nonetheless migration quickly became substantial.

BUMIDOM organised recruitment, selected and rejected migrants, paid part or all of their fares and provided employment, training and housing in France. Four centres opened in France, one designed specifically for women, to provide training in domestic and paramedical skills and give aptitude tests for more skilled training courses and employment. For two decades the BUMIDOM sponsored migration to great effect; in Réunion the number of sponsored migrants grew from a mere 135 in 1962 to about 3000 in 1968 and from 1974 to 1982 averaged around 4500 a year. In Guadeloupe and Martinique together, the total number mounted as high as 15,000 a year in the 1970s, though not all were sponsored migrants. Even with extensive emigration, unemployment in the Antilles rose as high as 30 per cent in the 1970s. During that decade, the great volume of emigration, without any return migration, meant that the population of each of these *départements* remained static. In the late 1970s sponsored migration began to decline, as unemployment levels in France rose. The BUMIDOM, which had organised about 16,000 migrants between 1963 and 1980, in 1982 was transformed into the Agence Nationale pour l'Insertion et la Promotion des Travailleurs d'Outre-Mer (ANT), no longer oriented to stimulating and assisting emigration but to enabling migrants already in France to obtain better employment and also to encourage some return migration.

BUMIDOM also followed a policy directed at family reunion, and over the period 1962–81, more than one-third of all migrants from the Antilles who entered the *métropole* were in this category. This resulted in more female migration and a newly balanced demographic structure. Family reconstruction within France, and marriages to spouses outside the community of migrants from the overseas *départements*, have emphasised the increased permanency of this migration, even in the face of racial discrimination and economic problems. It shows, too, the transition from organised to spontaneous migration and from labour migration to settlement. Movement between the DOMs and the *métropole* has been accentuated by other attempts to encourage migration, such as the establishment of a special school in Réunion to train seamen for the French merchant navy and a military academy that trains officers for the French army. Moreover,

the French middle class is encouraged to recruit maids from Réunion. The Catholic Church discreetly arranges marriages between French farmers in the more remote parts of France and girls from Réunion . . . Adoption of babies from Réunion is also encouraged.[58]

In various ways demographic pressure is eased and emigration becomes a matter of course.

Over time the character of migration to France has changed. In the early years most emigrants from the *vieilles colonies* were students, civil servants or other professionals, as well as soldiers, but as the trickle became a flood, the migrant stream included many young, unskilled workers psychologically ill-prepared for the cultural, and even the climatic, differences between France and the tropics; they quickly joined the ranks of the unemployed as metropolitan economic growth slowed. In the early years BUMIDOM, and French organisations such as the Comité d'Action Sociale en Faveur des Originaires des Départements d'Outre-Mer (CASODOM) and the Amicale des Travailleurs Antillais-Guyanais (AMITAG), were able to promote the welfare of new migrants, giving them an advantage over voluntary migrants from various parts of Africa. Later migrants found conditions more difficult as job opportunities declined and racial tension increased. Earlier migrants were recruited into service industries, notably the lower ranks of the public service, particularly the postal and hospital services. Later migrants have experienced competition from other migrant groups, principally from Africa. The Antillais' and Réunionnais' superior education and French nationality, which granted 'the most superficial equality',[59] have proved inadequate to guarantee employment comparable with that of the French population as a whole.

So substantial has emigration from the *anciennes colonies* been that at the time of the 1982 census, 282,300 migrants from the DOM-TOMs lived in France, the vast majority from Martinique, Guadeloupe and

Table 4. Population Born in the DOM-TOMs Resident in France, 1945–1982

Territory	1954	1968	1975	1982	Percentage change, 1975–1982
Guadeloupe	6,380	26,344	53,200	87,024	64
Martinique	9,240	34,816	62,265	95,704	54
Guyane	1,860	4,384	6,275	9,904	58
Réunion	3,180	16,548	34,985	75,724	116
All DOMs	20,660	82,092	156,725	269,112	72
TOMs	3,540	9,376	15,440	13,188	− 15
DOM-TOMs	24,200	91,468	172,165	282,300	64

Source: INSEE, *Les Populations des DOM-TOM en France métropolitaine* (Paris, 1985), p. 58. The decline of the population born in overseas territories between 1975 and 1982 is a result of changes in administrative statutes classifying the territories, which excluded the Comoros, Djibouti and Saint-Pierre and Miquelon. In 1982 the TOMs population resident in France was recorded as being born in Mayotte (344), French Polynesia (6,188), New Caledonia and Wallis and Futuna (6,656). A further 756 people were born in Saint-Pierre and Miquelon.

Réunion (Table 4). This total, 64 per cent greater than at the 1975 census, implies that more than one person in five born in the French Antilles now lives in metropolitan France. There is no indication that this rapid growth has slowed in subsequent years. Migrants are typically youthful; more than two-thirds live in the Paris region, mainly in the eighteenth and nineteenth *arrondissements* or the poorer northern suburbs, such as Saint-Denis.

The tentative support for return migration that marked the transformation of BUMIDOM in the early 1980s has failed to bear fruit. Most who have returned to their home islands, relatively few in number, have been those who have failed to find jobs or who have retired, and most have gone back to the towns rather than the rural areas. In Martinique, for example, many of those who have returned have been unemployed women without formal skills.[60] Those who have been successful in France have generally remained there.

Emigration to France has become a characteristic of the Antilles and Réunion, but has generally had little impact elsewhere. Guyane has lost a very substantial proportion of its population, indeed a proportion almost as great as that of Guadeloupe and Martinique, but it is more characterised by immigration than by emigration. In the overseas territories, emigration has been minimal; almost all of those born in the TOMs and resident in France (Table 4) were the children of temporary migrants from France. Only a tiny proportion represented the indigenous population of the TOMs. Very few Melanesians, for example, have left New Caledonia and almost none have moved permanently. Those who have gone have either joined the military, enrolled in tertiary education or have become professional footballers in France.

Beyond the *vieilles colonies* only one other area shows substantial emigration, but emigration has so transformed Wallis and Futuna that half of its population lives outside the territory. Even before the New Caledonian nickel boom, emigration marked Wallis and Futuna. Heavy population pressure in some areas, and lack of opportunities for earning income, led to emigration to the Franco-British condominium of the New Hebrides beginning in the 1950s. Employers sought a strong and stable plantation workforce, and Wallisian productivity in copra shelling was reported to be three or four times that of local Melanesians. These early migrants had no official papers, since the islanders of the New Hebrides were still without a recognised nationality; the Wallisians had no legal protection, they could speak no relevant language and were easily exploited. Because they had signed a labour contract and shipping services were rare, they were forced to remain in the New Hebrides. However, subsequent migration continued, and more than a thousand Wallisians were in the New Hebrides by the early 1960s, many working in the Forari manganese mine. Afterwards, the expatriate Wallisian population stabilised and fell, as New Caledonia became a more important destination. Already by 1959 about 2000 Wallisian migrants lived in New Caledonia, one-third that of the population remaining in the home islands; this proportion grew rapidly until after the nickel boom. Overseas migration increasingly represented the most attractive alternative to the subsistence economy, emphasised by the decline of the copra market. A further stimulus to emigration was the establishment of French national service in 1959. Military life provided wider geographical, social and economic horizons and fostered boredom with limited domestic opportunities. The conservative nature of society in Wallis and Futuna also influenced emigration; not only were there dissatisfactions with the limitations of subsistence life, but also social tensions within the fairly rigid hierarchical system and dissatisfaction with the 'quasi-theocracy' of the kings and priests. Few migrants have therefore voluntarily returned to Wallis and Futuna, despite the nickel bust and political tensions. Their remittances remain crucial to the domestic economy, being transformed into new houses and new forms of consumption. Indeed, so few economic opportunities exist in Wallis and Futuna that the Vice-President of the Territorial Assembly, Petelo Takatai, declared in 1985 that 'substantial return migration would be a catastrophe'. Without a substantial decline in the rate of natural increase and much greater economic development in Wallis and Futuna, return migration will be unlikely to occur.[61]

In a rather similar manner there has also been migration away from Saint-Pierre and Miquelon, as much in response to limited social opportunities as to employment possibilities. Unlike every other DOM-TOM, emigration has not here been oriented to France or the other DOM-TOMs, but to nearby Canada, where a range of socioeconomic opportunities exist in a partially Francophone context. In Montreal alone live more Saint-Pierrais than in the islands.[62] For more than half a century, until the 1950s, there also occurred substantial migration from Saint-Barthélémy, mainly to the American Virgin Islands; this movement resulted in the decline of the island population from 2174 in 1875 to 2079 in 1954, when growth resumed, following the development of tourism.[63] From Saint-Martin, too, migrants for years went to the United States, various parts of the Caribbean and, taking advantage of the divided island, to Aruba and Curaçao in the Dutch Antilles.[64] In New Caledonia, economic and political difficulties in the 1970s and 1980s also led to the migration of a proportion of the European population to the east coast of Australia.[65] Yet these migration streams are relatively small and demographically unimportant; migration, either temporary or permanent, has generally linked the DOM-TOMs more closely to France and reduced the significance of regional ties.

Emigration to France has encouraged assimilation, decreased unemployment and reduced discontent; for Michel Debré, the former RPR *député* for Réunion and prime minister, not only is migration crucial because of its role in incorporating the DOM-TOMs more firmly into France but 'the direct consequence of ending migration would be a revolutionary situation'.[66] Migration has fostered stronger ties between the *départements d'outre-mer* and France, including a significant flow of remittances from Paris to the periphery. In some respects BUMI-DOM encouraged the selective migration of the more skilled from the Antilles and contributed to their further training in France, absorbing semi-skilled workers and those with tertiary education and finding employment for them in the *métropole*.[67] Indeed, in Réunion, BUMI-DOM rejected as many as 70 per cent of all applicants for migration because of their limited academic achievements or lack of apparent aptitude for employment.[68] While emigration from the DOMs has been counterbalanced, and in Guyane dwarfed, by immigration, it has largely been the migration of bureaucrats and technocrats, an imposition that has been quite widely resented. Strong arguments have been made under the Socialist government against migration from the DOM-TOMs, and the Secretary of State for the DOM-TOMs stated in 1983 that 'the government regrets this economic migration which is proof of the lack of real development of the DOM economies ... Migration should be a free choice rather than an economic necessity'.[69]

But migration from the DOMs does not appear to have slowed substantially and, in the future, may also develop from the TOMs.

POPULATION CHANGE WITHIN THE DOM-TOMs

In the years before the Second World War populations within the DOM-TOMs did not increase; these were years of economic stagnation, few new settlers migrated overseas and the health and welfare system was generally inadequate to prevent high mortality rates and raise the life expectancy. In New Caledonia, for example, population grew from around 55,000 at the turn of the century to only 56,000 on the eve of the war. Elsewhere there had been rather more growth; in French Polynesia, over the same period, numbers increased from around 30,000 to 51,000. But in Guyane, the population actually declined from 33,000 in 1901 to 28,500 in 1946. From the end of the war, with the change in statute of the DOM-TOMs, the situation began to change and in some cases population grew extremely rapidly.

In the post-war years expansion of welfare services, from medical care to social security payments, brought a widespread decline in mortality. In Réunion, for example, the mortality rate fell from 19 per thousand in 1957 to 6 in 1981, an exceptionally rapid decline that coincided with the virtual end of tropical diseases, especially malaria. This decline in mortality, one of the most rapid ever recorded, raised life expectancy from 50.5 years in 1959 to 70.5 years in 1984, the latter figure not significantly different from that of metropolitan France.[70] Similar but less spectacular falls were recorded in the Antilles, where mortality in both Guadeloupe and Martinique decreased from around 14 to 6 per thousand over the same period,[71] and infant mortality similarly declined. In Guyane and the Pacific territories, with poorer facilities and more scattered populations, change was less rapid, but in each case mortality rates also eventually fell closer to 6 per thousand, a rate not much greater than that of France.

As mortality rates declined, population growth became rapid, especially in Guyane and New Caledonia, where it was accompanied by significant immigration. In the Antilles and Réunion, however, under the dual impact of emigration and the establishment of birth control programmes, a dramatic decline in the fertility rate occurred. Between 1965 and 1975, it fell by 25 per cent in Guadeloupe and 40 per cent in Martinique. Indeed the Antilles offers 'one of the few instances in which the French government abandoned its habitual devotion to demographic increase and actively encouraged contraception'.[72] The

population increase that followed declining mortality rates was can-
celled out, and there was considerable concern in the Antilles over the
long-term effects of these changes. From the early 1960s, the population of the Antilles has grown only slowly (Table 3). Beyond the
Antilles neither emigration nor family planning have induced demographic transition, and populations continued to grow; in Réunion,
despite emigration, fertility rates have declined more slowly than in the
Antilles, giving it 'the mortality rate of an advanced industrial country
without substantially affecting its fertility as a backward country'.[73]
Birth control is not popular and families with twelve to fourteen children are common. In Guyane, Mayotte and the two largest Pacific
territories the population has doubled or tripled in the post-war years.
Even for Wallis and Futuna, half of whose Polynesian population now
lives in New Caledonia, the population is twice that of the war years. In
every case population continues to grow.

Significant differences between population growth rates appear
within particular DOM-TOMs. Often these are regional, with emigration and mortality rates highest in more remote rural areas in New
Caledonia, Guyane, or Réunion, but they also vary between ethnic
groups. Such disparities are particularly significant in New Caledonia,
where the Melanesian population growth rate accelerated in the post-
war years to reach 2.5 per cent per year in the early 1970s and again in
the mid-1980s. By contrast, the European growth rate, influenced by
slowing immigration, has fallen below 1 per cent, whilst the Wallisian
and Futunan rate of natural increase in New Caledonia is more than
3 per cent. Such differences take on considerable significance when
ethnicity is not divorced from politics and economic development.
However, in New Caledonia, as elsewhere in the DOM-TOMs, immigration, especially in the 1960s and 1970s, has contributed to the
indigenous populations of the DOM-TOMs often becoming a much
smaller proportion of the total than variations in rates of natural
increase would otherwise ensure.

The post-war changes that encouraged population growth and, in
some cases, emigration also directly contributed to the urbanisation of
the populations of the DOM-TOMs, either in France or within particular islands. Employment growth increasingly concentrated in the
urban centres and was accompanied by the decline of the agricultural
sector and new aspirations for wage and salary employment. In the
Antilles,

with comparatively low salaries in the private sector, and extremely lucrative
ones in the public sector, young Martinicans are little inclined to seek employment in an ill-paid, socially unrewarding and generally exhausting occupation, such as cane cutting. The ideal job is that of the bureaucrat, the

fonctionnaire; the antithesis is the agricultural labourer. Since the generosity of the French government (including unemployment insurance) suppresses the need to work at any price, true unemployment is rampant, whereas job possibilities (at least in the primary sector) do exist.[74]

The decline of agriculture has thus been accompanied by migration out of rural areas (balanced, in the Caribbean, by some immigration) and the ageing of the agricultural workforce. In Réunion 'the rural population, for the most part, only work in agriculture because of the impossibility of finding stable and permanent wage employment'.[75] The young have little incentive to take up agricultural employment and the ageing labour force virtually ensures that the agricultural sector will decline further in the future.

Throughout the DOM-TOMs similar patterns of internal migration have occurred in the post-war years. More remote islands have lost population, a situation apparent in French Polynesia but significant also in the Loyalty Islands (New Caledonia) and the dependencies of Guadeloupe. Migration from outer islands has been most substantial in the outer islands of French Polynesia, where infrastructure and employment provision are extremely limited compared with Tahiti. This is especially true of the mountainous Marquesas, where even ports are inadequate, there is only one airport (completed only in 1979) and transport costs are prohibitive (despite subsidies to Air Polynésie). It is also true of the Tuamotu chain of atolls where, since the 1930s, at least six atolls have been completely depopulated,[76] and where a series of cyclones in 1982 and 1983 hastened emigration. The establishment of the Centre d'Expérimentation du Pacifique (CEP) in French Polynesia completely depopulated the atoll of Tureia; the resident population were relocated in Tahiti, a foretaste of the waves of migration that were to follow. By May 1985 it was estimated that migration had affected as many as 85 to 90 per cent of the whole agricultural workforce in French Polynesia.[77] Even in Saint-Pierre and Miquelon, tiny Miquelon has been increasingly deserted in favour of urban Saint-Pierre, just as the population of Wallis has grown relative to that of smaller Futuna.

Populations have also everywhere moved from isolated upland areas towards more accessible coastal locations. In 'Morne-Paysan', in the Martinique mountains, the 'population of 1650 persons has scarcely changed over fifty years; 98 per cent of its potential increase from declining mortality rates has been offset by a steady emigration to the estates, the city, and overseas. Immigration is minor.'[78] In Rapa, villages which in the last century were in the hills have now moved to the coast, and in New Caledonia isolated tribes have abandoned mountain fastnesses, 'the slow desertification of the mountainous parts of the territory'.[79] In every case these movements have accompanied the search for more accessible land for commercial agriculture, access to wage and salary employment and better infrastructure provision. Urbanisation has emphasised such trends, as the populations of the DOM-TOMs have increasingly concentrated at a single point in each state. Only in Mayotte and Wallis and Futuna do the bulk of the population remain in rural areas, though by 1985 more than a quarter of the Mayotte population lived in Dzaoudzi or Mamoudzou. Elsewhere at least half the population is now urban, a vast difference from the pre-war era of rural agricultural populations and quite different from nearby island states where urbanisation is much less substantial.

In the early post-war years urbanisation was limited, even in the administrative centres. With the sole exception of Guadeloupe, few centres existed outside the capital itself and even those scarcely displayed significant economic activity. One traveller's description of Marigot on Saint-Martin at the end of the 1940s is typical of this era:

> Marigot is a miserable town. Two hundred yards of dust, lined with wooden houses that have none of the charm of those of the other island towns . . . comprise the main street. At one end lay the quay, where a couple of fishing smacks lay at anchor, the other trailed off into rolling meadowland. . .with cows grazing under tame European trees. Only a single palm tree, and a few Negroes hanging listlessly about, hinted that we are in the tropics. And nothing else. Listlessness, we were to learn, was the essential characteristic of the town; that, and an absolute characterlessness that was so extreme that it contrived to develop from a negative attribute into something destructively positive.[80]

Albeit a negative view, this description was indicative of a period without economic development or the expansion of a bureaucracy in the rural centres and small towns of the DOM-TOMs. In the next two decades the situation changed quite drastically.

The concentration of infrastructure provision and more prestigious and better-paid employment, especially in the public sector, emphasised urbanisation. Virtually throughout the DOM-TOMs capitals became primate cities in the post-war years, dominating each of their regions; the sole exception is Guadeloupe, where Basse-Terre is an alternative urban centre with 'the extreme form of a "ville des fonctionnaires" ("bureaucrats' city").'[81] In French Polynesia, by 1967 half the population lived in Papeete; a decade later, this proportion reached 57 per cent. By the time of the 1983 census, the greater urban area held over 93,000 people; Papeete has continued to grow, even if it has not increased its proportion of the territorial population. In New Caledonia, Noumea had grown in a similar manner; by 1989 the greater Noumea area (including Dumbea and Mont Dore) held more than

91,000 people, some 56 per cent of the total population of the territory. (Neither of the next largest towns, Uturoa in French Polynesia and Bourail and Thio in New Caledonia, presently have even 3000 people.) In both Pacific territories, the urban population had been only a quarter of the total in 1946. Indeed in the 1960s urbanisation in New Caledonia was so limited that one scholar classified centres with populations of more than twenty-five people as urban.[82] The growth of Cayenne, in Guyane, has been even more explosive; its population doubled from 18,400 in 1961 to 38,100 in 1982 and has continued to expand at the same rate in more recent years. Migration to Cayenne in many respects defines the rationale for rapid post-war urban growth:

Most often rural migrants see living in Cayenne as achieving undeniable social mobility. Although most migrants join the ranks of the sub-proletariat they do not resent this situation. On the contrary they value the positive aspects and opportunities, especially for their children to whom they believe they have given the best possible education and training ... The young almost always think of the city as the only place where they can join the modern world.[83]

In Guadeloupe, Martinique and especially Réunion, where populations are much larger, and emigration has been substantial, primate cities appear less obvious and many small towns have grown in size over the past decade. This is especially so in Réunion, where Saint-Denis has little room for expansion on a narrow coastal site, but Saint-Pierre has spread on its coastal plain. Though much recent growth has been a function of the expansion of the public service outside the capital city, it is primarily a legacy of the series of small commercial centres that grew up during the long years of dominance by the sugar industry.

The majority of immigrants to the DOM-TOMs have become urban residents; indeed, in Guyane, New Caledonia and French Polynesia, many recent migrants have little familiarity with, or commitment to development in, the rural areas. The capitals of the DOM-TOMs are quite unlike their rural hinterlands; in New Caledonia, for example, Noumea represents 'an urban area, a small corner of the land but densely populated, living in semi-ignorance of the rest of the archipelago, but dominating it culturally, politically and economically'.[84] Noumea is also a predominantly white town, with Melanesians no more than a quarter of the population, in contrast to the bush, where they are dominant, and the islands, where there are virtually no Europeans. After the political crises of the mid-1980s these ethnic divisions have been reinforced, as Melanesians have abandoned the city and Europeans have fled the east coast and the north of the Grande

Terre. French Polynesia exhibits some of the characteristics of New Caledonia, with recent immigrants concentrated in Papeete (and Mururoa) and Polynesians dominant elsewhere, but the substantial *demi* population makes racial divisions less significant than in New Caledonia. In Guyane, fully 40 per cent of the population of Cayenne were born outside the *département*. Such ethnic divisions are rarely apparent elsewhere; Wallis and Futuna, however, contain two ethnically distinct populations, to the extent that the kings of Futuna sought secession in 1983; but this division has been largely unchanged from pre-colonial times because of minimal migration between the two islands. Capital cities in other DOM-TOMs have a cosmopolitan character denied to the small towns and the countryside; this further emphasises ties between France and the DOM-TOMs.

Migration to the DOM-TOMs, especially that of metropolitan public servants, has introduced new value systems and a new concept of poverty has emerged through comparison with these new migrants. In French Polynesia, there are also now many poor Tahitian families, according to one Tahitian cleric, because 'the established western system of values and the force of colonialism have contributed to the dispossession of their natural wealth'.[85] In urban areas, where this comparison is greatest, relative deprivation is acute; urban Tahitians have a 'standard of living not necessarily lower than their relatives in the outer islands yet they are poor in a special way. For their life takes place in the context of others, the *demis* and *popa'a* (Europeans) and the tourists who are so much better off than they are.'[86] Migration has thus contributed to the unequal integration of distant islands into the world system.

If affluence is concentrated in the capital cities, so too is poverty. In Papeete, shanty towns (*bidonvilles*) are common and have contributed to the pollution of land and lagoon. In 1970, urbanisation was seen as producing an 'eruption of shantytowns that are spreading like an uncontrolled rash',[87] and it has been suggested that as many as 20,000 Polynesians may live in 'shocking squalor'.[88] The growth of Papeete has given rise to economic changes, especially a recent growth in unemployment and the emergence of an informal sector, as well as to social changes, most dramatically increased violence, theft, delinquency and alcoholism.[89] Other social problems are more and more common in Papeete including drug abuse (usually of home-grown cannabis or 'magic' mushrooms) and child neglect. The emergence of youth gangs played a part in the destruction of the Papeete waterfront in the riots of October 1988. At the same time there exists enormous affluence in the prestigious suburbs on the mountain flanks and in the business centre of the city. One indication of the great contrasts within the urban areas of the DOM-TOMs, typified in Papeete, is that the cost of land in the centre of the city has been estimated to be more than that on the Champs-Elysées.[90] In Fort-de-France and Pointe-à-Pitre delinquency is associated with children from households where formal employment is absent, housing is overcrowded and bereft of amenities and incomes are inadequate.[91] Noumea has few squatter settlements, though they have multiplied in the past decade, but Melanesians are concentrated around Montravel, a grim suburb of tenement blocks in the shadows and pollution haze of the Doniambo nickel smelter.

Daubed with graffiti, stinking from inadequate waste disposal systems, these rented flats house some of the poorest Melanesians in New Caledonia. Many are unemployed but have chosen to remain in Noumea rather than return to reservations, where their social ties have been poorly maintained. They are the urban dispossessed.[92]

Many urban residents

live in a world with neither a past nor a future. They are adrift in the present . . . they live between two worlds. They like to go to the outer islands but they are soon bored there . . . they are only at home in their marginality.[93]

Urban life has also contributed to greater individuality, the breakdown of social cohesion and the decline in traditional systems of social control.

The expansion of the bureaucracy, and the shift from production to consumption, have underlined urbanisation in the DOM-TOMs. Where, as in New Caledonia, genuine production is also concentrated in a single city, the gulf between city and countryside is now enormous. Even before the nickel boom, 'all the dynamism of the island was concentrated in Noumea',[94] and, in economic terms, New Caledonia has become more and more 'Nouméa et le désert calédonien' ('Noumea and the Caledonian desert').[95] Incomes, living standards and amenities in the cities are vastly superior to those in the countryside, and even a flow of remittances to the rural areas has not redressed imbalances. As in French Polynesia, urbanisation has contributed to the impoverishment of the countryside:

Whilst new economic and social structures were established, mainly in the cities, rural areas experienced degradation of economic infrastructure and deterioration of social structures — the very power and integrity of which had contributed to giving people a place in their environment and had slowed the rural exodus. These changes were even more rapid because the old systems did not allow people to integrate easily with the new models exported from Papeete. Those who wished to adopt the new trends had no choice but to move to the city.[96]

In such circumstances, as elsewhere in the DOM-TOMs, development planning has subsequently given greater attention to rural development but the economic climate has limited success.

Though development policies have stressed decentralisation and agriculture, successful attempts to bring about rural economic growth have been few, and only part of the minimal return migration has been of a labour force committed to rural development. The Fonds d'aménagement et de développement des îles de la Polynésie Française (FA-DIP), created in 1981, has aimed at encouraging socio-economic development in outer islands, through various subsidy schemes and welfare programmes, including video television in the Marquesas, but success has been minimal. However, in the mid-1970s, a number of factors did lead to return migration to a few favoured areas. The principal influence was· the deterioration of employment prospects in Papeete, but rising copra prices (and support schemes), air transport improvements (and subsidies) and some successful development projects, such as pearling in Takapoto, led to a degree of return migration.[97] However, even in favoured islands such as Takapoto and Tubuai,[98] the particular conjunction of factors that have encouraged return migration are unusual and offer little hope of long-term economic growth in remote islands. In New Caledonia, too, a number of Melanesians left Noumea in the aftermath of the nickel boom, and many others left in the mid-1980s as political tension made the city uncomfortable. Yet though the ideology of migration remains one of return, most who have good jobs in the city think of returning 'home' only on retirement. The reality has increasingly been one of urban permanence. As migrants have become more urban, their sometimes distant rural ties have become more tenuous and the necessity to hold and retain paid employment has become greater. Thus those who have returned to rural areas are much like those who have returned from France: the old and the failures, and those who could no longer afford urban life.[99] Though the rate of urbanisation has declined, slowing urban economic growth has scarcely contributed to rural development. On balance migration has continued to drain the rural areas, and the DOM-TOMs in general, of their more dynamic people.

THE POLITICS OF POPULATION

Population growth, and especially the immigration that has contributed to the ethnic diversity of the DOM-TOMs, is not without strong political overtones. At different times and in different places, particular migrant groups have been favoured and encouraged, as emigrants or immigrants, and population policies, where they have existed, have focused on particular sectors or places. Within the DOM-TOMs specific policies have encouraged new geographical distributions. Nowhere is this more true than in New Caledonia, where in the early colonial years, both convicts and free settlers displaced Melanesians to the mountains and east coast and contributed to their declining numbers. Subsequent waves of Asians, Polynesians and others diversified the ethnic structure, yet suggested to conservative observers a 'Caledonisation' of the population, with different races and cultures fused together into a single harmonious society, so that the accidents of history could be ignored and no ethnic group accorded a special status. By contrast, for Jean-Claude Guillebaud, 'Noumea is probably the town [in the DOM-TOMs] where the colonial anachronism is most glaring. In Noumea the violence of white Caldoche society, obsessed with racial arithmetic that will one day put it in a minority, provides a situation that is openly racist.'[100] Hence, at the same time, there are persistent claims of a substantial *métis* population and arguments that Melanesians are not so distinct as they are sometimes assumed to be.

Neither in the census nor in social life are the *métis* of New Caledonia recognised as a distinct group; rather they label themselves as Europeans or Melanesians according to the context and consciousness of their own identity. Emphasis on either *métissage* or the variety of ethnic groups in New Caledonia is scarcely devoid of political connotations; arguments over the extent of *métissage* in New Caledonia, along the lines of Chirac's extreme claim that 'we are all *métis* now',[101] enables settlers, some of whom claim to be the first occupants of a particular tract of land, to demand 'in the name of what nation, what colour, through the first occupation of land, how can we possibly be separated?.'[102] Jean Guiart, however, has countered more bluntly that 'the line of separation in New Caledonia is due to history. It is between Melanesians and all others.'[103] Bernard Brou believes that Melanesians wholly aspire to imitate Europeans and that 'Caledonisation' has led to a 'general Creolisation' of society;[104] in the illustrations to Brou's monograph on population, many postcards and the judiciously chosen photographs in some official publications, the mixture and harmony of races suggests an ethnic 'melting pot' in New Caledonia. It has been

seriously argued by *Le Figaro* that all the prominent *indépendantiste*
leaders, Jean-Marie Tjibaou, Nidoish Naisseline and Eloi Machoro,
had mixed racial origins and hence, with 'widespread *métissage*, Kanak
culture was an invention'.[105] This argument is thoroughly rejected by
many Melanesians; in 1972 a Melanesian from Mare declared: 'We and
our land were believed dead, put to sleep for ever, anaesthetised by
modernisation and cultural assimilation. After 129 years we are now
awakening.'[106] Assimilation is no more than wishful thinking by those
most prone to reject Melanesian values. At the margins there are similarities and convergences in genetic structure and social organisation,
but ethnic divisions in New Caledonia have massive significance in
economic and political life.

The issue of 'Caledonisation' is important in one further way: the
insistence of many observers that history is irrelevant and that the contemporary population structure forms the reality around which all
political negotiations should take place. Europeans, Polynesians and
Asians in New Caledonia generally support this view, and a number of
political parties which have emerged in the past decade emphasise
racial equality as a key element in their platform, effectively denying
the possibility of redress of historical inequalities, especially access to
land. Every ethnic group, however small, has had some role in political
change. The ethnicity, and to a lesser extent the geography, of population are critical determinants of past and future in New Caledonia.
Marginal 'Caledonisation' has failed to erode major differences, and
many Melanesians (and also some Europeans) dispute the existence of
such convergence, arguing instead that Melanesians above all, but also
the Caldoche descendants of the early colonists, are 'victims of history'
and thus must be clearly distinguished from recent migrants of whatever race. Diverse and often conflicting economic interests have
ensured that divisions between ethnic groups are largely maintained;
recent claims in the 1980s, such as those by the Vietnamese, that intermarriage has blurred racial divisions, reflect the politicisation of population changes rather than real social evolution. Though many liberal
Europeans see integration as desirable and are attracted to the idea of a
harmonious multiracial society, such a melding, even if practicable,
would lead to further destruction of Melanesian traditions. Consequently opposition to assimilation and integration became bywords in
the struggle for independence. At the same time Wallisians, French
Polynesians and Asians oppose what they perceive as 'Kanak' independence.[107] In the last few years 'Caledonisation' has been shown to be no
more than a figment of conservative imaginations. Ethnic polarisation
is increasingly the reality.

Outside New Caledonia population issues are less obviously related to the politics of independence or integration, but the immigration of particular groups often provokes bitter opposition. Throughout the DOM-TOMs opposition has arisen to the migration of bureaucrats from France, since many senior administrators repatriate significant proportions of their incomes, return to France after brief service overseas and show little commitment to local development. Regular leave and plans for eventual retirement to France nurture old roots, and regional associations of Bretons, Corsicans and others sustain these attachments. The *fonctionnariat* includes few old people, and public servants' children often seek education in France; they form a working population in which both women and men take advantage of excellent opportunities to increase incomes at inflated rates of pay, with low taxation, earning money that will eventually provide a good life in France — all in a pleasantly tropical environment. Such bureaucrats are widely perceived, and disparagingly referred to, as *z'oreilles* or *cinq-cinqs*, those who migrated after hearing of high salaries and who remit more than half their earnings to France. The situation causes hostility among the local population, a discontent which can have nationalist repercussions:

Increasingly, especially in the Antilles, all racial groups including many white Creoles, have come together in opposition to the metropolitan invasion. This has not assisted the politics of assimilation. In fact the resentment and jealousy which it has provoked have, on the contrary, combined to make it more difficult, even impossible. It has given birth to a strident creole nationalism which is beginning to demand cutting the principal ties with the *métropole*.[108]

At least in the Antilles, the public servants ally themselves with the merchants to advance their common interests: 'Two worlds co-exist: that of the bureaucrats and businessmen, one living off the other, and that of the workers and peasants, in general four times poorer and the first to be hit by unemployment.'[109] New divisions have thus arisen in the DOM-TOMs and, ironically, local residents often find better professional opportunities in the *métropole* than in their own regions. A paradox emerges, in which skilled metropolitan migrants have blocked social mobility within the DOM-TOMs.[110]

Concern over metropolitan migrants and the resultant competition for jobs, status and even land is a new variant on historic concerns over uneven access to resources. Inequalities are the result of early immigration, and especially the divisions within the *vieilles colonies* that followed the migration of plantation owners and workers, and the subsequent construction of a hierarchical social structure. Despite socio-economic changes, especially in the post-war years, social divisions are often substantial. For example, in Réunion: 'A new elite of money, business and property income is replacing the old elite of the land and the cane fields';[111] traditional landowners have retained agricultural land, without undertaking investment, but they benefit from subsidies and so contribute further to the decline of the agricultural sector. In Martinique *Béké* plantations have been described as 'intact latifundia',[112] or large estates, and Réunion retains a society where 'almost all the large sugar properties and refineries are controlled by a small group of white Réunionnais who, despite internal divisions and conflicts, remain undivided in opposition to other social and ethnic groups.'[113] Many plantation families have kin in France, capital is transferred from France to ensure the continuation of the plantation system, and plantation owners are closely integrated into the islands' political systems. Small farmers have effectively been marginalised, technical change is concentrated on large landholdings and landowners have been able to discourage and prevent most social and economic reforms that would contribute towards equality. Such landowners are often prominent politicians, hence there is no power base for radical political change.

Land is extremely unevenly distributed in most DOM-TOMs. This is particularly the case in New Caledonia, where a small number of Europeans own most of the agricultural land while Melanesians own a very small proportion, less now per capita than at the start of the twentieth century. Land reform lagged behind demand for land, a situation which focused the initial demand for independence on land issues. Land reform initially accelerated in the 1970s only to slow after 1986 with, for a brief period, more land being redistributed to settlers than Melanesians.[114] In Martinique the uneven distribution of land meant that in 1981, 85 per cent of all holdings covered no more than 18 per cent of the agricultural area but a mere 127 holdings (0.5 per cent of the total) covered 42 per cent of the agricultural land;[115] a somewhat similar situation exists in Guadeloupe.[116] Réunion displays substantial differences between the small landholdings in regions dominated by 'poor whites', and the great properties more common elsewhere. Indeed, in the early 1970s, not only were there almost as many properties of more than 1000 hectares in Réunion as in France itself, but a mere 2 per cent of the properties encompassed more than half the agricultural land on the island:

Réunion is not only a French *département*; it is an underdeveloped country where a mass of small farmers and landless peasants, illiterate and discriminated against, are subject to the will of a minority of landowners and urban bourgeois closely tied to a distant *métropole*.[117]

In French Polynesia, despite various permutations in the form of land alienation, much land in Tahiti and in nearby islands was owned by metropolitan Frenchmen, Chinese or *demis* by the mid-twentieth century;[118] the Polynesians often retained poor-quality land or holdings in remote islands. Virtually throughout the DOM-TOMs land inequalities have followed a particular structure of migration and population change rather than being inherent in society or a result of technical and economic changes.

More generally social organisation is a function of population structure, as in the Antilles, where the social structure has been loosely described as 'a color-class pyramid: at the apex a white landed aristocracy, in the middle a colored middle class, and at the base a black proletariat.'[119] In reality social organisation is much more complex, though often quite rigid, but nonetheless everywhere it is influenced by the historic and contemporary structure of migration. In a similar manner to the situation in New Caledonia, there are strong arguments elsewhere that the DOM-TOMs have become melting pots of races and cultures, as in Réunion, where a similar social structure to the Antilles has also been championed as a 'harmonious society, a crucible of peoples and civilisations, a rare example of social concord', a conclusion at some remove from reality as considerable violence early in 1991 showed.[120] The 'melting-pot' view of DOM-TOM society differs significantly from a situation where emigration is considerable and immigration often a source of tension and opposition. Of the DOM-TOMs which were inhabited at the time of conquest, only Wallis and Futuna has a population of essentially the same ethnic composition as at the time of European contact. Three — Réunion, Saint-Pierre and Miquelon and, of course, the TAAF — were uninhabited, hence have wholly post-contact populations. Elsewhere migration has substantially changed population compositions, even if only New Caledonia is a genuine settler colony.

Population change and migration cannot be divorced from politics. In New Caledonia, migration was encouraged to dampen nationalist sentiments and, in the Antilles, BUMIDOM was established soon after the first pro-independence groups emerged. Ironically, Pierre Messmer, the architect of migration to New Caledonia, later lamented large-scale migration to France: 'This is a trap set by history. We in France and Europe have been accustomed to colonizing the world. Now the foreigners are coming here to us.'[121] In another sense, it was a French trap that tied the DOM-TOMs to France. Migration in both directions has fostered strong ties between France and the DOM-TOMs, encouraged assimilation (through new cultural ties and intermarriage), discouraged demands for independence and emphasised rapid urbanisation and bureaucratisation. In the post-war years this dual structure of migration, heavily criticised in some quarters — as in Martinique, where it has been viewed as 'the invasion of metropolitans and the haemorrhage of French West Indians'[122] — has emphasised the integration of the *départements* into France. Though the overseas territories have not yet followed, worsening economic problems could one day lead to a similar kind of evolution.

5

Economic Change: From Production to Consumption

THE ECONOMIC history of the DOM-TOMs is one of early ambitions for colonial treasure-troves of exotic products and great
profits, and later attempts to confront the difficulties of developing the
territories that had been acquired. Proposals for exploiting the
potential of colonies were not lacking, but relatively few initiatives bore
fruit, at least for a very long season. With few exceptions, the DOM-
TOMs in the later part of the twentieth century have failed as sources of
great production; their economies are dominated by the tertiary sector.
Instead of providing economic largesse for the *métropole*, they consume
vast quantities of imports and subsidies. Critics charge that, in an in-
version of the traditional situation in which the mother-country reaped
economic rewards from its colonies, the DOM-TOMs now rely on
France for the capital and commodities that support an artificially high
standard of living — the old producer colonies have become consumer
colonies, the old monopolies of the colonial pact replaced by a transfer
economy.

COLONIAL ECONOMIES

The European expansion of the 1500s was characterised by the search
for raw materials, preferably gold, that would directly contribute to the

growth of the colonial powers. In this sense the construction of France's first overseas empire was little different from that of other imperial powers, though strategic interests invariably combined with economic interests and the balance between these varied over time and space. The *vieilles colonies* were perceived as sources of wealth just as were other Caribbean and, to a lesser extent, Indian Ocean islands. In general, they were disappointments, providing little in the way of minerals but eventually becoming valuable producers of sugar and some other agricultural products. Colonial expansion in the Pacific was less obviously motivated by economic dreams but rather by unfocused aspirations for a global empire that might one day prove of value. French acquisition of both New Caledonia and French Polynesia owed much to the desire for naval bases that would prevent the South Pacific becoming a 'British lake', and even such small Polynesian islands as Rapa were accorded enormous, but unrealised, strategic significance.[1] In many cases colonialism was even reluctant, with the last small islands to come under colonial control exciting little or no interest in Europe.[2] Though France eagerly competed for the larger Pacific islands, such as Tahiti and the Grande Terre of New Caledonia, it showed less interest in the smaller outlying islands of these territories or in Wallis and Futuna. In a rather different way, the acquisition of the TAAF in the mid-nineteenth century was equally unmotivated by economic goals, but by the same vague scientific goals that had convinced other European powers to stake a claim in this icy, uncharted wilderness. By then the economic rationale for colonialism had largely died.

Anticipated economic profits provided a crucial motive for European expansion overseas, and the French activities in the colonies which became the DOM-TOMs were no exception. Private companies, policy-makers, colonial lobbyists and individual setlers all sought to exploit the potential of overseas possessions for production of tropical agricultural commodities, extraction of minerals, fishing and trading. Lack of markets, capital and labour frustrated development projects, and regular crises punctuated the economic history of the DOM-TOMs. What developed was a classic case of a colonial economy: primary products from the colonies were exchanged for manufactured goods and capital from France, with profits divided between metropolitan business interests and a local settler elite; the labour was performed by native populations or imported workers. Martinique, Guadeloupe and Réunion grew sugar, as well as bananas, pineapples and other tropical crops. Saint-Pierre's fishermen caught cod, and other fishermen occasionally worked the waters of the TAAF. The

Pacific islands exported copra to France. Vast profits remained elusive and the DOM-TOMs, despite the steady production of new materials, were far from being the jewels of the empire. Even at its zenith, production was sometimes slight and the economies of these territories were pale reflections of those of better-endowed colonies.

At the end of the nineteenth century the promise of economic growth had largely given way to disenchantment. Guyane and Wallis and Futuna showed virtually no sign of modern commercial development and elsewhere most early agricultural ventures had declined or disappeared. Both Guyane and New Caledonia were better known as penal colonies than sources of wealth. Remote markets, substitution and competition from better-endowed colonies in Africa and Asia had turned the islands into economic backwaters. By the twentieth century French imperialist interests, like those of Britain, had largely shifted from the small, distant and unprofitable islands towards the vast expanses of Africa, where the prospects of agricultural, timber and mineral wealth were more alluring. The *anciennes colonies* had failed to generate the wealth expected of them, and the costs of economic growth in the French Pacific remained considerable. Inevitably, without constant support from France, the export economy stagnated, a process that continued into the twentieth century.

In the Antilles a crisis of sugar overproduction occurred in the 1920s, only minimised by France's willingness to guarantee a market for a proportion of the sugar and rum exports. The institution of a customs union between France and some of its colonies in 1892 had led to the gradual elimination of economic activities in Martinique and Guadeloupe that might conflict with French metropolitan interests, and the quota system on sugar and rum 'demonstrated conclusively that, as far as France was concerned, Martinique was no more than an adjunct to the metropolitan economy and that in no circumstances would competition with metropolitan interests be contemplated'.[3] Yet the quota system preserved the agricultural economy and in the 1930s the agricultural decline that would otherwise have accompanied global depression was slowed by French preferences for colonial produce.[4]

Frustration with sugar cultivation encouraged numerous attempts to diversify agriculture in the twentieth century. Early experiments at planting cotton, cocoa, coffee and rice showed only episodic growth or marginal results. Bananas and pineapples in the Antilles represented partial exceptions, especially in the inter-war years, yet for all the attempts at diversification, in the 1930s sugar covered 50 per cent of the agricultural area of Guadeloupe and Martinique and sugar and rum constituted 90 per cent of exports.[5] In Réunion there was even less diversification and the economy of the *vieilles colonies* remained almost as dependent on sugar as it had ever been. The colonial plantation economy was far from over.[6] Elsewhere agricultural production was erratic, copra exports from the Pacific territories needed subsidies, and the grazing industry of New Caledonia traversed a long period of depression. Despite predictions of commercial success, the Pacific territories never lived up to expectation; markets were remote, labour unavailable and natural hazards often disrupted development. Even in Saint-Pierre and Miquelon the economic decline that accompanied competition to the local fishing industry was halted only by the successful establishment of contraband smuggling and, for a decade (1922–33), the unusual service industry flourished. In the TAAF the various marine industries and agricultural ventures had disappeared or lingered on unprofitably.[7] From Wallis and Futuna, Guyane and Mayotte little had ever been exported. Greater success came from mineral resources: New Caledonia was the world's largest nickel producer at the end of the nineteenth and in the early twentieth century; the Polynesian island of Makatea furnished phosphate. Miners largely depleted reserves of phosphate, and the gold of Guyane, but New Caledonia's nickel was the single most valuable export of the future DOM-TOMs.

Economic problems that had previously emerged in the *vieilles colonies* surfaced later in the Pacific, after the inevitable and necessary attempts to develop a colonial economy. Conclusions on the economic results of French colonialism in French Polynesia before the Second World War were quite abrupt:

On any rough cost-benefit analysis it is hard to see what France gained in the classic terms of 'economic imperialism' or even for the more atavistic urges of the 'national prestige' school of French expansionists. Most French capital came in the form of support costs for the officials and materials required to establish the post by war, and to maintain it, on a reduced scale, throughout the long decades of marginal development. The French government underwrote a market for foreign enterprise, missionary conversions and the islanders' access to the material goods and ideas of the outside world.[8]

Such a postscript on a period of colonial history applied far beyond French Polynesia. Profits were often no more than visions for speculators and colonial administrators, though colonialists constantly emphasised the importance of production. The bulk of the population remained employed in agriculture and fisheries. In an era when fortunes were made in Asia and Africa, the future DOM-TOMs contributed little to French coffers.

THE DECLINE OF PRODUCTION

Despite competition to the plantations of the *vieilles colonies*, sugar and its by-products such as rum remain the leading exports from the Antilles and Réunion. Fish continues to dominate Saint-Pierre and Miquelon. Pearls from the Tuamotus in French Polynesia, nickel from New Caledonia and perfume essences from Mayotte form those territories' major products. In short, the sorts of agricultural and mineral production pioneered during the colonial age have persisted in the latter half of the twentieth century, buffeted by changing market demand and often dependent on high levels of French subsidies.

A certain continuity in production, though with declining exports, has been counterbalanced by rapidly expanding imports. The era of production waned with the abandonment of arduous and unproductive agriculture, the shrinking of fisheries resources, the periodic 'busts' and 'booms' of mining or depletion of mineral deposits. These small colonies were becoming rapidly dependent on French finance already in the mid-twentieth century. At the end of the Second World War, the French geographer Jean Gottman concluded that the extent of dependence in Guadeloupe was 'certainly not the sign of a healthy territory'.[9] Similar observations were made about other colonies. Yet in 1946 the four *anciennes colonies* became French overseas *départements* and, in the Pacific, France reasserted more direct authority after the years of economic disorientation caused by the war and the presence of American troops. As this occurred, French funding steadily increased, and the DOM-TOMs entered a phase of change that quickly took them into a new sort of dependence.

Transformations of the global economy in the post-war years further weakened the ability of DOM-TOM commodity production to compete on world markets. For example, sugarcane production in the *vieilles colonies* could not even match that in relatively affluent and costly producing areas such as Hawaii, and banana production was in no better position. Substantial French transfers of capital, especially in the 1960s, attempted to revitalise the sugar industry through restructuring production and the modernising of factories, but decline could not be arrested. Public finance could only prevent the disappearance of these industries and slow the rise of overt unemployment.

Sugar production in Martinique registered a steady fall; in two decades, after 1963, the number of factories fell from eleven to one and the number of distilleries from thirty-one to twenty-one. As the area under sugarcane contracted, production declined from 89,000 tonnes to less than 2000 tonnes. Exports disappeared and were replaced by imports of sugar from Guadeloupe and from France itself. This occurred despite enormous French expenditure to 'save the sugar industry'.[10] Competition from European sugarbeet production, where there was mechanisation on vast areas of flat land, readily available fertiliser and accessible markets, emphasised the process of decline, accentuated by the emergence of a tertiary economy and society. Martinique, 'a colony that produced wealth for metropolitan consumers, has become a market colony for metropolitan producers'.[11] Despite exports of sugar from Guadeloupe to Martinique, a similar decline also occurred there: twelve factories closed between 1952 and 1980. Others were modernised, but two sugar development plans in the 1970s were unsuccessful; mechanisation failed and agricultural unemployment significantly increased.[12] Réunion did not experience a similar decline because the regeneration of sugar became the major endeavour of the post-war administration; new irrigation schemes doubled productivity, and production increased from 2400 tonnes in 1945 to 246,000 tonnes in 1984 only because Réunion secured almost three-quarters of the EC sugar quota that was given to the DOMs. With guaranteed prices, sugar became four times as profitable as any other crop.[13] Meanwhile, sugar never occupied more than a tiny area in Guyane; it brought little prosperity and by 1981 still occupied no more than 300 hectares, from which a small quantity of rum was produced.[14] Throughout the DOMs the sugar industry only survived because of substantial French financial support and EC preferences.

Other Antillais agricultural activities generally fared little better. Pineapple production, though still dominant to the extent that Martinique supplied 42 per cent of France's imports in 1962, substantially declined thereafter; the Ivory Coast became France's major supplier by the 1980s. Banana production continued, with exports from Martinique in the 1980s remaining at similar levels to those in the 1960s. In Guadeloupe banana production halved in the 1970s and only effectively survived as an economic activity through French willingness to reserve (from 1961 onwards) two-thirds of its domestic market for bananas from the *départements d'outre-mer*. Banana cultivation had foundered as wages increased, and it has survived through a series of state interventions to guarantee a minimum price and provide subsidies and indemnities. Ironically, however, Guadeloupe by the 1970s had become unable to produce its guaranteed quota in the French market. Several other crops completely disappeared in the French West Indies. Vanilla had vanished by the 1960s; coffee survived longer, but by 1980 the labour costs of harvesting exceeded the value of the crop and the end was nigh.[15] In the outlying islands the situation was worse. Cattle were exported from Saint-Martin at least until the 1950s, but this activity then ended; at about the same time production of the island's major exports, salt and lobsters, also ended. The emergence of tourism had destroyed the productive sector. By the start of the 1980s 'nothing remains of the economic basis of this once traditional agricultural society' beyond a few cattle and twenty full-time agricultural workers.[16] In nearby Saint-Barthélémy, where soils and rainfall were even poorer than on Saint-Martin, agricultural production disappeared even more comprehensively; only two full-time farmers survived by 1979.[17] Here, too, tourism displaced agriculture.

Outside the Antilles agriculture performed no better. Whilst sugar production survived in Réunion, less important crops often fared much worse. Several food crops, including some fruits and vegetables, and also meat and milk production, disappeared from the coastal plains, remaining only in the high mountains (*les Hauts*). Even farming of geraniums, once the second export crop after sugar, declined so dramatically that, by the 1980s, they represented only 1 per cent of all exports by value. Both geranium and vetyver cultivation have experienced strong international competition and, despite financial support for mechanisation and the introduction of new varieties, the two crops are rapidly being abandoned.[18] Réunion has again moved closer to monoculture.

The secession of Mayotte from the Comoros in 1975 had a belated but substantial impact on the agricultural economy. Vanilla production, hitherto a staple activity, declined drastically; coffee exports and copra sales ended. Maintenance of coconut plantations was neglected — a quarter of production was consumed by rats and flying foxes — and ylang-ylang, the principal export, faced difficult overseas markets. Land previously planted to ylang-ylang, especially distant, steep ground where production could not be mechanised, was sold or abandoned, as agricultural labour became more difficult to obtain.[19] Agricultural decline, accentuated by environmental degradation, has accelerated with a substantial growth in public service employment. Coffee and copra exports have become trivial. However, ylang-ylang, despite its difficulties, continues to contribute between a half and three-quarters of the value of all exports; production expanded in the latter half of the 1980s and some abandoned plantations were reopened.

In New Caledonia the agricultural economy stagnated after a temporary war-time growth when, for a brief period, New Caledonia became self-sufficient in food production. Export crops such as cotton, tobacco and sugar had already been abandoned, and European-style agriculture declined and reverted almost entirely to cattle-raising. Many farms verged on bankruptcy, the commercial and mining booms offered better prospects of urban employment and the 'mirage of Noumea' became a constant preoccupation as agricultural work lost its attraction. The last illusions of achieving a prosperous rural economy were laid to rest. Nevertheless great European cattle stations still dominate the west coast, while the tiny uneconomic cattle stations of small farmers occupy more remote northern valleys; Melanesians occupy many small cattle ranches, often symbols of modernity rather than real sources of income. Efforts to stimulate rice-growing, cereals, and market-gardening have met only partial success. Coffee and copra, the only two export crops of New Caledonia, produce an insignificant revenue and are now almost exclusively Melanesian economic activities;[20] for some years coffee has been imported from elsewhere in Melanesia so that New Caledonia's own coffee can retain its description of Café Mélanésien or Café des Iles. Copra, too, has been imported from Vanuatu to keep the Noumea copra mill in full production. Even the size and affluence of the Noumea market has not been sufficient to stimulate agricultural development in the face of high wages, remote markets and relatively cheap imports.[21]

In French Polynesia agricultural decline occurred rather later, but the arrival of the Centre d'Expérimentation du Pacifique (CEP) in the 1960s ensured that it took a similar form to that in other DOM-TOMs. As late as the 1950s, the majority of Polynesians in the Society Islands continued to supply much of their own requirements for food and shelter by their own gardening, collecting, fishing and craftwork. Islands as distant as Maupiti and Mai'ao regularly marketed vegetables, copra and fish in Papeete, and in Tahiti itself, Polynesians earned more from selling agricultural produce than from wages and salaries.[22] Outer Polynesian islands, such as the Tuamotus and Tubuai in the Australs, remained largely outside the commercial economy; even in the 1960s one observer noted that in Tubuai, 'with the exception of the growing reliance on western manufactured items, the rural household economy was in many ways not unlike what it had been prior to [European] contact'.[23] Much the same was true throughout the Australs and the Marquesas, as well as in equally isolated Wallis and Futuna and the Loyalty Islands, though in these remote islands migrant labour had contributed to a flow of cash income and substantial socio-economic change.

When change did occur in French Polynesia, it brought rapid results. Coffee exports peaked in 1957 but had completely ended by 1964; vanilla production peaked in 1949 and quickly fell away,[24] especially in Moorea and Tahiti. The long-standing pearlshell trade from the Tuamotus virtually disappeared at the same time, a victim of over-exploitation and the substitution of plastic. In the 1960s it appeared 'that French Polynesia's economy is approaching a dangerous climax, when century-old methods of cash-cropping on insecure tenure will no longer provide more than a fraction of exchange-earning exports'.[25] By 1980 little more than vanilla, pearlshells and copra oil were exported though in the mid-1980s the cultured pearl industry, based in such Tuamotuan atolls as Takapoto,[26] experienced a substantial growth; pearls now dominate French Polynesia's exports. The economy was transformed by four events which occurred more or less simultaneously: the emergence of relatively cheap jet air transport and mass tourism after the construction of an international airport at Fa'aa in 1960; the arrival of the CEP, in 1964, which led to new infrastructure construction (especially in Papeete), substantial immigration, the growth of a bureaucracy and the decline of traditional forms of social organisation; a rapid movement into the monetary sector and wage labour; and the closure of the Makatea phosphate mine in 1966. In no other part of the DOM-TOMs was economic transformation so rapid nor the decline in traditional agriculture so dramatic.

Throughout the DOM-TOMs various non-economic factors played a part in the decline of agricultural production. Cyclones, which once had no more than a cyclical effect, increasingly became catalysts for the abandonment of some forms of agriculture throughout the tropical DOM-TOMs. In Guadeloupe, seven major cyclones between 1963 and 1980 and the eruption of the La Soufrière volcano in 1976 severely damaged the agricultural economy.[27] In French Polynesia cyclones in 1982 and 1983 destroyed the production of copra in the Tuamotus and accelerated migration of the agricultural workforce in the towns.[28] Ultimately, however, it was the substantial transformation of the political economy of the DOM-TOMs that brought about the slump in agricultural production.

Some positive developments did occur in agriculture. Market-gardening activities have become profitable with the emergence of a well-paid public service and growing urbanisation. On many of the great sugar estates production continues much as it has ever done in the post-war years, and in rare cases, as at Petite Ile in Réunion, a particular combination of land reform and subsidised irrigation and fertiliser supplies have enabled the agricultural economy to diversify and production to increase. In Guyane, irrigated rice, introduced in 1982 from neighbouring Surinam, has become 'agriculture's only hope'[29] because of the high cost of agricultural labour and the necessity for subsidised mechanisation. At enormous cost Guyane has become self-sufficient in rice. Similarly in the Polynesian island of Tubuai, new agricultural schemes for vegetables and potatoes were introduced in the 1960s. In most of these situations, only subsidies, guaranteed prices or the free provision of machinery and seeds ensured that agriculture continued successfully. Even in the most remote islands the local population itself had little role in formulating development programmes 'which have been explicitly planned to meet regional level economic needs as they are perceived by officials in Paris and Papeete'.[30] Apart from the market-gardening industry, the destiny of the agricultural economy of the DOM-TOMs has been in every way shaped by the new financial structure of incorporation that has firmly tied remote islands to Paris.

Massive increases in the volume of food and drink imports, and the creation of an emerging food dependency, illustrate the decline in the agricultural economy. This accelerated substantially after 1945 and self-reliance now occurs only with the most trivial of food products. In New Caledonia, where the agricultural economy was once character-ised by pastoralism, meat must now be imported. In Martinique enough meat and poultry are produced to satisfy only about 30 per cent of market requirements.[31] Moreover, tastes have substantially shifted be-yond the ability of largely tropical islands to produce goods such as wine that have increasingly become perceived as necessities rather than lux-uries. The transition to French tastes has been particularly marked in French Polynesia, especially in the atolls which always provided a small range of food. By the 1960s, most Tahitian villagers had aban-doned the labour-intensive cultivation of root-crops, in favour of cash crop (copra) production or wage-earning, a move which had radically altered their diet from local fresh foods to rice and various wheat prod-ucts. Tahitians had become 'enthusiastic consumers'[32] and unen-thusiastic producers. A substantial proportion of expenditure was for imported alcohol; in parts of Tahiti such expenditure, by the mid-1960s, had for a defined group of 'drinking people' absorbed more than half their income and led to rampant alcoholism.[33] In the Tuamotus the transition to purchasing rather than growing food had begun as early as the 1870s, as monetisation enabled islanders to buy flour from passing schooners; taro production there was reported to have already disappeared by the end of the nineteenth century.[34] By the late 1950s food dependency was so well-established in the Tuamotus that a vil-lager from Takaroa atoll commented with unintended irony: 'We have little here. The water comes from what rains we are lucky enough to have. Sometimes we run out of flour before the schooner arrives and must eat coconut and fish.'[35] A similar situation occurred rather later in New Caledonia where, in the east coast blockades during the political troubles of 1984, there was an extensive return to the old consumption of garden produce — a withdrawal accepted by the old but hated by children, grown accustomed to a softer, sweeter diet.[36] These dietary transformations are the most visible symbols of the encroachment of consumer society and the consolidation of a new commercial economy.

The same broad changes transformed rural life virtually throughout the DOM-TOMs, whether villages were predominantly sugar, coffee or fish producers. The limited self-reliance and cooperative activities that characterised village life quickly declined. Agricultural employment dwindled and migration from rural areas followed. Once-isolated villagers were integrated into the local and international political economy, a situation graphically illustrated in 'the dark complete world of a Caribbean store.' In a single tiny, remote yet typical, rural Martinique store, in mid-1983, almost half of the items for sale came from outside Martinique, imported from thirty-one different countries and from every continent except Australia. 'The locally grown coffee was often unavailable, and the store sold instead stale coffee that had been grown in the Ivory Coast, processed in Switzerland, imported to France and then shipped to Martinique.' Many products had undergone similar itineraries before reaching Martinique. In short 'the products on its dusty shelves form a startling microcosm of the world-system, an astonishing testimony to the history of colonialism and the more recent organisation of international commerce.'[37] The goods in the village stores, and their distant origins, are the symbols and substance of the diverse structure of incorporation; the store, in itself often a recent incursion from another world, has incorporated hitherto remote islands into that world more effectively than either production or, later, migration was able to do.

The decline that has affected agriculture was less apparent in other sectors of production but, with the exception of nickel mining in New Caledonia and fishing in Saint-Pierre, other productive activities were always limited. In New Caledonia the rise of the nickel industry both emphasised and compensated for agricultural decline. The Second World War itself had given a boost to the mining industry, with an increased demand for nickel and chromium, and also to the commercial sector. In the post-war years nickel mining has come to dominate absolutely the productive sector of the economy and the Société le Nickel (SLN) pushed small mining companies into the background. The Korean and Vietnam wars stimulated new demand, migrants flooded out of the rural areas (abandoning agriculture) to Noumea and into New Caledonia from France and the other French Pacific territories. New Caledonia was still the second most important producer in the world, with 20 per cent of world production and 7000 employees in the boom years. The boom climaxed in 1971, but the subsequent decline became substantial only in the 1980s, as mines closed and employment contracted. Rises in the world nickel price in the late 1980s encouraged talk of a second 'nickel boom', and production grew by a quarter in 1988. Nickel production and prices then almost doubled the value of nickel exports to make New Caledonia's trade balance the best for fifteen years. Even after its long, now interrrupted, decline, New Caledonia is still the fourth-largest nickel producer in the world. Nickel has consistently constituted more than 90 per cent of exports and the SLN is the second-largest nickel-mining company in the world.[38]

In the other DOM-TOMs mining was either nonexistent or in decline. The Makatea phosphate mine closed in 1966 after more than half a century in operation, bringing to an end the mining industry in French Polynesia. At a stroke half the foreign-exchange earnings of French Polynesia (other than the then minimal input from tourism) simply disappeared.[39] Only in Guyane have there been other mining ventures. Various successes from the mid-nineteenth century onwards offered hopes and encouraged migration into the interior, to the extent that around 1930 there were some 10,000 miners in the territory; by the start of the 1980s only a few dozen remained. Prospects for any growth in the Guyane mining industry for either gold or bauxite are extremely poor.[40] Other than in New Caledonia, dreams of tropical mining riches in the DOM-TOMs have remained precisely that.

As the agricultural sector dwindled, so fisheries have stagnated in recent years except in Saint-Pierre and Miquelon. Despite numerous attempts to establish commercial fishing ventures, success has been slight, especially in the Antilles, where the coastal zone is particularly impoverished, and even small-scale fishing remains limited. In Martinique and Guadeloupe, about half of all fish consumed are imported. In Guyane commercial fishing has been moderately successful, though for a long time it depended on American and Japanese capital, only recently coming into French ownership.[41] Fish now provide the major export from Guyane, a measure of the lack of success of other economic sectors rather than the strength of the fisheries sector. In the Indian and Pacific Oceans commercial fishing has largely been unsuccessful, though small fisheries supply a much higher proportion of local fish consumption than elsewhere in the DOM-TOMs. In Réunion fishing activities have decreased in the past decade, despite distant deep-water fishing. In French Polynesia fish have occasionally been exported in the post-war years; a tuna cannery briefly operated, but recent attempts to establish an export industry have failed.[42] In New Caledonia, locally based industrial fishing began in 1981, but massive losses have led to closures of the principal companies. Nowhere in the Pacific have local ventures, with their high labour and fuel costs, been able to compete in protected markets. The abundance of fish stands out in sharp contrast to the minor significance of commercial fishing, despite the promise of the 200-mile exclusive economic zone. Aquaculture has known brief moments of success in New Caledonia, Guadeloupe and elsewhere, but optimism for the future of the industry has always outweighed any real success without vast subsidies. Indeed on a global scale it is invariably only in the subsidised DOM-TOMs that substantial attention is given to this industry. The black pearl industry of the French Polynesian atolls is one prominent exception to the lacklustre performance of the marine sector elsewhere; the industry has grown from nothing in the early 1960s to one of great significance. Pearls are some of the few exported goods whose value is still increasing. Nonetheless for what are primarily islands the resources of the sea have conspicuously failed to generate economic development in the DOM-TOMs.

Forestry continues to offer development prospects for Guyane, but valuable hardwoods are thinly scattered in the forests that cover the majority of the territory, rivers are inadequate for transport and the cost of providing a road infrastructure is considerable. Very little timber is produced — no more than 80,000 cubic metres in 1986 — to the extent that not only do Guyane's timber mills lack raw wood but timber imported from France is sold in supermarkets in Cayenne and Kourou, and is used for such basic items as telegraph poles. Even a woodburning power station has not been able to obtain adequate supplies.[43] Elsewhere, only in New Caledonia has there been serious consideration of forestry, since the Antilles and French Polynesia are too ecologically impoverished, dry or mountainous to offer real possibilities of development. New Caledonia exported timber in the immediate post-war years, but exploitation was so destructive that after the war little more than indiscriminate felling remained possible. Plans to re-establish a sandalwood trade and achieve reforestation have failed.[44] An economy dominated by the export of sandalwood in the mid-1800s now imports more than two-thirds of its timber.

With rare exceptions — nickel in New Caledonia, pearls in French Polynesia and fisheries in Saint-Pierre and Miquelon — the productive sector has declined and even disintegrated in the years after the Second World War in the DOM-TOMs, as a commercial and tertiary sector expanded. Vastly improved conditions in the expanding bureaucracy, the emergence of new 'artificial' activities, including tourism, and the increasing unwillingness of the young to work for low wages (or none at all) have contributed to this evolution. The decline of production was one element of the rapid change in the post-war economy of the DOM-TOMs, emphatically reducing any lingering hopes that they might one day prove profitable.

A manufacturing sector is everywhere conspicuous by its absence, often hindered by the absence of raw materials, a lack of technology and skills and the problems of scale of production on small and remote islands. Where some industrialisation has occurred, as in Guadeloupe, it has been incomplete and costly.[45] The entrenched local bourgeoisie, primarily oriented either to agricultural and mineral production or to commerce, showed little interest in encouraging industrialisation. In the Antilles the Creole oligarchy was particularly uninterested in becoming an industrial bourgeoisie; where industries did develop they were often associated with alliances between the Creole elite and different groups of French entrepreneurs. Most industries in Martinique, for example, were controlled by *Békés* in association with metropolitan administrators of important commercial organisations.[46] In the Pacific there was minimal industrial development. High wages, cheap imports and a preference for the status of imported French goods have discouraged industrialisation and diversification beyond some basic import-substitution industries, such as beer production.

Many of the industries that have developed have been primarily finishing activities, employing few people, using no local raw materials and having little if any link with the agricultural sector. Typical of such specialist industrial activities are glass-making (in Martinique) and the manufacturing of windsurfers, what one observer dismisses as 'pseudo-industrialisation.'[47] Most small industries 'have been annihilated by metropolitan competition.'[48] Almost all industrial production aims at the local market, the value added is minimal, it creates few new skills and provides little local employment. The cost of production discourages international competitiveness, and it is usually cheaper to import manufactured goods than produce them locally. Foreign investment in the manufacturing sector has generally been discouraged by France, though many Antilles rum companies are owned by international interests, including Cointreau-Dubonnet and Martini and Rossi. Throughout the DOM-TOMs the proportion, and even the number, of people employed in the manufacturing sector has diminished in the past two decades.

One semi-industrial sector that has grown substantially in the post-war years has been the construction industry; this has almost wholly depended on the transfer of capital to the DOM-TOMs, the expansion of the bureaucracy and, to a much lesser extent, the rise of tourism. Where tourism growth has been most spectacular, as in the Antilles, so the growth of the construction industry has been equally dramatic; by

1981 almost half the active workforce of Saint-Barthélémy had jobs in the construction industry.[49] Similarly there has been a growth of employment in the transport and energy sectors with the expansion of infrastructure. Even more than in the productive sector, much of the growth in these areas has been dependent on public funds, involves branches of metropolitan companies and has virtually no links with other sectors of the economy.

THE CONSTRUCTION OF A TERTIARY ECONOMY

The emergence of a tertiary economy ensured, hastened, and compensated for the decline of production. Three principal elements in this transition were the rise of the commercial and service sectors and the growth of the welfare state, with an accompanying expansion of the bureaucracy; the growth of tourism; and the construction in the DOM-TOMs of some key French strategic installations, specifically the facilities of the nuclear Centre d'Expérimentation du Pacifique in French Polynesia and the space-research and missile testing programme in Guyane. Rapid urbanisation went along with these developments as migrants moved into several of the DOM-TOMs and local workers sought to move out of the poorly paid productive sectors (especially agriculture) into the service sector, and from remote villages and islands to urban areas.

The most crucial element contributing to the transition from production to transaction has been the massive expansion of the public service in the DOM-TOMs. Not only is this now the most important sector of paid employment, but it also provides the highest wages and salaries. In parallel, grants, subsidies and welfare payments of several different kinds have expanded simultaneously, fostering dependence on the French state and a further decline in the productive sector. Transfer payments from the *métropole* have increasingly propped up local economies. Public sector growth and the transfer economy, for example, have created a ' "vicious circle" of dependence engendered by the contemporary agricultural system and which, far from leading to economic growth in Martinique, has reinforced its impoverishment through "false growth" with weighty consequences.'[50] Part of this bureaucratic expansion, and symptomatic of it, has been the emergence of various new institutions oriented to some aspect of development or change.[51] In the *départements d'outre-mer* the key institution influencing the rapid transformation of the political economy has been the Fonds d'Investissement pour les Départements d'Outre-Mer

(FIDOM), and the equivalent institution for the territories, the Fonds d'Investissement pour le Développement Economique et Social des TOM (FIDES). EC funding and individual ministry expenditure have also been substantial. Direct French state subsidies to the budget of each of the DOM-TOMs have been at least 30 per cent since 1945, and often much more in the 1980s. They have been further boosted by other state expenditures in support of particular programmes, such as education and health.[52] Such lavish resources fostered a new form of dependence and ironically contributed to the distortion of the sector that they had been intended to support.

The resulting expansion of the public service has been dramatic. Already by 1976 some 120,000 *fonctionnaires* worked in the DOM-TOMs, an unusually privileged workforce. Public servants benefit from a salary that is 40 per cent greater than that of their metropolitan colleagues and they enjoy various other advantages. In French Polynesia basic public-service salaries, already much higher than in the private sector, are swollen by particular loadings, including an 84 per cent supplement to the metropolitan base salary, a 1 million CFP (French Pacific francs) allowance for a distant posting and six months' paid leave after three years of service, with free transport to Paris.[53] At the same time the official minimum wage is lower in the DOM-TOMs than that in France, hence income disparities are substantial. In the Antilles a worker earning the minimum wage in the private sector must work four times as long as the lowest-paid public servant for the same income and in French Polynesia the difference is tenfold. This represents a legacy of the colonial era when *fonctionnaires* had to be offered substantial bonuses to serve overseas.

Senior public servants are often also distinct in ethnicity and in their attitudes from other inhabitants of the DOM-TOMs. In many respects the *fonctionnariat* has become a class apart[54] partly because of the significance of metropolitan migrants in the public service. Thirty thousand metropolitans work in the Antilles alone, mostly in the higher-ranking positions; in Réunion, Martinique and elsewhere virtually all the most senior positions with the best salaries were held by migrants until François Mitterrand became president in 1981 and the situation slowly began to change.[55] In New Caledonia, too, differences occur between Melanesian and European access to bureaucratic employment. Tentative recent attempts have been made to encourage greater Melanesian participation in the modern sector, almost entirely by accelerated promotion in the bureaucracy through a widely supported *promotion mélanésienne*. Nonetheless, throughout the DOM-TOMs there exists considerable inequality in access to this critical employment sector.

Large numbers of state employees are the key to the economic imbalance of the DOM-TOMs. For example, one observer has charged
that 'Guadeloupe, like the other DOMs but to such an extreme degree
that it has become a caricature, is a pretty holiday resort for *fonctionnaires* and, for the moment, nothing more'; he adds:

In a country which produces nothing, a privileged class tends to have a European standard of living thanks solely to subsidies from outside. In short, if the
DOMs before 1946 were colonies of France they have subsequently become
colonies of the Administration.[56]

The number of public servants is so large that fully a third of the
French metropolitan subsidy to the DOMs goes to cover the extra pay
given to the *fonctionnaires*. In Guadeloupe, for example, the public
sector in 1976 absorbed 55 per cent of the total wages and salaries,[57] a
proportion that has subsequently increased.

Beyond the direct funding of public-service salaries the provisions of
the French welfare state system were gradually extended to the DOM-
TOMs, and especially the *départements d'outre-mer*. Inevitably the
wholesale transfer of a welfare system appropriate for urban industrial
France to what were still predominantly rural agricultural societies
accelerated dependence on France, contributing to a

paradoxical situation, since these islands, that once produced riches for the
métropole, now in turn benefit from the advantages which they gain from a
society which is highly industrialised but with which they can only periph-
erally be involved.[58]

After *départementalisation*, for example, families in the DOM-TOMs,
just as in the *métropole*, received government allowances according to
the number of days worked and the number and ages of children; this,
in some cases, contributed to higher fertility rates.[59] These allowances
grew over time and aggravated instability in the workforce, as it became
easier to gain family allowances; old-age pensions were also introduced
from the age of fifty-five, or after twenty-five years in formal sector
employment. Other such payments, such as sick pay, emphasised the
welfare system and were relatively easily abused, as those on 'sick leave'
could easily work in their gardens or go fishing. In general this led to
the decline of certain kinds of employment since 'the social welfare
system gave workers the possibility of withdrawing their labour from
the plantations without losing any of their income.'[60] A further decline
followed the extension of unemployment benefits in 1980. Welfare
payments have simultaneously played an increasing role in household

income. In Réunion, in 1977, welfare payments represented more than 20 per cent of the cash income of all households and, by the early 1980s, were estimated to be more than 40 per cent of the incomes of agricultural households.[61]

In the Pacific territories access to welfare payments has been more difficult to obtain. In the outer islands of French Polynesia and New Caledonia welfare payments remained quite limited in the 1950s; in fairly typical parts of the Society Islands some residents were 'eligible for old age or welfare-type remittances but did not receive them, it was charged, because of official neglect or local ignorance of rights.' Nevertheless from the 1950s, welfare payments of various kinds had been introduced, including veterans' pensions, welfare payments and child-support allocations. In Papeete, however, welfare payments were much higher in the largely Polynesian suburb of Manuhoe, where child-support payments made up one-fifth of the community's income.[62] A similar situation existed in Noumea, where there even occurred intermittent migration from outer islands, such as Ouvea, to take advantage of welfare payments unobtainable in remote villages where the agricultural system was supposed to provide adequate support.[63]

Though a substantial proportion of government expenditure in the DOM-TOMs was absorbed in the wages and salaries of the bureaucracy, and for welfare payments, a vast and increasing sum went into the physical and social infrastructure, which between 1947 and 1960 made up more than half of all FIDES expenditure,[64] while less than one-fifth directly supported productive activities. The years after the Second World War witnessed massive improvements in communications between the DOM-TOMs and France, if more rarely between the DOM-TOMs and their immediate neighbours. Principally from the 1960s onwards new direct air links replaced inadequate and intermittent air and maritime links. In Réunion the Saint-Denis airport was reconstructed in the 1960s; the first direct air service from Paris began in 1966, replacing an indirect flight through Madagascar. Only Mayotte, Saint-Pierre and Miquelon, Wallis and Futuna and the TAAF are now served indirectly, and the other DOM-TOMs are connected by daily flights to Paris. In French Polynesia the ability of the new Fa'aa airport to take jets fostered the growth of the tourist industry and, in nearby Moorea, rapid socio-economic transformation in the island was also instigated by the construction of an airport. Outer Polynesian islands, such as the Australs and, to a lesser extent, the Marquesas, were belatedly transformed by the construction of airstrips, subsidies for flights from Papeete and, later, electrification. Saint-Martin went through similar changes, and in the Tuamotus and Australs long-term emigration was reversed by substantial infrastructure provision.[65]

Once-isolated colonies were more effectively incorporated into the cultural and economic ambit of France and outer islands given rapid access to the centre of their territories.

Airports and jets represent the most visible symbols of improved communications, but other areas of transport also improved. In Réunion the old port was renovated, then a new one built to accommodate a massive increase in imports, which by 1984 were eight times the weight of imports in 1939. In Tahiti the port was also twice upgraded in the post-war years. Throughout the DOM-TOMs, massive expenditure on roads and other transport systems linked all but the most inaccessible mountain areas and the more remote islands to urban centres. In New Caledonia, for instance, communes that could once only be reached by boat became accessible by road, and in Mayotte, a massive road-building programme in 1988 stimulated the expansion of the construction industry.

Improvements in telephone systems, radio and television communications have further stengthened cultural and economic contacts inside the DOM-TOMs and with France. News programmes have now reached the most remote districts; even Wallis and Futuna received a television service in 1986 and a satellite telephone link opened in 1989. Other infrastuctural improvements eventuated. Until 1957 Réunion had no reticulated water supply but by 1961 10 per cent of households had access to water supplies and by 1982 this proportion had grown to 70 per cent.[66] Similar changes occurred elsewhere; though the extension of services showed an acute urban bias, shanty towns sometimes remained without basic services. In New Caledonia, for example, water supplies were extended, but there remain enormous differences between Noumea, where virtually all households have piped water, compared with the Loyalty Islands, where only a quarter of houses are so provided. On remote islands like Ouvea and Belep, not one household has piped water. In Noumea 93 per cent of homes have internal toilets, compared with only 8 per cent in the Loyalty Islands.[67]

The consolidation of the tertiary economy has vastly improved income and social services throughout the DOM-TOMs, albeit at the expense of a more unequal distribution. Invariably income levels, education, health services and infrastructure of various kinds (such as roads, ports and electricity) are vastly superior to those of neighbouring independent states, and sometimes even parts of France. Such improvements have primarily occurred in the past two decades. In Martinique, for example, the number of doctors more than doubled from 1961 to 1979 and infant mortality dropped by half; in Réunion the number of physicians similarly grew almost fifty-fold and the infant mortality rate fell by nine-tenths.[68] In New Caledonia health services are maintained in Noumea at metropolitan French levels; even in rural areas, where standards are more like those of other Pacific countries, there are rapid transfers to urban hospitals. Specialised treatment can necessitate referral to Australia, and the emergency transfer of patients (*évacuations sanitaires*) is a customary feature of air services between Noumea and Sydney and a symbol of France's determination to ensure a high level of medical care. The health status of New Caledonia is much higher than that of neighbouring, though more tropical, Melanesian countries and the structure of disease closer to that of temperate metropolitan countries. The main causes of death have become 'modern' problems such as cardio-vascular diseases, traumatic injuries and alcoholism, rather than infectious epidemics.

Education has also undergone rapid change. In Réunion as late as 1970 no more than 58 per cent of five-year-olds were in school, but by 1982 all five-year-olds were enrolled; the illiteracy rate of 57 per cent in 1954 had fallen to 20 per cent.[69] Transformation has been less dramatic in the Antilles, since pre-war standards were superior to those of other DOM-TOMs. In the Pacific territories, by contrast, progress has been slower, and again demonstrates urban bias; in New Caledonia, inaccessibility, discrimination and uncertainty have limited Melanesian access to education, with repercussions in professional life. Secondary schools opened to Melanesians in 1958, nearly eight years after the first such school opened in Noumea, and not until about 1961 did the first Melanesian pass the *baccalauréat* (the high school leaving examination). In the early 1960s, the first Melanesian gained a university degree.[70] In the Antilles, Guyane and Réunion university centres were established in the 1960s and by the 1980s each enrolled several thousand students; more recently university centres have been set up in French Polynesia and New Caledonia. These changes emphasise comparisons between the tropical DOM-TOMs and their neighbours,[71] especially between New Caledonia and Vanuatu, in the provision of all forms of services: in every respect the DOM-TOMs enjoy better facilities than their independent neighbours.

Largely impelled by the expansion of the public service, the private service sector has grown rapidly throughout the DOM-TOMs. Nowhere was this more evident than in New Caledonia, where the presence of more than 100,000 Allied military personnel during the Second World War sponsored the first 'commercial boom.' More generally, commerce has expanded in the wake of the growth of bureaucracy, tourism, and trade.[72] In New Caledonia, the leading commercial entrepreneurs have made a transition from agriculture (and mining) to finance and commerce; for example, Jacques Lafleur, the leading RPCR politician and owner of one of the largest ranches on the main island, has diversified to become the principal owner of numerous banking, tourist and commercial activities.[73] In Martinique the *Békés* have been accused of abandoning the agricultural economy to make their fortunes in trading, import and commerce; a fraction of the class of indigenous whites, commonly referred to as 'the ten families', dominates the commercial sector. The rapid increase in incomes and expansion of the public sector has emphasised the growth of a consumer society to the extent that the DOM-TOMs, especially those in the Antilles, have been well and widely described as 'consumer colonies.'[74]

In many respects, the greatest benefit of *départementalisation* was the application, with only minor modifications, of the full weight of the extensive social security system of metropolitan France, and the construction of a comprehensive public welfare system. Subsequently a similar system was extended to the overseas territories. One casual observer commented of Martinique in the early 1960s:

Our first impression on landing was how much more civilised it was than other islands we had visited in the West Indies. Here were the same West Indian people . . . but better shod, better educated and more intelligent than any we had seen or met in other islands.[75]

Such general observations, typical of their time, hint at the transformation experienced in the two largest eastern Caribbean islands. The same was true in other oceans. In Tubuai, a relatively remote outer island in French Polynesia, a high school providing free education was opened in the 1970s and a doctor and dentist arrived on the island to provide free health care. A monthly family allowance subsidy, worth about $US25 per child, was instituted to improve the health and welfare of children. Beyond these direct subsidies, many jobs became available involving unskilled manual employment on public works, which 'greatly increased the previously negligible employment opportunities and offered high salaries.'[76] In short, in rather less than a decade, the complete panoply of a welfare state had emerged, here as elsewhere in the DOM-TOMs. Cash incomes and welfare improved simultaneously. A new political economy had been constructed, well summarised by the distinguished Martiniquais writer Edouard Glissant, who recognised the benefits but also pointed to the psychological cost: 'Here are the contemporary structures of alienation: the town hall, the social security system, schools, garages, supermarkets, associations, political and administrative bodies, stadiums, credit institutions.'[77] In no more than a quarter of a century the socio-economic organisation of the DOM-TOMs had been transformed from production to consumption.

TOURISM

One particular aspect of the transition from production towards a transfer economy has been the growing significance of tourism; a common image of the DOM-TOMs is that promoted by tourist brochures — the picture of warm, tropical islands and relaxing resorts, exotic food and exotic people, in a pervasive French ambience. Image became a version of reality in the years after the Second World War, especially from the 1960s onwards, in part as a response to the disappointment of other economic sectors. So successful has tourism been in the Caribbean and Tahiti that it is one of the few economic success stories of the DOM-TOMs. Yet tourism depends on the fluctuations of the global economy and is concentrated in only four of the DOM-TOMs. Guyane, Mayotte and Wallis and Futuna either lack hotels or air communications, are remote from markets or promise few scenic or cultural attractions, while Saint-Pierre and Miquelon[78] and the TAAF are beyond the normal climatic range of mass tourism. Mayotte and Wallis and Futuna had a total of only seventy-nine hotel rooms in 1988.

In most of the DOM-TOMs substantial public investment flowed into tourism in the 1970s. In the Antilles French investment followed the decline in agricultural development,[79] while in New Caledonia it succeeded the collapse of the nickel boom; in French Polynesia and Guyane it represented much-needed diversification. For the same reason attention has been given to developing tourism in Réunion, although the tourist industry there remains quite small, especially in comparison with neighbouring Mauritius. Everywhere airports were reconstructed, hotels built and golf courses and marinas added to the landscape; ports were also rebuilt to enable the docking of cruise ships which, especially in the Antilles, bring in the most visitors. The growth of the industry was thus consequent on new infrastructure. In the Caribbean tourism has been heavily oriented towards France, which provides more than half of all tourists; the bulk of the others come from North America. In the Pacific tourists are more likely to arrive from countries other than France: Japan (in New Caledonia), the United States (in French Polynesia) and Australia.

The opening of an international airport on Tahiti in 1961 (and the relative decline in international air fares) provided the most critical influence on the growth of tourism in Polynesia. The legendary island paradise of Tahiti could be reached from the United States in a few hours, and from Tahiti tourism rapidly extended to Moorea, Bora Bora and to other nearby islands. Remoteness of Tahiti from European markets (alongside high costs) prevented rapid growth of the tourist industry, however, and tourists tended to be unusually wealthy.[80] Nonetheless the number of tourists in French Polynesia grew spectacularly, from a mere 1472 in 1959 to 77,988 in 1973, but since then numbers have grown more slowly to peak at 161,000 in 1986. An incomplete hotel and the closure of the Club Méditerranée in Bora Bora testify to the decline, but the opening of a direct air connection to Japan in 1989 provided new stimulus to Tahitian tourism.

In New Caledonia tourist numbers jumped from 16,000 in 1969 to 92,000 in 1984. By then it had become the only growth sector in the territory, and was second only to nickel mining as the major industry. Yet, until the collapse of nickel, there had been no official interest in tourism. Afterwards jumbo jets brought a massive increase; commerce grew and the number of tourists tripled in only five years. New Caledonia became the third most important tourist destination in the Pacific, after Fiji and Tahiti. Club Méditerranée opened there in 1980, but the tourist boom was already slowing. By the end of 1984 it had been dramatically affected by political upheaval and the negative perception of New Caledonia in nearby Australia and New Zealand;[81] only Japanese tourists enabled the industry to survive as the number of tourists plummeted from its 1984 peak to 48,000 in 1985. Though again growing, tourism in New Caledonia has not regained its former heights; if it does not, that failure will be attributed to changing tourist promotion and preferences in metropolitan countries, violent political disturbances and distorted media coverage.

Throughout the DOM-TOMs tourism has been primarily an urban or peri-urban phenomenon, which contributed to the growth of cities like Noumea and Papeete, but emphasised rural-urban disparities. Only at Pointe-du-Bout in Martinique was tourism significantly divorced from the existing urban economy, though islands like Bora Bora and Moorea (on both of which Club Méditerranée constructed holiday resorts) were transformed by tourism even, in the latter case, leading to the development of a small local market-garden industry.[82] In New Caledonia international tourists rarely see more of the countryside than the scenery that borders the drive from the airport to the city; about three-quarters of all hotel rooms, and all the major hotels, are in Noumea, and only in the Isle of Pines and Lifou is tourism organised around small Melanesian hotels. Otherwise tourism, in New Caledonia as elsewhere, is marked by unequal benefits and uneven development.

Tourism has everywhere emphasised socio-economic inequalities; where local capital is present in the industry, it is necessarily contributed by the elite. Even in the larger *départements*, such as Guadeloupe, just as in the public service, some 15 per cent of all employment in tourism is of 'outsiders', mainly in the more senior positions.[83] The environment has occasionally suffered damage by the expansion of the tourist industry.[84] If tourism scarcely benefits rural areas, or many of the local population, there must also be doubt as to how much profit from the industry is retained locally; tourism is classically an industry where profits filter back from small-country destinations to metropolitan nations. Most hotels are just one branch of an international chain, passengers travel in international airlines (and the French airlines Air France and UTA have a major share in the tourist industry), with passages booked elsewhere; they consume food, drinks and souvenirs that are largely imported. Moreover, most of the hotel construction materials, especially in the Antilles, are imported from France; only 6 per cent of tourist expenditure there is on local goods (generally alcohol and handicrafts).[85] There are also social costs in the emergence and expansion of particular forms of personal service provision, congestion and crime. Tourism, however, has contributed to economic growth, production and employment and has also moved the DOM-TOMs economy even closer to consumerism. It has reconstructed the economy of the Antilles and Tahiti by providing employment in the industry itself and related service sectors to become one of the principal sources of locally-generated income. That contribution often remains slight in comparison with other income sources; in French Polynesia, for example, tourism has rarely contributed more than 3 per cent of the GDP because of the importance of the revenue generated through nuclear testing. Tourism is a fragile infant industry vulnerable to politics and economics, but which offers one of the few opportunities for local development.

TOWARDS AN ARTIFICIAL ECONOMY?

The growth of the bureaucracy, fuelled by French finance, and the later development of the tourist industry were two phases of a trajectory of development that moved the largest DOM-TOMs away from production to a new service economy. Though the speed at which these two growth areas moved ahead was considerable, as were the changes in employment that they engendered, they were not in themselves very different from similar changes in other parts of the world. What did transform the DOM-TOMs, specifically French Polynesia and

Guyane, was the imposition of two large projects which simultaneously wholly restructured employment, further undermined the productive sector, encouraged urbanisation and promoted what were increasingly becoming artificial economies.

The most dramatic socioeconomic transformation in any of the DOM-TOMs has occurred in French Polynesia, with the construction of nuclear-testing facilities. The independence of Algeria forced France to choose a new site for its nuclear programme and at the end of 1962 the French government decided to create the Centre d'Expériment-ation du Pacifique (CEP), a decision that immediately caused concern in French Polynesia. It also encouraged some of those who had previously been hesitant about independence to advocate it more strongly, while others, fearing that an independent state would not be viable, sought to use the CEP as a bargaining tactic to increase French funding for development in French Polynesia.[86] In 1964 the French government obtained sovereignty over the two key atolls of Mururoa and Fangataufa, where the tests were to be conducted, and a construction boom began.

Nuclear testing led to substantial migration from France, improvements in infrastructure (in both Papeete and on the atolls), a dramatic increase in employment (with 3000 people initially working directly in association with nuclear testing, primarily in the service sector), and much higher wages. New installations were constructed on the Tua-motu atolls of Mururoa, Fangataufa and Hao, and a support base grew up in Papeete. A new port, hospital and radio stations, roads, airstrips in the outer islands, water supply and sanitation programmes expanded the infrastructure, accompanied by a building boom, as new migrants and bureaucrats had to be supplied with offices and housing. Commercial development followed the increase in incomes. The traditional Polynesian economy was effectively destroyed, as agricultural wages were quickly forced up fourfold to compete with those paid by the CEP; ironically, as a new and wealthy market grew, the volume of local produce in the Papeete market fell. Migration to work in CEP activities created salary increases and inflation; workers flocked to urban employment, while landowners could no longer afford scarce labour. Furthermore, migration depopulated atolls and led to uncontrolled urban growth in Papeete and much urban land speculation.[87]

Between 1962 and 1970 per-capita income in French Polynesia increased 3.5 times, a rate more than 50 per cent faster than in France itself. From 1964 onwards, CEP expenditure was more than four times greater than that of the territorial budget. By 1970 wages and salaries paid by the administration constituted one-third of all household incomes, and more than half of this derived from CEP employment and activities. Growth, tied to public expenditure, even reflected the rhythms of the tests themselves.[88] Nevertheless massive increases in incomes led to a dramatic consumer revolution with a consequent increase in imports; conversely it accelerated the decline of the export economy and established a substantial and persistent trade imbalance. Within a decade the now urban economy had become a service economy almost entirely dependent on French expenditure. French Polynesia had become, to some, the world's first 'nuclear colony'[89] and the material advantages from nuclear testing had virtually destroyed any prospect of self-reliance or future economic independence. A territory of considerable size and diversity had gone 'from copra to the atom.'[90]

For all the rapidity of the expansion of employment with the CEP, and the accompanying growth of commerce and the bureaucracy, the boom could not be sustained indefinitely. Nor could it keep pace with population growth. By the end of the 1960s the nickel boom in New Caledonia was being viewed by the French Polynesian territorial administration as 'a safety valve for the state of employment.'[91] Though French Polynesians became more prosperous, they also became more differentiated, as disparities widened between rich and poor, centre and periphery. Frustrations eventually began to mount. After 1975, when nuclear testing went underground and the military presence in French Polynesia declined, the transformation of the French Polynesian economy had largely been completed. The territorial administration sought agricultural, fisheries and industrial development, with little success (other than the establishment of the pearl industry in the Tuamotus), since by 1977 more than two-thirds of the labour force were employed in the more prestigious and better-paid tertiary sector.

On the other side of the world a somewhat similar transition took place. Guyane, once a small sugar and rum economy, is also now dominated by a single activity: the space centre at Kourou. This 'ghetto of white expatriate technicians guarded by French Foreign Legionnaires' is the key to Europe's space effort,[92] a place marked by the 'recyling of a forgotten colony from Green Hell to Outer Space.'[93] The Centre Spatial Guyanais (CSG) began operations in 1964 just outside Kourou, a site chosen because of its latitude and the availability of a wide sector in which launching was possible, and the project became operational in 1968. From 1979 onwards the programme became oriented to the European Space Agency's Ariane rocket which now launches half the world's satellites into orbit. This cooperative project enabled France's *aventure spatiale* to be valued for its symbolic role in fostering European unity.[94] Thus the CSG has become a pivot for

France's European policy, a site for substantial expenditure and the basis of the Guyanese economy.

Just as with the CEP in French Polynesia, the space programme in Guyane produced an enormous construction programme, one eagerly sought by the politicians and bureaucrats of the *département*. A new town grew up at Kourou and expanded from fewer than 4000 people in 1974 to 8500 in 1983; those directly employed in the space programme totalled 7000 by the latter date.[95] Outside Kourou the Centre National d'Etudes Spatiales (CNES) financed new roads, bridges, ports, airports, two hotels and a number of schools, an expenditure of 80 million francs. The programme encouraged migration from rural areas, agricultural decline, the growth of commerce and a swollen bureaucracy. If the impact was much less than that of the CEP in Polynesia, the establishment of the space programme has been the principal element in French socioeconomic policy in Guyane. Little survived of the traditional economy. The 'terre du bagne' ('penal colony') became a 'terre de l'espace' ('space colony') and Guyane, in its turn, became a consumer society.[96] This unique transition has been

a key element in the process of *départementalisation*, and in the socio-political orientation which it has recently displayed. The creation of the space centre and modern city at Kourou is in a way the crowning achievement of a politics of prestige, which had led to a different form of development. This has been stimulated by financial support as massive as it is unproductive, intended to make Guyane 'a French showcase on the American continent', a place for exhibition rather than production.[97]

Other variations of such 'artificial economies' have been established in the uninhabited DOM-TOMs. In the TAAF, at the request of the International Civil Aviation Organisation, France began in 1949 to construct meteorological observation posts to monitor Indian Ocean weather. And, with the subsequent impetus of the International Geophysical Year (1957–8), France initiated a complex and diverse programme of scientific research in the Antarctic region,[98] based in Port-aux-Français, Kerguelen.

The unusual transformations of French Polynesia, Guyane and the TAAF have been substantial. They may ultimately be transient. There is widespread opposition to France's South Pacific nuclear testing programme; rumours abound that Mururoa is crumbling and that testing operations may be transferred to equally isolated Kerguelen in the Indian Ocean.[99] The future of the space programme is not necessarily secure, whilst the technology of meteorological forecasting is constantly changing. The new activities are of international and military importance and they have contributed to a greater French overseas military presence; a strategic economy has evolved in these DOM-TOMs. In some respects nuclear and space testing are the direct contemporary parallels of the historic policies which saw the location of such activities as penal colonies on the remote frontiers of empire. Consequently critics charge that the impacts of the CEP and the CSG are artificial and exploitative but, economically, they have created great wealth and standards of living that the DOM-TOMs' neighbours cannot match.

THE STRUCTURE OF EMPLOYMENT

The transition from production to consumption inevitably influenced both the structure of employment and the new attitudes that accompanied and contributed to this change. It also led to the emergence of more overt unemployment, first, because increasing numbers of workers entered the market economy and were registered as salaried or unemployed and, secondly, because the decline of agriculture could not be matched by the growth of tertiary employment, especially when population growth was rapid. Almost universally those young people able to obtain work welcomed and accepted new formal sector employment. The arrival of the CEP and the expansion of employment appeared 'to Polynesians if not as a liberation, at least as an increase in opportunities, despite the alienating effects of wage labour, of which people quickly became aware.' Even as far away from Papeete as Moorea, villages became virtually dormitory settlements during the week, followed by the return of migrant workers at weekends. Daily life became a product of the rhythm of wage labour.[100]

For the young especially, the urban economy represented a form of liberation from the social constraints of rural life and the limited economic opportunities it offered. Salaried urban employment also offered an alternative to farming and promised quick rewards:

'Money work' yields what Tahitians call 'fast money' that comes in every week on pay-day as opposed to 'slow money' that comes in at long and irregular intervals from cash crop harvests. It is 'fast money' that enables Tahitians to meet their motorcycle time payments, to live off imported foodstuffs and frequently buy beer.[101]

Such opposition to farm work was not limited to Tahiti. In Guadeloupe and Martinique the young were so reluctant to be employed in agriculture that West Indians from nearby St Lucia and Dominica have flocked to the islands to find jobs as agricultural workers. In Guyane employment in agriculture is dominated by Hmong migrants or Indians and the forestry industry by either Indians or migrants from Brazil and St Lucia, whilst the fishing industry is manned by migrants from Surinam. Creoles and metropolitan French, by contrast, find employment in the public service and the space industry. In Guadeloupe, after a series of strikes in the sugar industry, Haitians were recruited after 1975 to work in the sugar plantations and banana cultivation; Guadeloupeans work in the bureaucracy or other tertiary activities. Neither in Martinique nor Guadeloupe do local residents, whatever their origin or skin colour, willingly cut cane or perform menial jobs; the heritage of slavery makes plantation labour anathema to Antillais, as well as Réunionnais.

The construction of an increasingly 'artificial' economy drastically increased the volume of employment in the bureaucracy and, by ensuring that employment conditions were superior, emphasised the 'modern' sectors to the detriment of agriculture and fishing. Even those who remain in agriculture perceive its rewards as exceptionally poor. In Réunion, by the mid-1980s, almost 60 per cent of the heads of agricultural households also took part in some other economic activity, often as their principal source of income. Public service employment, even in the most rudimentary form, offers enormous advantage over farming. Even by the 1960s on remote islands such as Rapa (French Polynesia), public works employment was the second most important source of income (after coffee cultivation), and the men on the island frequently rotated between agriculture and the bureaucracy to assure that all had some opportunity to earn wage income.[102]

The employment transition can be formally traced through statistics. In Réunion, agriculture accounted for two-thirds of the workforce in 1946, primarily in the sugar industry, but by 1974 only 14 per cent of workers remained in the primary sector, as substantial a decline as has occurred in any of the DOM-TOMs; by contrast the tertiary sector employed 69 per cent of the workforce. This move towards services continued, albeit at a declining rate, in subsequent years. Martinique, with 74 per cent of its active population in the tertiary sector in 1976, epitomises the extreme form of this transition. In New Caledonia as late as 1956 the agricultural sector made up half the workforce, but by 1983 it accounted for less than a quarter of employment and no more than 5 per cent of the paid workforce. By contrast more than 60 per cent of the paid workforce was concentrated in the service sector. Even in Saint-Pierre and Miquelon, where fishing characterises the economy, fully 68 per cent of the population worked in the tertiary sector in 1985. Only in Mayotte and Wallis and Futuna are the bulk of the population still in the agricultural sector and outside the paid workforce; even so, in the latter case, the public sector employs more than 60 per cent of salaried employment, and virtually no wage employment exists outside the tertiary sector.[103] Such transformations are quite different from those of neighbouring states; New Caledonia, for example, now has one of the smallest proportions of workers in agriculture of any state in the South Pacific.[104] Exactly the same situation is true in the French Antilles by comparison with other states of the Caribbean and for Réunion in the Indian Ocean.

Although in the decade 1970–80 France's budgetary expenditure in the DOMs alone went from 2 to 10 billion francs,[105] such lavish public expenditure has not resolved development problems. The *vieilles colonies* have experienced substantial unemployment (and underemployment) for a quarter of a century, despite significant emigration. In Réunion falling sugar prices, mechanisation and the restructuring of the economy from plantations to a service economy hastened the movement of the workforce into other economic sectors and also created a substantial increase in formal unemployment. Unemployment grew from 13 per cent in 1967 to fully 31 per cent in 1982.[106] Similarly in Martinique, the absolute number of employed people fell from 96,080 in 1972 to 88,780 in 1980, a decline in the proportion of the working age population from 50 per cent to 42 per cent: 'Barely one-half of the active population hold full-time jobs. The most generous definition of employment (which includes the officially underemployed) still gives a 1980 unemployment rate of 28 per cent',[107] a level which has subsequently increased. A similar situation exists in Guadeloupe, emphasised by high rates of natural population increase. Such unemployment breeds frustration and emphasises other inequalities. Various incidents in past decades emphasise underlying social (and racial) tension in France's DOM-TOMs, both in the Antilles and the Pacific, partially linked to problems of unemployment.

In French Polynesia the employment situation reached a crisis in 1987, marked by considerable violence by striking dockers. After a long period of growth and then consolidation, the highest recorded level of formal employment was reached in August 1987; in the following ten months, until June 1988, the private sector lost 3000 jobs and the public sector a further 500 posts. Employment declined by around 9 per cent in less than a year in a context where economic growth was no longer the norm. In Réunion conflict over the closure of the pirate station Télé-Free-DOM in February 1991 led to the death of eleven people in bomb attacks and arson in which numerous shops were destroyed. Angry youths attacked the symbols of their frustration — the *gendarmeries* and stores and showrooms of expensive imported goods. In New

Caledonia youth unemployment similarly prompted unfocused riots. The provisions of the Matignon Accord which were designed to train and employ young Melanesians in the provinces may arrest this situation but at the expense of a further increase in the size of the bureaucracy. The future, therefore, depends not on the revival or expansion of agriculture, nor on industrialisation, but on the transfer of resources from France. There is no internal dynamic to economic growth.

A TRANSFER ECONOMY

Four very broad economic periods have marked the DOM-TOMs. The initial period of colonial economic development saw the production of substantial volumes of export commodities in the *vieilles colonies*, which lasted until the abolition of slavery, and the nickel and copra booms of the 1800s in the Pacific colonies. This era was characterised by dependent development, as the *métropole* extracted a surplus from the colonial periphery; this situation differed little from that of other colonies of the time. A second period, when disillusionment and doubt discouraged investment, characterised the DOM-TOMs from the nineteenth century to the Second World War, when the future of these tiny colonies seemed bleak. The post-war years of new political statutes have witnessed a wholly different economic structure, even a 'crisis of accumulation', with the shift from production to consumption and the emergence of a bureaucratic transfer economy. With rare exceptions, the companies established in the DOM-TOMs in this era, unlike those of earlier periods, neither extracted substantial profits nor invested their surplus locally. More generally economic growth depended on subsidies from France. This third phase has given way, more obviously in the DOMs, to a fourth period in which, despite the rapid expansion of the tertiary sector, there has been substantial unemployment. This 'destabilisation of assimilationist development'[108] has been most visible in the *vieilles colonies* and, more recently, in French Polynesia and New Caledonia. Growth has continued but with little broadly based development or diversification; it is increasingly dependent on metropolitan transfers and subsidies to individuals, industries or political entities.

Nevertheless, the structure of growth and development has taken different forms in each of the DOM-TOMs. Martinique, Réunion and Guadeloupe have now reached economic crisis, with the collapse of the sugar industry and the failure of diversification, aggravated by high population densities, unemployment, a chronic balance-of-payments deficit and urbanised societies that rely heavily on French aid.

Agricultural decline has sparked union-sponsored land occupations and strikes, such as those which opposed the mechanisation of the Réunion sugar industry in 1984.[109] The terms of trade have worsened throughout the *outre-mer*. Imports into Réunion, for example, are now eight times the value of exports. The French Caribbean has been an 'economic fiasco: a society which consumes but which produces practically nothing.'[110] More than two-thirds of all employment in each of these *anciennes colonies* is in the tertiary sector. Salaries account for more than half of all government expenditure. High standards of living, amongst the highest in the Caribbean and the Indian Ocean, often hide huge income disparities between French bureaucrats and the white land-owning bourgeoisie on the one hand, and farm labourers on the other. Caribbean pro-independence activists argue that only secession can destroy the 'feudal' powers of colonial oligarchies propped up by the French state;[111] such dissidents, however, remain a tiny minority in the Antilles and are virtually non-existent in Réunion.

New Caledonian development has been exceptionally uneven by place and race. Melanesians, the indigenous population, were incorporated into the periphery of the New Caledonian economy through wages, taxes, pensions, medical assistance and a variety of legal and institutional means. Yet this has sharpened perceptions of relative deprivation. 'Traditional' self-reliant Melanesian economies have disappeared in the wake of this incorporation. Regional and ethnic economic inequalities have changed little in the past two decades. Disparities of development also characterise French Polynesia. Shanty towns housing migrants to Papeete from rural districts and outer islands contrast with the tourist image of Tahiti and point to enormous inequalities in a territory where Mercedes taxis are the norm and the per capita consumption of champagne is reputedly the highest in the world.[112] A decline in employment in the nuclear industry and tourism worsened the economic situation by the mid-1980s. In Guyane a similar transition followed the development of the space programme, but on a much smaller scale.

Rapid change in economic structure has also occurred in Mayotte, which once had an almost wholly agricultural economy and very little other employment. Agricultural exports have declined since 1981 and imports now amount to more than thirty times the value of exports. This massive trade imbalance must be supported by French assistance. France directly provides almost half Mayotte's budget, much of which is directed towards building up the bureaucracy and creating an infrastructure, turning what a decade ago was a largely subsistence economy, with a substantial degree of self-reliance, into a virtual welfare state. Standards of living, educational services and medical care have certainly improved. But, in less than a decade, the island that was once the poorest in the Comoros has become the richest and most dependent.

Wallis and Futuna similarly moved from an almost wholly subsistence economy (with minimal exports) to one reliant on external finance, either direct subsidies from France or remittances from kin who have migrated to New Caledonia. Even more so than in Mayotte, there was no intervening period of agricultural exports, merely a direct transition from subsistence to subsidy. Of all the DOM-TOMs (other than the TAAF) Wallis and Futuna has the most dependent economy. Its exports are by far the smallest, amounting to only 1.5 tonnes of trochus shells in 1983. Imports total more than a thousand times the value of exports. Though the subsistence economy remains in place (despite high population densities), cash crops have been unsuccessful, tourism is less significant than anywhere else in the South Pacific and the first bank opened only in 1977. No development plan existed until 1979, when the nickel crisis in New Caledonia brought emigration to a virtual standstill. Though France has established a comprehensive social welfare system, aid to Wallis and Futuna has been much less than to most other DOM-TOMs, partly because of its low absorptive capacity. There appears little prospect for the emergence of a productive economy; the description of the territory as being a case of 'total dependency' is apt.[113]

Of all the DOM-TOMs, Saint-Pierre and Miquelon appears the most obviously productive because of the fishing industry. Yet even this is partly an illusion. Though the productive economy depends primarily on fishing, alongside a tiny tourist industry, imports are now twice the value of exports, and the whole economic structure relies on French finance. Most employment is in the bureaucracy. Even in Saint-Pierre the tertiary sector now dominates.

The move from production to consumption has paralleled the 'tertiarisation' of other Western economies, and in this evolution the DOM-TOMs differ little from France. The tertiary revolution has brought benefits of greater wealth, improved services and migration opportunities. But it has also created economic (and perhaps psychological) dependency on France. The paradox of contemporary development is ultimately a simple one: the less the DOM-TOMs produce, the more income they receive and the more they consume.[114] France absolutely dominates a trade that is increasingly unidirectional. Only Saint-Pierre and Miquelon receives the majority of its imports from another country (in this case, Canada). Each of the three Caribbean *départements*, as well as Réunion and Mayotte, receive about 60 per cent of their imports (by value) from France; in New Caledonia and French Polynesia the proportion is around 55 per cent. Not only does the volume and value of imports invariably dwarf exports, but the imbalance has substantially increased; in Mayotte, for example, the trade imbalance climbed from a deficit of 56 million francs in 1979 to 140 million francs four years later. Only in Saint-Pierre and Miquelon are exports valued at more than 15 per cent of imports. This trade imbalance again demonstrates the new consumer society of the DOM-TOMs. One polemical observer described the situation in emotive terms, referring to a

delirious world with supermarkets filled with imported consumer goods, luxury cars, luxury villas surrounded by fallow land, abandoned or dilapidated sugar refineries, masses of men and women who each year swell the ranks of the unemployed. It is a world turned upside down, plunged into 'abundance' and the increasing loss of its productive activities, which hides its destitutes behind a veneer of general prosperity. A consumer country, but an unproductive one. A country of *fonctionnaires* and rich bourgeois, but also of the underprivileged, existing on the fringes of employment and survival, other than through welfare subsidies. A country of the well-to-do but also a country of the 'handicapped' in permanent quest for assistance. A country of waste, of frustration and precariousness.[115]

Yet another paradox is that the income and welfare situation in the French DOM-TOMs is far superior to that of their independent neighbours in the Caribbean, South America, and the Indian and Pacific Oceans. Such a situation is only rendered possible through a transfer economy with ever-reinforced ties to a wealthy developed nation.

The DOM-TOMs, through French investment, trade, transfer payments, migration and remittances have become ever more firmly tied to France and almost isolated from their neighbouring regions. Guyane is a classic enclave economy, with virtually no links to the rest of South America, but increasingly oriented to France. Until the 1980s modern communications linked Wallis and Futuna with no Pacific state other than New Caledonia. Mayotte has broken many of its ties with the Comoros. The DOM-TOMs are less 'windows' on these parts of the world than termini for the largesse of France. Without France the current structure of development would disintegrate. In the post-war years the populations of the DOM-TOMs have become clients of the French state.

Initially *départementalisation* of the *vieilles colonies* brought the four largest *départements* (in terms of either population or land area) much closer to France, a result of their long historic ties and the growing recognition that, at relatively little expense, their economy and society could be transformed. Rather later the Pacific territories went through the same process. The necessity to satisfy local demands, and perhaps the desire also to ward off discontent and upheaval, and feelings of responsibility for improving standards of living and completing the 'civilising mission', brought increased financial resources, migration and also the strengthening of the military presence. The smaller DOM-TOMs followed suit.

Visions of the emergence of a productive export economy, apparent in every development plan for the DOM-TOMs, remain rhetoric. The relative lack of valuable natural resources (except in New Caledonia), vast distances to export markets (except in the Caribbean), extremely high wages and new attitudes to employment all discourage production. The relationship between France and the DOM-TOMs, in which grandly conceived plans for future development have not been matched by reality, is no longer the old structure of colonialism, nor even the extensive neo-colonialism that characterises so many newly independent states, but a more subtle yet thoroughly pervasive structure of dependence.

Proposals to minimise dependency, as well as imbalances among ethnic groups, economic sectors and geographical regions, relate to ideology. The problem is often simply seen as fundamentally an economic one, that of moving away from an unproductive economy based on subsidies and an inflated public sector, with all its negative consequences; this therefore demands a technocratic solution with, perhaps, a change of statute. It does not necessarily imply a disavowal of capitalism, but the need for greater economic and political decentralisation that would provide the possibility of confronting inequalities of income and development, an attempt to channel public funds into long-term development, and efforts to remedy a situation in which 'the system of subsidies from the *métropole* . . . ends up as the transformation of a large part of the public expenditure into private profit.'[116] The DOM-TOMs are littered with the reminders of elegant grandiose schemes that flourished briefly, only to be abandoned because of escalating costs, inappropriate techniques, limited labour supplies, ecological degradation or changing governments. Typical of such schemes was the Green Plan for Guyane announced in 1977 by Olivier Stirn, the DOM-TOMs Minister, which has left a wasteland of former livestock ranches and woodlands; no paper was ever produced from the pulp mill and only a handful of plots remain from the reforestation scheme.[117] Various grand schemes have been introduced everywhere in the DOM-TOMs, usually calling for replacement of imports (particularly food) with locally produced items, the setting up of free-trade zones and high-technology industries,[118] the development of tourism (especially where it is currently minimal), the building of better port facilities and more suitable airports, increasing exploration of submarine resources (e.g. polymetallic nodules), and the establishment of subsidies and tax incentives for production. Such projects have seldom been put into practice. Moreover development objectives have never been able to escape from the assumption that merely achieving locally-based economic growth, even if possible, would meet the needs of the whole population. Nor have they been able to achieve any sort of development which can bypass significant injections of French capital hence, at least in the short term, reinforcing dependency. Yet those who suggest a radical alternative, such as independence and the establishment of a different economic system, have not proposed alternative sources of capital, technology and labour. Nor can they demonstrate that residents of the DOM-TOMs, accustomed to high levels of social services, multiple consumer goods, access to France and other DOM-TOMs for migration and relatively high standards of living, would be willing to forgo these advantages. In short, the very success of the increased dependency of the post-war years creates a dilemma from which few economists and planners can see any escape. In these circumstances new structures of development are rarely sought after and optimism about change is largely misplaced. A new form of development has become ideological rather than economic, a myth which unsuccessfully competes with a new political economy of dependent development.

6

Culture, Identity and National Consciousness

THE QUESTION of cultural identity forms a central and continuing theme in the history of the DOM-TOMs. Thousands of kilometres distant from Europe but closely linked to France, and home to a variety of racial and cultural groups, the DOM-TOMs' cultures show the mark of diverse heritages. Patterns of family and community links, music and art, language and literature, religion, food and clothing contribute to defining traits of local identity but also have a political dimension. Cultural attachment to metropolitan France is championed by many who defend the maintenance of close institutional links with the *métropole*, whereas arguments about the existence of separate cultures and national identities are used by those who desire greater autonomy or outright independence. Culture thereby becomes a stake in elections and public life, and the search for a 'national' identity constitutes a major preoccupation for the intellectual elite in the DOM-TOMs. In recent years, a cultural revival in the French overseas regions, notably in the Antilles, has accompanied and inspired new assessments of the relationship between the DOM-TOMs and the 'mother country'. But writers and musicians from the DOM-TOMs, almost all from the Antilles, have also won great acclaim in France. At best, cross-fertilisation and exchange have marked cultural connections between France and its outposts; at worst, French administration of the former colonies has led to continued cultural imperialism and the stifling of indigenous creativity.

In the period of classical colonialism, French administrators and settlers denigrated non-European cultures. They frequently misunderstood elements of local cultures which they found primitive and uncivilised, and viewed the world through Eurocentric glasses, often unable to see foreigners except in terms of exotic and mysterious Levantines, voluptuous Polynesians, or savage Melanesians. Until the beginnings of modern anthropology and ethnography in the twentieth century, and the 'discovery' of 'primitive' art by contemporary artists, Europeans set no value on the culture of the Africans and Pacific islanders who form the majority of the population of today's DOM-TOMs. Missionaries regarded tribal customs as heathen and barbarian, and administrators feared that native cultures could be dangerous bases for rebellion. France's vocation, apostles of colonialism argued, was a *mission civilisatrice* (civilising mission) to bring Western science and learning to the 'savages', convert them to Christianity, cover their nakedness and reform their morals.[1]

In the nineteenth century, French policy towards the indigenous populations was, in theory, 'assimilation'; 'it meant that the colony should become an integral, if not contiguous, part of the mother country, and its society and population made over — to whatever extent possible — in her image.'[2] This proved manifestly impossible and colonialists replaced it in the 1890s with a policy of 'association', a less strict, less ambitious means of attachment of the colonies and their populations to the *métropole*. Both policies, in practice, dispensed French culture to a selected elite in the colonies and tolerated, in an often debased and sometimes clandestine form, the persistence of pre-contact customs and traditions of the masses. Neither approach considered indigenous cultures of overseas areas as valid and valuable in their own right, except in the case of highly structured civilisations whose literature and architecture the French could admire and study (as was the case with Islam). Cultures with fewer recognisable forms attracted less attention and esteem. The mosques of the Maghreb and the Buddhist temples of Indo-China impressed Europeans, but the art and ceremonies of black Africa, the Antilles and the Pacific struck them as only sorcery and superstition.

Colonial rulers found it impossible to eliminate native cultural practices, and judged it useful to allow the indigenous population to maintain at least some of their beliefs and traditions. Doing so, however, often blocked access to social advancement, education and justice in the Western system. The state offered French citizenship only to those who learned French, abandoned polygamy and agreed to be judged by French law rather than traditional regulations. From the beginning of colonisation, therefore, the dominated peoples were caught between remaining true to their own cultures, 'converting' to French language, religion and behaviour, or trying to find some elusive compromise between their historic traditions and new foreign customs. Only in rare cases was *francisation*, the adoption or imposition of French culture, total.

Few traits of European society were transferred to the colonies more successfully than Christianity. Bastions of Islam, such as the Comoros, resisted conversion, and Christian practices were often only a veneer on traditional beliefs and forms of behaviour, but the precepts of Christianity affected vast regions, as administrators, teachers, and missionairies often reinforced each others' activities. Sundays became clearly differentiated, and forms of clothing and consumption were transformed, whilst new religious discord accentuated and sharpened historic social divisions and later emphasised political conflicts.[3] In several DOM-TOMs, notably New Caledonia, the churches were at the forefront of pressure for social and political change and in the 1970s radical Christian groups, especially in the Antilles, pressed for independence. In New Caledonia religious adherence has affected the course and structure of the independence movement.

Access to French culture was limited in the colonies. Education provided the *entrée* to culture and political life, and the school was the primary institution for the *francisation* of colonised peoples. Few schools for native peoples existed, and until the twentieth century these depended largely on Catholic mission teachers. Lack of literacy kept doors to white-collar professions closed. Those who received an education could generally hope only to complete primary school and had little chance of advancing successfully in the highly competitive secondary and tertiary systems. The courses complied with the classical syllabus used in metropolitan France, including the study of ancient languages and history lessons that for many years began with discussions of 'Our ancestors the Gauls.' Enrolling in higher education meant travelling the great distance to an often inhospitable 'mother country' and attempting the difficult examinations that characterised France's elitist schools. Only the advantaged, persevering and intelligent could aspire to the higher levels of education. In fact, the colonial education system was designed precisely to encourage the clever sons (and, more seldom, daughters) of the native elites, training them to become either teachers or assistants to white public servants in the colonial administration.

Despite the difficulties, a number of indigenes of the French empire succeeded. These educated Africans and Asians served as intermediaries between the European rulers and the masses of illiterate peasants. Some became articulate representatives of their own ethnic groups and

cultures or theorists of new artistic movements. Educated colonials
such as the black Guyanais Félix Eboué won appointments as administrators in the Empire, while others, such as Habib Bourguiba, Aimé
Césaire, Léopold Sedar Senghor and Ho Chi Minh, became spokesmen
for nationalist demands. Such men became the leaders of colonies
which gained their independence and remained the dominant political
figures in those possessions which remained attached to France as
DOM-TOMs.[4]

Only after the Second World War did education become more widespread in the DOM-TOMs. This was especially the case in the DOMs, a
key gain from *départementalisation*, which required the establishment
of schools in all areas and the enforcement of mandatory education
laws. The state made efforts at improved education in the TOMs, but
progress was slower. A cultural and geographical hierarchy remained:
DOM-TOM residents of more modest backgrounds, those living in
peripheral areas (rural regions, outer isles) and those who did not bow
to the strict intellectual discipline of French education had fewer
chances for schooling and the career opportunities which education
provided. In New Caledonia the first Melanesian did not graduate from
secondary school until the 1960s. In the 1980s, only a handful of
Mahorais and Melanesians had earned university degrees, and only one
Melanesian practised medicine (and then in France rather than in New
Caledonia). Glaring disparities continue to exist among social groups;
in New Caledonia, for example, the Caldoches' children still enjoy a
much better chance of success in completing secondary education than
do their Melanesian neighbours.[5]

Even those with little access to formal education at an advanced level
have been greatly affected by the contact between French and non-
European cultures. Increased newspaper circulation, as well as a variety of radio and television programmes, diffuse metropolitan culture,
and the frequent sojourns of many inhabitants of the *vieilles colonies* in
the metropole further acquaint them with various facets of French
culture. Pop musicians, comic books and the latest style of jeans are as
familiar to French children of the Indian Ocean or the Antilles as to
those of the provinces of metropolitan France. Consumer culture has
brought many of the same foodstuffs, consumer durables and luxuries
to the French overseas populations. The *baguette* has become a staple of
diets, as well as a symbol of French culture, around the DOM-TOMs,
and many residents prefer imported food to locally-produced commodities. Structural changes in French society and culture such as
urbanisation and secularisation have affected the *outre-mer* as well,
although always at different speeds and to different degrees. Only the
most romantic observers imagine that any of the DOM-TOM residents

are completely cut off from the products of modern French consumer society or popular culture — or want to live in an isolated world relying solely on their 'traditional' ways and regional products. Yet many changes have been both recent and superficial. Furthermore, they give rise to charges of imperialistic consumerism and materialism, mediocrity and continued alienation of local populations from their indigenous cultural roots. Television-watchers from Mayotte to Polynesia can even see dubbed American serials, European variety shows or French literary discussions, but local content is limited to brief newscasts and there is rarely, if ever, any regional content. This explains the recent success of the unlicensed Télé-Free-DOM in Réunion, where local issues were discussed in Creole. Bookshops and record stores stock the most recent French books, newspapers, magazines and recordings, at sometimes substantially higher prices than in the *métropole*, a situation that reinforces French dominance of popular culture.[6]

Cultural diffusion from France may take quite different forms. Throughout the DOM-TOMs the structure of sport follows that of the *métropole*, except in New Caledonia where the early influence of the London Missionary Society was such that cricket is still the principal summer sport, though with Melanesian embellishments that distinguish it from the now classical form. Cycling dominates sporting calendars; the Tour de Calédonie has become so important that early Kanak militancy in 1984 was symbolically directed to its disruption. Caldoche reaction resulted in the official cancellation of the football matches that predominate in the Melanesian world. If Wallisians are known outside the Pacific, it is simply because for years they have dominated all French javelin-throwing competitions, whilst Alain Lazare from New Caledonia is the French marathon champion. But cultural ties are most apparent in football, where the French cup is unique in that the first round incorporates the champions of each of the DOM-TOMs who either fly to France or welcome the great teams of France at home. Although the champions rarely proceed beyond the first round, their participation symbolises the direct ties between centre and periphery in an area that has enormous popular support.

Side by side with the variants of 'high' culture and 'popular' culture imported from overseas are specific local cultures. In some DOM-TOMs, cultures substantially predating European contact have survived, while in others, the blending of different civilisations has produced new, syncretic cultures. But time and distance have wrought cultural changes even in those islands which are the most European outposts of France overseas. The populations of Saint-Pierre and Miquelon and Saint-Barthélémy — not coincidentally, almost all Caucasian — are closest in culture to their metropolitan compatriots.

Yet they display particular cultural traits, variation in language and customs derived from their ancestors and transplanted to the western hemisphere. In Saint-Pierre, various old Basque customs are still observed, as are a number of Norman traditions in Saint-Barthélémy, but culinary and dress habits have adapted in different ways to suit the climates of North America.[7] The white settler populations of other DOM-TOMs have also diverged from the metropolitan norm. Most of the Antillais and Réunionnais *Béké* families, some of whom have lived in the tropics for more than four centuries, have special vocabularies, observances and traditions foreign to metropolitan France.[8] The language of the Caldoches has borrowed words from Australian English, for instance,[9] but the Saint-Martin population is perhaps even further removed from the norms of the mother country. There the first language and the language of communication is English; French is learnt at school and is rarely used.[10]

The Mahorais of Mayotte are a contrast to other more obviously assimilated groups. Almost all are Muslim, which sets them apart from the residents of most other DOM-TOMs. Few speak even rudimentary French, and even fewer have received a French education. Traditions remain strong, and women preserve the dominant role they have always enjoyed in Mahorais society.[11] Urbanisation has had less effect in Mayotte than in most other DOM-TOMs, and few Mahorais migrate to France. A very similar situation occurs in Wallis and especially Futuna; despite the long influence of Catholicism, French is poorly understood and rarely used, Polynesian customs are pre-eminent in social life and exchange ceremonies are oriented around a subsistence, root-crop economy. Such lack of 'acculturation' to French life, however, has not limited support among Mahorais voters for their island to become a fully-fledged *département* of France, or support of the status quo in Wallis and Futuna, and demonstrates that cultural dissimilarity is not necessarily a motive for independence.

The TOMs of the Pacific, with their Oceanic cultures overlaid by the French presence, and the DOMs, which have a particularly vibrant and dominant Creole culture, are quite separate cases. They also form the two groups of DOM-TOMs where questions of cultural identity have been most often posed, often in an inflammatory manner, and where culture has been most politicised.

CREOLE CULTURE IN THE *VIEILLES COLONIES*

Réunion was uninhabited when the Europeans arrived; in Guadeloupe and Martinique, the native Arawak and Carib Indians were almost all killed; the Indians of Guyane continued to live largely in isolation in the Amazonian forests that dominated the colony. The four future DOMs, therefore, were to some extent *tabulae rasae* on which the French created new societies. Foreign populations imported into the *vieilles colonies* included Indians, Chinese and, later, other Asians and Middle Easterners, but African slaves formed the dominant group in the plantation societies. The Africans came from different tribes and regions, bringing with them their own languages, religions and cultures. Some customs fell into disuse on the new plantations, and the slave masters repressed many traditions. Gradually a new culture evolved. The Creole language, a version of French with African and other foreign words incorporated, became the lingua franca for communication between slaves and between the slaves and their owners. Most slaves converted to Christianity, but, to varying degrees, maintained non-Christian beliefs and ceremonies.[12] Europeans tried to impose their strictures on sexual and family life and end what they considered the promiscuity and unbounded sexual activities of the slaves, though this did not restrict the men from contracting liaisons with slave women which led to the emergence of the substantial *métis* populations of the *vieilles colonies*.

After 1848, the path of social mobility in the plantation economies lay in *francisation*: the adoption of French language and learning, Christian practices and patterns of behaviour that resembled those of the Europeans. The *métis* showed themselves particularly skilled at making these changes. While the *Békés* were content to dominate the economy, and the full-blood Africans remained an agrarian proletariat marked by Creole culture, the *métis* enrolled in schools and achieved professional successes. Already in the nineteenth century, *métis* Antillais, Guyanais and Réunionnais became lawyers and doctors, professors and administrators, *députés* and mayors. To succeed, however, they had to speak French rather than Creole, abandon any practices which the French might consider 'uncivilised', and in effect, be more French than the French. In addition, a lighter skin colour was beneficial, and Antillais families always hoped that their children would marry lighter-skinned partners to whiten their progeny further.[13]

The *métis*, therefore, valued everything French and devalued the African part of their heritage. Rejection by whites resulted in self-denigration of black skin and African culture. Until well into the twentieth century, the African heritage was neglected or denounced by whites and many *métis*. Africa was considered a land without history, and Africans overseas a people without culture or roots. However, some black writers made an effort to rehabilitate their African heritage. Precursors, such as W. E. B. DuBois's *Souls of Black Folks*, published in the

United States in 1902, and the writings of Haitian intellectuals in the early 1900s, began the process and influenced intellectuals in the French empire. New studies in the social sciences, and cultural interest in African art, slowly allowed Europeans to look at African art and African society with a less jaundiced eye. A group of black writers from the French colonies, in articulating the concept of *négritude*, played a decisive role in the rehabilitation of the African heritage and the creation of a new black identity among the French-speaking black populations of the world.

One of the early influences on the emergence of *négritude* was René Maran, a Martiniquais writer, who lived most of his life in Paris but who had spent thirteen years as a French colonial administrator. His novel *Batouala*, which won the prestigious Prix Goncourt in 1921, stirred considerable controversy because of its account of colonial life in the Central African Republic. Maran was the first black writer to use literature to oppose the practices of incompetent colonialism though he was not opposed to colonialism itself.[14] The main figures in the establishment of *négritude* were Aimé Césaire, teacher, poet and later doyen of political figures in the French Antilles; Léon Damas, a Guyanais novelist; and Léopold Sedar Senghor, future president of Senegal and member of the Académie Française. Each later attested to the significance of Maran's work on the development of black consciousness. They met in the 1930s as students in Paris, where they came into contact with the new historical and anthropological writing and the works of English-language black authors. In a journal called *L'Etudiant noir*, in the 1930s, Césaire launched the term *négritude*. For Senghor, *négritude* was simply: 'all the values of black civilisation.'[15] It implied a new appreciation of African history; the young intellectuals argued that Africa had a history of its own, and moreover that there existed a united African history, despite tribal and regional variations. An African philosophy also existed, which Senghor identified as based on intuitive reason, a pluralistic dialectic, indigenous forms of religion and black humanism. African music, art and dance, the writers argued, had enjoyed widespread influence — for instance, the spread of African musical forms into Arabic and then European music. Each could legitimately be considered a culture of its own. Africans, in short, were not barbarous, ahistorical people devoid of culture, but the repository of an evolving, structured and sophisticated history, philosophy and art.[16]

Négritude aspired to incorporate African themes into the culture of black artists and writers both in France and elsewhere. 'We naturally expressed ourselves as Negroes, taking inspiration from and thinking in the authentic style of our people, whether Antillais or black African: energy, conviviality, community', said Senghor. *Négritude* was, therefore, essentially a cultural programme, but, 'its significance moved towards a struggle for liberation from the chains of cultural colonisation.'[17] *Négritude* also, and inevitably, took on political connotations, since the idea was directed against colonial control of culture. Césaire, in 1947, published a seminal work in Caribbean literature, *Cahier d'un retour au pays natal* (*Notebook of a Return to the Native Land*), in which he used an innovative poetic style to celebrate West Indian life but also to castigate French colonialism, the poverty and backwardness of his native Martinique and the cultural frustrations of a black Frenchman. With this work, Césaire became widely recognised as the most important writer in the French Antilles. Moreover Césaire was already a political activist. At first a Communist, he broke with the French Communist Party in 1956, writing in an open letter to its head, Maurice Thorez, that the Communists did not take account of the struggles of blacks but subsumed the concerns of colonised peoples to the dialectic of class struggle. His political career saw him espouse *départementalisation*, flirt with independence and advocate autonomy for the DOMs, but his demands were always rooted in a sense of the cultural particularity of the Antilles, and the contribution of African roots to that identity and the philosophy of *négritude*.[18]

An even more piercing critique of colonialism came from Frantz Fanon, a black psychiatrist from Martinique, whose works appeared in the late 1950s and early 1960s during the difficult days of the Algerian War. In *Peaux noires, masques blancs* (*Black skin, white masks*), published in 1952, Fanon argued that blacks in the colonies had been transformed into 'obsessive neurotics' and that Antillais society was itself 'neurotic.' In the mythology of whites black is identified with evil, but also with orgiastic pleasure. Racism had made blacks hate themselves and deify whites, to the point that light skin and a mastery of classical French — and thus betrayal of African origins — became the aim for the colonised black: a strategy which Fanon termed 'lactification.' Blacks, alienated from their African background, were incapable of merging into white French society because of white racism. Fanon argued for the independence of Algeria and other French colonies, but so deep was the neurosis in the Antilles that he argued that it was first necessary to question stereotypes and establish a new identity.[19]

The ferment of the 1960s — decolonisation, student demonstrations, the emergence of counter-cultures — spread some of the new political doctrines, such as the ideas of the 'new left', to the Antilles. Groups of intellectuals began to explore further methods of analysing the situation of the Antillais and articulating a new identity. For instance, a group of young writers founded a new social science journal in

Martinique, *Acoma*, which published articles concerning Antillais alienation. They linked race and class, arguing that the colonisers had assimilated blacks and slaves and warned that the colonial system was now reaching its highest stage, a complete depersonalisation of West Indians.

Particularly important in the new cultural ferment of recent decades has been the work of Edouard Glissant, novelist and theoretician of *antillanité*. Glissant's *Le Discours antillais*, published in 1981, summed up some of the new ideas and represented an implicit critique of Césaire's *négritude*. For Glissant, African roots were not unimportant, but the dominant cultural trait of the French Caribbean islands was their *antillanité*: their unique mixture of French, African and Caribbean cultures. Glissant strongly opposed the cultural 'balkanisation' of the West Indies and sought stronger links between the Anglophone and Francophone Caribbean. *Négritude* seemed old-fashioned and backward-looking, and what was needed was a new cultural creativity which would develop the Antillais identity.[20]

For many who shared Glissant's view, only political independence would allow the genuine development of cultural creativity and identity; shackled to the French political system, the Antillais remained tied, as well, to French systems of thought and art. The Antillais must decolonise themselves, and the implicit message was one of political protest and rebellion. This message was not necessarily a call to revolution, but it did pose the question of whether any *département*, with the integration which that statute implied, could ever be anything other than a colony.

More recently, partly inspired by Glissant's work, a renewed interest in Creole language and literature has emerged. Creole, previously denigrated as the language of poor and illiterate blacks, and forbidden in government and school, now attracts much attention from linguists and other authors. Attempts have been made to systematise what was essentially an oral language; novelists and poets publish in Creole, claiming it as the authentic language of the DOMs and the necessary vehicle for a 'national' cultural identity. Such writers as Raphaël Confiant and Patrick Chamoiseau have won great praise, in the West Indies and in France, for novels which draw on the Creole language (even when they are not written in Creole) to translate the life and concerns of the ordinary people of the Caribbean.[21]

A recent book, *Eloge de la créolite* (*In Praise of Creole Culture*), affirms: 'Not Europeans, not Africans, not Asians, we proclaim ourselves Creoles.' The authors pay homage to Césaire — 'To a totally racist world, torn apart by colonial divisions, Aimé Césaire restored mother Africa, the African womb, black civilisation.' But they accuse him of making Antillais into Africans by using an African reference for local aspirations, revolt and identity; they also disagree with his view of Creole as only an oral language of emotion, rather than a written language of reflection. Edouard Glissant, they argue, in proposing the concept of *antillanité* recognised the uniqueness of the West Indian islands, and with him, 'we declare the primary aesthetic base for knowledge of ourselves and the world' to be *créolité*. This is more than just a language: '*Créolité* is the interactional and transactional aggregate of Caribbean, European, African, Asian and Middle Eastern cultural elements, that the yoke of history has brought together in one place.' *Créolité* is specific to the Antilles, Guyane and other regions where these elements come together, and the very mixture of them is its strength: '*Créolité* is a rejection of false universality, monolingualism and homogeneity.' It forms the common heritage of the residents of those islands, whatever their ethnic background or skin colour; the authors claim as one of their own the Guadeloupean *Béké* poet and Nobel prize winner Saint-John Perse. But *créolité* aims to affirm, in a fashion different from that of mere regionalist and local colour authors, and in opposition to those who would make the Creole islands culturally tributary to Europe or Africa, a nascent and original identity.[22]

The authors of the *Eloge de la créolité* also address the question of politics. They stress that *créolité* is not just an aesthetic movement but has ramifications for politics and economics: 'It is structured around the claim for complete sovereignty for our peoples, without identifying itself with any of the different ideologies which until now have promoted this claim.' They distance themselves from both orthodox Marxism and populist nationalism, particularly of the sort which seeks to divide the Antilles into separate independent states. Their ultimate political aim is to establish a federation of Caribbean islands, a goal for which 'mono-insular' independence may, however, be a step.[23]

For other authors cultural identity is also tied to political status. French domination of the Antilles was a product of cultural and political assimilation and hegemony, so a recovery and proclamation of authentic cultural values must include political control. Nationalism in Martinique and Guadeloupe is political activism based on cultural identity.[24] Creole is an authentic national language, potentially rich enough to be used for science and learning as well as for everyday life, the language of intellectuals as well as the masses. Use of Creole, for example, by the pro-independence Guadeloupean trade union (the Union des Travailleurs Agricoles) or in the courtroom by political dissidents arrested and brought to trial, becomes a real and symbolic representation of opposition to the French state and the hegemony of French culture. Particularly in Guadeloupe, since 1970, the Creole language has increasingly become a political and symbolic stake in social relations . . . and it appears certain that recognition of Creole as an official language would risk subverting the social order to the same extent as a barbarian invasion.[25]

If *créolité* is anchored in language, it implies an affirmation and recognition of a variety of cultural particularities in the Antilles and other Creole regions. 'Creole' is a whole culture:

Contemporary Antillo-Guyanais civilisation is characterised by the presence of cultural syncretism, where the originally conflicting cultural relations of European colonisers and West African slaves have been reconciled more or less harmoniously in a Caribbean island or coastal context.[26]

What exactly are the components of this Creole culture? Certainly the landscape, the volcanoes and flora and fauna of the tropics contribute a distinct physical and artistic element, different from the images of French life portrayed in the school books in wide use in the DOM-TOMs. So, too, are various forms of music (such as the gwoka and zouk of the Antilles),[27] an oral tradition of story-telling, the highly spiced cuisine and the old costumes featuring madras fabrics. But there exist, as well, different forms of social organisation,[28] such as patterns of marriage. In the Western Christian tradition, marriage was ideally a lifelong and monogamous institution. However, slavery worked against the establishment of long-lasting and stable families. Slave owners encouraged black women to bear children, and sometimes themselves seduced or raped their slaves. Virginity was not so highly prized as in the West. Consequently, sexual and marital relations took on a different form in the Creole countries and, more widely, in the Caribbean. Relatively common pre-marital (and extra-marital) relations and short-term liaisons left many women in charge of single-parent families. Legal marriage, when it occurred, often came after a long period of cohabitation and sometimes the birth of several children. Though to moralists such behaviour smacked of promiscuity, it represented an alternative form of social organisation. Creole behaviour or customs also differed from those of the *métropole*, or at least traditional French society, in attitudes toward work, politics and religion. Contemporary Antillais attitudes and practices may find roots in the slave era. Ostentatious consumerism could be tied to the slave's need to prove his dignity, liberation and *francisation*.[29] Religious behaviour in the Antilles is a syncretic blend of Christian and non-Christian customs. Even in Westernised Martinique and Guadeloupe, superstitions abound, herbal medicines are widely used, and many people resort to shamans and folk-healers (*quimboiseurs*) to treat illnesses or resolve personal problems. Some observers dismiss this as evidence of incomplete conversion to Christianity or the survival of pagan vestiges, but for others it represents a distinct form of religious belief combining elements of Christian and non-Christian African religions.[30] Psycho-social behaviour, finally, displays particular patterns related to the historical context of island societies.[31]

In sum, attempts to make Antillais, Réunionnais and Guyanais into French citizens with different-coloured skins have not been successful. They have provoked a reaction against French assimilation (and the restrictions on possibilities for acquiring it) and a search for a corporate identity, especially in the Antilles. Ironically, some of the intellectuals and artists most successful in the French system of education have spearheaded the revival of local culture and 'nationalist' demands. Only in recent years has Paris accommodated this movement, for example, by allowing Creole as an examinable subject for school-leaving certificates, encouraging research into Creole culture and establishing regional cultural councils. Individuals in the DOM-TOMs may feel the mixture of cultures as alienating or clashing,[32] but many move easily between the metropolitan and Creole worlds.[33] Still others may adopt somewhat peripheral imported beliefs or cultures, such as varieties of fundamentalist Protestantism.[34] Claims of cultural identity and particularity are now widely accepted, whatever their form, even by those who do not agree with the arguments of the *indépendantistes*. But the precise place of Antillais culture in a France still marked by cultural centralism and ideals of universality remains uncertain, as also does the issue of whether cultural and political autonomy must go hand in hand.

OCEANIC CULTURES

In the islands of the South Pacific, France encountered cultures very different from those it had previously known, and the people of Oceania became both the very French image of the noble savage (in the case of Polynesians) or the primitive brute (the Melanesians). Such distinctions have long characterised, quite erroneously, these two vast cultural regions.[35] At the time of formal French takeover, both New Caledonia and French Polynesia had already witnessed several decades of contact with European traders and missionaries. Neither Polynesian nor Melanesian culture still existed in a pristine pre-contact state; Tahiti, where the London Missionary Society had a Protestant mission from the 1790s, was quite thoroughly Christianised. Wallis and Futuna quickly converted to Catholicism after the arrival of the first Marist priests in the 1830s, though not before Futunans killed Pierre Chanel, who became the first Pacific saint. New Caledonia, however, remained apart: contacts with Westerners were more episodic, and missionaries less successful during the first years of French control, except for the successes of the London Missionary Society in the outlying Loyalty Islands.[36]

Polynesia and to a lesser extent Melanesia had highly structured, well-ordered societies, although the Europeans made little effort to understand them.[37] In Polynesia there existed a hierarchical social structure of an elite, the 'gentry' or nobles, and the common people. Priests preserved the polytheistic religion and in eastern Polynesia, carried out worship at stone altars (*marae*). Sexual roles were also strictly defined. Various restrictions (the *tapu*) regulated social and cultural life. Arts and crafts included carvings, clothing, jewelry, story-telling, singing and dancing. The missionaries had restricted some of these activities, but others survived the English, then the French, presence. Many customs fell into disuse, particularly among those who had converted to Christianity and adopted French manners and morals. Anthropophagy and infanticide were strictly forbidden, nakedness gave way to Western clothing — such as the 'mission dresses' worn by women — and hymns replaced the old songs as the major form of music. Social controls broke down, although some of the chiefs found new influence as government officials or church officers, and the daughters of noble families intermarried with the prosperous merchant class. The Tahitian language remained in use, gradually triumphing in the other archipelagos, although French became the language of education and administration. No pidgin language similar to Creole developed, but a powerful group of mixed-blood Tahitians (the *demis*) emerged.[38] In fact, the key cultural effect of the first decades of European presence was a demographic and cultural *métissage*, a blending of European and Polynesian blood and beliefs that was so apparent that, for some, it seemed that the islanders had colonised the Europeans rather than the other way around.[39]

The nature of Tahitian society — and the lure of the Polynesian isles — attracted scholars and social commentators to the South Seas, as well as the writers and artists who made Tahiti famous. Already in the nineteenth century, observers mourned the disappearance of the old Tahitian culture, pollution by Westernisation and lack of creativity among the population. Gauguin's painting at the end of the century, showing Tahitians apparently unsure of where they had come from or where they were going, propped against religious carvings but smoking Western cigarettes, became common portrayals. Later observers also suggested that Westernisation had a 'fatal impact' in the Pacific islands, beyond the solely demographic, though this argument has been disproved by serious study of the survival and transformation of old cultural forms through syncretism of Oceanic and Western cultures in Polynesia.[40]

Nevertheless, foreign presence devalued and diluted much of precontact culture. The French did little to encourage use of the Tahitian language, and the education system, in Polynesia as elsewhere in the French empire, aimed to produce graduates conforming to the metropolitan model. Artwork shifted to the production of curios for tourists. Dictionaries and Bibles were published in Tahitian, but little else. The *marae* fell into disuse. For the first century of French colonisation, Polynesia produced no great intellectual movement or call for a reclamation of Tahitian culture; there was no equivalent of *négritude* in Polynesia.

Lack of cultural renewal can be explained by the great distance of Polynesia from the world's intellectual centres, the very small number of students who continued their education at university level in France, and the lack of a catalyst for cultural debate such as the Antillais had received from Haitian and American black authors. The small population of French Polynesia, scattered and divided over hundreds of islands, and dominated by a francicised elite, perhaps made for less contact between cultures. This *demi* elite became francicised but, unlike the *métis* of the Antilles, did not react against European culture and attempt to revivify their Oceanic identity. Residents of outer islands, less touched by European colonisation, clung to a Polynesian culture which gradually atrophied. Though the Tahitian language has overwhelmed the distinctive languages of the outer island groups of French Polynesia, it never successfully made the transition from an oral to a written language, though there are texts in Tahitian, plus the obligatory synopsis of texts in Polynesian. Yet the very persistence of a Polynesian culture obviated the need to create a concept similar to *antillanité*.

In recent years the young in particular have made an effort to recover Polynesian culture, what is termed the *ma'ohi* heritage, and to use it as a basis for cultural and political consciousness.[41] Specific endeavours have included the establishment of a Polynesian Cultural Centre and a Tahitian Academy in Papeete. Tahitian is now recognised as an official language of the territory, and official documents are printed in both languages. Political parties (and other organisations) carry Tahitian names. The mixed-blood *demis*, who often shunned speaking Tahitian in the past and emphasised their 'Frenchness', now make a point of speaking Tahitian in public and stress their Polynesian heritage. Some of the pro-independence parties have sought to reclaim their Poly-nesian culture and to attack the French heritage of cultural alienation. Yet the French government has also promoted contacts between Tahiti and other Polynesian countries and supported moves to establish a 'Community of Polynesian Peoples.'

France's other Polynesian territory, Wallis and Futuna, was para-doxically the most quickly and thoroughly changed by Catholicism, yet also the one where other elements of French culture have been slowest to infiltrate. Both groups of islanders almost unanimously converted to the Catholicism brought by the Marist priests, who established a virtual theocracy that lasted in Wallis and Futuna until the 1940s. The priests served as advisers to the traditional chiefs, intermediaries between the Polynesians and the French administrators, and the sole teachers. The law code of the islands, still in force in the 1940s, imposed fines for blasphemy, improper dress and behaviour, and various other offences against Catholic morals. In the years after the Second World War, rela-tively little change took place in Wallis and Futuna, other than the migration of islanders to New Caledonia. Polynesian social structure changed much less than in Tahiti; the contemporary kings retain con-siderable authority and power, and there is a stronger attachment to traditional modes of behaviour and customs than in most parts of Poly-nesia. Wallis and Futuna are still among those Pacific islands least touched by 'Westernisation.'[42]

The social structure and culture of Melanesians in New Caledonia was little understood by the French, as neither colonists nor social scientists took great interest in social systems regarded as difficult of access, primitive and in the process of becoming extinct. Those who did comment were often wrong; early visitors to New Caledonia, not rec-ognising strong chiefs with great power and the outward insignia of office which they identified in Polynesia, assumed that Melanesian society was egalitarian and unstructured. Even Maurice Leenhardt, the first ethnologist to study New Caledonia, wrote during the 1930s and 1940s that Melanesians had no notion of time, nor precise distinctions between past and present and between individual and group. Sub-sequent research proved that such estimations of Melanesian cos-mology were false.[43] Difficulties in making any generalisations about Melanesian culture, in fact, resulted from the division of indigenous society into several dozen tribal groups and over thirty language groups.

Melanesians traditionally had a complex society based on the identi-fication between clans, groups which claimed a common ancestor, and territory, the site with which the clans identified. Historic migration meant that individuals and clans had moved away from their traditional homelands, yet they preserved precise genealogies and a sense of identification with a particular area of land on the Grande Terre of New Caledonia. The French policy of *cantonnement*, placing Melanesians in reserves, often removed from their traditional clan territories, therefore represented an especially blatant and destructive attack on Melanesian social structure, where identity was 'written on the ground.'[44]

Melanesians in New Caledonia had some elements of a hierarchically organised society, notably in the Loyalty Islands and to some extent on the east coast, where there had been Polynesian influences. The most powerful figure in the community was the 'master of the land', the resident whose family first arrived in the area and who thus enjoyed a right of precedence. The authority who decided on the division of land for use by families in the community, he also enjoyed other ceremonial and sacred rights. The 'chieftainship', by contrast, was an honorific position sometimes even conferred on an outsider. He received homage from his 'subjects' but reigned rather than ruled; the chief was an arbiter, the guarantor of the unity of the community, sometimes an intermediary between the community and the outside world and, above all, 'the personification of the power and prestige of the group.'[45] The French often misunderstood this role, assuming the chief to be the real ruler. Moreover, the French generally appointed an administrative chief as its delegate within a tribe, although such a chosen chief might have neither the prestige nor the power of a traditional chief or the master of the land.[46]

Like most other cultures, Melanesians had a tradition of oral history, often tied to the myths of origin of the tribes, and the spiritual ties between the living and the dead. Complicated genealogies, cosmologies and records of migration were handed down orally from one generation to the next. Melanesians also had traditions of art and architecture — the carving of the totems, door-posts and lintels which festooned houses, the spatial organisation of villages (itself a representation of the various roles of inhabitants in village society), the masks which symbolised the chief, and various artisanal products. Particularly important in binding together Melanesian society was *coutume* (custom), ritual gift-giving to the elders and chief, the presentation of gifts (an expression of respect) by outsiders entering tribal areas and particular forms of behaviour at ceremonial and everyday occasions.

In the nineteenth century, collectors carried off many Melanesian artworks and even the heads of leaders killed in revolts to museums in France and elsewhere. Even in the twentieth century Melanesians were exhibited at the Paris Colonial Exhibition of 1931 as living relics of primitive societies. Missionaries tried to prohibit the making of objects perceived as heathen and attempted to substitute Christian practices for pre-Christian ones. Melanesian cultures were thus devalued, and such activities as carving often fell into disuse. What remained alive, however, were the cosmologies and genealogies, the attachment of Melanesians to ancestral land and a deferential attitude towards the elders and chiefs. The marginalisation of Melanesians in reserves, the limited extent of 'Westernisation' and a relative lack of *métissage*, all encouraged the survival of this culture. The very isolation and physical marginalisation of Melanesians by colonial authorities helped preserve both that culture and the grievances of those who felt that no account of it had been taken by the French.

The demands of contestatory groups in New Caledonia in the 1970s and 1980s consequently included not only return of land, political self-determination and changes in the economy, but a recognition of Melanesian culture and identity. One of the most important expressions of Melanesian identity in New Caledonia came with the 'Melanesia 2000' festival, organised in 1975 by Jean-Marie Tjibaou, future leader of the FLNKS. The participating artists presented Melanesian culture to a wider audience, and the festival sparked new cultural efforts, including writings by Tjibaou on Melanesian identity. A Melanesian priest, Apollinaire Anova-Ataba, authored a study of the 1878 revolt which remains one of the most important pieces of Melanesian writing and proclaimed the rebel chief, Ataï, a hero for contemporary fighters for independence. The independence party LKS promoted research into Melanesian culture, and such political activists as Déwé Gorodey published poetry in which cultural identity and political struggle were linked. The *écoles populaires kanak*, set up by the independence movement as alternatives to the French state education system, taught Melanesian languages and traditional values. Films and publications concerning the independence movement highlighted the particularity of Melanesian culture and the nature of the cultural revival.[47]

The dimensions of this cultural renewal remain uncertain. Many younger Melanesians felt uncomfortable with the acceptance of authority (and the primacy of men over women, elders over the young) which the traditional hierarchy demanded.[48] But certain elements of Melanesian behaviour — such as political decision-making by consensus rather than by majority vote — have been retained in contemporary activities. Melanesian political gatherings are still symbolically marked by the ritual 'custom' exchange of gifts. At the same time, most Melanesians did not reject the French language, Christian religion or European cultural heritage, and even the most ardent independence leaders affirmed that these would have a place in a future sovereign state of 'Kanaky.'

CULTURE, SOCIETY AND POLITICS

The difference between the DOM-TOMs and metropolitan France is particularly evident in the ethnic background of most of the overseas residents in comparison to the majority of their compatriots in the *métropole*. Attempts to make them into carbon-copies of Frenchmen — or, in the case of the Melanesians, to marginalise them until they disappeared — did not succeed.[49] The cultures of the Melanesians, Polynesians and Mahorais (as well as those of smaller groups, such as the various Indian populations of Guyane) have survived the imposition of French language, religion and culture. More recent migrations, such as that of the Hmongs to Guyane and Vietnamese and Wallisians to New Caledonia, merely emphasised diversity. The educational system imported from Europe was unsuccessful in eradicating the differences between the white and the non-white French populations. In the *vieilles colonies*, an authentic, unique and especially vibrant culture emerged from the mixture of Europe and Africa, but it took Creole culture several generations to define itself and win recognition from the *métropole*, and the advocates of *créolité* admit that it is still a culture in germination. Polynesian and especially Melanesian culture never acquired even the limited 'respectability' of Creole culture; even hotels in New Caledonia generally provide Polynesian music and dance entertainment. Yet Pacific islanders have never needed to search for the identity that has eluded the black Caribbean population. The exact place of these peripheral cultures, whether as folklore, legitimate regional cultures, or bases for nationalism, remains to be fully defined. But the reactions to imposed and imported French culture, and attempts to revive or create a new one inspired by ancestral roots, have been powerful ingredients in most expressions of recent political sentiment. The *prise de conscience* in the DOM-TOMs has been, at least in part, a cultural one.

Culture in the DOM-TOMs, for many, provided a reason for continued attachment and even increased ties to France. Cultural differences do not necessarily imply independence, as proved by the cases of Mayotte and Wallis. But in the Antilles, New Caledonia and French Polynesia, cultural differences have provided a peg on which to hang demands for autonomy, self-determination and independence. Culture has been a key vector for the transmission of French 'civilisation' to the colonies and the *francisation* of diverse groups from different backgrounds. But the older cultures which have been preserved, and the new ones which have been created, have sometimes also turned against the assimilationism, centralism and 'cultural imperialism' of France.

7

The Shape of Politics
in the DOM-TOMs

THE INSTITUTIONS of the French Republic provide the basic
structure for politics in the *outre-mer* but allow a flexible application of constitutional and administrative provisions and a large area
of manoeuvre for ideologies, parties and individuals. The system, however, does not always function straightforwardly in practice. What
William Miles and Maurice Satineau call the 'paradox' of politics in the
DOM-TOMs is that the structure designed for the *métropole* does not
necessarily match the realities of the overseas *départements* and territories, which have a different cultural, political, economic and social
structure from that of European France. Alain Miroite even speaks of a
'dysfunction' of metropolitan political models in the *outre-mer*. Politics
in the DOM-TOMs has different contours from those of the *métropole*:
usually greater degrees of abstention in voting, a marked clientelism
and personal control of politics, compromises between local elites and
the centralised state, and a strong influence for numerically marginal
parties. Furthermore, the small size of the DOM-TOMs, rather than
simplifying politics, creates fragmentation of parties and ideological
cleavages, and the different levels of political authority (municipal,
departmental and regional, or territorial) fosters competition for leverage among politicians and parties.[1]
   Politics in the DOM-TOMs is often analysed solely in terms of asym-
metrical relations between a dominant centre, the *métropole*, and a
subjected periphery, the overseas *départements* and territories.[2] Such an

approach takes account of the great power Paris wields over the DOM-TOMs, but it fails to understand the 'domestic' political factors inside each DOM or TOM, which are often immensely complex. Nor does it consider the quite significant latitudes for the leaders of the DOM-TOMs to collaborate with, resist or manipulate politicians at the 'centre'. In short, seeing political relations between Paris and the DOM-TOMs merely in terms of colonialism or neo-colonialism leads to a mistaken perception of political realities. Questions on the nature of links between the DOM or TOM and metropolitan France are rarely absent in political debates, and the issue of the precise statute for each DOM and TOM — *départementalisation*, greater autonomy, independence or some other option — is never far removed from discussion. However, politics in the French *outre-mer* is not simply a matter of whether each territory should or should not accede to independence. Even if almost every round of voting becomes, at least indirectly, a mini-referendum, a plebiscite on continued attachment to France,[3] politics in the DOM-TOMs is more complicated than this single proposition.

Because of the constitutional and institutional variations between DOMs, TOMs and *collectivités territoriales*, each of the entities has its own history, social structure and set of political particularities. Furthermore, political scientists have rarely studied the politics of the DOM-TOMs; much of the available literature is made up of partisan (and often polemical) statements and memoirs by actors in the political contests themselves. Only New Caledonia and the Antilles have received significant attention; conclusions about the Antilles are often applicable to the other DOM-TOMs, but, as recent events in New Caledonia have shown, politics in both short-term and medium-range can take on a special cast depending on the context and the moment.[4]

TRAITS OF POLITICAL LIFE

One of the most obvious characteristics of DOM-TOM politics is the high level of abstention in elections. Seldom do fewer than 20 per cent of the electorate abstain, and in many national elections 40–50 per cent or more of the voters do not cast a ballot. In Martinique, in the 1981 presidential elections, 52 per cent of the electorate abstained in the first round of voting and 45 per cent in the second round; in the first round of the legislative elections in the same year, 64 per cent abstained, followed by 54 per cent in the second round. These proportions resemble those in the other DOMs, if not the TOMs: in the second round of voting in the 1981 legislative elections, 48 per cent of the DOMs' electorate did not cast a ballot; by contrast, only 25 per cent of the electors in the *métropole* did not go to the polls in the parliamentary elections, and only 16 per cent did not vote in the presidential second-round balloting.[5]

The reasons for such high levels of abstention are multiple. With the large-scale migration of around 300,000 people from the DOMs to the *métropole*, many voters remain registered in the overseas *départements*. Without changing their electoral residence, they are ineligible to cast ballots in the *métropole* and do not bother to vote by proxy in the DOMs. This percentage of the electorate has been estimated at 5–10 per cent but may well be much higher. Rather more importantly, a certain proportion of eligible voters in any society in which voting is not compulsory do not cast ballots; perhaps half of those who abstain in the DOM, a proportion that is equivalent to the abstention rate in the *métropole*, fall into this category.[6]

Specific reasons for abstention also exist in the DOM-TOMs. On various occasions, political parties call on their supporters to boycott elections. Typically, far left-wing and pro-independence parties in the *vieilles colonies* boycott balloting. In the French Antilles, such groups as the Parti Communiste Martiniquais, the Groupe Révolution Socialiste, the Union Populaire pour la Libération de la Guadeloupe and the Mouvement Indépendantiste Martiniquais have sometimes (but not in all elections) refused to participate in the balloting, which they claim is part of the colonial system they oppose. In New Caledonia, the call of the Front de Libération Nationale Kanake et Socialiste to boycott the election for the presidency and the parliament in 1988 meant that some 40 per cent of the voting population, four-fifths of the Melanesian electors, did not participate in the election.[7]

Abstention should not be interpreted, however, as always expressing radical or pro-independence sentiment. It often indicates only apathy, or *anomie*, a feeling of powerlessness or a view that elections are irrelevant. Voters thousands of kilometres from Paris may be less than enthusiastic to turn up to voting booths to elect representatives to a distant parliament, especially when the popular vote and the voice of those representatives may be drowned in the masses of the *métropole*. Electors in the DOMs have the right to vote for *députés* to the European Parliament, but this, too, may seem of less than immediate concern (despite the impact of European Community decisions on the DOMs) and the abstention rate is invariably higher. The higher voter turnout in local elections, especially communal elections, confirms this interpretation. Similarly, a high participation rate in some elections in New

Caledonia shows that voters are willing to turn out when crucial matters are at stake.[8]

The DOMs have a high level of unemployment and underemployment, estimated at as much as 40 per cent of the work force; the unemployed are less likely to vote than those with jobs. In the TOMs (with the exception of Saint-Pierre and Miquelon) a significant number of residents live on the margins of the Europeanised economy and political system. Except in New Caledonia, these electors may feel less than a pressing urge to participate in polling, even as a vote of protest. They leave political matters to the more urbanised, integrated parts of the population. The population of the DOM-TOMs is very young, and in the Antilles especially this group is little politicised and thus apt to abstain.[9] In the DOMs, historical circumstances partially explain levels of abstention. The major aim of the black population in the DOMs in the nineteenth century was the abolition of slavery, not the right to vote; the two were granted at the same time in 1848, though women could not vote, but this degree of freedom did not automatically politicise the black populations.[10] Abstention may even represent a kind of twentieth-century *marronnage*, a flight from European society and its institutions first practised by runaway slaves.[11]

A second trait of electoral politics in the DOMs and, to a lesser extent, in the TOMs, is *légitimisme*, the tendency to vote for incumbent candidates. This may symbolise an acceptance of the legitimacy of the institutions and personalities holding power, a wish for continuity and confidence in the familiar.[12] It may also result from a certain sense of security which the *métropole* and its institutions represent by comparison with neighbouring (or unknown) political systems. Most leading politicians in the DOM-TOMs are mayors of prominent municipalities. *Légitimisme* has contributed to the longevity of such DOM-TOM political leaders as Aimé Césaire in Martinique, Michel Debré in Réunion, Jacques Lafleur in New Caledonia and Gaston Flosse in French Polynesia, in spite of the great ideological differences among them. For anti-independence groups in the DOM-TOMs, voting for the conservative political candidates of the Gaullist and centrist parties has meant that the respective DOM or TOM would not be forced into unwilling independence; votes for conservative candidates in national elections — though not necessarily in local ones — from 1946 to 1988 were indications of support for continued attachment of the DOM-TOMs to France. This explains the opposition to the Socialist candidate François Mitterrand throughout the DOM-TOMs (other than Saint-Pierre and Miquelon) in the 1981 presidential election. The Parti Socialiste was widely seen, and exaggeratedly portrayed by its opponents, as favouring the 'abandonment' of the DOM-TOMs and the

financial benefits which accompanied French administration.[13] However, the increased support for the Socialists in the legislative elections
of 1986 and the presidential and legislative elections of 1988 showed
that these fears had not been warranted. The *décentralisation* of 1982
was seen to have benefited the DOMs, as had the increase in social
services during the Mitterrand presidency.[14] Mitterrand, and his Parti
Socialiste, had thus earned legitimacy in the eyes of the electors, so a
vote for the Socialists and their supporters (such as Césaire's Parti
Populaire Martiniquais) was now also considered one in favour of
stability, continuity and republican legitimacy.

The influence of the media on the perception of political parties,
policies and candidates in the French *outre-mer*, as in the *métropole*, is
considerable. Moreover there is a virtual monopoly of press information in several of the DOM-TOMs. The only daily newspaper in
Martinique and Guadeloupe is *France-Antilles*, which belongs to the
powerful chain of newspapers controlled by the conservative press
magnate and political figure Robert Hersant; *France-Antilles* consistently supports conservative political candidates, and the paper refuses
to hide its sympathies behind 'objective' journalism. Critics have
charged that *France-Antilles* gives little coverage to opposition parties
and has violated restrictions on partisan coverage in the period from the
official close of campaigning to the actual elections. Similarly, in
Mayotte the only regular newspaper, the weekly *Journal de Mayotte*, is
an ardent advocate of *départementalisation* and favourable to the
right-wing and centre. Réunion has two daily newspapers, the *Journal
de l'Ile de la Réunion*, which has conservative sentiments, but also
Témoignages, published by the Parti Communiste Réunionnais. French
Polynesia is dominated by a conservative daily, *La Dépêche*, generally
favourable to the RPR-affiliated Gaston Flosse. In New Caledonia, the
only daily, *Les Nouvelles Calédoniennes*, makes no pretence to objec-
tivity. The paper is opposed to independence and the position of the
FLNKS; especially since 1984, its often violently polemical tone has
been judged by critics as a campaign of disinformation. In French
Polynesia and New Caledonia, repeated efforts to establish opposition
daily newspapers failed because of boycotts (sometimes under pressure)
by local advertisers. Opposition periodicals exist throughout the DOM-
TOMs, but with some exceptions (such as *Antilla* in the Antilles, and
the Front National's *L'Objectif* or the Union Calédonienne's *L'Avenir*
in New Caledonia) they appear only infrequently or irregularly and
have small circulations.[15]

The electronic media have also enjoyed a monopolistic position.
Until the liberalisation of the 'audio-visual landscape' in France in
the early 1980s, all radio and television stations were government

controlled. The only television station in the DOM-TOMs, FR-3 (now called Radio Télévision Française Outre-mer — RFO), presented programmes and points of view sent from Paris. Very little local content was included (although this had begun to change), and political coverage favoured the party in power in Paris and its supporters in the DOM-TOMs. Private radio stations operated illegally as 'pirate' stations, then after the Mitterrand reforms, as legally approved channels, though they generally lacked the transmission powers and staffing of RFO. Liberalisation also meant access for conservative groups to the airwaves. In New Caledonia, for instance, in addition to the state radio stations, there now exists an alternative station close to the local conservatives, Radio Rythme Bleu, as well as a pro-independence FLNKS-affiliated station, Radio Djiido, whose wavelengths have at times been jammed by conservatives, and whose programmes are ignored in the press. However, until the 1980s, such a spectrum of broadcasting options was unknown in the DOM-TOMs.

The government has also used its power of pork-barrelling to influence elections in the DOM-TOMs. Just before polling, France can release huge credits or speed up the delivery of social security payments; this happened in the Antilles just before the 1981 presidential balloting, when payments which had sometimes been blocked for years suddenly arrived in voters' letter boxes. French governments have also courted favour among both political figures and their electorates. For instance, in the 1970s, the government created communes in the former Inini territory of Guyane and wooed notables. In the commune of Papahiston, the building of a town hall and a *gendarmerie* increased the prestige of the state and the local Boni chieftain, who received an invitation to Paris to meet President Georges Pompidou. The Boni chief subsequently changed the name of his commune to 'Pompidouville' and ensured the loyalty of his voters to the Gaullist party.[16] Pre-election times have also been opportune for the announcement of new projects for socio-economic development, often by politicians flying in from Paris to campaign for their parties' candidates.[17] Political parties (particularly in New Caledonia) have been charged with coercing voters, making outright gifts or payments for votes or threatening those who violate boycotts. In 1984, for instance, figures associated with the FLNKS captured and destroyed ballot boxes and tried to keep voters out of polling stations. In the Antilles and in French Polynesia, fraud has been widely rumoured, and several DOM-TOM elections have been annulled because of fraud. Fraud seems less prevalent now than in the 1950s and 1960s, when charges of double-voting, stuffing of ballot-boxes and falsification of results were numerous.[18]

The government has also acted against dissident political figures.

A 1960 law made it possible for the *préfet* of a DOM to expel *fonction-naires* whose political opinions or statements were considered incompatible with their job. The law, not repealed until 1975, allowed the expulsion of a number of left-wing and pro-independence political figures. A nineteenth-century statute on 'foreigners' was even unearthed to expel the Martiniquais writer and public figure Edouard Glissant from Guadeloupe in the 1970s. In the 1950s the dissidents Pouvana'a a Oopa in French Polynesia and Maurice Lenormand in New Caledonia were arrested on trumped-up charges of terrorism. Pouvana'a was deported to France and kept under virtual house-arrest for a decade. More recently pro-independence politicians have been arrested, such as the late deputy leader of the FLNKS, Yeiwene Yeiwene, and the prominent Guadeloupean radical Luc Reinette. A leading figure in the FLNKS, Eloi Machoro, was killed by French *gendarmes* in a shoot-out in 1985; much controversy surrounded the government's claim that the attack on pro-independence rebels was in self-defence. Unsuccessful attempts were also made in 1985 to 'deport' five members of the extreme right-wing Front Calédonien to France. In the Antilles, the government outlawed the Alliance Révolutionnaire Caraïbe, which advocated violent overthrow of the French government in the Caribbean DOMs, and various other pro-independence groups have been harassed.[19]

Extraparliamentary groups also play a role in DOM-TOM politics. Such quasi-official organisations as Chambers of Commerce, which group together entrepreneurs and other notables, may exert influence on public opinion and generally support centrist and conservative parties. By contrast, labour unions often, but certainly not always, contest the established order, and dissident unions have spearheaded autonomist and pro-independence movements in several of the DOM-TOMs. In particular, the Union des Travailleurs Agricoles in Guadeloupe has been in the forefront of political activism in that *département*, and the Union Syndicale des Travailleurs Kanaks et Exploités was part of the pro-independence FLNKS coalition in New Caledonia until late in 1989. Similarly, the Protestant churches of New Caledonia and French Polynesia — which count half of the Melanesians and two-thirds of the Polynesians of these territories among their congregations — have openly criticised the French government, disapproving of nuclear testing in French Polynesia and favouring independence for New Caledonia. By contrast, in Wallis and Futuna the Catholic church has had a powerful and conservative influence on political and economic development.[20] Occasionally, extraparliamentary politics boils over into violent confrontation — and the strikes that have been a constant phenomenon in the post-war history of the

Antilles, the hostage-taking and assassinations that have troubled New Caledonia since the mid-1980s and the riots in Tahiti in 1987 and in Réunion in 1991. Such clashes may promote the demands of rebel groups and ideologies, but may also provoke a reaction against their stances and thus aid in the polarisation of politics.

Finally, there are groups in the DOM-TOMs whose lack of political participation may itself contribute to the results of formal decision-making. Residents of outer islands and the remote interior, including less Westernised populations (such as some of the Amerindians of Guyane) usually play a smaller role in political life than do their compatriots. Some more established ethnic minorities do take part in local politics; these include the Indians of the Antilles and Réunion — where a number of important politicians are the descendants of contract labourers brought from the Indian subcontinent — and the Chinese in Tahiti; others, however, such as the Indonesians and Vietnamese in New Caledonia, are more discreet in their political activities, and still others, notably the Hmongs of Guyane, are almost entirely absent from the political scene. The largest demographic group in the DOM-TOMs, women, has also played only a small role in politics. Despite the activities of several noteworthy women politicians, such as Lucette Michaux-Chevry in Guadeloupe (a former Secretary of State for Francophonie), successful women politicians are the exception rather than the rule. Women's political groups have formed, and all political parties have made an effort to include token women among their leadership; the FLNKS coalition included a tiny women's group until it faded away through inactivity. Although women do indeed vote in large numbers, possibly weighting their vote in favour of centrist and conservative parties, they have not yet found a political voice or identified distinctive issues commensurate with their proportion in the population.

Such characteristics as abstention, *legitimisme* and the absence of women from politics are not unique to the DOM-TOMs, but they are particularly marked there. They give a different tenor to politics in these regions and suggest structures and undercurrents which raw election results, for parties which seem analagous to French counterparts, do not reveal. For some they bespeak outright corruption and coercion, for others a particularistic cast to politics in the French *outre-mer*.

RACE AND CLASS IN POLITICS

Certain forms of political behaviour, and loyalties to individuals and parties, are sometimes connected with race and class. In the *vieilles colonies*, however, class has not been of great importance in politics. Though there are great inequalities of income and status and relatively well-defined bourgeoisies and peasantries are identifiable, a classic factory proletariat does not exist. If classes do exist, they may differ from traditionally defined ones.[21] In Guyane, for instance, there is no proletariat, and the peasantry is becoming extinct. Yet a new pseudo-'class' is emerging, the unemployed. For one observer, Guyanais social structure is polarised between the bureaucracy, 'la caste des bureaucrates', and the others.[22] Yet in general, an absence of class cohesion marks the DOMs.[23] Socialist parties in the nineteenth century and Communist parties in this century have tried to call on class loyalties, or attempted to create class consciousness, but with little success. This results partly from the old notion of political (and cultural) assimilation, which, in theory, held open the benefits of French civilisation to all who strove for it. But it is linked as well to the great individualism of politics, and life in general, in the DOMs. This influences group loyalty but also personal strategies for advancement. As Fred Constant, an Antillais political scientist, concluded: 'people do not want to change society but simply their position in it. The vision for change is much more directed to individual enrichment than towards social development.'[24] The accessibility of social promotion, the benefits of consumer society and progressive *embourgeoisement* of DOM-TOM populations work against militant class loyalties and help account for the weakness of the pro-independence movement in several of the DOM-TOMs. Certainly, the Communist Party is strong in the DOMs (particularly in Guadeloupe and Réunion) but the basis of its power is not its class base or its class analysis; similarly, pro-independence groups draw what support they enjoy from their status as pressure groups rather than from ideological or class identifications with their goals.[25]

Race, at least in the nineteenth and early twentieth century, was a different issue. Descamps suggests that the question of race 'replaced that of class as the means and ends of political acts and conflicts.' Racial antagonism in the pre-emancipation period grew from the hostility of whites to blacks and mixed-race Antillais, Guyanais and Réunionnais. The emerging *métis* class added another element to this bipolar antagonism, and the new racial and political division was made up of the white *Békés*, the *mulâtre* middle class and the black labourers;[26] the *métis* in the Antilles and Réunion became the political class *par excellence*. Racial concerns, which have not disappeared in the DOMs, intermix with economic and cultural situations and the search by many militant intellectuals for a 'national' identity.

Elsewhere in the *outre-mer*, racial questions are also present. In Mayotte, almost all of the population is composed of dark-skinned

Islamic indigenes; however, *métropolitains* have a strong presence in
the technical and administrative elite, a situation which has not caused
problems. Similarly, in Wallis and Futuna, the mass of the population is
Polynesian, and there are also few *métropolitains*. In French Polynesia,
a *métis* Polynesian-European group (which also includes those with
Chinese blood), the *demis*, dominates politics while the pure-blooded
Polynesians remain somewhat peripheral to both political and economic life. Racial questions take on the greatest importance in New
Caledonia, pitting the majority of Melanesians against the European
Caldoches and their Polynesian and Asian supporters. Political div-
isions in New Caledonia often seem to coincide with racial divisions
and the quest for a new statute for the territory and possible indepen-
dence. Racial questions, therefore, add a different texture to DOM-
TOM political life than that of the *métropole*.[27]

POLITICAL PERSONALITIES, PARTIES AND THEIR STRATEGIES

Political loyalties in the DOM-TOMs, in addition to class and race,
include components of ideology, geographical, social and ethnic affiliation and the role of powerful personalities.[28] The power of individuals
is remarkably strong. Constant has emphasised the 'personalisation' of
politics in Martinique, and Rodolphe Alexandre went beyond this to
record the 'shamanism' of politics in Guyane, where ideology is often
subordinated to charismatic leadership.[29] Political scientists concur on
the role of the *'grand personnage'* in DOM politics, whether the strong
metropolitan figure enjoying great local appeal, such as de Gaulle, or
the local politician who wins support himself. The measures of political
decentralisation of 1982, according to Constant, have only increased
the role of these local notables.[30]

The most powerful politician in the *outre-mer* has long been Aimé
Césaire. As a young intellectual in the 1940s, Césaire became one of the
major apostles of *négritude*, and his poems, essays, plays and speeches
have made him a well-respected intellectual figure in the Antilles and
in France. Césaire's oratorical talents are legendary, and he is capable
of mixing Latin quotations, literary allusions and biting wit. *Député* to
the French parliament and mayor of Fort-de-France since 1944, he has
also served on the *Conseil général* and the *Conseil régional*. Césaire was
one of the architects of the *départementalisation* legislation of 1946 in
the Chamber of Deputies. He also founded the Parti Populaire Martiniquais, which has dominated politics in Martinique. Increasingly

disenchanted with *départementalisation*, by the late 1950s he advocated 'autonomy' for Martinique. This remains his official position, although in 1981 and 1988, Césaire supported Mitterrand and the Socialist Party, and after 1981 declared a 'moratorium' on the question of the statute of Martinique. In his seventies, Césaire remains the dominant figure in the French West Indies.[31]

Elsewhere in the Antilles and Guyane, strong political figures have similarly wielded great and lasting influence. Guyanais politics has witnessed a succession of influential and often controversial figures. In the early twentieth century, René Galmont led dissident political movements and demanded greater government concern with the development of the colony — activism which led to his arrest and assassination. His ideological descendant, Joseph Catayée, organised the modern socialist party in Guyane and spoke fervently against *assimilation*. A Martiniquais, he dominated politics in Guyane from the early 1950s to his death, in an aeroplane crash, in 1962.[32] On the other side of the spectrum, the Guyanais Gaston Monnerville sat for twenty years in the French Senate and, as President of the Senate, ranked in the French political hierarchy second only to the President of the Republic.[33] Figures like Victor Sablé held office literally for decades, both as mayors and as representatives in the parliament. The longevity of such leaders is remarkable; in the *Conseil général* of Martinique, the average term of office is fourteen years.[34] The tenure of such local political figures contrasts with the brief tenures of government-appointed *préfets*. Despite their powers, *préfets* can therefore seldom match the political and cultural strength of local figures in the Antilles and Guyane.

In Réunion the dominant figure has been Michel Debré, de Gaulle's former prime minister 'parachuted' into a legislative seat in the 1960s, a post which he held until 1988. In the French parliament, Debré, variously described as a 'Gaullist of the first hour' and the 'Gravedigger of the Fourth Republic', was one of the major and most articulate spokesmen for the retention of ties between France and the DOM-TOMs, and he used his considerable influence among Gaullists to orient DOM-TOM policy and obtain advantages for Réunion. His main opponents in the island — Raymond Vergès, his son Paul, and the other leaders of the Réunionnais Communist Party — have also been noteworthy for their powers to retain control and recruit supporters. Former French prime minister Raymond Barre, who represents Réunion in the parliament, has also wielded power on the local and national scene for many years.[35]

The Pacific TOMs are also replete with powerful figures. In the 1940s, Pouvana'a a Oopa was the first Polynesian politician to attract attention; building on his record as a soldier in the First World War and his talents as a public speaker (in Tahitian), Pouvana'a mobilised Polynesian opinion, as he moved from demands for greater self-government to a position favouring independence. Government harassment of Pouvana'a made him something of a martyr for his supporters, and when he returned to French Polynesia in 1968 after his exile in the *métropole*, the now aged figure was greeted as a hero and elected to the French Senate. His successor in political influence in Tahiti, from the opposite end of the political spectrum, has been Gaston Flosse. The most prominent businessman in Tahiti, Flosse is the long-serving mayor of Pirae, a suburb of Papeete. Flosse's conservative party, Tahoeraa Huiraatira, from the 1960s to the mid-1980s was the dominant group in the Polynesian Territorial Assembly. Flosse served as a *député* in Paris, where he helped draw up the 1984 statue of autonomy for French Polynesia. He headed the new government in Papeete, then became Jacques Chirac's Secretary of State for the South Pacific and a roving French ambassador in the region from 1986 to 1988. Flosse's star fell when a palace coup ousted him from the Tahitian government and the RPR's defeat in national elections deprived him of his ministerial portfolio, but he returned to power in Tahiti in 1991.[36]

New Caledonia has produced a conservative dynasty in the Lafleur family. Henri Lafleur, nickel magnate and importer-exporter, led New Caledonian politics as *député* and mayor of Nouméa in the 1950s; on his death he was succeeded by his son Jacques, head of the RPCR, the local conservative party affiliated with the RPR, and *député* in Paris. Jacques Lafleur has been the head of the anti-independence cause in New Caledonia and was the RPCR signatory to the Matignon Accord of 1988. On the other side of New Caledonian politics, the key figure in the 1950s was Maurice Lenormand, a pharmacist from the *métropole* who moved to Nouméa, where he organised the reformist Union Calédonienne. This party, which grouped together Caldoches and Melanesians to work for progressive self-government and political decentralisation, in the 1950s included a variety of New Caledonian political figures who subsequently dispersed; Henri Lafleur was at one time a member. In 1984, the Union Calédonienne became the major force in the FLNKS coalition under the leadership of Jean-Marie Tjibaou. Tjibaou, a Melanesian scholar and former Catholic priest who was mayor of Hienghène, remained the leader of the pro-independence forces until he was assassinated in 1989. Tjibaou maintained his local tribal position, with support among a wide variety of Melanesians, alongside his institutional position (he served briefly as head of the New Caledonian territorial assembly in the early 1980s) and sometimes seemed to hold the divergent groups in the FLNKS together by the sheer force of his will.[37]

There have also been long-established political personalities in the smaller DOM-TOMs. Saint-Pierre and Miquelon is dominated by Albert Pen, mayor of Saint-Pierre and, at different times, *député* and Senator. Wallis and Futuna's *député* for several decades, until his defeat in 1989, was Benjamin Brial. In Mayotte, politics is almost totally dominated by Senator Marcel Henry and the *député*, Henri Jean-Baptiste (who, is Martiniquais).

Somewhat ironically, however, while DOM-TOM politicians have enjoyed influence in their home regions, they have been unable to, or uninterested in, acquiring power or even taking part in debate on a national level. Their activities in parliament are largely confined to DOM-TOM issues, and none has ever played a significant role in a metropolitan political party. Those politicians from the DOM-TOMs who have held office as ministers, Debré and Barre, did not owe their success or fame to their positions in the DOM-TOMs, while the secretaries of state from the DOM-TOMs have been appointed to essentially minor posts, Gaston Flosse with a portfolio on Pacific affairs, Lucette Michaux-Chevry on Francophonie. The only member of Michel Rocard's government who is from a DOM-TOM is Roger Bambuck, an Antillais former champion athlete who is Secretary of State for Sport.

Several of these politicians have displayed a great ability to bend with the wind. Césaire moved from *départementalisme* to autonomy and has alluded to independence for Martinique; Sablé, Pouvana'a and many of the politicians of the Union Calédonienne changed camps over time. More recently, Michaux-Chevry of Guadeloupe, mayor, *député* and a junior minister, has had a career marked by conversion from socialism to Gaullism. Such metamorphoses indicate the evolution of ideology and the relative situation of the DOM-TOMs in the Republic, the sensitivity of local politicians to changing attitudes among their electorate and the manner in which dominant personalities have been able to swing local support behind their changing ideological positions.

Represented, too, is the succession of different generations in DOM-TOM (and metropolitan) politics.[38] The generation of the 1940s and 1950s was that of the *Résistance*, *départementalisation* and an attachment to French language and culture; by the late 1950s, a new technocratic generation was taking its place, a group preferring greater autonomy to total integration with France.[39] In the 1960s and 1970s a younger group of militants came onto the scene, those who had grown up in a consumer society, and were often influenced by the ideals of the New Left and the 1968 radical movements emanating from French universities. By the 1980s, however, they too seemed somewhat anachronistic or utopian. The new generation, perhaps adhering to Césaire's 1981 call for a moratorium on the independence debate, has favoured working with Paris to accomplish practical goals. However, the ideas and men of the older generation, such as Césaire, have been rejected by some younger and more militant leaders.

The background of political figures is revealing about the role of politics in the DOM-TOMs. Many of the political figures, at least in the DOMs, come from the worlds of academia, the public service or medicine. The phenomenon of intellectuals in politics means that politicians often formulate theories of DOM-TOM politics or culture. Politicians who have written books or academic articles about their regions include Descamps, Bangou, Césaire, Sablé and Tjibaou. These accomplishments often give the writer-politicians added status in their electorates (and certainly beyond), particularly in the Antilles, where great value is placed on education and culture. However, it may also indicate a certain cleavage between the politicians and their electorate, notably in the case of the pro-independence leaders, the majority of whom are young university-trained teachers or *fonctionnaires* who pitch their campaigns at a more working-class or rural audience.[40]

Everywhere in the *outre-mer*, political leaders have consolidated their positions through various strategies. Many combine a local authority power-base, generally as mayor, *conseiller général* or *conseiller régional*, with a position in the French Chamber of Deputies or Senate, and draw on special social or ethnic groups for support — the Caldoches for Lafleur, Melanesians for Tjibaou, the *demis* of Polynesia for Flosse and the *métis* of Martinique for Césaire. Each of the key figures exhibits a special style which appeals to his electorate, symbolised by the different oratorical strengths of Pouvana'a, Césaire and Debré. Each defines an ideological position on the relationship of his DOM or TOM with the *métropole*: anti-independence for Lafleur and Flosse, independence for Tjibaou, *départementalisation* of Mayotte for Jean-Baptiste and Henry, *départementalisation*, then autonomy and finally a moratorium on the question for Césaire. Most politicians have called on their affiliations with national political movements to give them patronage and leverage in Paris. And each has used his powers and relationships to create client relations and dispense benefits.

Less well-known political figures in the DOM-TOMs replicate these general strategies and have used ethnic or geographical foundations to launch their campaigns. For instance, Nidoish Naisseline in New Caledonia has combined his position as high chief of the island of Mare with his French education and the ideological heritage of the 1960s, when he established one of the first radical Melanesian groups, to attain prominence as head of the Libération Kanake Socialiste, a pro-independence group which has remained outside the FLNKS. In Polynesia, Oscar Temaru has used his base as mayor of the commune of Faaa to promote his pro-independence ideas; his electoral base, in fact, does not extend beyond his municipality. In Martinique, the Mouvement Indépendantiste Martiniquais finds a geographical base in the city hall of Rivière-Pilote and the Groupe Révolutionnaire Socialiste in the commune of Ajoupa, just as Césaire's support is concentrated in Fort-de-France. In both Guadeloupe and Réunion, politicians of Indian ancestry have used their ethnic background to recruit support, so much so, in fact, that in Réunion, the Indian population has been accused of 'municipalism' and an effort to dominate communal politics through ethnic voting.[41] In the June 1989 territorial elections in New Caledonia a new party, Union Océanienne, representing Wallisians and Futunans, gained two members in the Assembly, the first time a party representing this minority group had been successful. Despite this trend, however, and the composition of the predominantly Melanesian FLNKS coalition, politics in the DOM-TOMs has not generally been characterised by voting following ethnic lines.

CLIENTELISM

The key element in DOM-TOM politics is probably clientelism: the politics of the pork barrel. An analysis of DOM-TOM politics in terms of clientelism also provides an approach which goes beyond the simplistic, and somewhat worn, ideas of exploitation and oppression of the periphery by the centre; it forms a post-colonial, and a post-anti-colonial, interpretation.

Despite the centralisation of France, local politicians retain significant political and financial powers. More precisely, they can provide employment. With high unemployment in the DOM-TOMs, this power assumes pronounced importance. Furthermore, the expansion of the bureaucracy means that the government has become the major employer; government jobs are highly sought after and, with various salary and other fringe benefits, extremely lucrative. In Fort-de-France, for instance, the municipal government alone, with 4000 jobs, is the major employer in Martinique, hence appointment to most jobs can be made by the mayor and the government. Appointment often becomes either a reward for or an inducement to political support. Municipal employment allows a politician to form and maintain a network of alliances and electoral loyalty. The fact that most such municipal employment is temporary, part-time and non-tenured reinforces the need for job-seekers to be on good terms with their employer, the mayor's administration.[42] On a smaller scale clientelism is just as important at village or commune level.[43]

Clientelism and patronage therefore underpin politics in the DOMs. Indeed, the roots of clientelism lie in the history of the Antilles. In the

1800s and 1900s, the underdevelopment of Antillais economy and society created a need for individuals to secure patrons able to further their interests; those who received benefits paid with personal and political loyalty. This, therefore, was a *clientélisme sur misère* ('a clientelism of servitude').[44]

Justin Daniel recorded a historical compromise, a group trade-off between political and economic power in Martinique that followed *départementalisation* in 1946. In this arrangement, which is

one of the fundamental characteristics of *départementalisation*, a clear choice has been made by the central authorities in collusion with local officials, in favour of a redistribution of resources (subsidies and welfare payments) to the detriment of an (official) redistribution of power.

Political elites in the DOMs received financial and administrative powers delegated by Paris in return for renunciation of sovereignty. The local bourgeoisie in the Antilles, the *bourgeoisie de couleur*, holds the reins of political power, and thus receives the primary benefits of metropolitan transfers, which it passes on to its supporters. In return, it allows the heights of the local economy to be commanded by the old *Békés* (in Martinique) or by metropolitan businesses (in Guadeloupe); and it allows Paris to retain the international prestige and the strategic and other advantages of possessing outposts in the Caribbean. This perspective is widespread even among those with autonomist or pro-independence sentiments. Daniel summarises this argument:

Early on political elites . . . decided upon their strategy: to gain the maximum benefits from belonging to a wider society, by demanding social equality, even at the cost of increased dependence on the centre. Deprived of economic power . . . having political power appeared to this *bourgeoisie de couleur* as the best way of exercising its authority and becoming a political class . . . However incoherent such a strategy might seem it aimed at nothing less than profiting from a system of dependency.

This trade-off or compromise thereby became the foundation for the patron-client political system of the DOM. But it also increased the significance of local office-holding. Administrative positions serve as intermediary links between the centralised power and the local population, but they are also fortresses in themselves, places from which the leaders can resist, manoeuvre or compromise with Paris. Césaire explained in 1977:

For us progressive politicians, for myself as a democrat, for me as a man from a colonised country — because we are in a colonised country — for me who knows that real power is in the hands of the *métropole* and its representatives here, I can only consider local government as a contestatory form of power — a 'counter-power.'[45]

The locus of power in the DOMs, therefore, is the *bourgeoisie de couleur*, which functions as an administrative and political elite.[46] This it does with the tacit collaboration of the central state, using the financial resources put at its disposal by Paris. Finance from Paris is the most critical form of state intervention and because of the role of local officials as intermediaries, these financial flows reinforce their power and prestige. This situation places the notables in a position where they are able to grant favours and form local alliances. Such personalised networks are 'more important than any connection between socio-economic status and illusory political choices' in explaining DOM politics.[47]

Local politics in the Antilles is more complex than merely the manifestation of relations between the centre and the periphery. In case studies of two communes in Martinique, the political elite was based among the *bourgeoisie de couleur*, particularly from the *fonctionnariat* (including teachers), irrespective of ideological orientation. Strong, articulate candidates manoeuvred to gain maximum advantage from the possibilities for political and economic power open to them. On the basis of their personal and client relations — rather than their ideologies — they gain and retain power. There exists little class consciousness, and ideological commitment is trivial in comparison with the need to form these politico-economic alliances. In short, 'candidates are less the representatives of a particular social class than they are key figures in specific social networks.'[48] Politics in Martinique, as elsewhere in the DOM-TOMs, is based on social organisation rather than philosophy or economic relations.[49]

Such a view is consistent with the more evident traits of abstention, *légitimisme*, even pressure and fraud, which can underpin and reinforce clientelism. This does not empty politics of ideological value, but points to particular overlays of political motives in the DOM-TOMs. Even in New Caledonia both pro- and anti-independence groups construct networks of loyalties, and regional, ethnic, religious and personal allegiances come into play. Even if such aspects of politics do not entirely differ from the shape of politics in the *métropole*, the heritage of colonialism and continued economic dependence places them in high relief.

Clientelism also allows for mutual manipulation by politicians and parties in the *métropole* and the *outre-mer*. Paris has the upper hand, but local politicians can also weight the balance. Loyalty to the national party and to the French Republic must be courted, rewarded and sometimes bought.[50] Local politicians with the personal power of a Césaire or a Lafleur, who can choose among various reactions to French initiatives and local disputes, force Paris to beware of them. If Paris wants to retain their support, if France wants to continue to benefit from the advantages of having the DOM-TOMs, it must agree to the social transfers, financial subsidies, cultural recognition or political decentralisation demanded in one or another DOM-TOM. If these demands are at least partially satisfied, criticism and discontent may be quietened and compromises accepted. The lack of greater pro-independence feeling in the DOM-TOMs, and the absence of demands in France for decolonisation of the DOM-TOMs, result from negotiated compromises on political and economic power and the advantages each side gains.

At the administrative level, DOM-TOM politicians can therefore 'use' Paris, but on the political level, it also means that the politicians and parties in the *métropole* and the DOM-TOMs can 'use' each other. DOM-TOM parties give or withhold their support and votes to the various national groups, and in close elections, as is increasingly the case, the *outre-mer* vote can be of considerable electoral importance.[51] The metropolitan parties can also use the DOM-TOMs to their campaigning advantage. New Caledonia is exemplary. The RPR in the 1980s posed as the defender of the interests of the anti-independence loyalists in New Caledonia, the upholder of one-person, one-vote democracy, and the force opposing radical terrorism. The centrists of the UDF, with a more moderate approach, were able to use the New Caledonian issue both to ally with the RPR and to distance themselves from their coalition partner. The Socialists championed the cause of decolonisation within the institutional framework of the Republic and the Parti Socialiste thus seemed, to some, as the supporter of the Melanesian cause. The Communists continued to denounce colonialism. Other parties also make particular claims: the Front National as the defender of the French settlers in danger of being sold out by the mainstream conservatives, the far left as the opponent of a neo-colonial sell-out by the Socialists and the Communists.[52]

Complementing reciprocal manipulation is the permeability of parliamentary and extraparliamentary politics. Extraparliamentary politics takes many of the same forms in the DOM-TOMs as it does elsewhere, including strikes and riots and terrorism. In particular, pro-independence groups enter and leave the institutional system. Several of the pro-independence parties in the Antilles call for abstention in presidential elections, then take part in legislative and local elections. In New Caledonia, the FLNKS boycotted legislative elections in 1984, participated in local elections the following year, boycotted a referendum on independence in 1986, did not take part in presidential and legislative elections in 1988, voted in a nation-wide referendum on

New Caledonia in 1988, and took part in local elections in 1989. Such changes in strategy relate to the perceived significance of elections and possibilities of victory, but also represent an attempt to obtain maximum advantage from the state itself: this, too, is a form of clientelism. Extraparliamentary politics, therefore, enters into this general compromise between the state and political parties, between Paris and the DOM-TOMs.

The exceptionally complex nature of political life in the DOM-TOMs results from the heritage of the colonial era, the institutional framework of the French Republic, and the local sociological and anthropological context of politics. The question of the statutory relations between the DOM or TOM and France is ever-present: independence or continued attachment, and if so, what kind of links? Paris holds the dominant position, and political life in the DOM-TOMs often takes place in reaction to what goes on in the *métropole*, sometimes with a delay, or sometimes even in advance.[53] Possibilities for compromise and accommodation remain broad and numerous.

POLITICAL CURRENTS

The grid of DOM-TOM politics can be read in terms of either the specific political history of each DOM or TOM or common trends in the French *outre-mer*. The latter approach shows the existence of local branches of metropolitan parties or variants and, also, of indigenous political movements. (Conversely, there are no national parties based in the *outre-mer*, such as a national pro-independence party or a DOM-TOM party.) Some metropolitan groups are notable by their absence in the DOM-TOMs; the tiny monarchist groups in France are not represented overseas, although the monarchist Action Française and its newspaper *Aspects de la France* have been among the most ardent champions of Mayotte's remaining in the Republic. Far-right-wing groups are less important in the *outre-mer* than in the *métropole*, with the notable exception of New Caledonia, where they are more important. The anti-independence Caldoches have flocked to the banner of the Front National, and similar parties, in New Caledonia, giving Jean-Marie Le Pen's reactionary and racist party some 20 per cent of the vote in recent New Caledonian elections. The Front National has accused other parties of betraying the white New Caledonians and pronounced itself whole-heartedly in favour of continued ties between New Caledonia and Paris. Such strong support appeals to New Caledonians who feel threatened by Melanesian nationalism, the signing of the Matignon Accord and metropolitan disavowal or lack of interest. Not coincidentally, supporters of the Front National in New Caledonia include a number of *pied-noir* migrants to the Pacific. Elsewhere, however, the Front National lacks strength and encounters opposition; when Le Pen tried to visit Fort-de-France, Martinique, in 1988, protesting airport workers kept his plane from landing.

The conservative Rassemblement pour la République (RPR) party, by contrast, enjoys widespread support in each of the DOM-TOMs through its branches in the DOMs and its affiliated parties in the TOMs, such as the Rassemblement pour la Calédonie dans la République (RPCR) in New Caledonia and the Tahoeraa Huiraatira in French Polynesia. It draws on the genuine popularity of de Gaulle, who made triumphant tours of the French overseas areas in the 1960s, and, among older residents, memories of the Resistance and the 1946 *départementalisation*. The RPR continues to present itself as the defender of Republican legitimacy, parliamentary rule and refusal of Paris to 'abandon' the DOM-TOMs. Between 1986 and 1988 prime minister Jacques Chirac tried to underline its support for the DOM-TOMs by making the overseas frontier a 'priority' of the government, giving increased financial credits, and seeking to establish centralised law and order and eliminate pro-independence groups in New Caledonia.

In uneasy coalition with the RPR has been the centrist party, the Union pour la Démocratie Française (UDF). The UDF has sometimes had difficulty in differentiating its approach to the *outre-mer* from that of the RPR, although it promotes a less heavy-handed and more developmentalist policy. The UDF has won particular support in Mayotte, partly because of local anger at the RPR's failure to fulfil its promise to make the island a *département*, and in Wallis and Futuna, where the UDF existed as the liberal alternative (in the absence of other parties) to the RPR. The personal popularity of Raymond Barre has helped the UDF's cause in his native island of Réunion.

The RPR-UDF alliance (and the conservative-centrist coalitions which preceded it) has been the majority political force in the DOM-TOMs from the 1960s to the 1980s. Election victories in national polls and, less often, in local balloting, renewed RPR control in almost all of the French overseas regions over much of the last three decades.

Socialist parties were established in all of the DOM-TOMs late in the nineteenth century but the Parti Socialiste (PS) has not been so successful in implanting itself as have other groups.[54] The branches of the PS in the Antilles and in the Pacific territories are small and lack influence. The main reason lies in the inability of the Socialists to find political space among the autonomist, pro-independence and Communist movements on the left and the RPR-UDF coalition on the right. The Socialist movement in Guyane has been troubled by ideological conflict and scission.[55] Similarly, in New Caledonia, it has split into pro- and anti-independence groups, amongst others. The Socialists are charged by their opponents with being either too reticent to change neo-colonial ties or too ready to 'abandon' the DOM-TOMs. The lack of support for the PS in the 1981 elections provided proof of the problems facing the Socialists overseas, but the presidency of François Mitterrand inspired much hope among reformist politicians (some of whom subsequently expressed disappointment with the results).[56] New Caledonia was again an exception; conservative voters reacted violently to the Socialist government plan for 'independence in association with France.' The vote registered by the PS in the DOM-TOMs (other than New Caledonia) consequently increased in the 1988 elections. However the Socialists have done markedly better in local elections than at the national level in the DOM-TOMs. Several DOM-TOM politicians have given their support to the PS, although they are not members of the party; notable among them are Césaire in Martinique and Albert Pen in Saint-Pierre and Miquelon.

The Parti Communiste Français (PCF) has been far stronger in some of the DOMs than in metropolitan France, even if it is now non-existent in the Pacific territories and Mayotte. In the years immediately after the Second World War, the PCF benefited from its record in the Resistance and, afterwards, from its opposition to colonialism. Politicians like Aimé Césaire, a party member until 1956, bolstered its influence. The PCF also gave total independence to the Communist parties in the DOM-TOMs, and dealt with them as equals; this allowed members to set their own agendas and wield local authority. In Réunion, especially, the Communist party had great success, often being the biggest vote-getter in elections. The Communist parties were early advocates of autonomy and independence for the DOM-TOMs and support for self-determination has been maintained. The Communist parties also promoted local 'national' identities against the centralising assimilation of Paris, and this too increased their popularity. The Communists have been marginalised in recent French elections, but their strength in several of the DOMs, although also diminished, remains strong.

The Communist parties of the *outre-mer* are similar to the indigenous parties in that they set their policy according to local demands and differ with the national PCF and each other on various positions. Even more particularistic are the parties in the DOM-TOMs which have no official ties with metropolitan groups. The most significant of these is Aimé Césaire's Parti Populaire Martiniquais (PPM), founded in 1956. The PPM espoused many of the social goals of the Socialists and Communists but anchored itself in the island. Since its founding, the party has advocated autonomy for Martinique, although the exact nature of autonomy has been carefully left undefined. Officially, the party sees autonomy as 'une étape vers l'indépendance' ('a step towards independence') but it works firmly within the structures of the Republic. Césaire's support for François Mitterrand in 1981 and 1988, and his declaration of a 'moratorium' on the question of the institutional status of Martinique, according to the party, do not mean abandonment of the goal of independence, but that it is no longer viewed as a priority.

Several other parties in the DOM-TOMs advocate autonomy. In the *territoires d'outre-mer*, autonomy is not a radical position. In French Polynesia, for example, Flosse's Tahoeraa Huiraatira promoted the 1984 autonomy statute. The conservative RPCR in New Caledonia also prefers autonomy, so long as the Caldoches retain the upper hand in political affairs. In Mayotte, a group led by Colonel Bamana advocates autonomy to strengthen ties with France since *départementalisation* does not seem immediately achievable. In the DOMs calls for autonomy had looked more radical in the context of the 1946 and 1958 constitutions. However, since Mitterrand's decentralisation, they seem less so and may be put forward as ways of maintaining peaceful links between the *métropole* and the DOMs rather than steps towards sovereignty.

Perhaps the most vocal political groups in the *outre-mer* have been the pro-independence parties, although in each of the DOM-TOMs, they are a minority. In New Caledonia, support for the pro-independence FLNKS and LKS comes from about a third of the population (although from a substantial majority of the Melanesians). In French Polynesia, up to one-fifth of the electorate have voted for pro-independence parties; in most of the other DOM-TOMs, independence movements attract much less than one-tenth of the electorate. Independence movements do not exist in Wallis and Futuna or Saint-Pierre and Miquelon; in Mayotte, also, there is no independence party, although one party advocates union of the island with the Republic of the Comoros. Furthermore, independence parties are fairly recent groups. Most date from the 1970s, influenced by the ideology of the 1960s and decolonisation of most other European possessions. These groups were highly fragmented among Communist, Trotskyist, Maoist and other influences; some were affiliated with such metropolitan parties as the Trotskyist Ligue Communiste Révolutionnaire. They agreed neither on how independence should be achieved, whether immediately or after a period of transition, nor the means of economic and political transformation, whether at the ballot box or through extra-parliamentary tactics. The clientele for *indépendantiste* parties also varies; several pro-independence parties in the Antilles have support from agricultural workers, while there and elsewhere the leaders are generally young intellectuals. Often they are linked to specific geographic locales or influential political figures.

Despite their lack of success, the pro-independence movements have great importance in DOM-TOM politics. They are the most vocal challengers to French rule and put forward denunciations of French colonialism in the *outre-mer* in part or in whole which even some of their other opponents find hard to reject. They organise demonstrations and publish newspapers and broadsheets, participate in international meetings outside France (and are sometimes charged with collaborating with foreign governments eager to destabilise France) and they have initiated contacts among themselves and organised conferences on the 'dernières colonies françaises' ('the last French colonies').[57] Some of the groups, such as the now outlawed Alliance Révolutionnaire Caraïbe in the Antilles, have resorted to acts of violence and terrorism to promote their message. Less dramatically, they serve as advocates for local grievances, pressure groups for particular interests and thorns in the side of the body politic, constantly reminding leaders of their failure to bring French ideals to fruition.

The most successful of the pro-independence groups has emerged in New Caledonia, the territory where ethnic strife has been most violent and metropolitan neglect most obvious. The first calls for autonomy for New Caledonia came from the Caldoches in the late 1800s; the multiracial Union Calédonienne in the 1950s began to ask for greater self-government, although not then independence or even autonomy. Melanesian nationalism, as a separate force, did not develop until the 1970s, when the first Melanesian political figures began to demand independence. A decade later this became a more concerted pressure for a 'Kanak and socialist' independence in which the future of non-Melanesian residents of the territory seemed uncertain. These calls struck a responsive chord among Melanesians who suffered the heritage of the *réserves* and the *code de l'indigénat* and have been marginalised from economic and political power in New Caledonia. About one-fifth of the Melanesians did not support the independence groups, and very few of the non-Melanesians did so, but the pro-independence groups won majority support from the indigenous inhabitants of the islands. In New Caledonia, therefore, independence has been an ethnic as well as a nationalist struggle in a way that is not possible in the *métissé* populations of Polynesia or the Antilles, Réunion and Guyane.[58] Elsewhere in the DOM-TOMs, these ethnic and racial cleavages are not so great. In the Antilles and in French Polynesia, pro-independence leaders, as well as those opposed to independence, both come from the groups of *métis*, even though the pro-independence groups make claims to represent authentic Creole or Polynesian identities, respectively, rather than colonial French cultures.

Support for political parties is not altogether random, but neither is it entirely predictable.[59] Metropolitan Frenchmen in the DOM-TOMs generally vote for conservative parties; in Guyane, 'the *métropolitain* overseas generally votes in a colonial fashion. When he [*sic*] votes it is simply to affirm "the maintenance of the French presence" in the territory.'[60] Given the large number of public servants and technicians attached to the space centre, such a vote is far from inconsequential in that *département*. Those who have benefited from the presence of France, older residents and those who have moved from one DOM-TOM to another are more likely to vote for parties which promise to maintain the status quo. Other voters choose their allegiances on varied grounds which only a thorough electoral sociology could unravel.

On the surface DOM-TOM politics operates in a similar fashion to politics in the *métropole*, with a spectrum of parties and ideologies, most of which adhere to the practices of parliamentary democracy. Beneath the surface, local conditions restructure politics, add new elements and often decide issues and elections. DOM-TOM politics are no longer simply colonial politics, as they were before 1946, but have evolved into something more than just regional politics within the French state. They are expressions of manoeuvrability on the two levels of local and national considerations (and sometimes on an international level as well) in a situation where *départementalisation*, cultural assimilation and Jacobin centralism were unsuccessful in creating far-flung political clones of European France. The changes of the 1980s, both *décentralisation* granted by France and the rise of more militant local movements based in a search for particularistic cultural and political identities — the word 'nationalism' is not inappropriate — have altered the stakes and the strategies of politics in the *outre-mer*.

8

Towards Independence?

THE WINDS of change that blew through Africa and Asia, sweeping a variety of colonies to independence, did not avoid the French colonies. Yet decolonisation was never a process that France embraced enthusiastically. In protectorates such as Syria and Lebanon, France had little choice but departure. In Indo-China and Algeria, however, only sustained warfare forced it to relinquish its colonies. In sub-Saharan Africa, France's departure was much more like that of Britain. Though it unsuccessfully sought to weld the future independent states into a French commonwealth, the new black African states remained closely tied to France; a neo-colonialist relationship replaced colonialism and the political basis for Francophonie was established.[1] For France decolonisation was virtually over by the early 1960s, yet already there had been demands for independence in the Pacific territories, and elsewhere in the DOM-TOMs the French presence was contested in more muted form. Efforts to transform islanders into Black Frenchmen had been more successful in Réunion and the Caribbean.[2] At that time, few observers believed that small island colonies, such as the present DOM-TOMs or the remaining British colonies, possessed the resources or capabilities for independence.

For the two decades to 1990, France took little interest in further decolonisation. After the 1960s it gave independence only to the Comoros (but not Mayotte), Djibouti (the Afars and Issas) and, most recently and reluctantly to Vanuatu, but it retained close control over its other overseas territories and *départements*. So close was this control that in 1981, despite the movement towards independence of many smaller territories, New Caledonia and French Polynesia even 'seemed likely eventually to become Overseas Departments'.[3] In the joint Condominium of the New Hebrides (Vanuatu), France strongly resisted decolonisation, despite British and local pressure, and fostered opposition and a violent secession movement centred on the island of Espiritu Santo. Even when inevitable, French acceptance of the independence of Vanuatu in 1980 was no more than grudging; shortly beforehand, Paul Dijoud, the Secretary of State for the DOM-TOMS, stated in Noumea:

Since the British government has already advised Parliament that it is prepared to accept this date, the French government will not take the risk of seeing our friends in other Pacific countries imagine, even for a moment, that we do not wish to give the New Hebrides their independence or that we are holding it up ... but I will state clearly that France declines the moral responsibility for what happens in this country and that after Independence we will only be able to regret what happens.[4]

This was a thinly veiled warning that France would not tolerate independence in nearby New Caledonia. The decolonisation of the New Hebrides proved to be the catalyst to strengthening French resolve to retain control of its remaining Pacific territories and dampening nascent independence sentiments elsewhere. There have been few recent suggestions from Paris that the present status of the DOM-TOMs is likely to change.

THE QUEST FOR INDEPENDENCE, 1950–1980

Various groups in what are now the DOM-TOMs, chafing under French centralisation, had called for greater autonomy as early as the nineteenth century. In general, they were privileged settler elites who saw their advantages being eroded by French tariff policy, the emancipation of slaves, male suffrage and the parliamentarianism of the Third Republic. The blacks and *métis* of the Antilles and Réunion favoured closer ties with France to protect themselves against exploitation by the *colons*. In the Pacific colonies, settlers similarly preferred some degree of autonomy while the marginalised indigenous islanders lacked a political tribunal. The early twentieth century saw little change in these positions, and the question of significant autonomy, let alone independence, did not emerge until after the Second World War. The earliest demands for independence came from one of the most unlikely regions, the South Pacific, where the first island state (Western Samoa) did not become independent until 1962. Such calls issued from French Polynesia, even though that territory had little tradition of political discussion and dissent, and the distant archipelagos remained only thinly incorporated into what passed for a national polity. Yet in the immediate post-war years some politicians began to demand greater autonomy for French Polynesia, led by the first prominent Polynesian politician, Pouvana'a a Oopa. A powerful orator and charismatic figure, previously jailed by France and confined during the war to his home island of Huahine, Pouvana'a was elected to the French parliament in 1949. His party, the Rassemblement Démocratique des Populations Tahitiennes (RDPT), won fully 70 per cent of the votes in French Polynesia in elections in 1951, advocating a radical policy to transform the territory into a Tahitian republic. The principal early goals of the RDPT were already familiar calls for greater autonomy, civil rights and equitable treatment for Tahitians, and a decreased number of metropolitan *fonctionnaires*. Over time its programme became more radical and anti-French, as the party demanded that Tahitians replace expatriate bureaucrats, that they take over the local bank and Chinese-run commerce, that Tahitian be the official language and that a Tahitian flag replace the French flag.[5] Most support for Pouvana'a and the RDPT came from rural Tahitians who believed that economic life would be improved since a more autonomous state could by-pass France and sell copra and vanilla directly to the United States, and hence obtain higher prices by cutting out the French middlemen. They also thought that following the replacement of metropolitan officials, local salaries would significantly increase. At the 1958 constitutional referendum, which allowed French colonies to vote on their future status, Pouvana'a campaigned fervently in favour of independence. But factional strife had divided the RDPT, Pouvana'a was denied access to government radio and two-thirds of the electorate voted in favour of remaining with France. By then it had already become apparent that the islands would be economically vulnerable if metropolitan subsidies were to cease after independence. Aided and abetted by French manipulations, this realisation led to the downfall of Pouvana'a and the decline of the independence movement in Polynesia. Pouvana'a, who had been harassed by the French administration throughout the 1950s, was now exiled to France for a decade. At its peak in the early 1950s the independence movement had been much the strongest in the South Pacific but, before any island state in that ocean had become independent, the time had passed for French

Polynesia. Nevertheless, France, which gave full citizenship to the residents of French Polynesia, New Caledonia and Wallis and Futuna, as well as granting them representation in the French parliament, had pursued a form of political integration that no other imperial power in the Pacific (or elsewhere) had attempted.

In the aftermath of the 1958 constitutional referendum a new *indépendantiste* party formed, the local assembly solemnly stated that French Polynesia wanted to 'remain an integral part of the French Republic' and France, having lost its nuclear test sites in the Algerian Sahara, moved the site to Mururoa. John Teariki, the new RDPT member of the French Assembly, strongly opposed the establishment of the Centre d'Expérimentation du Pacifique (CEP) and expressed the first concerns that Tahitians, like the Japanese, would become victims of radioactivity. That opposition was ignored and the RDPT was dissolved by de Gaulle, only to be replaced by a new party, Pupu Here Aia (The Group of Those Who Love the Homeland), established by Teariki.

Expansion of employment and incomes in the era of nuclear testing resulted in the decline of the independence movement in the 1960s. By the early 1970s local concern centred primarily on problems that would follow the possible end of nuclear testing. There was no longer significant interest in independence, and only a minority expressed concern over either the extent of dependence or the impact of nuclear testing.[6] In the mid-1970s, as testing went underground, the mushroom clouds and aerial fallout disappeared along with both local concern and reactions from other Pacific states in the region. For almost a decade local and international opposition was largely silent.

Though the demand for outright independence weakened, there was always a substantial autonomist movement, associated with Pouvana'a and his successors, Francis Sanford, who established the party Ea Api (The New Way), and John Teariki, and which was concentrated in Tahiti and the other Society Islands. Pouvana'a, allowed to return to Tahiti in 1968, Teariki and their associates published a manifesto which began: 'If the present relations between Paris and Tahiti do not improve, Polynesia will not remain French much longer. When will the French government learn something from all its missed opportunities to decolonise?' The central element was even more strongly worded:

Nothing else can be more dangerous in Polynesia, or elsewhere, than to refuse the irresistible march of the colonial peoples towards greater freedom and democracy. The present French government condemns itself by trying to arrest this movement with quickly forgotten promises, legal infringements and threats against our persons. This is a much too fragile dam against the torrent of freedom that will rapidly destroy it and sweep away not only the rotten structures but also those which might have been worth preserving. The French government is keeping control over Polynesia in order to avoid having to undertake unpopular nuclear tests at home, and because these 800,000 square kilometres of oceans surrounding our islands contain enormous mineral resources, coveted by French mining companies. But these desperate efforts will come to nothing.[7]

Sanford sought a referendum on independence. France eventually agreed to a greater degree of autonomy, but this changed relatively little, as France remained in control of defence, foreign affairs and the budget. Nonetheless the new statute undercut the independence movement and the more radical supporters of autonomy. More overtly *indépendantiste* parties did appear, such as Charlie Ching's Taata Tahiti Tiama and Ia Mana Te Nunaa (Power to the People), established in 1975, which was committed to socialism, independence and the end of nuclear tests. Ia Mana Te Nunaa pressed for economic independence as a precursor to political independence and gradually grew in strength. Pouvana'a died early in 1977, Teariki was now old and Sanford frequently ill, and more radical leaders temporarily came to the fore, including Pouvana'a's nephew, Charlie Ching, who was jailed for several years for breaking into a French army depot. Several of his followers, members of the Toto Tupuna (Blood of Our Ancestors), carried out various violent acts, including the bombing of the Papeete telephone exchange and the murder of a French businessman and they, as well as Ching, were jailed. In response to the granting of greater autonomy to French Polynesia in the 1980s, the principal conservative party, Gaston Flosse's Tahoeraa Huiraatira, moved much closer to support for autonomy, stealing the ground from under the feet of Teariki and Sanford, weakening the already fragile autonomist movement and making the divisions between *indépendantistes* and others more acute. In the French national elections of March 1978 pro-independence candidates gained 15 per cent of the vote, and in the 1981 elections that proportion had increased to around 20 per cent, marking the further growth of the independence movement in French Polynesia.

In New Caledonia the emergence of nationalism was contemporaneous with that in French Polynesia. The first significant multiracial party, the Union Calédonienne (UC), was founded in 1951, and its mild reformist policies attracted substantial Melanesian support. The UC, in fact, won majorities in elections to the territorial assembly for almost two decades from 1953 to 1971. However, Melanesian frustrations with the slow pace of reform, racial discrimination, and continued opposition to their aspirations towards greater autonomy eventually produced a radicalisation of politics. Demands for greater autonomy paralleled those in French Polynesia to the extent that in 1968 the two territories sent a joint delegation to Paris which the Minister for the DOM-TOMs simply refused to receive. Roch Pidjot, later to be a prominent supporter of independence, commented that

the demand for autonomy by the Polynesians and ourselves is due to our disgust with the ill-will and stupidity of a colonial administration attached to a mandarinate which dates from the age of sailing ships and kerosene lamps. The Polynesians, like the Melanesians, feel immensely frustrated. Neither of us wants independence, which is too often illusory, but a new contractual relationship which will give us full internal autonomy.[8]

Continued rejection of demands for autonomy pushed the UC in a direction that ultimately led to a demand for independence.

Radicalism emerged at the end of the 1960s, stimulated by the transformation of the economy and unionisation in the nickel boom, regional echoes of the student and worker demonstrations in France in 1968 and, eventually, disappointment with the limited achievements of UC reformism. There were two important elements in the growth of radical nationalism: the attempt to rediscover and assert Melanesian identity and culture, symbolised in the restoration of the hitherto derogatory word 'Kanak', and the pressure for land rights. Confrontations between militant Melanesians (Kanaks) and the administration focused on land rights, and a number of wholly Melanesian parties broke away from the UC or were created spontaneously. Consensus dissolved as new Melanesian parties sprang up, based on regional and religious differences rather than on ideological issues. To prevent further fission the UC itself became more radical, resulting in the loss of most of its European support. Melanesian attitudes gradually became more radical. The first demand for independence came in 1975 from Yann Celene Uregei, who had already broken with the UC, but the more radical Parti de Libération Kanake (PALIKA), founded in 1976, soon afterwards sought a 'Cuban-style socialist society' and 'Kanak independence'. In opposition to the emergence of more radical Melanesian parties, the fragmented conservative parties consolidated into the Rassemblement pour la Calédonie dans la République (RPCR), a primarily European party, and New Caledonian politics gradually polarised.[9] By the end of the 1970s each of the predominantly Melanesian parties had come out in support of independence.

Land issues dominated politics and emphasised divisions between the European settlers (Caldoches) and Melanesians, who had not been legally allowed to move from reservations until after the Second World War. Kanaks pointed out that Melanesians still owned little property, the economy was totally controlled by European interests, and Melanesians were absent from the economic, political and cultural elite: the first Melanesian to be awarded a high school diploma graduated in the 1960s. In many Melanesian reservations land pressures were aggravated by natural increase and return migration which limited the potential of cash cropping and cattle ranching and stimulated demands for land reform. Though the speed of restoring land to Melanesians increased in the 1960s and 1970s, it was still far short of Melanesian expectations and needs. In the second half of the decade, Melanesians mounted direct action to regain land by occupations. Increased amounts of land were purchased by the government and returned to Melanesians, but invariably too little and too late to defuse tension and political pressure. Indeed Melanesians had no more land per capita in 1980 than at the start of the century.[10] By then demands for greater autonomy and land rights had given way to calls for independence. Land issues were symbol and substance in the struggle for independence, and slogans stressed the continuity of the contemporary struggle with that of the 1878 revolt and century-long Melanesian resistance to French colonialism.

French plans for economic reform remained inadequate, belated and a source of further division between Melanesians and Europeans, who feared they would lose land, privileges and subsidised wages and services. Asians and Polynesians, whose employment seemed to depend on the French presence, supported the status quo. The population composition of New Caledonia ensured that as long as Europeans voted for retention of ties with France, and gained support from the Asian and Polynesian electorate, Kanak demands for independence could not to be satisfied through the ballot box. Despite amalgamation of pro-independence parties into a loose Front Indépendantiste coalition for the 1979 territorial election, the pro-independence vote reached only 34 per cent. Kanak electoral frustrations led to more direct action and there occurred confrontations between militant nationalists and extremist right-wing groups antagonised by Kanak radicalism.

Outside the two largest Pacific territories demands for independence have been less strident and opposition to France has taken quite different forms. In Wallis and Futuna and Saint-Pierre and Miquelon, such demands have been wholly absent. In the Caribbean and Réunion, only a tiny minority have ever voted for independence, in part because of 'an attitudinal framework emphasising security-mindedness and materialism, and the lack of a visible and charismatic pro-independence leader'.[11] However, contestatory groups have regularly sought greater autonomy. In the Antilles such demands found stimulation from the ideology of Frantz Fanon and Aimé Césaire. Though time and power have tarnished the idealism of Césaire, more recent West Indian writers like Edouard Glissant have continued to emphasise issues of culture and identity, and in both Guadeloupe[12] and Martinique cultural issues have strongly influenced attitudes to the political relationship with France.

Various violent events in the Antilles, including the killing of striking workers at Le Carbet (Martinique) in 1948, Moule (Guadeloupe) in 1952 and Le Lamentin (Martinique) in 1961, emphasised the discontent in the Caribbean and the strong-arm response of the French state. Radical movements later sought part of their legitimacy in this repression.[13] From about 1956 criticism of *départementalisation* began to appear in the Communist press, becoming a constant theme in the politics of the *vieilles colonies*. It was most strongly embodied in the establishment of the Parti Progressiste Martiniquais (PPM) in 1958.[14] Other autonomist parties, the Parti Communiste Martiniquais (the rump of the French Communist Party) and the Parti Socialiste Martiniquais, subsequently aligned themselves with the PPM. The basic position of the PPM was well expressed in its journal, *Le Progressiste*, in 1977:

An increasingly clear national consciousness has asserted itself in recent times, and it is an article of faith for the most enlightened amongst us that the Martinican people with its territory, its ethnic and cultural particularity, its distinctive language (Creole), its specific economic, social and cultural problems, constitutes a distinctive human society: a specific nation. Martinican society, the nation of Martinique, cannot be confused with any other nation whatsoever. Martinicans are neither Europeans, Africans nor Asians, but something distinctive. It is therefore essential that this distinctive national entity should be organised, planned and directed in accordance with lines chosen by itself. It is essential that Martinican affairs be run democratically, that is by Martinicans elected by the Martinican people and responsible to it. This demand is healthy and natural. Indeed, what would be the reaction of the people of the Gironde, of Brittany, Lorraine and Corsica if the direction of the economic, administrative and cultural affairs of their regions was entrusted to Martinicans or Guadeloupeans?[15]

Cultural identity was thus explicitly linked to nationalism. Throughout its existence the PPM has sought greater self-determination for Martinique and in the 1970s, as we have seen, characterised autonomy as a 'step towards independence'. However, it carefully distanced itself from positions advocating any significant change in French sovereignty over Martinique and only elliptically and theoretically did Césaire entertain the notion of an independent Martinique.[16] More typically he stated in 1971 that

France has been in this island for three centuries and that is not negligible. Nobody denies it: extremely strong cultural and sentimental links, incontestable links, have been forged and all the reasons I have just invoked clearly indicate, therefore, that there is no question of the French West Indies and of Martinique in particular breaking the links that bind them to France.[17]

Independence was regarded as so distant and so improbable that some form of continued association with France could be the only realistic policy.

In Guadeloupe the powerful Parti Communiste Guadeloupéen (PCG) filled a similar role to that of the PPM in Martinique, distinguishing itself from the French Communist Party, pressing for greater autonomy, and giving no support to independence. In thinly populated Guyane, there was a weaker demand for autonomy, a function of its more limited social and economic development. Even this limited pressure largely faded when Justin Catayée, leader of the Parti Socialiste Guyanais, who had argued that departmental status was worse than being in a prison colony, was killed in a plane crash in 1962.[18] In Réunion the first emphasis on autonomy came from the Parti Communiste Réunnionnais (PCR), led by Paul Vergès, which in 1959 reversed its support for *départementalisation* and separated itself from the PCF. Broadly the PCR's support for autonomy was similar in principle and practice to the PPM's in Martinique: opposition to the perceived exploitation and insensitivity of the sugar planters and to the links between the planters and the bureaucracy, and reaction to the lack of understanding of Creole values and susceptibilities. The PCR constantly distinguished between autonomy and independence, recognising that the economic link with France ensured that independence was not feasible. Wilfred Bertile's small Parti Socialiste Réunionnais also sought greater autonomy but, despite some pressure on France, support for *départementalisation* was too powerful to be successfully challenged.[19]

The first pro-independence group emerged in the Antilles in 1959 in the wake of Castro's revolution in Cuba, the Algerian war and the steady progress of global decolonisation. In Martinique an Organisation de la Jeunesse Anti-Colonialiste Martiniquaise was established and in Guadeloupe there was the Groupe d'Organisation Nationale de la Guadeloupe (GONG). Both were Marxist organisations seeking local revolutions; harried by the authorities they dissolved after internal dissent within a few years. In France, the Association Génerale des Etudiants Guadeloupéens (AGEG) formed in 1963, and the Association Génerale des Etudiants Martiniquais (AGEM) set up in 1967; also radicalised by events in Indo-China and Algeria, and by earlier revolutions in China and Cuba, they began to press for independence at home.[20] Throughout the Antilles pro-independence parties have been strongly left-wing. In Martinique in the 1970s the principal independence party, and the only well-organised one, was the Trotskyist Groupe Révolution Socialiste which had links to a similar group in Guadeloupe. Primarily supported by young middle-class intellectuals, it enjoyed limited though not negligible working-class support. A second Trotskyist group, Combat Ouvrier, founded in the mid-1960s and established in both Martinique and Guadeloupe, had less support and was more concerned with internecine disputes rather than promoting a revolutionary struggle for independence.[21] For these and other even smaller groups, independence without socialism was inconceivable.

The most vocal of the legal pro-independence parties has been the Mouvement Indépendantiste Martiniquais (MIM), founded in 1972 by a teacher, Alfred Marie-Jeanne, later the mayor of Rivière-Pilote, and which was originally known as La Parole au Peuple; it rejected both the Marxist analysis of the Trotskyists and the 'neo-colonialism' and 'reformism' of the autonomists, and boycotted French presidential and legislative elections in the 1970s. The MIM argued that both Martinique and Guadeloupe were separate nations, whereas the Trotskyists conceived a single Martinique-Guadeloupe nation. Though Miles has suggested that the MIM policy 'demonstrates that logical purity may result in political self-denial',[22] its support has been so small that political recognition could never have been probable. Nonetheless its intransigence to all other parties and its absolute and sole demand for unconditional independence, though preceded by autonomy, marginalised and eroded the movement into inconsequence.

The principal pro-independence party in Guadeloupe, the Union Populaire pour la Libération de la Guadeloupe (UPLG), was founded in 1978 tracing its descent from GONG; it found support from trade unionists engaged in agriculture and education and *fonctionnaires*. Most of the radical unions which supported UPLG had themselves formed in the early 1970s.[23] The UPLG denounced assimilation, emphasised the role of Creole (which was introduced to school curricula in 1983) and called for abstentions in French elections. From 1970 a series of land occupations was carried out, under the direction of the Union des Travailleurs Agricoles (UTA) and the Union des Paysans

Pauvres de Guadeloupe (UPG) and supported by the UPLG, especially around Sainte-Rose, but in a range of areas on the north coast. Some 645 acres was occupied, about one-third of which was planted in sugar, some retained for grazing and other areas used for market gardening. Despite this support for direct action, the UPLG had still to define a practical and theoretical programme in 1981, though, as elsewhere, it argued that economic restructuring should precede independence.[24]

The first small independence party appeared in Guyane in 1974: the Mouvement Guyanais pour la Décolonisation (MOGUYDE), strongly supported by the Union des Travailleurs Guyanais (UTG). In the same year two new left-wing journals, *Jeunes Gardes* and *Caouca*, also emerged.[25] Amongst the Boni people, on the banks of the Maroni river, a Mouvement de Libération Boni was established in 1976, and fared well in local elections. In 1980 and 1981 a number of pro-independence activists, mainly associated with the pro-independence Front National de Libération Guyanais (FNLG), were arrested after bombings in Kourou and Cayenne. The principal pro-independence party was the Marxist Unité Guyanaise. However, despite the existence of other small radical groups, overall support for independence was even less than in the Antilles, and the structure of a post-independence Guyane was barely considered.

In Réunion equally tiny and radical groups also sought independence. In the 1970s the Maoist Organisation Communiste Marxiste-Léniniste de la Réunion (OCMLR) and Georges Sinamalé's small Jeunesse Marxiste, argued strongly for independence, gaining a much wider audience in radical African circles than they could gain within Réunion, but ensuring that there was occasional debate on the idea of independence, rather than more vague discussions on the structure of autonomy. However, since the PCR was in favour of nationalisation of the sugar industry, large-scale land reforms, full employment and Réunionnais control of the economy,[26] its programme was substantially more radical than autonomist parties in the Antilles, leaving little distinct ground for the *indépendantistes*. Consequently for an island of its population size, Réunion has been the least troubled by demands for independence.

From time to time, in each of the *vieilles colonies* and in French Polynesia, *indépendantistes* have been elected to positions of power, for example, as mayors in some small towns. In the Martinique municipal elections of 1977 *indépendantistes* gained 9 per cent of the vote and two *indépendantiste* mayors were elected, though both fought on local issues. In the small town of Rivière-Pilote, Alfred Marie-Jeanne, the leader of the strident MIM, was elected mayor in 1981, though 87 per cent of the urban population voted for Giscard as president. Beyond local elections, however, candidates supporting independence have fared badly; in Martinique in 1978 and 1981 the two proponents of independence in the legislative elections scored 1.9 per cent and 1.5 per cent of the total vote.[27] *Indépendantistes* thus have fared well electorally only when independence was not an issue. Only in New Caledonia was the situation different: there *indépendantistes* consistently won seats at all levels, and in all institutions, though pressure for independence was not always the sole or even the most important election issue.[28] In the presence of a conservative government in France, the independence movement outside New Caledonia failed to gain significant converts in the 1970s, despite the growing conservatism of established autonomist parties, such as the PPM, whose emphasis shifted from nationalism to more pragmatic support for such economic goals as agricultural diversification, small industry development and increases in the minimum wage. Even in an era of global radicalism, many of the tiny parties sank into oblivion. However, the inauguration of a Socialist government in France in 1981 appeared to offer some prospects of significant political evolution, including changes in the status and statutes of the DOM-TOMs.

THE FIGHT FOR KANAKY

Though intermittent violence had already marked early struggles for independence in the Antilles, it was in New Caledonia that the demand for independence prompted a genuine upsurge of nationalism, a more coherent political programme and a mass movement that effectively challenged French hegemony. The roots of this lay firmly in historic land alienation, nurtured by a radicalism ironically imported from France, and nourished by the failure of French authorities to carry out even relatively mild reforms. Over time, as other parts of the South Pacific became independent, especially neighbouring Vanuatu in 1980, and a Socialist government took power in France in 1981, there were renewed Melanesian expectations for independence. Such hopes were quite quickly shattered. A government which was expected to be sympathetic to the independence aspirations of Kanaks turned out to be little different from its predecessors.

The unsolved murder of the Secretary-General of UC, Pierre Declercq, in 1981 demonstrated the strength of opposition to Kanak independence and there was no sign that the Socialist government intended to move towards independence for New Caledonia. The Front Indépendantiste briefly gained power in the Territorial Assembly, in alliance with the last remnants of a centre party, as tension and violence mounted and France attempted to devise a new statute for New Caledonia. The statute satisfied few, and Kanaks were angry that no electoral reform was proposed (to disenfranchise recent arrivals and enable Melanesians to achieve a majority) and that there was no time-table for independence. They came together in 1984 in a new coalition, the Front de Libération Nationale Kanake et Socialiste (FLNKS), to demand immediate independence for the state of Kanaky. As the Kanak position hardened, the conservative stand became increasingly extremist, and new right-wing parties, including the Front National, formed to oppose the FLNKS. The stage was set for further confrontation.

The emergence of the FLNKS heralded an escalation of conflict as Kanaks abandoned the unbalanced struggle for constitutional change, ignored the French government and embarked on direct and violent action to secure Kanak independence. The FLNKS boycotted the November 1984 elections and through roadblocks and the destruction of ballot boxes ensured that the boycott was 'active'. The RPCR inevitably won the election, the FLNKS undertook more direct action (barricades on roads and the occupation of town halls and gendarmeries), briefly held the small town of Thio and declared a provisional government of the Republic of Kanaky with Jean-Marie Tjibaou (of the UC) as president. Violent conservative reaction followed; ten Kanaks were killed in an ambush and ten more Kanaks and Europeans lost their lives in various incidents. The French government sent Edgard Pisani as a special envoy and new High Commissioner to devise a peace strategy. The essence of Pisani's proposals was for independence in association with France, with France retaining control of defence and foreign affairs, French citizens having special status, and New Caledonia moving to independence in 1986 if a referendum approved the plan. The proposals attempted to reconcile three conflicting interests: Melanesian claims to independence, the rights of French settlers (Caldoches) and French strategic interests. The FLNKS were unenthusiastic about a 'neo-colonial' solution, with the franchise barely changed, and withdrew from negotiations after the death (in a police raid) of their most militant leader, Eloi Machoro, Minister of Security in the provisional Kanaky government. The military presence was strengthened, right-wing opposition to Kanak militancy grew and, without French or urban support, Kanak militants were unable to gain power. Pisani's proposals, increasingly viewed by conservatives as lavishly over-generous to the FLNKS, were ignored. The French prime minister, Laurent Fabius, devised new proposals which divided New Caledonia into four regions each with its own council responsible for a range of development planning issues. The FLNKS eventually accepted the basis of this plan, though they continued to distrust the French government. Disappointment over unresolved negotiations and discussions, misery over the death of a disproportionate number of Melanesians, recognition that direct action would not guarantee independence, and fatigue, all contributed to a less idealistic vision of the future of an independent Kanaky and a more pragmatic recognition of the necessity to negotiate. Conservatives, increasingly well-armed, were concerned about these developments but confident that in March 1986 a more conservative government would gain power in France and abandon the 'conciliatory' mood of its Socialist predecessor.

As the French government stepped up its military presence, and the RPCR organised and armed its private militias, so the FLNKS withdrew from violent action and sought to develop a more self-reliant Melanesian society and economy in rural areas, in preparation for regional councils and eventual independence. Kanak alternative schools (the *écoles populaires kanakes*) were established[29] and cooperative agriculture was encouraged in a futile bid to destabilise the economy of Noumea. French subsidies ensured that this had little effect. In the elections for the regional councils in September 1985 the FLNKS won three of the four regions, though the RPCR won so comprehensively and expectedly around Noumea that it retained control of the Territorial Congress. The election was fought solely over the issue of independence; some 38 per cent of the voters, mainly on the east coast and in the islands, in the highest turnout in history, supported independence and 61 per cent were opposed. These broad proportions, maintained for a decade, demonstrated the continued improbability of independence being gained through the ballot-box without some dramatic restriction of universal suffrage. FLNKS successes in the regions prompted right-wing violence and there were sporadic bombings, mainly of institutions such as the Lands Office which were broadly supportive of Melanesian development, or of the homes and cars of FLNKS supporters in Noumea. In rural areas Kanak destruction of settlers' property also continued sporadically, largely out of frustration, and the new regional councils were without funds to implement policy. The FLNKS coalition became weaker, as the most important party within it, the UC, chose a policy of greater compromise, whilst others, especially the Front Uni de Libération Kanake (FULK), wished to maintain a more confrontationist position.

The 1986 elections that brought Jacques Chirac to power in Paris were boycotted by the FLNKS, hence the new and extremely conservative RPCR-Front National coalition swept the territory by gaining 89 per cent of the vote though the participation rate was only 50 per cent.[30] The effect of the FLNKS boycott was to ensure that, for the first time, the RPCR had two representatives in the French parliament. Though the FLNKS had succeeded in demonstrating that its support was maintained, it was at the expense of losing its seat in Paris, and thus its sole constitutional representation outside New Caledonia. Chirac quickly emphasised the new French conservatism. Bernard Pons became Minister for DOM-TOMs and Lucette Michaux-Chevry, from Guadeloupe, was appointed as Secretary of State, in charge of Francophone affairs. Indicating Chirac's determination to retain control of the Pacific, a new position of Secretary of State for the South Pacific was created for Gaston Flosse, newly re-elected President of French Polynesia, and an ardent supporter of the French presence in New Caledonia and confidant and colleague of the conservative RPCR politicians, Dick Ukeiwe and Jacques Lafleur. The fact that Flosse was both a member of the French cabinet and President of French Polynesia demonstrated the increased strength of French political control in the South Pacific.

The specific proposals for New Caledonia that followed emphasised that no movement towards independence, or even greater autonomy, would now be contemplated. Although the regional councils remained in place, their funds were effectively frozen by the new concentration of power in the hands of the Territorial Congress (controlled by the RPCR) and the French High Commissioner. This shift of authority removed the possibility of FLNKS regional governments adopting radical initiatives towards developing real regional economies. A further package of economic measures was proposed that, whilst formally directed at reducing unemployment by encouraging economic growth, would tie New Caledonia yet more firmly to France. Pons made no reference to any Melanesian demands, either political or economic, specifically abolishing the Lands Office (although a land reform programme officially continued). He commented that 'New Caledonia is French because its inhabitants wish it to be', a clear denigration of the historic basis of Kanak nationalism. He also offered the prospect of further immigration. Troop numbers were increased and some of the 6000 troops in New Caledonia were dispersed throughout the countryside, in a policy of 'nomadisation' previously practised before independence in Algeria. Regiments of marines patrolled rural areas, maintaining a military presence, providing such technical assistance as road construction and contributing to tension. The immediate result of these changes was that the FLNKS effectively lost almost all its limited power in the regions, the only places where it had legal and constitutional authority, and was constitutionally reduced to an ineffective minority in the Territorial Congress. Its minor achievements had largely disappeared though its support had not been eroded.[31]

Denied success within New Caledonia, the principal goal of the FLNKS has increasingly become to gain international support within the Pacific region and beyond. In March 1975 a delegation first went to the United Nations to attempt to have New Caledonia considered by the United Nations Committee on Decolonisation. However, it was not until the South Pacific Forum, an annual assembly of independent states (including Australia and New Zealand) in the Pacific region, agreed to raise the issue collectively after its 1986 meeting, that action appeared likely. The leader of the FLNKS and its largest component party, Union Calédonienne, Jean-Marie Tjibaou, argued that a 'new strategy' would be adopted since New Caledonia had moved into a situation like that of Algeria before independence and sought further support in Europe and elsewhere. With reference to the referendum he stated: 'The people concerned by independence are the Kanak people. The French are independent. I don't think it is necessary to consult them or know whether they wish to remain French or not.' France launched a diplomatic offensive in the United Nations, aimed at the sponsoring countries (particularly Australia) and argued for the pluri-ethnic character of New Caledonia, the absence of separate development and the post-contact growth of the Melanesian population (contrasted directly with that of Australian Aborigines). But in December 1986 the United Nations General Assembly voted 89 to 24 (with 34 abstentions) in favour of referring New Caledonia to the Committee, effectively classifying New Caledonia as a colony. France predictably rejected the decision, went ahead with its proposals to organise a referendum on independence and refused the admission of UN officials to monitor the referendum. Following South Pacific sponsorship of and support for the UN resolution, France also launched retaliatory measures. The Australian Consul-General in Noumea was expelled and France briefly broke off ministerial contacts with Australia in January 1987, though without provoking any response. Those countries in the region that supported independence in New Caledonia (and opposed nuclear testing in French Polynesia) saw reductions in bilateral aid. By contrast, the Cook Islands, which has generally supported all aspects of France's presence in the region, received increased bilateral aid, as France sought to divide the states of the region.

The French conservative government moved forward with plans to hold the referendum in 1987 and the proposal was finally approved by the French Senate in May 1987, in the face of Socialist opposition. The sixth annual FLNKS Congress predictably voted to boycott the referendum in order to 'destabilise the strategy of the colonial government' and subsequently embarked on a series of pre-referendum protests leading to strong repression from the French riot police. At the same time, the South Pacific Forum, meeting in 1987 in Western Samoa, described the referendum as a 'senseless exercise' and a 'recipe for disaster.' The referendum, held in September 1987, resulted in 57 per cent of the electorate voting in favour of remaining with France. Almost all the remainder of the electorate did not vote. Once again, but for the first time in a referendum, the population had firmly voted against decolonisation though no more than about 20 per cent of Melanesians voted against independence. Chirac declared in Noumea, four days after the referendum: 'You have said yes to France and France is happy and proud to keep you close to its heart.' Jean-Marie Tjibaou, however, maintained that as long as there were Kanaks in New Caledonia, France would continue to have problems,[32] and vowed that the unequal struggle would continue. President Mitterrand for his part expressed his reservations about the utility of the referendum.

Soon after the vote, Bernard Pons introduced a new statute for New Caledonia. Executive authority was transferred from a High Commissioner, responsible to Paris, to a ten-member Executive Council, consisting of the presidents of the four regions and six other members elected by the Territorial Congress. The boundaries of the regions were redrawn to produce quite different units so that the FLNKS would be likely to control only two rather than three regions, and communes were given extra responsibilities. Though undemocratic, in that much more than half the population (in Noumea and the south) had only one council, the regional councils enabled Kanaks to play some formal part in the development of the rural areas in which they lived and suggested the promise of future constitutional evolution. The demise of the old regions, alongside Kanak electoral boycotts, left Kanaks powerless and with little incentive to take part in a reconstruction devised in Paris and determined in Noumea. The new statute withdrew powers from the Territorial Congress. Control of the 200-mile Exclusive Economic Zone, the public service, the remaining postal and telecommunications functions were all effectively transferred to France, so reducing the autonomy of the Territorial Congress. Other elements of the new statute also threatened Kanak interests. The Council of Customary Chiefs was abolished but there was to be a new Customary Assembly of nominees who were not traditional leaders. Melanesians would no longer have any distinct civil status but would be entirely subject to French law and traditional land rights (the basis of the clan system) were to be radically transformed. Such threats to land and society were bitterly resented. Tjibaou accused France of 'cultural genocide', noting that the statute 'would mark the end of the Kanaks as people.' The proposed change in civil statute implied that Kanaks seeking independence would now become an illegal secession movement, comparable to Basque and Corsican groups, indeed the 'separatists' that conservatives called them rather than '*indépendantistes*.' Tjibaou consequently called for a 'muscular mobilisation' to oppose the statute which offered no concessions to Kanak aspirations, and the FLNKS refused any dialogue on the terms of the statute. The RPCR was generally satisfied with the new statute though there was inevitable concern that the FLNKS would have any role in decision-making in New Caledonia. The Front National rejected the statute, claiming that it was non-democratic and would lead to 'institutionalized destabilization' and the partition of New Caledonia.[33]

The political situation in New Caledonia deteriorated as land conflicts surfaced again on the east coast, and the seven men accused of the murder of ten Kanaks in 1984 were acquitted by a jury that contained no Melanesians. The number of soldiers also increased. Chirac appeared determined to intimidate and marginalise the FLNKS by public demonstrations of troop activities in rural areas, rather than seeking to convince uncommitted Melanesians that their future lay with France. The Seventh Congress of the FLNKS in February 1988 vowed to oppose the Pons statute and, in a press conference after the congress, Tjibaou concluded that the future will bring 'a strong and determined mobilisation, as a function of a different balance of forces to that of 1984. The responsibility for working out the ways and means belong to the Comité de lutte [the organising committee] in each commune.' Acute frustration and despondency had again brought the FLNKS to a position where it appeared that only a violent struggle could convince France of the gravity and legitimacy of their claims and again draw the attention of the world to one of the last inconclusive struggles for independence. Only one channel of dissent and debate was left open.[34]

Chirac set both the French presidential elections and the New Caledonian regional elections for the same day in April 1988, a decision which angered the FLNKS. As the two sets of elections went ahead the French government, fearful that violence might be repeated, saturated New Caledonia with more troops and gendarmes, bringing the total eventually to more than 9000. Léopold Jorédié, the secretary-general of the UC, warned that New Caledonia was 'sliding into an Algerian-type situation' and that 'the government will have to face the consequence of what will happen in the territory next month.' Thus warned, but without any information on what 'muscular mobilisation' might imply, the French government took precautions, though it was to little avail. Two days before the elections, a commando group of Kanaks made a dawn raid on the gendarmerie at Fayaoue on Ouvea island, killing four gendarmes and taking twenty-seven hostages. Some were released a few days later, but other police and officials who subsequently arrived were taken hostage, and transported to a coral cave. Kanaks then made demands for the cancellation of the Pons statute and the regional elections, the withdrawal of the military from the island and a new referendum supervised by the United Nations. The hostages were deemed 'prisoners of war' and it was claimed that they would be held for six months.

Conservatives in New Caledonia were incensed at the turn of events. Jacques Lafleur, president of the RPCR and *député* in the French parliament, who accused the FLNKS of 'terrorist' methods and described its members as 'subversives', repeated his demand for the dissolution of the party. Conservative politicians in Paris joined the call, and Chirac spoke of Kanak 'savagery and barbarism.' Dick Ukeiwe, the most prominent Melanesian in the RPCR, a senator and now president of the newly elected Territorial Congress, declared that the 'Kanaks who are holding the hostages should be treated as outlaws.' Justin Guillemard, a leader of the local Front National, claimed that 'he would rather die with a gun in his hand than submit to the Kanaks.' Guy George, also of the Front National, pointed out that if Mitterrand won the elections there would be civil war, since settlers now had well-organised 'self-defence groups to meet fire with fire.' The right therefore appealed for adherence to the law, stressed the necessity to give the new Pons statute a chance to succeed, campaigned against the election of Mitterrand and sought to detect Libyan involvement in New Caledonia. Mitterrand refused to respond to the right-wing, before or after the first round of the presidential elections. Jean-Marie Tjibaou, interviewed shortly after the hostages had been captured, observed:

My first reaction is that it is saddening to observe the results of the partisan, cynical and despicable policy of the RPCR ... This Pons statute is the final touch in a system of refusal to take the Kanak people and its claims into consideration. And this has been ordered by the local clique which has grabbed the land, hunted the Kanaks from their own homes, taken control of the mines and of commerce. It is these people who are setting themselves up to give us a lesson and who made no such fuss over the murder of 10 people at Hienghène ... They must bear all the consequences for what is happening, just as they must bear the consequences of 1878, 1917, the deaths at Hienghène, of Eloi Machoro and the others. Attention must not be drawn away from the real problem.

Once again the FLNKS sought its legitimacy in history and traced the history of nationalism back over 110 years. Violence was attributed to those who, over the decades, had provoked this 'colonial war.'[35]

As the hostages remained in Ouvea, the first round of the presidential elections went ahead, disturbed by a series of events in different parts of New Caledonia. Ouvea was not therefore an isolated incident but was probably the catalyst for further actions. Other local 'struggle committees' effectively forced the evacuation of Canala, barricaded many highways and later executed José Lapetite, one of the defendants of the Hienghène massacre. Police were fired on, a Melanesian woman was killed by a stray bullet at Canala and pro-French Melanesians were harassed. At Canala, Henri Morini, organiser of the RPCR militias, was shot and seriously wounded. Voting went ahead with 31 of the territory's 139 polling stations closed, a similar proportion to that in 1984, and about 56 per cent of the population voted. The RPCR gained 64 per cent of the votes and thirty-five of the forty-eight seats in the Territorial Congress whilst the Front National substantially increased its support, especially in Noumea. In the presidential elections, Chirac gained 75 per cent of the vote in New Caledonia, Jean-Marie Le Pen of the Front National gained 12 per cent and Mitterrand received a derisory 5 per cent. Two days before the second round of the elections, with Mitterrand apparently well ahead of Chirac, crack army units stormed the cave, rescued the remaining twenty-three hostages and killed nineteen Kanak militants, including their leader Alphonse Dianou. Two soldiers were also killed. Once again violent events had led to the deaths of many more Kanaks than any other ethnic group. As the evidence trickled in that three militants were killed after their capture, napalm bombing had been contemplated, and that the hostages were almost certain to have been released after the second round of the presidential elections, Kanak anger and resentment resurfaced. In the immediate aftermath of the deaths an FLNKS press release promised that 'neither deaths, tears, suffering or humiliation will stifle the cry for freedom.' Bitterness was the dominant sentiment.[36]

The calculated political expediency of the raid, which coincided with the negotiated release of French hostages from Lebanon and the return of the *Rainbow Warrior* bomber, Dominique Prieur, from her exile on Hao atoll in French Polynesia (in breach of a United Nations agreement), failed to convince the French electorate which returned President Mitterrand on 8 May with a substantial majority of the vote. Chirac's desperate and lethal gamble had failed. Even the supporters of Le Pen, for whom the gesture was surely intended, may not have rallied their support behind Chirac. And, insofar as election issues can be disentangled, the evidence suggests that on New Caledonia the French electorate preferred Mitterrand's promise of renewed dialogue with the FLNKS to Chirac's aggressive opposition. Yet New Caledonia is remote and tiny, there are normally few votes for particular Pacific initiatives and the presidential elections centred primarily on metro-politan concerns.[37]

The re-election of President Mitterrand under the slogan 'La France unie' ('France united') brought an immediate end to the hard-line confrontationist policies of the Chirac era, undercut conservative forces in France, and dismayed New Caledonia 'loyalists' but it created an atmosphere where there was more prospect for tolerance and con-sensus. The new Prime Minister, Michel Rocard, held talks in Paris attended by both the FLNKS leader, Jean-Marie Tjibaou, and the RPCR leader, Jacques Lafleur, which led to the signing of the Matignon Accord; the Accord established direct rule from France for a year, divided New Caledonia into three new regions (two of which were to be controlled by *indépendantistes*), established new economic devel-opment strategies for the Melanesian areas and proposed a second referendum on independence in 1998 with a new electoral system. Rocard described his proposal as 'decolonisation within the framework of French institutions.' Much of the new French financial support was directed to training Kanak bureaucrats. Without policies of localisation Kanaks are conspicuously absent from the higher echelons of the pub-lic service. 'The training and placement of Kanak cadres must surely be a pressing priority for a new government. For it is in giving the settler community the direct experience of sharing power with, and being governed by, Kanaks that independence becomes a viable option.' This was the optimistic view of those in the FLNKS, like Tjibaou, who saw in the new regions the opportunity to demonstrate their legitimacy and effectiveness in power. An alternative view was that if further substan-tial economic resources were diverted from Paris to rural New Cal-edonia, an even more artificial economy would be created and many Kanaks would achieve positions of power, status and high income in the emergent economic system, so creating more Melanesians (like their predecessors from parts of the Isle of Pines and the Loyalty Islands) who are no longer interested in independence, especially if it means reduced foreign aid levels. Whereas the previous FLNKS strategy, repeated at regular intervals over the past decade, was to set an independence date and then seek to construct the basis of an indep-endent state before that deadline, the Accord reversed this procedure and in so doing reduced the probability of independence.[38]

The proposal for a new referendum on independence in 1998 also resulted in substantial discussion. There was widespread surprise that, on behalf of the FLNKS, Tjibaou would even contemplate postponing the next debate on independence for a decade. Underlying this pro-posal was the decision to 'freeze' the electorate at its present size, subsequently to be expanded only by adding descendants of electors currently living in New Caledonia. This would radically change the structure of the electorate to give greater effective weight to the Melanesian population than had ever occurred before, and going beyond the September 1987 referendum when the electorate had to have been resident in New Caledonia for at least three years. However, demographic projections give little support to the possibility that the Melanesian electorate will be a majority in 1998. Moreover, perhaps the most difficult task of all for the FLNKS will be to convince those Melanesians who now vote against independence to change their position. Tjibaou expressed his own belief that it would be easier to gain the votes of sympathetic Europeans:

We have to convince the 20 per cent of Kanaks [who vote with the Right]. With that 20 per cent we would have a majority. But I am more confident of achieving this by increasing the [pro-independence] five per cent among the Europeans ... Why? Because many Kanaks follow their masters who give them a living, while the Europeans, the Chinese and other Asians are more independent.

Consequently the FLNKS sought, again unsuccessfully, to restrict the future electorate to those born in New Caledonia, and also asked for a range of policies discouraging immigration from France (a policy supported by the Front National) and new measures to ensure that people do not vote against independence for economic reasons; these include the abolition of privileges designed to attract French public servants (such as salary bonuses and a 75-per-cent top-up on retirement benefits for those who stay in New Caledonia), and a currency devaluation.

There was serious concern in the FLNKS that, at the very least, independence had been postponed for a further decade, and this delay was unacceptable after so much previous discussion, violence and bloodshed, in which the victims had been predominantly Melanesian. Ten more years seemed to represent minimal commitment to the principles and practice of decolonisation. Tjibaou too was unconvinced: 'The root of our claim to independence has still been left in abeyance.' Representing the Union des Syndicats des Travailleurs Kanaks et Exploités (USTKE), the trade union component of the FLNKS, Louis Kotra Uregei summarised the dominant sentiments in the FLNKS:

In Kanaky we have just signed an accord with our colonialists. This accord is a victory for us. It is a response to our struggle of recent years, to the sacrifice of so many of our brothers and sisters. But we are the first to recognise that it is a compromise, a necessary compromise, which allows us to continue our struggle on a different plane. Independence is our objective. We have not won it yet and we do not think that France will hand it to us easily. Independence is what we want and we will win it, perhaps even before the ten years are over.

For its part the RPCR was unconcerned about a referendum in another decade. By then the Socialist government could well have been replaced by a new government more ideologically sympathetic to their aspirations. Ten years is a long time in politics.[39]

The small Kanak party FULK, often at odds with the body of the FLNKS after Yann Celene Uregei, its leader, had been disciplined for his links with Libya, was hostile to the Accord and sought to move a censure motion against Tjibaou. However, most FLNKS supporters welcomed the Accord, as well as Tjibaou's role in achieving this agreement, in the slow but peaceful process of dialogue and possible decolonisation. Recognising that the demand for independence could not easily be allayed by the slow constitutional process that the Accord outlined, Tjibaou stressed that the FLNKS would be constantly vigilant that the proposals were working appropriately and called for continued 'militant mobilisation' to ensure that the FLNKS could never be ignored. A national referendum on the Matignon Accord in November 1988 had a turnout of only 37 per cent, the lowest turnout for any French national election or referendum since the Second World War. Some 80 per cent of those who voted were in favour of the new statute. In New Caledonia the turnout was much higher though it still reached only 64 per cent of the electorate. Moreover, while 57 per cent of those who voted approved the new statute, some 43 per cent voted against it, a very large proportion which raised serious doubts in the FLNKS over the future of the independence movement. In six communes in the south — Noumea, Mont Dore, Dumbea, Farino, Bourail and La Foa — a majority voted against the statute. Elsewhere there was a majority in favour of the proposals, though there were high abstention rates in the Loyalty Islands. Despite their concerns, the bulk of FLNKS supporters voted in favour of the proposals. Though many Europeans deserted the RPCR to oppose the proposals, those Melanesians, Wallisians and Futunans who have conventionally supported the RPCR mostly voted in support. The referendum overwhelmingly demonstrated the lack of metropolitan interest in New Caledonia and the very substantial concern within New Caledonia that, whatever the merits of the new proposals, they nonetheless opened the door to some kind of eventual independence. Nonetheless the signing of the Matignon Accord brought a period of peace to New Caledonia.[40]

That peace was rudely shattered exactly a year after the violent events in Ouvea when, at a memorial service for the victims of Ouvea, the FLNKS and UC leader, Jean-Marie Tjibaou, and the deputy-leader, Yeiwene Yeiwene, were murdered by a dissident member of the FLNKS, angered over the signing of the Accord. The assassinations emphasised divisions within the FLNKS, and these divisions increased further, as the FLNKS failed to organise a congress to elect a new leader, FULK was marginalised, and USTKE withdrew from the coalition.[41] The UC elected a new leader, François Burck, who quickly emphasised that independence was not solely for Kanaks but would involve everyone and that 'independence means changing our relations with France — no longer colonial relations but a partnership. Independence means being able to choose interdependence. And the partner that we must look towards is France.'[42] It appeared to be a withdrawal from historic aims. Despite some local election successes, the loss of the sole leader who had been able to unite the FLNKS again emphasised the task of a divided independence movement, supported by a minority of the New Caledonian population, to achieve its goal.

THE NEW CALEDONIAN 'CONTAGION'?

The dramatic development of the New Caledonian independence movement in 1984 and 1985 had widespread repercussions throughout the DOM-TOMs, though much of the impact was towards strengthening ties with France, in the face of the possible 'loss' of New Caledonia. However, the existing independence movements gained strength from the events in New Caledonia and their claims became more vocal and violent, so much so that in the French parliamentary debate on the Fabius Plan, a Réunion *député*, Michel Debré, accused the government of 'wishing to create in all the DOM-TOMs a conflict situation, an attitude favourable to separatism' and, speaking of Guadeloupe, he accused the government of 'letting the insurrection become mistress of the streets.'[43] Symbolic of this renaissance of support for independence, in Guadeloupe the Union Populaire pour la Libération de la Guadeloupe organised an international conference opposed to French colonialism in April 1985, attended by parties from other DOM-TOMs, except Mayotte, Wallis and Futuna, Saint-Pierre and Miquelon and French Polynesia, although the latter territory intended to be represented, and the Comoros was present in the form of the Front Démocratique. This conference aimed at 'coordinating and reinforcing the solidarity of the people of the last French colonies and informing international opinion on the problems of their decolonisation', stressed common future programmes of non-alignment and self-reliance, and was specifically designed to press for the inclusion of the DOM-TOMs with the UN Committee on Decolonisation.[44] For all its novelty, the 'First Conference of the Last French Colonies' was a tiny meeting and international opinion took little notice. Subsequently there have been less ambitious conferences, with fewer DOM-TOMs participating, though occasionally with Corsican delegates.[45] Otherwise, particular movements continued to struggle for independence in their own distinctive ways.

In French Polynesia, despite the change in government, nuclear testing continued through the 1980s as France, under governments of different persuasion, pushed ahead with the expansion of the nuclear programme, incorporating the neutron bomb, and regional concern again grew, accompanied by local protests from Polynesians who had missed out on the material benefits of the programme. The principal *indépendantiste* party, Ia Mana Te Nunaa, gained support, winning three of the thirty seats in the Territorial Assembly in 1982. Ia Mana Te Nunaa sought economic and political independence, directed to the establishment of an egalitarian socialist state, through land reform and the introduction of progressive income tax and opposed nuclear testing. Much of its support came from impoverished urban Polynesians. The elected representatives immediately transformed discourse in the Assembly by speaking Tahitian. Other radical groups emerged. Oscar Temaru had earlier established Tavini Huiraatira no Polinetia (the Polynesian Liberation Front) which also sought independence by legal means. In 1983 Temaru was elected mayor of Fa'aa, a poor Tahitian suburb on the fringes of the international airport, primarily because of his promises to reduce unemployment. The visibility of his party significantly increased and, over time, these two new parties, once widely regarded as too idealistic, gained significant popular support especially amongst urban Tahitians. As in other DOM-TOMs, a number of tiny *indépendantiste* parties appeared and disappeared and, as in New Caledonia, were supported as much through religious and regional sentiment as political ideology.[46]

The form of independence sought by Ia Mana Te Nunaa was similar to that demanded by most parties within the FLNKS. Jacqui Drollet, the Secretary-General, has stated:

In economic matters we favour a turning back, a complete change of direction. . . . In order to achieve independence we must change direction, pull the tertiary sector back to a reasonable level, and concentrate our activity on reviving the primary sector, developing agriculture to achieve self-sufficiency, developing fisheries in collaboration with certain other countries to earn foreign exchange, developing tourism — not a capitalistic tourism . . . — and developing renewable energy sources to achieve independence in matters of energy. . . . Independence must be based on the development of our natural resources, on our prospering on the things that we have, living at a level more worthy of us and of the Polynesian reality.[47]

As in New Caledonia this is not the socialism of state control, but one built on a greater respect for local identity, language and resources, and aimed at regional linkages rather than association with a distant European state. Other parties in French Polynesia had barely defined a future programme.

As the independence struggle in New Caledonia intensified at the end of 1984, it gained widespread support from *indépendantistes* in French Polynesia, who were more familiar with the nature of the struggle, and equally widespread opposition from conservatives. While Gaston Flosse, the president of the Territorial Assembly, fearing a 'Caledonian contagion', signed an alliance with Dick Ukeiwe, the conservative Melanesian president of the New Caledonian Assembly, 'to defend their common interests and promote joint action in political administrative, economic, cultural and social matters', the *indépendantistes*, led by Oscar Temaru, saw common cause in Kanak aspirations. Temaru pointed to a similar history of 'domination and exploitation', an imposed colonial power, European monopoly of great stretches of land, settlers importing foreign labour, multinational phosphate mining and tourism and a refusal 'to undertake serious decolonisation; the only small difference is one of numbers; we are not yet quite as dominated and submerged as our Kanak brothers in New Caledonia.'[48] Temaru also sought to use the same tactics of appealing to the United Nations Committee on Decolonisation. The principal *indépendantiste* party, Ia Mana Te Nunaa, at its Fifth Congress, expressed unconditional support for the FLNKS and denounced Messmer's letter of July 1972 encouraging immigration, fearing that one day in Polynesia too 'the legitimate people would find themselves a minority in their own land.'[49] The reduced importance of migration, the arithmetic of race and the loss of land in French Polynesia have ensured that though there is sympathy for the Kanak cause, and the independence parties have drawn strength from it, the differences between the two independence movements are substantial. One major difference is that in French Polynesia all 970 local councillors are either Polynesians or *demis*, a situation quite different from New Caledonia.

Greater Tahitian support for the independence parties followed the Socialist government's emphasis on institutional rather than political reforms in the DOM-TOMs, resulting in changes to the statute of French Polynesia in 1984, and its unwillingness to adopt any policies that might put its national defence policy at risk. The conservative party, Tahoeraa Huiraatira, continued to stress the need for autonomy, effectively outflanking the autonomists within the Territorial Assembly, and facing opposition principally from Ia Mana Te Nunaa. In 1983 Teariki was defeated, after thirty years as Mayor of Moorea, and died the following year. Sanford retired, after electoral humiliation, and the old autonomist parties disintegrated. Oscar Temaru, and another party member, were elected to the Territorial Assembly in 1985, whilst Charlie Ching, whose electoral support had faded, was jailed for two years for staging an unauthorised demonstration and inciting violence. However, late in 1987, breakaway members of Flosse's Tahoeraa Huiraatira, led by Alexandre Léontieff, established a coalition government, incorporating Ia Mana Te Nunaa, with Jacqui Drollet as Minister of Health. Demands for independence have largely been submerged in pressure for greater autonomy and the reduction and end of nuclear testing, but all parties have stressed the necessity for the French presence to be retained until a more self-reliant economy can be developed. Four of the forty-one members of the Territorial Assembly support independence (and oppose nuclear testing); however, Ia Mana Te Nunaa in government lost its influence, gave less emphasis to the necessity for independence, and lost all its seats in the 1991 territorial elections. In 1989 Oscar Temaru's Tavini Huiraatira no Polinetia led a hunger strike against testing. Jacqui Drollet challenged France to provide the health files of all those who had worked at Mururoa and Fangataufa; Daniel Millaud, Senator for French Polynesia since 1977, warned about the risk of French Polynesia becoming a dump for EC nuclear waste after 1992. The government coalition favoured autonomy and greater self-reliance, demanding, paradoxically, that this be achieved by greater French expenditure to ensure the viability of French Polynesia if and when nuclear testing was phased out.

The end of nuclear testing in French Polynesia would increase the probability of independence in this remote, fragmented, unproductive and exceptionally dependent colony, where French public expenditure is double that in New Caledonia. Yet, at the same time, there is widespread acquiescence towards the French presence, a situation unlikely to change in the future as the demand for improved employment and income-earning opportunities mounts. Though there is a surprisingly widespread view that independence will eventually follow genuine self-government,[50] it will occur only if France abandons its strategic interests in the South Pacific, a prospect unlikely in this century.

In the Antilles, as in the Pacific, the arrival of a Socialist government suggested the possibility of significant political change. However, the more established Caribbean independence movements were not optimistic over the directions of change. Supporters of the UPLG feared that opportunists would desert the cause of independence and by 1982 recorded that 'nothing, absolutely nothing has changed since 10 May 1981.' Political, cultural and economic repression were argued to be as strong as they had ever been, hence the demands of *indépendantistes* remained unchanged.[51] The first two years, with Régis Debray as Mitterrand's adviser on Latin American affairs and Henri Emmanuelli the Secretary of State for the DOM-TOMs, saw some decentralisation of power and, though the possibility of movement towards independence gained greater ideological respectability, it still lacked support in the Caribbean. Aimé Césaire, the leader of the PPM, had however announced that

François Mitterrand's victory is an opportunity for Martinique. A unique opportunity, an exceptional opportunity, an historic opportunity that we must seize, that we must take account of . . . today I proclaim a public moratorium on the question of the legal status of Martinique.[52]

This suggestion of a more obvious movement towards independence was not in tune with the aspirations of most PPM supporters, who were generally reformists and, in a French context, had been happy to vote for the conservative Giscard. Between the choice of an unpopular nationalism, without the economic means to achieve it, and the vague promise of long-term independence, the PPM eventually returned to the reassuring and dependent option of welcoming the 'good intentions of a socialist government, open to dialogue and discussion, convinced of the need for progress and change in Martinique.'[53] Though this was no abject submission to the policies and practice of the French government, as the PPM continued to seek appropriate forms of decentralisation, it left scope for more radical parties to demand greater autonomy or independence.

In Martinique the French Socialist government's promise of decentralisation was universally opposed by every independence group — MIM, GRS, Combat Ouvrier, Parti Communiste pour l'Indépendance et le Socialisme (PCIS) and the Maoist, 'Asé pléré, an nou lité' ('Enough weeping — onto the struggle') — as simply a means of opposing decolonisation. The MIM stressed again in 1983 that even in a Socialist France, Martinique remained 'a colony, politically dominated, economically exploited, culturally oppressed and occupied militarily',[54] and argued that decentralisation would not change the fundamental balance of power, but would merely strengthen the position of a bourgeois elite which would continue to act as an intermediary between the French colonial state and the Martinique people. Typical of this view was that of the PCIS which sought in 1984

the establishment of an independent, sovereign and socialist Martinique state on the basis of a planned, self-reliant economy oriented to the satisfaction of the needs of Martinique, through land reform, modernisation of agriculture, industrialisation, the exploitation of our natural resources, the nationalisation of banks and the control of credit.[55]

Few of these socialist *indépendantiste* parties sought success in territorial or French elections and there was little evidence that this form of socialist idealism had any significant support.

Unable to gain substantial popular support, and unwilling to recognise and participate in the existing democratic institutions, many *indépendantistes* turned to alternative forms of influence, specifically violence. In both Martinique and Guadeloupe the smaller parties came together in new alliances, the Conseil National des Comités Patriotiques (CNCP) in Martinique and the Mouvement pour l'Unification des Forces de Libération Nationale de la Guadeloupe (MUFLNG) in Guadeloupe. This new and tentative solidarity did not prevent some erosion of local support, though the independence movement, and specifically the UPLG, sought to gain new legitimacy by identifying parallels with New Caledonia. This emphasised the international nature of the struggle for decolonisation. They also attempted to have the Antilles recognised by the United Nations Committee on Decolonisation. A new slogan, 'Guadeloupe, Kanaky: the same enemy, the same struggle', became popular but, beyond slogans, there was little to unite disparate movements in a global struggle against French colonialism. In the more liberal Socialist environment, where there was greater autonomy, decentralisation and liberalisation of local cultural policies and social institutions, the independence parties had no successful candidates in a series of elections between 1981 and 1983. In this climate radical nationalists chose 'the only recourse still available — political violence.'[56] In Guadeloupe, where shootings, bombings and kidnappings have been endemic to the political scene, political violence was well under way by 1981. In 1982 two members of the Groupe de Libération Armée de la Guadeloupe (GLA) were arrested. The GLA expressed its opposition to both the Parti Communiste Guadeloupéen and the UPLG and to 'French capitalism and colonialism' and emphasised that its revolutionary violence was in opposition to metropolitan institutional violence, in education and language. Both Combat Ouvrier and the Groupe Révolution Socialiste were broadly sympathetic to the GLA's aims.[57] As in New Caledonia, a fraction of the independence movement had been pushed to the brink.

Violent attacks against 'the occupying power and the symbols of colonialism', as the Alliance Révolutionnaire Caraïbe (ARC) termed it, multiplied in the first half of the 1980s. Although they had considerable physical effect, they weakened the limited support already accorded to the *indépendantistes*, despite most groups denying their support for the ARC. Ironically, one of President Mitterrand's first acts had been to grant an amnesty to twenty-five political prisoners, including ten Guadeloupean and Guyanais *indépendantistes*, as a gesture of conciliation to regional and ethnic nationalists. One of those released was Luc Reinette who, on his return to Guadeloupe, founded the Mouvement Populaire pour la Guadeloupe Indépendante (MPGI). After a brief lull, terrorist activities began again in Pointe-à-Pitre in 1983, as the ARC established a new bombing campaign, primarily in Guadeloupe, but spilling over into Martinique, Guyane and Paris. The campaign continued for a year, with bombings of various institutions, including the United States consulate in Fort-de-France, but more generally of the establishments of French business and institutional interests. The ARC was banned in 1984 and Luc Reinette jailed for seven years. A new campaign of bombing began a year later. Three people were killed in a Pointe-à-Pitre restaurant, and Reinette escaped from jail. At the end of the era of Socialist government, the situation was as bad as it had been for years: 'The ideologues cannot bring independence, the local independence groups have small followings, and the pragmatists cannot resolve the Antilles' socio-economic problems.'[58] Any initial idealism of the Socialists had foundered.

Under the new conservative regime in Paris, violence declined and Luc Reinette was eventually recaptured in St. Vincent in 1987. Reinette, the most important figure in the ARC, the 'militant wing' of the MPGI, articulated the sentiments of those who sought a violent solution; in his 'Message à la Guadeloupe' the opposition to colonial oppression was set out:

French colonialists in their souls remain racists and slavemongers. . . . If today we are runaway slaves, this is because a slave society still exists in Guadeloupean daily life, disguised by glittering facades and hypocritical institutions. No longer do physical chains shackle our bodies, but invisible chains bind our spirits. . . . Our cause is just: this land to which we were deported more than three centuries ago, that our fathers and our mothers enriched with their sweat and blood, this land of Guadeloupe is ours, wholly ours. . . . Guadeloupeans are not French, they never chose to be so and cannot be so by history, geography or culture.[59]

Much of the literature of the independence movement in the Antilles has been expressed in similar vein: a powerful, rhetorical opposition to all the trappings of colonialism, an assumption that only false consciousness prevents the widespread recognition of injustice and the necessity for change, and the assumption that only a socialist independence can genuinely transform the Caribbean. After two decades, and in opposition to different French governments, the basis of the independence movement had never changed.

Of all the pro-independence parties in the Antilles the Union Populaire pour la Libération de Guadeloupe (UPLG) is the largest and best organised, with the most widespread popular support, especially from unions such as the Union Générale des Travailleurs de Guadeloupe (UGTG); it has its own radio programme and weekly journal, *Lendependans*. Unlike the other more theoretical independence groups, the UPLG has a broad threefold strategy, and has rejected the violence of ARC or the 'Algerian way' while supporting a 'popular violence' through mobilisation in support of particular issues, and is oriented towards obtaining working-class support. Firstly, the UPLG has emphasised the need to transform the dependent economy and ensure working-class agricultural production, through occupying unused land, establishing cooperatives of both factory workers and agriculturalists, opposing '*blancs créoles*' and ensuring that sugarcane remains the base of the agricultural economy. The UPLG has attempted to ensure that sugar factories are kept in operation since 'cane is inscribed in our culture',[60] sugarcane can be developed further (for example, through rum and alcohol production and the extension of irrigation) though other crops, such as yams and potatoes, could diversify agricultural production. Agricultural development is thus given priority in opposition to extension of industrial development, the form of which introduced European business, fiscal changes, French banks and stronger links to the European Community, and in opposition to the bureaucracy, where high salaries have distorted the economy, pushed up prices and raised consumption levels with 'transit money' which 'does nothing to develop Guadeloupe.' Secondly, at the political level, UPLG has focused on raising 'national' consciousness in Guadeloupe, emphasising the necessity to boycott elections, supporting ARC members deported to France (without supporting violence itself) and opposing the 'reformism' of the Parti Socialiste and the PCG, which increasingly emphasised local social issues. At the international level UPLG began in 1981 to try to establish Guadeloupe with the United Nations Decolonisation Committee and found, as the FLNKS had previously done, that Guadeloupe and *indépendantiste* aspirations were barely known elsewhere. Thirdly, there has been a strong emphasis on cultural issues, especially the written and spoken use of Creole, and support for local literature and music.[61]

After 1986 the Chirac government sought to bring the Caribbean DOMs closer to France, primarily through more wide-ranging fiscal incentives to local economic development. Decentralisation was no longer emphasised and, in some respects, the political parties in the Antilles again adopted the perspectives they had held in the 1970s. The independence movement did, however, increasingly emphasise the need to achieve decolonisation before the *départements* became integrated into Europe, and a new form of 'colonisation' was imposed. Where they competed in elections the *indépendantiste* parties retained their tiny proportion of the vote, in support of the candidates' municipal achievements as much as through support for independence. Even in traditional strongholds, *indépendantistes* never reached 5 per cent of the total vote. Parties like the MIM continued to seek boycotts of French elections and, when normally high abstention rates grew, claimed that this represented a success in terms of the rejection of French institutions and that those who had voted were 'anti-Martiniquais', a result of either false consciousness or external pressure.[62] High abstention rates were more likely to be a function of uninterest in elections where the result was often a foregone conclusion. Independence through the ballot-box was as distant as it had ever been, and revolution was implausible. Without exception the Antillais parties continued to stress the necessity for socialist independence, arguing, as did the UPLG, that 'the most acute form of the class struggle is the struggle for independence.'[63] Recent *indépendantiste* tracts have not challenged this basic assumption,[64] though there has been some attempt to broaden the scope of the independence movement. The major parties continued to emphasise autonomy as a possible transitional stage towards independence. Though in 1988 the powerful Parti Communiste Guadeloupéen (PCG) replaced its long standing demand for 'democratic and popular autonomy, a step towards a socialist independence' with the goal of 'a national independence with a socialist orientation [attained] according to stages democratically chosen by the Guadeloupean people',[65] it was little more than a cosmetic change, and an attempt to win over some *indépendantiste* support. After two decades of minority pressure for independence, very little had changed.

In Réunion the violence of the Antilles was largely absent, despite some gesture of support for independence from Libya's Colonel Gaddafy, and Georges Sinamalé's new Mouvement pour l'Indépendance de la Réunion (MIR) remained tiny and unimportant, never challenging the status quo in elections. It gained brief publicity in 1986

compare the quality of life to that of their former compatriots who chose independence.'[69] Since France initially refused aid to the independent Comoros and embarked on an extensive public works programme in Mayotte, these disparities have grown substantially. Most of the population would prefer formal *département* status. Though attitudes might eventually change, the present processes of economic incorporation will defer any demands for independence, or ties with the Comoros, into the indefinite future. In each of the three smallest DOM-TOMs attitudes are very firmly in favour of stronger political and economic ties with France.

The opening address by the UPLG to the Conference of the Last French Colonies noted the necessity to seek a political solution to the problem of decolonisation for the various 'confetti de l'empire' and 'danseuses de la France' ('French dancing girls') but noted that acquiring national independence was ultimately 'a process internal to each people. This process was not imported and it will not be exported.'[70] With the exception of significant ties between the independence parties of Guadeloupe and Martinique, where the socioeconomic structure is similar, each of the 'last colonies' has separately sought its own road to independence, based on the particular local situations, and outside New Caledonia the local situation has only exceptionally stimulated significant support for *indépendantiste* parties. Despite attempts by *indépendantiste* parties to emphasise global similarities in the struggle for independence, the 'New Caledonian contagion' has been more evident in the increased strength of the opposition to independence. Calls for decolonisation have fallen largely on stony ground.

THE END OF EMPIRE?

French sensitivities over the loss of territory are unusually strong, historically emphasised by the reacquisition of Alsace and Lorraine at the end of the First World War and the occupation of France itself during the Second World War. Even the hexagon of 'metropolitan France' is a relatively recent phenomenon. The Comté de Nice (Nice and its surrounding area) has been part of France only since 1860, when it was annexed from the House of Savoy; it is, therefore, a more recent acquisition than most DOM-TOMs. Moreover, Nice often chooses to see itself as somewhat different to the rest of France, and its former mayor, Jacques Médecin, suggested with tongue in cheek that 'Nice is France's most recent colony. Perhaps we might accept a proposal of independence-association like the one the French government has offered the Kanaks.'[71] Not until around the turn of the century was the Third

Republic able to turn 'peasants into Frenchmen', to impose the French language on the provinces and create a popular national identity;[72] hence both ethnicity and what is perceived as secessionism are widely viewed with suspicion. Except for a brief period in the 1980s, when Pisani presented his proposals for New Caledonian independence in association with France, no interest has been displayed by either French Socialist or conservative governments in New Caledonia or any other DOM-TOM in achieving a greater degree of independence. Commenting on the Matignon Accord, even before it had been signed, Michel Rocard emphasised that the option that he preferred was that in the long term New Caledonia would remain part of France: 'That's my dream, I'm working towards that end.'[73] Thus despite the novelty of the proposals in the Accord, the individual most closely responsible for them prefers one particular solution. Despite substantial Melanesian support for independence in New Caledonia, an intermittently violent struggle and occasional external pressure on France to continue the process of decolonisation, there is no obvious likelihood of independence occurring in any DOM-TOM in this century.

The Algerian war and subsequent independence dealt a blow to the concept of a united and indivisible French republic: 'Having set its boundaries in north Africa, the political class had to accept decolonisation as dismemberment, making it more difficult to sustain the myth.'[74] But for conservatives it has been crucial that the myth be sustained; the merest hints of independence in New Caledonia have provoked instant reflection on the enormity of Algerian parallels. One of the strongest opponents of New Caledonian independence, the Corsican-born Senator Charles Pasqua, proclaimed that 'the defence of Bastia begins in Noumea'[75] and Jacques Chirac, in response to Pisani's proposals, warned of problems not only in the DOM-TOMs and Corsica, but amongst Bretons and Basques. Despite the 'loss' of Algeria, and other parts of Africa, the essential message for conservatives was that the remainder of the French Republic must remain inviolate, hence even the independence of the jointly-administered New Hebrides in 1980 was constantly considered to be a special case of joint decolonisation that provided no precedent. Almost all arguments for the retention of the DOM-TOMs, and especially New Caledonia, 'in the bosom of France', have thus been couched in metropolitan terms, with the local population, black or white, no more than bystanders in the construction of these scenarios. The former French Front National *député*, Jean-Claude Martinez, has neatly summarised these kinds of perspective for New Caledonia: 'Whatever legitimate aspirations some of the 61,870 Melanesians have, the France of the future (*la France millénaire*) cannot compromise its destiny as a great power to satisfy them.'[76] Though not the official view, this naked vision strongly informs a perspective which places national and international concerns above local and regional ones.

By far the most important impact of the 'Kanaky factor' has been renewed demands for closer incorporation in France, demands that are irresistible in Paris. The encouragement of migration from and also to the DOM-TOMs, lavish financial support alongside the decline of the productive economy, and the construction of a massive centralised bureaucracy have ensured incorporation and maintained dependence, especially in the absence of real cultural or economic nationalism outside the South Pacific. The material advantages of DOM-TOM status have discouraged independence movements, which have tended to focus on cultural aspirations, relative deprivation, unemployment, land tenure and inequality, self-reliance and self-determination, rather than on economic gains from local control of the economy. This is most apparent in French Polynesia, where the independence movement was strongest before the start of the nuclear testing that transformed the economy, and in the Caribbean, where independence is as much a cultural as a political or economic issue. The structural problems of the economies of most DOM-TOMs have resulted in high levels of unemployment, emphasised in periods of economic crisis, which, rather than stimulating demands for an independent economy, have often underlined the strengthening of ties with France to ensure the maintenance of a subsidised consumer economy.

Opposition to any hint of independence is strongest in outlying islands throughout the DOM-TOMs, where economic fragility, the regression of rural development, and dependence are usually greatest. In French Polynesia, the first independence party emphasised Tahitians, rather than outer islanders, and the Marquesas are the strongest bastions of support for France; Wallis and Futuna, in some respects 'outer islands' of New Caledonia, are wholly opposed and, in New Caledonia, Melanesian support for France is greatest in the Loyalty Islands and the Isle of Pines.[77] In the distant Guadeloupe outliers such as Saint-Barthélemy, 'the islanders are afraid of being transformed into a defenceless minority under the authority of the "big black island". Without doubt the "Saint-Barts" will do all they can to stay French.'[78] And in Saint-Martin, islanders also fear independence in Guadeloupe, preferring a separate referendum that would enable them to become more directly tied to France, and become what one former mayor called 'little jewels in the showcase of France.'[79] In Désirade too there is very strong opposition to nationalism and consequent support for the French presence.[80] The independence movement has shaped a new political geography of the DOM-TOMs.

For similar reasons there have often been suggestions that, if any independence movement appeared on the verge of success, partition would follow, as occurred in Mayotte and was overcome in Santo, Vanuatu. In French Polynesia, it is strongly believed that the Marquesas would be persuaded to remain French,[81] and in New Caledonia there have also been fears of fragmentation, with Noumea and the south remaining 'loyalist.'[82] Those areas that have fared best under France would hold firm.

Much of the literature of the *indépendantistes* exhibits concern over some regressive aspects of independence. John Teariki commented on French Polynesian independence:

It would be difficult now as the people aren't ready for independence. The Tahitians live an unnatural life now. They live off imported goods, tinned food and other things. There would be struggles, unemployment, all possible things.[83]

In Guadeloupe the UPLG stress, 'we must prefer liberty with its difficulties' or even 'dignity and deprivation'[84] and Burton concluded that in Martinique,

the one hope is that the different factions of the Martinican left will unite and tell the Martinican people, honestly and forthrightly, that, although independence will undoubtedly cause grave disruptions, it is ultimately better for the island to produce its own life, however modest, than to consume the tablescraps vouchsafed it by an alienating neo-colonialism.[85]

Like many before and after him, John Teariki pragmatically recognised that this kind of withdrawal would not command electoral support and chose to support autonomy; in the Antilles, ideological austerity and minimal support have tended to prevail. Not surprisingly the MIM has cautioned against crude measures of development such as per-capita income[86] and, with much of the independence movement, has focused on more personal and spiritual aspects of liberation. In fact, few of the *indépendantiste* movements have put forward cogent plans for economic development after independence, and most of their suggestions rely either on continued high levels of foreign support or on some vague and rather idealistic 'socialism.'

If the literature of the *indépendantistes* occasionally touches on economic difficulties, that of their opponents is replete with potential problems contrasted with the economic certainties of the French presence. In the 1988 referendum, New Caledonians were warned that a stark choice must be made between the continuation of the French presence and independence without French financial aid. This was a new version of an old theme. In 1958, de Gaulle had posed the same alternative to African countries voting on continued ties with France. In the 1970s Pierre Messmer warned 'pas de divorce avec pension' ('no divorce with alimony')[87] and Bernard Stasi, the Secretary of State for the DOM-TOMs, stressed: 'One cannot claim a right to both independence and social welfare.'[88] Threats emphasised economic certainties. A parallel theme of those opposed to independence was the difficult situation of neighbouring independent states. 'Loyalists' in New Caledonia have constantly pointed to problems in Vanuatu, with the implication that rejection of a prolonged French presence was the cause. Large numbers of illegal Haitian and Dominican migrants in the Antilles, and of Comorians in Mayotte, provided tangible evidence of economic stagnation; hence in Martinique 'independence is equated with Haiti, with material poverty, with political oppression; overseas department means France, security and (relative) prosperity.'[89] It has even been suggested that, in some circumstances, such as in Guyane, independent states might simply be annexed by larger neighbouring states.[90] This assertion seems unrelated to reality.

Arguments for and against independence, and autonomy, emphasise the inevitable unease at peripheral incorporation in a distant European state, with a quite different climate, economic structure and racial composition, and the additional unease of a new and wider European community. Yet there is much greater discomfort at the prospects of some form of disincorporation, for tiny dependent states without natural resources in the midst of island micro-states, many characterised by economic stagnation, political tension and emigration, and sometimes subject to such natural disasters as hurricanes. Tensions are ever-present since few residents of the DOM-TOMs are certain of the long-term value of French threats and promises. After all, the DOM-TOMs are largely unknown to the French public. Indeed, de Gaulle's famous statement, 'Mon Dieu, comme vous êtes français' ('My God, how French you are!'), on his arrival in Martinique in March 1964, has been variously interpreted as being one of either surprise, delight or amazement. A quarter of a century later few in the DOM-TOMs are quite sure of their place in the national or international community.

More than a decade ago Burton concluded for Martinique that 'the emergence of a race-based, non-socialist (even anti-socialist) independence movement, possibly "populist" and "Africanist" in character, may be anticipated.'[91] It did not happen there, but in New Caledonia, which has seen the only genuine popular movement in favour of independence. Melanesian nationalism simultaneously appealed to tradition, history, and progress, and stressed the need to construct a new egalitarian structure of development, founded on traditions of cooperation, but adapted to the presence of a mining industry; the FLNKS effectively called only for greater Melanesian participation in the economy without any structural transformation. The claims to unity that characterised Kanak nationalism are relatively permanent features, such as ethnicity, values, territory, language and history, and the belief that nation and state should coincide and enable social justice, status and power in a Melanesian land, over Melanesian society, economy, political system and destiny. 'Socialism' is no more than a rejection of a colonial capitalism from which Melanesians were largely excluded. In an independent Kanaky, Melanesian rights to land would be restored and agriculture would be more important; but otherwise the economy would be unchanged, tourism and mining would continue and further, and more diverse, foreign investment be encouraged. Kanaky would thus be much like the independent Melanesian states to the north where, despite a similar loose socialist rhetoric, capitalist development has continued and intensified and foreign investment everywhere increased.[92] Yet the independence movement in New Caledonia has used quintessential European concepts (such as nationalism) and strategies.

In French Polynesia and the Antilles similar but narrower claims were made, in situations where the distinction between 'coloniser' and 'colonised' was never the same as in New Caledonia. Consequently outside New Caledonia independence movements have focused primarily on a trilogy of issues: language, culture and national consciousness; wages and unemployment; and inequality. Nowhere have independence parties been alone in concern with these issues, which have often been adopted by autonomist and even centrist parties. Already tiny parties have experienced intermittent dissolutions, fission and fusion and, occasionally, the desire to share power by directly participating in government. Demands for independence are almost entirely those of small urban groups, more a protest against inequity than support for a coherent political programme. The struggle for independence has often been a lonely one, even the preserve of 'a handful of gloomy, pessimistic, alienated intellectuals'[93] intent on achieving new forms of education and consciousness, rather than direct action or even electoral participation. Yet in all but the three smallest DOM-TOMs there are independence movements, a *cri de coeur* against peripheral incorporation and a necessary thorn in the consensus of dependent development.

Réunion, the largest in population of the DOM-TOMs, has been one of the least troubled by any pressure for independence. Though there have been demands for greater autonomy, the independence movement is largely conspicuous by its absence, a function certainly of a situation where an isolated island has received massive financial assistance from France, more so per capita than any state in Africa, and welfare services are superior to those in some *départements* within the hexagon. More than elsewhere, it is in Réunion that decolonisation has been argued to concern not independence but integration; the Réunion senator, Albert Ramassamy, has said that 'for the old colonies that have become *départements*, integration is a means of decolonisation, just as much as independence for those who have chosen that.'[94] Hence in Réunion political pressure is principally for greater assistance from France. For Guyane, the historian Serge Mam-Lam-Fouck has also stressed that *départementalisation* was decolonisation,[95] a theme that has been less strongly promoted in the Antilles. This represents the most contemporary version of a historic French policy and tradition that envisaged the goal of colonisation to be the creation of a Greater France, through the integration of colonies into the *métropole* and the transformation of a dominant relationship to one of equality. Decolonisation would be an individual rather than collective goal.[96] Not only has this been a historic policy but it has also been precisely this perspective that has shaped much of contemporary French policy towards the DOM-TOMs. Bernard Pons, the Minister for DOM-TOMs under Chirac, stated: 'There are two ways of ending decolonisation: secession or the achievement of full French citizenship.'[97] Implicitly, 'secession', rather than 'independence', would be an illogical and foolish choice. In Réunion, and in the other DOM-TOMs, there is widespread support for this view.

When decolonisation was under way in Africa in the late 1950s, the *vieilles colonies* had already become French overseas *départements*, tied extremely closely to France. Assimilation and economic dependence triumphed over incipient nationalism and certain deprivation. When decolonisation occurred in the Caribbean and the Pacific in the 1970s, the Pacific territories had, in their turn, been firmly integrated with France, though early pressure for independence in French Polynesia had been rebuffed. In the *vieilles colonies* especially many residents perceived themselves foremost as French citizens and saw few similarities between their status and that of residents in nearby British colonies in the Caribbean, South America or the Indian Ocean, where independent states were being constructed. It was not until the 1980s, and then only in the territory of New Caledonia, that even *indépendantistes* drew the most mild parallels with nearby independent island states, a measure of the very different colonial histories and linguistic isolation. Though the Comoros, Djibouti and the New Hebrides (Vanuatu) belatedly gained independence, they were each exceptional cases; moreover both Djibouti, where a substantial French garrison is present, and the Comoros, invaded by French troops late in 1989, remain closely tied to France. There are no longer such exceptions. Hence the consolidation of the independence movement in New Caledonia in the 1980s was, in many respects, too late. It is an irony of history that the most vigorous independence movement in the South Pacific has not achieved its aim and is unlikely to do so and that, throughout the DOM-TOMs, the heyday of the independence movement is over.

The only conceivable scenario for independence in any of the DOM-TOMs would be one of French origin, based on some combination of economic crisis, in which the excesses of the transfer economy were no longer possible, combined with a reduced global strategic presence, in which, amongst other things, nuclear testing in a distant ocean would no longer be relevant or feasible. There is little prospect of a ban on nuclear testing being thrust upon France; nor is there any real prospect that economic depression would lead to the abandonment of the last 'confetti of empire.'

9

The DOM-TOMs and the Wider World

A MAJOR REASON for acquiring overseas possessions in the colonial period, in addition to the raw materials and markets they were seen to provide, was to establish bases at strategic points on the globe from which to further a nation's interests. This early role has endured into the contemporary world of the DOM-TOMs, which provide an international presence for France in all the oceans of the world and bases for a variety of French activities.[1] The DOM-TOMs are 'a valuable base for monitoring these regions which gives France an exceptional capacity for involvement there'. Because of the DOM-TOMs,

France's frontiers are not those of the *hexagone* but its independence begins in Noumea, Fort-de-France, Saint-Denis, Kourou and Mururoa. This French presence . . . gives our nation a global dimension and necessitates a political strategy that is world-wide.[2]

For Senator Paul Moreau of Réunion,

they ensure that France has a more than symbolic presence in every region of the world and particularly in the most strategic ocean areas. Economically they allow it to have a commercial presence in various parts of the world. They also ensure France a political presence and the perpetuity of *Francophonie*.[3]

And for Jean Maran, a *député* from Martinique: 'the DOM-TOMS are crucial bases for the French military and merchant fleets around the world and ensure its territorial and political security and its economic independence.'[4]

A number of commentators argue that the DOM-TOMs are both useful for France's international presence and essential for it to maintain its global role. Senator Albert Ramassamy of Réunion believes that 'the DOM-TOMS are not indispensable for France to remain a world power. But without them its place in Europe and the world would be much less important.'[5] Michel Renard argues that 'the DOM-TOMS are not only necessary but indispensable for France to remain a world power',[6] and Senator Marcel Henry of Mayotte fears that 'in the unlikely event that the DOM-TOMS choose or meet a separate destiny from that of the *métropole* then France would lose one of the most precious assets that enable it to remain a global power.'[7] Jean-Paul Vié, a former government official in the DOM-TOMs ministry, says straightforwardly: 'It is partly thanks to the existence of the *départements et territoires d'outre-mer* that France has not declined to the status of a second class world power.'[8]

Such sentiments reflect French global ambitions. One of the constants of French policy since the end of the Second World War has been the goal of maintaining its international position. As one of the permanent members of the United Nations Security Council, a founder of the European Community, a nuclear power and the fifth-largest economy in the world, France wields enormous clout in international affairs. Even after the 'loss' of much of the empire, Paris reiterates its right and determination to be a major actor in world affairs. More particularly, France views itself as a major second-ranking power, just after the two superpowers. By distancing itself from the policy of the United States and the Soviet Union, it acts as an alternative to the two. France champions its role as a patron to the Third World, and especially its former colonies, a source of exports, aid and culture to which Third World countries can turn rather than subordinating themselves to the Soviet Union or the United States. France has also tried to play an intermediate role between Europe and Africa and between Europe and the Islamic world.[9]

France performs these international roles in a variety of ways. The French military might is critical and is centred on its nuclear capacity and the efforts to keep this potent and up-to-date through nuclear testing in French Polynesia. Some 40,000 French soldiers stationed abroad — both in the DOM-TOMs and in independent countries with which France has signed agreements — back up the nuclear arsenal and the conventional forces in the *métropole*. France also has the financial means to make its influence felt; it is one of the world's largest aid donors and a major trading partner of many countries, especially the Francophone African states. Paris has an important voice in international assemblies and organisations, most notably the European Community, where it has often taken the leading role. Finally, France possesses important cultural links with overseas countries, providing them with educational and technical assistance, and is the key player in the Agence de Coopération Culturelle et Technique, the principal institution of Francophonie. Structuring the edifice is France's simple projection of itself as a world power. Whereas other European states, such as Germany, Italy and the Netherlands, have a relatively low-key international presence, and such other former colonial powers as the United Kingdom express their international might only episodically, France continually manifests its desire to remain present around the world.

The DOM-TOMs represent a particularly important component of this internationalist policy. They provide the sites for the space station in Guyane and nuclear testing in French Polynesia and are 'windows on the world' in their respective regions, showplaces for the French political system, culture and technological sophistication and bases from which to observe and win influence. For instance, in 1978, the French Secretary of State for the DOM-TOMs, Paul Dijoud, said that Réunion was 'one of the bases for French development and economic penetration of the Indian Ocean.'[10] And even tiny and isolated Saint-Pierre and Miquelon has been described as a window on North America.[11]

This international aspect of the DOM-TOMs has aroused particular controversy. The level of economic development and the high standard of living in the DOM-TOMs, by contrast with the modest conditions or outright poverty of their neighbours, excite envy and frustration. Such disparities are often glaring. Martinique and Guadeloupe have one of the highest standards of living in the Caribbean, while nearby Haiti remains the poorest country in the western hemisphere. Infant mortality is 12.6 per thousand in Martinique, while it is 30.1 in the neighbouring island, St Lucia. The gross domestic product (GDP) per capita in Martinique rises to more than five times that of St Lucia, almost eight times that of Dominica and thirteen times that of Haiti. In the Indian Ocean, the GDP of Réunion is more than three and a half times that of Mauritius and ten times that of Madagascar.[12] This relative deprivation can incite hostility towards the French presence among some politicians and nations, especially when prosperity is largely credited to financial transfers and subsidies from France, yet it can also engender migration from neighbouring states to the French territories.

The DOM-TOMs' neighbours have contested the legality of several French holdings, particularly uninhabited islands in the Indian Ocean and the French claim in Antarctica. France and Vanuatu have disputed the ownership of the Matthew and Hunter islands, which lie between Vanuatu and New Caledonia.[13] In the North Atlantic, France and Canada regularly argue about fishing rights in the waters around Saint-Pierre and Miquelon and neighbouring Newfoundland. This quarrel has been particularly animated because inhabitants of both the French territory and the Canadian province largely depend on fishing for their exports and livelihood.[14]

Other actions of France in the *outre-mer* provoke opposition, none more so than the nuclear testing in Mururoa. In the 1970s, Australia and New Zealand took France to the International Court of Justice in opposition to the nuclear experiments in French Polynesia, and several international organisations regularly condemn France for the tests, although such pronouncements have little effect.[15] In 1985, a group of South Pacific nations meeting at Rarotonga, in the Cook Islands (a territory of New Zealand), drew up a treaty making the South Pacific a nuclear-free zone. The treaty was directed at the United States and, rather more consciously, at France, but even some of the Oceanic states refused to sign the document. Although the treaty promoted regional solidarity and increased moral pressure on Paris, it has proved ineffective in achieving its main objective.

More generally, France's entire sovereign presence overseas is challenged by some neighbouring states, several international organisations, and such regimes as that of Libya. For these groups, the DOM-TOMs are nothing more than colonies in which France exploits natural resources and labour, pollutes the environment and oppresses subject populations. Calls for 'decolonisation' of the French *outre-mer* have become regular pleas at meetings of the Organisation of African Unity, the South Pacific Forum, the Non-Aligned States and the Decolonisation Committee of the United Nations. Most such demands are merely formal, and France's influence with the major powers and many small states means that such calls can be ignored, even though they provide a continual annoyance to policy-makers in Paris.

The DOM-TOMs thus provide France with a series of international bases but their continued existence is also a major ground on which France's international policy is criticised; such a conjunction is perhaps inevitable. Furthermore, both the structure of France's international interests and the nature of France's interventionism and 'colonialism' attract both support and opposition inside the DOM-TOMs and in the *métropole*. The DOM-TOMs have thus become an ideological stake in France's global presence.

Several areas of France's international relations are of particular and recent relevance to the DOM-TOMs. One is French cultural *rayonnement* and the concept of Francophonie. Another is the creation of exclusive economic maritime zones (EEZs) and the potential exploitation of ocean resources. A third is the role of the DOMs (and, to a lesser extent, the TOMs) in the European Community and the relationship between the DOM-TOMs and their neighbouring states. Finally, there are the particular regional relations which surface in the Caribbean, Pacific, Indian Ocean and Antarctica, concerning security and strategic issues. Each of these areas demonstrates the ways in which the DOM-TOMs are both a benefit but also an area of challenge to France's international actions and intentions.

FRANCOPHONIE

The DOM-TOMs are vehicles for the *rayonnement* (or dissemination) of French language and culture around the world. The French have always vaunted their language as an international tongue and argued that French culture is universalistic. The colonial effort included in its programme a *mission civilisatrice* to bring Western culture to non-Europeans. Paris continues to promote French culture by granting subsidies to the hundreds of branches of the Alliance Française around the world, setting up cultural centres, sponsoring *lycées* (high schools) and sending technical and teaching personnel (*coopérants*) to Africa, Asia and the Pacific. 'Francophonie' is the ideological and institutional link between France and other countries where French is spoken and often recognised as an official language. The Francophone nations organise regular summit meetings, work together in such organisations as the Association de Coopération Culturelle et Technique and sign bilateral agreements for cooperation.[16]

France disavows using Francophonie for overt political purposes, although some countries (notably Algeria and Madagascar) have refused to join certain Francophone organisations, charging that they are agents of French neo-colonialism. The Francophone movement itself, which dates from the early 1960s — the time of decolonisation of the largest French overseas possessions — began as a cultural alliance but is gradually evolving into a French parallel to the British Commonwealth with a more formal and permanent structure and more political goals.

A number of Francophone states are neighbours to the DOM-TOMs and were once French colonies: Dominica, St Lucia and Haiti in the Caribbean, Mauritius, the Comoros, Madagascar, the Seychelles and Djibouti in the Indian Ocean region and Vanuatu in the South Pacific, as well as Saint-Pierre's giant neighbour, Canada. In the DOM-TOMs, the French administration often organises schools and training programmes for language teachers and other specialists from surrounding countries and even organises university courses in other countries (as in the case of Mauritius and, in the future, perhaps Vanuatu). France has set up universities in the Antilles, in Réunion and in Oceania. Regular subsidised festivals of Francophone films and literature are held and there are tours by French performing groups. French radio and television is broadcast to surrounding areas from transmitters in the DOM-TOMs.

The cultural activities of France are designed to reinforce the *francisation* of the DOM-TOM populations and also make the DOM-TOMs displays for French culture in their respective regions. But this policy also aims at winning support for France's continued administration of its overseas *départements et territoires*. For instance, France has cultivated the French-speaking population of Mauritius partly to ensure acceptance for the departmental status of Réunion.[17] In the South Pacific, French support for the French-speaking minority of Vanuatu, roughly one-third of the state's population, has been seen as a way of gaining support for Paris' policy in New Caledonia and of sustaining opposition to Anglophone political leaders who have strongly criticised the French role in the South Pacific.[18]

The French cultural presence also draws tourists to the DOM-TOMs. Advertisements entice potential Australian and New Zealand vacationers to the distinctive French ambience of Tahiti or New Caledonia, and lure Americans to the French West Indies and South Africans to Réunion; the message they promote is that French *haute cuisine* and *haute couture* are near at hand. Tourist brochures meanwhile also hint to metropolitan residents that they can holiday in the French *outre-mer* without being too disoriented since they can enjoy the tropics while speaking their own language.

French culture in the DOM-TOMs has come under attack from those who argue that France has only imposed its language and culture by overwhelming and suppressing other traditions. The contemporary revival of indigenous cultures has created a counterweight to more traditional French culture.[19] In some of the more remote regions of the DOM-TOMs, such as the outer islands of French Polynesia and many parts of New Caledonia, French culture and language, in any case, have never become well established.[20] Nevertheless, in the Caribbean, the Indian Ocean and the Pacific, the DOM-TOMs both embody and channel French language and culture in the eyes of neighbouring peoples and serve as a cultural agent of France's global presence. They therefore provide a means of competing with a global Anglo-American domination and of exporting French culture. For example, in 1989 a Francophone film festival was organised in Saint-Martin, where the lingua franca of both the French and Dutch zones is English. An official commented on the links between culture and politics, but also pointed to French cultural neglect of its smallest overseas outposts:

It is our geographical location and the absence of French cultural institutions that have encouraged us to struggle for Francophonie. We are the forgotten people of our cultural *métropole* and totally swamped by American culture. Our wish to have a Francophone film festival in Saint-Martin clearly expresses our political intention.[21]

At least in theory, the DOM-TOMS also provide an environment for a mixing of European and non-European cultures. Only Mayotte and Guyane are not bordered by Anglophone states. It has been said of New Caledonia,

this territory might become a meeting place of Oceanic and European cultures and a place for cooperation with English-speaking groups of the Pacific. The Pacific people would like this in order to avoid the monotony and the danger of strictly Anglophone relationships.[22]

What remains unspecified are the advantages specifically accruing to France from that development.

REGIONAL ACTION

France's successes and failures in international activities depend partly on regional conjunctures. With the DOM-TOMs, France is present in several crucial zones of the world, yet that presence is not equally exercised or appreciated. The Caribbean is perhaps the area where France is best regarded as a good 'neighbour'; by contrast in the Pacific many perceive France to play a largely negative role. Elsewhere there is a more ambivalent concern over France's regional role, and even in the North Atlantic there are occasional collisions.

Saint-Pierre and Miquelon

The tiny remnant of France's North American empire, Saint-Pierre and Miquelon, has sometimes seemed a thorn in the side of Canada. Franco-Canadian relations, normally cordial, have occasionally been troubled both by French sympathy for nationalist movements in Quebec and by controversy surrounding fishing rights in the waters around Saint-Pierre. De Gaulle's 1967 cry of 'Vive le Québec libre!' ('Long live free Quebec!') in Montreal caused a rift between the two countries as did later French support for the separatist Parti Québécois. With the decline of the nationalist movement in the 1970s and early 1980s, and greater Canadian efforts to put into practice a policy of bilingualism, however, this issue faded. Conflicts over fishing rights have continued to fester.

In 1972, France and Canada signed a treaty for the use of maritime resources in the area, but Canada soon charged that French fishers were violating the accord by exceeding their quotas of fish. In 1977 Canada and France extended their claims over international waters to two hundred miles, obviously creating a clash in the area. Furthermore, rumours of petroleum deposits between Saint-Pierre and Newfoundland inspired prospecting activities, and Canadians objected to oil exploration by French companies. Meanwhile, to complicate the situation still further, Saint-Pierrais fishermen complained about metropolitan French trawlers, under licence from the government in Paris, fishing in 'their' waters.

In 1986, when certain articles of the 1972 agreement expired, and the French and Canadians began to consider new provisions for fishing in the north Atlantic, tension increased. Early the following year, the two states worked out an agreement for sharing catches, with the French agreeing to take a smaller harvest from the Gulf of St Lawrence in return for larger quotas from the waters northeast of Newfoundland. The arrangement suited no one. Charges of French overfishing continued to be made, and the premier of Newfoundland convinced Ottawa to ban French fishing vessels from Canadian ports as a protest. He argued that if this measure proved unsuccessful, Canada should withdraw its ambassador from Paris and proceed with retaliatory trade measures including even the use of the powers of the Canadian navy.

For his part, the Senator from Saint-Pierre, Albert Pen, suggested to visiting President Mitterrand that the French adopt the same strategy towards Canada that England had taken towards Argentina over the Falkland Islands; the French president rejected such a response. Pen warned that the Canadians might eventually want to annex the French islands, but he also criticised the French government for failing to support the economic development of Saint-Pierre. He refused to receive the visiting French prime minister and wrote a provocative article in Le Monde comparing Saint-Pierre with New Caledonia and asking,

'Et pourquois pas l'indépendance de Saint-Pierre-et-Miquelon?' ('Why not independence for Saint-Pierre and Miquelon?')

In early 1988, Pen went to Ottawa and began a hunger strike, though without great effect. In April, he and three other elected officials of Saint-Pierre and a few French fishermen were arrested by the Canadian coast guard on charges of trespassing in Canadian waters and imprisoned for three days in Newfoundland. The French were obliged to pay 2.9 million francs in bail for the release of the men. The following month the French Navy took a Canadian fishing vessel into custody off the coast of Saint-Pierre and obliged Ottawa to pay bail. Politicians in Canada and France called for trade sanctions and other retaliatory measures. The affair soon blew over, and what journalists labelled the 'cod war' between France and Canada did not escalate. Yet the long-term division of maritime resources between the two countries remains unresolved, proving the potential for conflict resulting from the overseas presence of metropolitan powers in even their smallest territories.[23]

The Caribbean Basin

The Caribbean was the first area of the western hemisphere to attract the attention of European expansionists, and the 'sugar islands' became the most precious colonies in the overseas empires of the seventeenth century. Since that time, various powers have striven for influence at this crossroads of the Americas and Europe. The United Kingdom and the Netherlands, as well as the United States, still administer islands in the Caribbean Sea.[24] The Soviet Union's support of the regime of Fidel Castro challenged Western strategists and led to the Cuban missile crisis of 1960. More recently, American troops have intervened in the Dominican Republic and invaded Grenada to maintain the influence of the United States in the region which Washington has considered its sphere of influence since the proclamation of the Monroe Doctrine in the early nineteenth century.[25] American intervention in Grenada was officially condemned by President Mitterrand, though the representatives of France in the Caribbean as well as most of the Antillais local leaders and populace generally approved the invasion. Indeed the dispute in Grenada reminded Martiniquais across the political spectrum that, on their own, their island might be no less hotly contested by the superpowers.[26]

American hegemony in the Caribbean has restricted French influence and also limited the French military presence to levels much below those of many other DOM-TOMs. But it has probably also safeguarded France from greater criticism of its presence in the DOMs there. Denunciation of France is not likely to come from those other territories attached to European states or the United States. Criticism of French 'colonialism', therefore, is a strictly formalistic pronouncement by 'progressive' regimes and pro-independence parties inside the DOMs themselves.

Most Caribbean islands, whether independent or dependent, have maintained the relations established in the colonial age with their metropoles, and regional cooperation in the Caribbean has consequently been difficult to achieve. The political integration of Martinique, Guadeloupe and Guyane with metropolitan France and the importance of transfer payments and subsidies from Paris have particularly reinforced the 'enclave' nature of French DOMs in the West Indies. Trade with other Caribbean islands is insignificant; the proportion of their exports to the rest of the Caribbean are 4 per cent for Martinique, 9 for Guadeloupe and 2.5 for Guyane. The French *départements* are not members of any of the regional economic organisations, notably the Caribbean Community (CARICOM), and they have not received concessions or payments under the American Caribbean Basin Initiative scheme set up in 1984.[27] However, since the 1980s there has been a series of private visits between the Antillais *départements* and their neighbours, an embassy was established in St Lucia in 1984 (accredited to each of the independent states between St Kitts-Nevis and Grenada), and France has become a significant donor of aid and technical assistance to several independent Caribbean nations, especially the nearest Creole islands of Dominica[28] and St Lucia, as well as Haiti. The Antilles university centres have begun a Caribbean agricultural development programme and are training students from several Caribbean island states, including Trinidad.

France stations troops in the Caribbean DOMs and a detachment of Légionnaires guards the space station at Kourou. In 1980, the French Caribbean troop strength totalled 3000 soldiers, and the Secretary of State for the DOM-TOMs affirmed: 'France is one of the rare countries in the world capable of transporting to the Antilles and Guiana, in ten hours, a division and a half of crack troops.'[29] Cuban encouragement of rebel activities in the Caribbean concerned France, as did a strong Libyan presence in Surinam, but the government of François Mitterrand also took a sympathetic stand towards the Sandinistas in Nicaragua and dissidents in El Salvador, and Mitterrand met Grenada's socialist leader, Maurice Bishop, in 1982. Invasion of the French Caribbean DOMs is unlikely, and French soldiers have not been deployed outside the French *départements* except in April 1982, when the conservative government of Eugenia Charles in Dominica was threatened with overthrow by dissident elements. Since then France has also undertaken the training of the Dominican police force, and provided army relief after Cyclones David and Frederic devastated Dominica in 1983 and 1985.[30] The military bases in the French islands protect them, and they also serve as back-ups for Guyane. Kourou has considerable strategic value, has been an enormously expensive construction and is carefully guarded against any attempted espionage or sabotage. The troops in Guyane also patrol the ill-defined and sometimes fragile frontiers with Surinam and Brazil, and numbers have increased in recent years to cope with problems posed by the substantial incursion of refugees and others from Surinam.

The exploration and use of outer space forms a key element in French policy, and France is one of only three nations in the world with a comprehensive space programme. In 1962, Paris set up the Centre National d'Etudes Spatiales (CNES) to promote space exploration and, indirectly, to compete with the then more advanced efforts of the United States and the Soviet Union. The French launched their first satellite in 1965 from a base in Algeria, which they continued to use until 1967. In 1964, faced with being deprived of the Algerian base which they held under the Evian accords, Paris decided to create a new space centre in Kourou, Guyane. The Centre Spatial Guyanais (CSG), closer to the equator than either the American Cape Canaveral or the Soviet Baikonur range, is technically ideal and has the advantage of being located in a thinly-populated and easily-secured region over which France enjoys legal sovereignty. The first rocket test took place at the CSG in 1968, and the first launching followed in 1970. Since that date, Ariane rockets have sent into orbit satellites for France, foreign governments and also private firms. Meteorological and telecommunications satellites have joined other scientific and military orbital vehicles launched from Kourou. The space programme, a major employer in Guyane, has produced great business activity; in 1985, official sources estimated the turnover realised from the French space effort at 5.8 billion francs. The programme serves as proof of French technological prowess and modernity and provides another justification for France's status as a world power. Furthermore, France has spearheaded the European space effort. A founding member of the European Space Agency (ESA), France provides much of the technological expertise and funding for a variety of programmes. Notable among these is the Hermes programme (for which France contributes over 40 per cent of the budget) which will put a manned space vehicle in orbit in coming years. The French have also cooperated in manned space missions with the Soviet Union and the United States.[31] Along with the nuclear testing at Mururoa, Kourou forms the most dramatic representation of precise French interests in the *outre-mer* and the international role they allow France to play.

Indian Ocean

For centuries, the Indian Ocean has been a crossroads for world trade; and the pioneering of a sea route around the Cape of Good Hope by Vasco da Gama in the 1490s inspired European interest and established Portuguese rights in the area. The great East Indies Companies of the 1600s chartered vessels to buy the spices and silks of the Orient, and the Dutch founded a colony in southern Africa and gradually outdistanced the Portuguese. But the British became masters of the Indian Ocean by the mid-1700s, and the vast possessions on the Indian subcontinent formed the heart of the British empire. Only the good grace of the British allowed the Portuguese to retain Goa and the French to stay in their five tiny Indian outposts, Pondichéry, Karikal, Yanaon, Mahé and Chandernagor. (The Dutch, meanwhile, restricted their activities to the East Indies.) The southwest Indian Ocean, however, became a pre-serve of the French, who won control of Réunion, Mauritius and the Seychelles. The Napoleonic Wars deprived France of the last two of those possessions, although Mauritius and the Seychelles preserved French culture and language under English sovereignty. Later in the nineteenth century, France expanded in the Indian Ocean with the conquest of Mayotte and the other islands of the Comoros chain and finally took the 'Grande Ile', Madagascar. In addition, France acquired several uninhabited islands in the Mozambique Channel, the 'Iles Eparses', and other unpopulated islands in the southern Indian Ocean. France also took increased interest in some of the countries on the littoral of the Indian Ocean, evidenced most notably by the French construction of the Suez Canal, which opened in 1869.[32]

Britain's reign over the Indian Ocean outlived the independence of India, Pakistan and Sri Lanka, as well as the independence of Kenya and Tanzania on the African coast of the Indian Ocean. In 1966, a British defence report recommended that the British withdraw 'west of Aden', a policy which became effective in 1971.[33] Britain divested itself of its remaining possessions, granting independence to Mauritius in 1968[34] and to the Seychelles in 1976 and retaining only the so-called British Indian Ocean Territory, several islands making up the Chagos archipelago. The Portuguese and French territories in India were retroceded to India, and in 1960, France granted independence to Madagascar. Paris, however, retained control of the Comoros until

1975, and even after the independence of that state held on to Mayotte, the Iles Eparses and the Austral Islands, as well as Réunion.

The British withdrawal from the Indian Ocean created what was perceived as a strategic vacuum in the region after two centuries of 'pax Britannica.' The Americans stepped in. The British government leased Diego Garcia, the largest island of the British Indian Ocean Territory, to the United States. The move provoked great opposition, especially from Mauritius, from which the islands had been bought for a derisory sum just before the independence of that country. Furthermore, the thousand or so residents of Diego Garcia were all removed from their island, forcibly taken to Mauritius and given little hope of an eventual return; they remain poorly integrated into Mauritian society.[35]

The United States installed a major military base on Diego Garcia, which serves as the headquarters for the American Indian Ocean fleet and air force and houses some four thousand American military personnel. The French also retained a military presence in the Indian Ocean with bases in Réunion and in Madagascar and Djibouti, both before and after the independence of those two states. However, the French military presence in the southern Indian Ocean suffered a blow in Madagascar. In 1972, the pro-French regime in Madagascar was overthrown, and the new pro-Soviet government forced the French to evacuate their base at Diego Suarez (Antseranana) on the northern tip of the island. Meanwhile, the Soviet navy became interested in the Indian Ocean in the 1970s, obtaining port rights in Somalia (that were subsequently revoked), South Yemen and Ethiopia (after a pro-Soviet coup there). The Soviet Union allied with six 'progressive' regimes in southern Africa and the Indian Ocean, and such states as Mozambique and Madagascar signed agreements of cooperation and aid with East European nations, Cuba and North Korea. The radicalisation of politics in the Indian Ocean together with the new Soviet interest concerned Western powers and ensured that France kept its strategic interests there.[36]

The new geopolitical and economic importance of the Indian Ocean caused some concern over a clash of superpowers in the region. The main stakes were the primary resources which existed in the areas bordering the Indian Ocean, especially after the oil crises of the 1970s. The countries of the Arabian Gulf contain 60 per cent of the world's known reserves of oil. Through the Indian Ocean pass half of all petroleum deliveries to Western Europe, 90 per cent of those to Japan and 80 per cent of the oil provided to the African states. The Indian Ocean littoral also has some of the world's richest deposits of minerals, particularly in South Africa and Australia. Europe imports from countries bordering on the Indian Ocean 44 per cent of its manganese, 40 per cent of its chrome, 47 per cent of its cobalt, 58 per cent of its uranium and many other mineral resources.[37] The possibility of exploiting underwater deposits of minerals and other maritime resources adds to the economic interest of the region. The uninhabited Iles Eparses and the Austral Islands, through the large exclusive economic zones which they provide for France, could be potentially useful for such resources. Furthermore, attempts have been made to use Port-aux-Français, the 'capital' of the Kerguelen islands and the TAAF, as a registry for French ships. Such a registry exempts French vessels from obligations to hire French nationals as a certain proportion of their crew.[38] Finally, the Indian Ocean countries, especially such giant population centres as India and Indonesia, represent vast potential markets for French exports.

The Indian Ocean region in the 1970s and after has been battered by war and domestic upheaval. India suffered the assassination of its prime minister, Indira Gandhi, and ethnic violence in the Sikh regions; civil war between Tamils and Sinhalese has torn Sri Lanka; rebels campaign for independence in the Ogaden and Eritrea regions of Ethiopia; and the struggle of black nationalists for majority rule continues in South Africa. Somalia, Mozambique, Myanmar (Burma), Pakistan and Bangladesh have witnessed turbulent times. Since independence, the Comoros has witnessed two coups and, in 1989, the assassination of its president; there was a coup in the Seychelles in 1977, and an attempted coup in the Maldives in 1988. From being a tranquil backwater of the globe, the Indian Ocean began to seem a tinderbox for strife.

The French presence in the Indian Ocean has endured and even been reinforced, despite some challenge to that position. In the early 1970s the Organisation of African Unity and conferences of leftist political parties from the Indian Ocean states regularly condemned continued French control of Réunion and Mayotte, charging France with colonialism and exploitation.[39] Until the independence of Djibouti and the Comoros, French administration there was regularly castigated, but such criticisms have become muted. The neighbouring states of Somalia and Ethiopia both claim Djibouti, but its independence and the French military presence serve as a guarantee that neither nation will be able to take over the contested area.[40] The Comoros government has never abandoned hope for a reunification of the archipelago under its control, but also uses Mayotte as a bargaining card to solicit everincreasing aid from Paris. Madagascar, for its part, rejects French control of Mayotte but has not wished to see the power of the Comoros, a traditional rival, grow stronger in the region.[41]

An effort was made in the 1970s to declare the Indian Ocean a nuclear-free and even demilitarised zone, and the United Nations General Assembly voted in favour of such a proposal. The nuclear powers were opposed, however, as were several states in the region interested in developing their own nuclear capacity. The project has come to naught and is no longer pursued by the groups which first pushed it.[42] In any case, France has always affirmed its sovereign right to station nuclear-powered vessels and to carry out other activities connected with military or civilian uses of nuclear energy in its territories.

French sovereignty over the uninhabited islands of the region remains contested. Both Mauritius and Madagascar claim the Tromelin reef north of Réunion but have made little effort to recover control from France.[43] Madagascar claims the Iles Eparses, which indeed came under the administration of the French government in Madagascar before its independence. The Malagasy government which came to power after 1972 claimed that French sovereignty is illegal and issued proclamations about extending its control over the Iles Eparses; in response the French in 1974 stationed a small contingent of soldiers on several of the islands to preclude any intervention from Madagascar. A modus vivendi now seems to exist concerning the islands, several of which are also claimed by the Comoros Republic.[44] The potential economic significance of the exclusive economic zones has made rival claims much more than ritualistic statements.

French aid to the nations of the southwest Indian Ocean has grown, and France is now the largest aid donor and trading partner of the island states of Mauritius, the Seychelles, the Comoros and Madagascar, as well as Djibouti.[45] Though Mauritius is heralded as one of the newly industrialising countries and has achieved political harmony and economic development,[46] the other island countries are in dire straits. Madagascar, the Maldives and the Comoros are among the poorest countries in the world and each faces severe environmental problems including, for the Maldives, the long-term greenhouse effect; Madagascar's population has suffered from a major epidemic of malaria and lives on the borderline of famine. In such circumstances, French aid is even more vital. France's strong voice in the European Community is also important for these countries, all of which (except the Maldives) are members of the African Caribbean Pacific (ACP) group of countries receiving special subventions and prices under the Lomé conventions. Partly for these reasons, France has been welcomed as a member of the Indian Ocean Commission.[47] Indeed, opening his electoral campaign in Réunion in November 1985, Raymond Barre stated: 'Never forget that there is no other representative of Europe in this ocean.'[48] France's links with Djibouti are also crucial for that small and arid country. The French military base there forms the state's primary resource; expenditures by expatriates and aid from Paris contribute greatly to the country's welfare.[49]

In short, despite some regional opposition to French control of its DOM-TOMs in the area, and the existence of a tiny pro-independence movement in Réunion, France has largely achieved recognition of its sovereign position as a nation of the Indian Ocean. France's international interests in the region are multiple and the maintenance of a French sovereign presence probably ensures that France does more for the other states of the region than it would otherwise.[50]

France's strategic mission is to safeguard its Indian Ocean territories against invasion or attack, and also to protect its citizens living in independent states of the region, who number more than 40,000.[51] Geopolitically, France has a number of other concerns, of which the main one is the desire to safeguard the maritime routes essential for the delivery of its petroleum supplies. France relies on minerals from countries bordering the region, and access to such strategic resources as uranium must be maintained.[52] France also seeks to secure the sea lanes through which it delivers armaments. France is the world's third-largest exporter of armaments (after the United States and the Soviet Union); it has significant clients among states of the Third World, including such nations on the border of the Indian Ocean as India and Iraq.[53] Finally, France has seen its role in the Indian Ocean as that of a third global superpower, a buffer between the American and Soviet presence and a patron of the states which maintain neutrality or which have loosened their ties with the superpowers: 'In "occupying the land" France limits the incursions of foreign powers into the region and contributes to its security and stability.'[54] France's Indian Ocean presence represents both a cause of and a justification for its claims to remain a global power.

About 7000 French troops are stationed in the Indian Ocean region.[55] France's military strength consists of a major base in Djibouti, which is the main refuelling and provisioning port for the French Indian Ocean fleet and base for 3500 soldiers. At the end of 1987 President Mitterrand stressed: 'Djibouti is one of the principal places where France, the third most important military power in the world, affirms its global presence.'[56] In Réunion, France maintains about 3200 military personnel and approximately 350 in Mayotte, including a regiment from the Foreign Legion. Between ten and twenty French soldiers and a gendarme are posted on each of the main islands of the Iles Eparses (Juan de Nova, Europa and the Glorieuses).[57] The primary aim of the military is to defend French territories and France's wider interests in the Indian Ocean but, it has also been hinted, the soldiers are a reserve force in case of any domestic trouble in Réunion or Mayotte.[58] Complementing the soldiers are the French ships which patrol the Indian Ocean. According to the head of the French navy, in 1977 the French fleet was the largest in the Indian Ocean with its twenty-three ships and 4500 sailors.[59] That strength has since been somewhat reduced, but the French naval force in the Indian Ocean remains at the level of around twenty ships carrying as many as 3000 sailors. 'Zone No. 5', the French military command for the Indian Ocean, in addition to these sailors, includes 6000 shore personnel and 1200 aviators and aircraft technicians, a total of 9800 personnel (with a possibility of reinforcement by a further 2000).[60]

In the Indian Ocean France benefits from the ties established with former French colonies, the *tiers-mondiste* policy (focused on aid delivery and technical assistance) and the independence from both superpowers which make it a partner for Third World countries in the region and enable substantial acceptance of France's sovereign rights as a full-fledged state of the Indian Ocean.

Antarctica

The frozen continent of Antarctica has become a new frontier for overseas expansion, currently in the political sphere and in future perhaps in an economic realm.[61] France is one of a number of countries with claims on the Antarctic mainland and also a number of sub-Antarctic islands. French sovereignty over the Austral Islands of the southern Indian Ocean is not contested in the international arena. There are few plans for development of these islands, but the islands give France a stake in the southern Indian Ocean which might conceivably be of strategic significance on southern sea routes particularly for the monitoring of movements of other nations' navies. Correspondingly Réunion provides relatively easy access to the TAAF. Construction of a military base on Kerguelen would be feasible, but unlikely, according to French observers.[62] Other commentators, on the basis of circumstantial evidence, suggest that France might have plans for transferring its nuclear tests to Kerguelen.[63] For the moment, the French Austral Islands — like others in the region which belong to different powers — create little strategic concern or debate.

France, along with Australia, the United Kingdom, New Zealand, Norway, Argentina and Chile, claims a region of Antarctica.[64] The 1959 international treaty on Antarctica, however, did not officially recognise such claims and agreed only to freeze discussions of sovereignty for the next thirty years. The expiry of that treaty, and new consideration of exploiting the mineral resources of Antarctica, renewed interest in the region. The 1959 treaty specifically demilitarised the Antarctic continent and prohibited any power from establishing military bases, stationing troops or weapons, or undertaking military tests in Antarctica, a ban apparently followed by all the countries which maintain scientific bases there. The dividing line between military and non-military activities, however, is difficult to determine and all activities in this region are difficult to verify.

The various stakes in Antarctica have been challenged, and there have been calls for the continent to be internationalised so that individual sovereignty claims would be forbidden. However, the growing scientific and potential economic significance of Antarctica work against such a harmonious resolution. Promoters of Antarctic development argue that new technology would make it possible to tap mineral and oil resources underneath the ice cap, that maritime resources (especially krill) in the waters surrounding the continent could be exploited, or even that bits of icebergs could be broken off and hauled northwards to provide fresh water for arid countries. However Paul-Emile Victor, the founder of the French Polar Expeditions in 1947 and dean of French Antarctic specialists, judges that the resources of the Antarctic and the problems of exploiting them 'do not justify the unbounded and feverish excitement which ... has caught hold of governments.'[65]

France's main activity in the Antarctic has consisted of regular scientific experiments at the Dumont d'Urville station in Terre Adélie, the French portion of Antarctica. Controversy has arisen concerning French plans to build the first airstrip in Antarctica (the Piste du Lion) near its base. Authorities say that the airstrip would ease access for scientists, lengthening the time research could be done during the southern summer from one and a half to four or five months. Direct air connections would also make it possible to transport staff and materials with greater ease and, ultimately, more economically, than by ship from Réunion; despite the cost of the airstrip it would thus save money in the long run. Opponents have argued that the airstrip would harm the environment of Antarctica and, in particular, endanger a large colony of nesting penguins by blocking their migration routes. By contrast, Victor rejected such arguments, pointing out that the penguins have various migration routes and that the species is not endangered; others, notably the French oceanographer Jacques Cousteau, have opposed the airstrip and warned of irremediable damage to the continent.[66] Several conservation groups, notably Greenpeace, have attempted to disrupt work on the airstrip and harass French scientists in Antarctica. Actual construction of the airstrip began in 1981 but was soon interrupted and began again only in 1989. The French government remains committed to the project, and opposition has been primarily confined to ecological groups and traditional opponents of French overseas policy.

Pacific Ocean

France is present in the Pacific Ocean principally through the three TOMs of French Polynesia, New Caledonia and Wallis and Futuna, yet nowhere has France's overseas presence been so hotly contested in recent years nor have domestic problems in the *outre-mer* reached such levels of upheaval and violence. These troubles have occurred at a time when the Pacific has assumed greater importance in world affairs and even been hailed as the 'new centre of the world.' The rapid economic growth of Japan, the development of the newly industrialising countries of east Asia, the Soviet policies of *perestroika*, *glasnost* and the reconstruction of Vladivostok, and China's emerging regional presence have focused attention on the Pacific basin. Trans-Pacific trade now exceeds trans-Atlantic trade in value and volume, and the mineral resources of Australia and the technological expertise of the American west coast complement the economic achievements of the Asian countries. Geopolitical concerns have spread to the Pacific as distant powers express a greater interest in the region and the Pacific is increasingly perceived as a new stage where many of the major contemporary economic, political and strategic struggles are being played out. Across the whole political spectrum there is a widespread view in France that the Pacific is 'the Mediterranean of the twenty-first century' and that France therefore has a duty to be there, alongside other democratic states, to share responsibility for the defence and economic development of the micro-states. In this scenario France would be an exporter to the region, a major investor, a guaranteed source of energy and a participant in technological and scientific development.[67]

The South Pacific in the 1960s and 1970s was championed as a haven of peace, and little turmoil surrounded the birth of the new micro-states of Oceania. Consensual politics, racial harmony and a degree of self-reliance seemed to reign in most islands, supposedly exemplifying 'the Pacific way.' Political systems were broadly democratic and there were few real diversions from the 'Westminster model.' Occasional problems troubled Oceania, but these generally related to natural disasters. The problems that followed American nuclear testing in Bikini (Marshall Islands) and difficulties surrounding the independence of the former Franco-British condominium of Vanuatu in 1980 seemed to be the exceptions which proved the rule.[68]

In the 1980s the situation changed. The campaign for independence by Melanesians (Kanaks) in New Caledonia exploded into virtual civil war and guerrilla warfare in the French territory. Fiji suffered two military coups in 1987, the first ever in the independent island Pacific, and the new regime in Fiji set out to limit the political rights of the Indian majority in the archipelago's population. In 1988, an unsuccessful coup in Vanuatu pointed to the deep cleavages which exist among different cultural groups and political factions in that nation. In Papua New Guinea, political instability, government corruption, rising crime rates and violence on the mineral-rich island of Bougainville emphasised the country's social and economic problems. The ANZUS military alliance of the United States, Australia and New Zealand broke apart over New Zealand's opposition to the visits of American nuclear-powered warships in its ports, bringing into question the American security umbrella which had been erected over the islands of the South Pacific ever since the defeat of the Japanese in the Second World War. The Soviet Union, China and Japan began taking a larger role in South Pacific affairs. In particular, the USSR signed short-lived fishing treaties with Kiribati and Vanuatu, and opened an embassy in Papua New Guinea; in a much-discussed speech in Vladivostok, the Soviet leader affirmed his nation's desire to play a role in the South Pacific. Japan increased its fishing activities and its commercial presence and became the largest aid donor in the region. The Libyan government provided some encouragement and support to one pro-independence group in New Caledonia, and various observers became worried about the intervention of these and other outside nations in South Pacific affairs.[69]

France has been at the centre of much debate on the South Pacific.[70] Opponents of French administration of its DOM-TOMs accused France of exploitative colonialism.[71] The micro-states with support from Australia and New Zealand convinced the United Nations that New Caledonia should be relisted on the roster of non-decolonised regions; the South Pacific Forum, an association of mainly independent nations, which refused to grant observer status to France at its meetings, regularly condemned French policy in New Caledonia. The violence in that territory, culminating in the taking of hostages and military siege in Ouvea in 1988, shocked regional opinion. Nuclear testing in French Polynesia provoked similar opposition from Australia, New Zealand and the other Pacific island states, many of which signed the 1985 South Pacific Nuclear-Free Zone Treaty (the Treaty of Rarotonga). Among the most vocal protesters against continued French tests was the international ecology organisation Greenpeace, and in 1985 French secret agents sank a Greenpeace vessel, the *Rainbow Warrior*, in the harbour of Auckland, New Zealand, killing one person, an act that provoked outrage in the Pacific and for which France eventually agreed to imprison the perpetrators and pay reparations.[72] During much of the 1980s, in short, France was treated as the pariah of the Pacific for its 'colonial' presence and its intransigence on nuclear testing, and often became a scapegoat for various political critiques.[73]

The French government, especially during the prime ministership of the conservative Jacques Chirac from 1986 to 1988, responded in an arrogant and uncomprehending manner, accusing critics of simply trying to evict France from the Pacific and interfere in France's own affairs. More reasonable communication gave way to emotional polemics and mutual distrust and denigration. Within the Pacific region the neighbouring Melanesian states of Papua New Guinea, Solomon Islands and Vanuatu came together from 1986 onwards as the Melanesian Spearhead group, perceiving themselves as frontline states in geographic and diplomatic terms in opposition to French actions in New Caledonia.[74] Only since mid-1988 has the climate improved; regular French ministerial visits to the independent states of the South Pacific have resumed, governments have largely agreed to disagree on the question of nuclear testing, and the South Pacific Forum has approved the terms of the Matignon Accord as a long-term move towards independence in New Caledonia. France has meanwhile made a special effort to cultivate favour among the micro-states of Oceania, especially Fiji, through more substantial aid; the effort has met with some success. The visit of French prime minister Michel Rocard to Australia and Fiji in August 1989 symbolised the improved relations between France and the states of the region. Although defending French policy, including nuclear testing, Rocard adopted a conciliatory approach and met with a warm reception.[75]

France has seen its actions in the South Pacific as appropriate for a sovereign power in the region, a necessary part of France's global strategy in protecting its geopolitical and economic activities, and a counterbalance to American and Soviet interests. Much as in the Caribbean or the Atlantic, the French territories of Oceania are both justifications and bases for France's international role, and France reacts strongly against attempts either to deprive it of those bases or to deny it that role, especially at a time when French Pacific promoters underline the stakes the Pacific holds for the future.[76]

Central to France's Pacific presence — and to opposition to French policy — is nuclear testing. French authorities argue that such testing is vital to the maintenance of French defence capacity and the continual modernisation of military forces. France first experimented with nuclear devices in the Saharan desert, but the independence of Algeria made the transfer of the test site necessary. President de Gaulle chose to relocate it on two small and remote atolls in the Tuamotu chain of French Polynesia, Mururoa and Fangataufa, with the island of Hao as a back-up base and much of the administration of the Centre d'Expérimentation du Pacifique (CEP) located in Papeete. The first atmospheric tests occurred in 1964; in 1973, France discontinued atmospheric testing and has since pursued underground testing with several experiments a year. The testing has become a major economic activity in French Polynesia and a prime source of funds for the territory.[77]

Opponents of nuclear testing argue that the explosions are destroying Mururoa atoll by undermining its basaltic base, thus allowing radiation to escape. Furthermore, they suggest that the sea around Mururoa is already polluted, and that radiation has poisoned fish and seeped into the food chain. They support such claims with statistics on levels of cancer, ciguatera and other diseases which might be associated with radiation. French officials reply that stringent safety tests, which are continually carried out, prove that there is no environmental damage because of the testing. France brought a team of Australian, New Zealand and Papua New Guinean scientists to Mururoa in 1983 to complete independent experiments, which concluded, on the basis of limited access to sites and data, that the nuclear testing was not dangerous. The French counter arguments that the tests pollute the 'backyard' of Australia (and other Pacific states) by pointing out that Mururoa is further from Australia than is the Soviet test site, and that not nearly as many people live in the vicinity of French tests as in the immediate range of American or Chinese tests. The French also reject suggestions that the tests be moved to the *métropole*, although the idea of transferring them to the Kerguelen Islands in the southern Indian Ocean has been mooted.

A considerable number of troops and support personnel are stationed in French Polynesia to protect the test site (including a detachment of Légionnaires in Mururoa). The French maintain a major fleet in the South Pacific, divided between French Polynesia and New Caledonia. In the mid-1980s different French governments sought to increase the military presence in New Caledonia, even talking of turning the island into a gigantic 'aircraft carrier.' Because of the internal troubles in New Caledonia, in the 1980s France also stationed as many as 9000 soldiers, riot police and *gendarmes* there. Critics charge this represents an unacceptable militarisation of the Pacific. France claims that it is necessary to preserve law and order in New Caledonia and protect France's wider interests in the Pacific TOMs. France states, however, that no nuclear weapons are deployed in the Pacific territories, although nuclear-powered French ships and submarines pass through the region.[78]

French military withdrawal from the Pacific, and the ending of nuclear testing, would undoubtedly have a major effect on the economies of French territories. Such a move, however, does not seem immediately likely, despite recent changes in European politics, as all major political parties in France (with the exception of the Communists) affirm the necessity of continued nuclear testing, and the ecological and peace movements in France are weak. Indeed the military presence increased during the 1980s and there was some reference to Wallis and Futuna, a major military base during the Second World War, and even Clipperton, hosting military forces.[79] The Treaty of Rarotonga is a 'toothless tiger', though it gained more signatories in 1989 and 1990, and France's friends and clients in international organisations are unwilling to risk an all-out attack on French policy. Even in the unlikely event of French Polynesia becoming independent, France would not have to relinquish its testing sites, as the islands of Mururoa and Fangataufa were officially ceded to the metropolitan government by an act of the French Polynesian assembly. A change in statute for French Polynesia or New Caledonia would also not necessarily preclude the sort of defence agreement that France arranged with Djibouti, and other former colonies in Africa, which enabled it to retain and even expand its overseas military presence.

THE DOM-TOMs AND THE SEA

All the DOM-TOMs, including Guyane and Terre Adélie, have vast maritime exclusive economic zones (EEZs) and extensive coastal waters, hence a particularly important aspect of their value to France is their maritime potential. The resources of the sea have always provided foodstuffs for DOM-TOM residents and products for export. Some 80,000 tons of fish are caught in the French *outre-mer* annually, half of which is taken by French vessels. Cod is the only commodity produced in Saint-Pierre and Miquelon and rights to fish for prawns off Guyane, and tuna around the Austral Islands (French Polynesia) are leased out. The sea provides other resources as well, notably the pearls found in the Tuamotu chain of French Polynesia, which now make up that territory's largest export, and the trochus shells, which are Wallis and Futuna's only export besides handicrafts.

A more significant long-term development may be the exploitation of submarine resources within the EEZs of the DOM-TOMs, following the Law of the Sea convention signed in 1982 by 120 nations (but not the United States). The convention recognises a limit of 12 nautical miles for territorial waters around a country and its possessions, plus a zone of a further 188 nautical miles in which that nation enjoys a monopoly on use of the sea and its resources; together these 200 miles form the country's exclusive economic zone. Through the DOM-TOMs, and especially the most isolated, France is in a particularly good position to benefit from the new arrangements. France's EEZ in Europe amounts to only 340,000 square kilometres, but the DOM-TOMs give France a total of 11 million square kilometres of EEZ; the EEZ of tiny Clipperton Island, at 440,000 square kilometres, is larger than that of metropolitan France. France, therefore, enjoys the third-largest EEZ in the world, after the United States and the Soviet Union, and is the only country to have significant EEZs in the Atlantic, Caribbean, Mediterranean, Indian Ocean, Pacific and the Southern Ocean of Antarctica. France's holdings, recognised under international law, are little contested by other nations.[80]

The immediate advantage of the EEZs is the right to the exclusive use of maritime resources and there is also the possibility of leasing out fishing, mining, exploration or other rights to different agents. Great hopes, however, are placed on the future exploitation of even more profitable resources. Geologists have discovered significant deposits of minerals in the continental shelf which is contained within the EEZs of the eastern Pacific, and these 'polymetallic nodules' are especially rich around volcanic islands, where a 15–30-centimetre crust contains such minerals as manganese and cobalt. Prospectors also hope that the continental shelf and ocean floor will eventually yield deposits of petroleum, that hydrothermal sources of energy may be put to use and that minerals may be extracted from the sea water itself.[81] However, technology, capital and entrepreneurship are not yet readily available, successful development has not been apparent elsewhere and there are major doubts surrounding the costs of exploiting submarine resources.

The EEZs have now become a major stake in France's desire to retain the DOM-TOMs and even to tighten its hold on some of them. Moreover, they have given the uninhabited islands — Clipperton, the Iles Eparses, the Antarctic Islands and various other offshore islands of the DOM-TOMs — previously unexpected potential. Loss of the Pacific EEZs, it is claimed, 'would compromise France's place in the global oceanological competition.'[82] They provide an 'atout océanique de la France' ('an oceanic advantage for France')[83] of special interest to the merchant marine and the French Navy. Furthermore, France carries out much oceanographic research through such institutions as the Institut Français pour la Recherche et l'Exploitation de la Mer

(IFREMER),[84] which centralises French research, and through private explorers, the most famous of whom is Jacques Cousteau. Some of this research remains purely theoretical but other projects, on such subjects as nutritional resources, weather prediction and mineral research, promise practical applications.

Nevertheless, the EEZs create several legal and political problems. The Law of the Sea agreement leaves certain questions unanswered, for example, whether waters between two neighbouring states should be divided equidistantly (and, if so, what exactly constitutes the farthest limit of a country's shoreline) or whether an effort should be made to divide the resources of the zone equitably between the states. This has been an issue in the conflict between France and Canada over fishing rights near Saint-Pierre and Newfoundland, but is critical wherever island territories are in proximity (for example, in the Antilles and in the Mozambique Channel). A further issue that affects France is the extent to which an EEZ can be claimed around islands that are not 'effectively occupied.' Clipperton Island has had no permanent population, since intermittent mining occupation between 1892 and 1917, hence one analysis of France's claim to an EEZ around the island is that it 'seems inappropriate that France should be able to claim an exclusive economic zone and continental shelf on behalf of this remote and seemingly uninhabitable atoll. It is surprisng that no nation has complained about France's action, and that even Mexico seems willing to go along.'[85] Within France concern has also arisen over the leasing out of rights, especially when they are given to 'unfriendly' foreign states. Some French geopoliticians feared that leasing fishing rights to the Soviet Union by Kiribati and Vanuatu would constitute the start of Soviet penetration of the South Pacific, but remained untroubled about the French giving fishing rights to the Soviets around Kerguelen. Whatever the eventual value of the EEZs, however, current agreements give France, somewhat ironically, an exclusive maritime area almost exactly equivalent to the land area of the French empire before postwar decolonisation and provide a new and powerful rationale for continued connections between the DOM-TOMs and France.[86]

THE DOM-TOMs AND EUROPE

Another international aspect of the DOM-TOMs is their connection with the European Community (EC). The Treaty of Rome, which set up the European Economic Community in 1957, in Article 227, associated the French DOMs (and Algeria) with the new organisation, and in 1978 the 'Hansen decision' of the European Court of Justice declared that all EC regulations applied to the DOMs. Both, however, made provisions for the adaptation of EC legislation and rules to the specificities of the DOMs.[87] They are therefore, completely assimilated into the EC and residents vote in elections for the European Parliament.[88] Somewhat paradoxically, these French *départements* in the Antilles, South America and the Indian Ocean are legally European. The TOMs, along with other overseas territories such as the British Virgin Islands and the Netherlands Antilles,[89] are not fully integrated into the EC, but have full voting rights in European elections and receive benefits from their relations with the Community.

The European dimension of the DOMs has become an object of contention. French authorities have championed the links between the *outre-mer* and the EC. The then Minister for the DOM-TOMs, Bernard Pons, told the Commission of the EC in Brussels in 1987: 'If Europe is an opportunity for the DOMs, the DOMs are an opportunity for Europe.' He added that with their EEZs, the DOM-TOMs brought to Europe an immense maritime zone: 'These regions offer Europe a global arena for scientific research, oceanic exploitation, telecommunication, and maritime, air and future space links.' Furthermore, with their ethnic and cultural diversity, 'they can serve as a link with neighbouring countries, opening the way for programmes of economic, scientific or cultural cooperation, so giving Europe undeniable assets.'[90] Pons and others have also spoken of the DOMs as a 'Europe tropicale.' France has emphasised that such projects as the space station in Guyane and regional cooperation between DOMs and neighbouring countries are European and not merely French undertakings.

By contrast, Ernest Moutoussamy, a *député* from Guadeloupe, perceived a new European imperialism in the DOMs. With closer integration of the *départements* into the EC, 'Europe will bring about profound and disorienting socioeconomic changes in order to create a flourishing parasitical tertiary society where productive employment and national identity will have no place.' He argued that 'Europe's goal ... is to get the most out of the DOM-TOMs, to turn them into an "ornamental wreath around Europe" and to Europeanise their cultural heritage.' Europe sought to use the DOMs as 'bases for trade and services, as tourist resorts and as disposal stores ... collective colonies of Europe whose local populations will be swamped by European migrants.'[91]

The debate took on new urgency with the acceptance of the Single European Act by the French Parliament in December 1986. The Act, scheduled to take effect in 1992, will create a vast European market with free movement of capital, goods and labour across the frontiers of the twelve member states. Customs duties will be almost entirely eliminated; the value-added tax will be harmonised; professionals, companies and other organisations will be able to move freely within the EC; and various regulations and qualifications (for example, higher education diplomas) will be standardised. Through their integration into the EC, the arrangements will also be implemented in the DOMs and, to a lesser extent, in the TOMs.

Within the DOM-TOMs fears of the Greater Europe have arisen on several accounts. Critics such as Moutoussamy believe that the migration of numerous Europeans to the DOMs, attracted by warm climates and economic possibilities, could swamp the local populations and reduce the cultural importance of the African and Asian elements of those populations. Such new arrivals, possibly with superior skills, would also provide competition for local workers in situations where unemployment is already considerable. Transnational corporations from Europe might also move into the DOMs, extracting natural resources with little benefit for local populations. This new demographic and economic 'imperialism' might only aggravate disparities between the DOMs and other members of the EC. Such disparities are already great, both individually and nationally. The average annual per-capita revenue in Guadeloupe is one-third that of Denmark. In 1985, the members of the EC (excluding France) sold 2176 million francs worth of goods to the French DOMs but bought only 309 million francs worth of goods in return.[92]

A more particular issue is the end of the *octroi de mer* in the DOMs. This tax, established in the 1800s, is levied on all products entering the DOMs, irrespective of their origin; even goods produced in other parts of France must pay the tax. The *octroi de mer* provides the bulk of finances for communal budgets. In December 1988, the Commission of the EC adopted a Programme d'Options Spécifiques à l'Eloignement et à l'Insularité des Départements d'Outre-Mer (POSEIDOM), which foreshadowed some financial assistance to the DOMs, as well as greater regional cooperation in the Caribbean and Indian Ocean, but also mandated the freezing of the *octroi de mer* at current levels until the end of 1992, followed by suppression of the tax. The proposal caused such an outcry in the DOMs that the Commission was forced to revise its position, stressing that some sort of tax, destined for regional development, could be envisaged as a replacement although the *octroi de mer*, in its present form, violated the provisions of the free European market legislated by the Single European Act. The issue remains unresolved, although a complete end to the *octroi de mer* would represent a financial loss to the DOMs and the dissolution of a powerful financial instrument used by DOM-TOM mayors and other politicians.[93]

The DOMs have already benefited from European subsidies, and

French authorities press for more EC aid to the *outre-mer*. Three sources of aid, in particular, have been available to the DOMs. The Fonds Européen de Développement Régional (FEDER) contributed 2007 million ecus to the DOMs from 1975 to 1984; the Fonds Européen d'Orientation et de Garantie Agricole (FEOGA) has provided money for irrigation, estate improvement and modernisation of farming techniques in agriculture in the DOMs; and the DOMs have received finance (amounting to 46.8 million ecus in 1983) from the Fonds Social Européen (FSE).[94] Nevertheless, politicians in the DOMs complain that they have been disadvantaged in the EC. The Common Agricultural Policy of the EC was designed primarily to protect the farm products of temperate climates, not the tropical products of the DOMs. For export of such commodities, the DOMs suffer from competition with the African, Caribbean and Pacific (ACP) countries which benefit from the provisions of the Lomé treaties. Under the terms of these treaties, some of the agricultural products of the ACP nations, among the poorest and smallest in the world, enter the EC duty-free, although no arrangement exists for a reciprocal free entry of European products into these markets. Many of the ACP countries export the same products as the DOMs, notably sugar and tropical fruits, yet their overheads and production costs are much lower. The EC has consequently agreed to a scheme to support the production of sugar, rum, bananas and tinned pineapple and to assure a portion of the European market for these commodities to DOM producers. Such price supports have been legally challenged in the European Community, and competitors (even some inside France) continually attempt to break through the trading arrangements of Lomé. DOM farmers also fear competition from low-cost producers of southern Europe in a European Community which now includes Greece, Portugal and Spain.[95]

France uses the DOMs as bases for displaying and selling its products to their neighbours in the Caribbean and the Indian Ocean (and, for the TOMs, in the Pacific) and as bases for regional cooperation. Yet the attachment of the DOMs to the EC and the inevitable competition between them and the ACP countries creates a clash of interests, which highlights the difficulties the DOM-TOMs face in being at the same time Caribbean, Pacific or Indian Ocean islands, French *départements* and territories, and, in the case of the DOMs, and to a lesser extent the TOMs, members of the wider European community. The European card, however, is one that can be played by France in attempting to win support inside the EC, and attempting to gain approval for its continued administration of the *outre-mer*. It can also be used by DOM-TOM politicians ready to bargain their location and resources for benefits and anxious to maintain and improve their positions inside an EC which can use the DOMs to stretch its frontiers beyond Europe.

FRANCE, THE DOM-TOMs AND THE WORLD

The international dimension which the DOM-TOMs give France provides the key to understanding metropolitan interest in maintaining French sovereignty over these far-flung *départements* and territories. They have increasingly become centres for the diffusion of French language and culture and constitute an integral part of Francophonie; they form French strategic bases and, in providing nuclear testing sites, the foundations of its military might; they are links in a network of regional and global alliances and cooperation; and their value can be extended to make them European, as well as French, outposts. Michel Debré, former prime minister and *député* from Réunion, has summed up this internationalist dimension: 'With the DOM-TOMs, France has a solid base for participation in global affairs. This means that France is not merely a small parcel of Europe.'[96] Furthermore, a certain continuity exists between the colonial and post-colonial periods for France's worldwide role: 'From the sixteenth century to the present, possession of overseas territories has been an important if not the most important factor in the global influence of a country which is also heavily involved in its role as a major European power.'[97]

In this kind of perspective the DOM-TOMs are seen to be linked together in a manner that does not exist for the dependent territories of other metropolitan powers. For conservative commentators especially, the 'loss' of a single DOM-TOM would be a major blow to France's economic and political ambitions. In this perspective 'the current political status of New Caledonia . . . enables France to take an important place in the path to the heavens and the future race to the stars.' If New Caledonia were to become independent,

this unique and iniquitous precedent would have an obvious chain effect in Tahiti and Kourou giving already active minorities the opportunity to go through the same motions . . . Indeed, after giving up Noumea, how could Mururoa and Kourou not be given up?[98]

Beyond this invocation of the domino principle, economic interests reinforce strategic interests. As Dijoud explained in 1981, in the context of the future prospects for the Pacific territories:

Why disguise the fact that our national interest is to stay in the Pacific? Thanks to our territories and their zones of sovereignty, France has the third largest maritime economic zone in the world. The core of humanity's hope lies in the sea and under the sea. What's more the major powers of the 21st century are to be found in the Pacific: the United States, the USSR, Japan and China, Indonesia and so on. So it's natural that France should be.[99]

Natural or not, this determination to have a global presence has strongly influenced French policy in the contemporary DOM-TOMs and contributed to the vision of at least a thread of French culture, technology and military might encircling and civilising the globe for the remainder of the century.

Such a diverse and comprehensive role has its risks and stimulates the rivalry and jealousy of other powers and the opposition of dissidents inside the country. In the 1800s, opponents of empire argued that France should channel its energies into maintaining its position on the European continent, defeating its European economic rivals or treating the 'social question.' Critics of the policy of expansion said that France should look towards recapturing the provinces of Alsace and Lorraine taken by Germany in 1870; hundreds of coloured 'domestics' overseas could not replace these two 'daughters.' In the 1960s, the French opponents of empire, the Cartierists, again argued that France should retrench itself behind its European frontiers.[100] Yet a surprisingly wide spectrum of public opinion, and most political parties, have always rejected the notion of a 'smaller France.' Current political opinion likewise holds that France's proper stage is a global one, and the DOM-TOMs provide both a justification for and a demonstration of that international position.

10

The Ties that Bind

THE DOM-TOMs are a diverse groups of islands and continental territories scattered around the globe in every ocean from the tropics to the poles. They are, however, united by their attachment to France; the influence of French control on the development of their economy and society, politics and culture; the role they play in France's global policy; and the very fact that they are grouped into an administrative unit by the French government. The nature of France's presence in every ocean is both critical to the understanding of France's overseas possessions and a unique element of its contemporary policy. Even to speak, for example, of 'France in the South Pacific' distorts a situation where French attitudes and strategies are global rather than regional.

Many observers do not hesitate to label the DOM-TOMs 'colonies', referring to them as the 'confetti of empire' and France's last overseas imperial domains. The argument that 'while most constituents of the old empires had been shunted into the post-colonial age, there were always enough awkward survivals to keep alive befuddling myths and rhetoric'[1] is nowhere more apparent than in this vestigial empire, even if 'from the man-in-the-street to the politician, French decolonisation has been completed.'[2] Such judgments are both hasty and simplistic, yet indicate the seemingly anomalous status of the DOM-TOMs in a post-colonial world.

Colonies in the classical periods of European expansion, the seventeenth and nineteenth centuries, were always marked by several traits which do not obtain in the contemporary DOM-TOMs. They enjoyed no political representation in national assemblies, but came under the direct rule of an appointed governor and had a distinctly inferior status to the colonial power. Since 1946, however, the DOM-TOMs have elected *députés* and senators to the French parliament, as well as representatives to their own local assemblies, and elections have been carried out with the same universal franchise as that of the *métropole*.[3] Certainly, actual political power has sometimes been arbitrarily exercised, and the French administration retains final decision-making authority (and still occasionally exercises direct rule), enabling it to over-rule local assemblies and retain significant centralised powers; but the institutional structure for parliamentary government exists. In particular, the DOMs have a system, for better or worse, which replicates the republican institutions of France. Classical colonies were also marked by legal differences among various categories of residents, with political and some civil rights generally denied to the indigenous population. This has changed in the post-war *outre-mer*; for three decades, the populations born in the DOM-TOMs have been French citizens. Economically, classical colonies existed to contribute wealth to the mother country by producing raw materials, buying manufactured goods, facilitating international trade and allowing for investment and settlement. The DOM-TOMs barely satisfy any of these requisites now, and, even in the past, rarely proved to be profitable ventures. The tropical agricultural commodities they produce could be provided to France at least as cheaply from other sources, and only the nickel of New Caledonia now forms a major mineral resource. European 'settlement' primarily consists of bureaucrats, a vastly different situation from that of the colonial age, when a range of settlers reshaped the cultural and physical landscape. The large costs incurred in the social security system, subsidies, administration and the transfer economy mean that the DOM-TOMs are a cost on the French economy, if only a relatively minor one — probably less than 5 per cent of the French gross national product.

Yet the DOM-TOMs retain elements of a colonial system, as even proponents of continued French administration admit. Their economies are dependent on the *métropole*, none of the DOM-TOMs is self-sufficient, the administration represents the largest employer and the French financial lifeline continues to be crucial to their survival. Moreover, France's construction of transfer economies in remote and largely unproductive islands that were increasingly closely tied to the 'hexagon', at a time when other colonial powers withdrew from their empires and France itself was decolonising in Indo-China and Africa, appears paradoxical. Although French law is theoretically applicable throughout the DOM-TOMs, various anomalies also mean that justice is sometimes unequally administered.[4] Informal and unofficial discrimination against certain groups appears obvious in some of the DOM-TOMs, notably in the marginalisation of the Melanesian population of New Caledonia and the Indians of Guyane, and the socio-economic hierarchy in most of the DOM-TOMs is partially based on racial and ethnic backgrounds. The enormously heavy weight of colonial history — including the penal colonies in Guyane and New Caledonia, the phenomenon of slavery in the *vieilles colonies*, the *indigénat* and the banishment of Melanesians to *réserves* in New Caledonia — continues to weigh on current concerns. French assimilationism and centralism have only recently begun to come to terms with expressions of 'national' identity and culture. All the DOM-TOMs remain enclaves in their respective regions, and their attachment to France (and the French language) limits possibilities for regional cooperation, and despite selective French aid, incites opposition from neighbouring countries. The TOMs especially display particular anomalies in the French system, for example, the maintenance of traditional Islamic law in Mayotte, the influence of the three kings in Wallis and Futuna and the civil status of Melanesians in New Caledonia. Balancing what is national and 'French' with what is local and particularistic remains one of the biggest questions facing the DOM-TOMs in order for them to maintain their cultural and social identity and, at the same time, profit fully from their affiliation with France.

The DOM-TOMs are far from homogeneous. Indeed the extraordinary heterogeneity of their landforms and climates, ethnic groups, land areas and population sizes, histories and contemporary structures of development suggests that only their apparent colonial status links them together. Over time these differences have diminished as distant places have become more closely integrated into France. Yet there remain many inconsistencies in the contemporary status of the DOM-TOMs, including the manner of their incorporation into France. Even in the DOMs, in principle totally assimilated to metropolitan institutional and financial norms, illogical exceptions exist. In Saint-Barthélemy, for instance, personal income taxes are not collected, despite a ruling by the *Conseil constitutionnel* that they are applicable. Residents of French Polynesia and Wallis and Futuna also pay no income taxes. The French minimum wage in the Antilles and Guyane is almost one-fifth less than the metropolitan rate and in Réunion it is about one-quarter lower.[5] These disparities, and more obvious historical differences, make generalisations difficult and ensure exceptions to most rules.

THE 'THEORY' OF THE DOM-TOMs

The existence of the DOMs and the TOMs represents two conflicting political ideologies in France. The DOMs, constitutionally as much a part of France as Paris or Corsica, are, in theory, totally integrated into the French system, although law and tradition have led to certain variations from metropolitan norms. It is readily apparent that all the DOM-TOMs, except Saint-Pierre and Miquelon, are culturally very different from the *métropole*. The centralising and universalistic stream in French history, however, has tried to make them overseas extensions of France, and the *départementalisation* of 1946, sponsored by leftist politicians whose intellectual ancestry goes back to the Jacobins, consecrated this arrangement. The residents of the DOMs became, again in theory, full French citizens, and the laws and institutions of the Republic were supposed to end the power of the *Béké* oligarchy. The French state was, therefore, an enforcer of legal equality and a guarantor of democratic representation. The institutions that accompanied *départementalisation*, allowing more comprehensive education, better medical care, higher salaries and social welfare payments, were intended to reinforce the attachment of the DOMs to France and to narrow the gaps between underdeveloped colonies and the modern *métropole*. Even steady migration typified the free access to France which overseas citizens enjoyed and cemented ties between the DOMs and France itself. *Départementalisation*, and the social and economic changes which accompanied it, represented the apogee of French assimilationism.[6]

The status of TOMs, however, represented a different trend, allowing the constitutional possibility of independence from France, specifically-designed institutions and laws, and considerable autonomy. The statutes for the *territoires d'outre-mer* were, somewhat ironically, therefore more 'colonial' than those for the DOMs in that they did not pretend that these regions formed integral parts of France. But the 'colonial' statutes were revised, in most cases, to incorporate universal suffrage, political representation and many of the benefits of the French state. The TOMs (just as the aborted French Union and Community) represented an embryonic Commonwealth with possibilities for self-government and local control under the watchful eye of Paris.

Although policy-makers soundly rejected federalism, in practice the TOMs represent a French version of it.

Over the past decade the two trends of centralism and quasi-autonomy have become linked and sometimes confused. The *décentralisation* of the early 1980s reduced the role of the central authority in French *départements*, not only those of the *outre-mer* but also metropolitan France. Corsica, for instance, acquired a special statute and particular institutions without a change in its constitutional status. Saint-Pierre and Miquelon became a *département*, then a *collectivité territoriale*, an ambiguous category into which Mayotte also falls. In the Pacific, French Polynesia gained a new statute of autonomy in 1984, while New Caledonia staggered from a large degree of local self-determination to a kind of federation among several provinces to direct rule from Paris and back to a renewed federalism.

Such institutional changes, however, did not necessarily imply a rearrangement of dependencies. French Polynesia, which has the greatest degree of autonomy among the French DOM-TOMs — and displays some of its symbols, including a territorial flag — is one of the most economically dependent on the *métropole*. The Melanesians of New Caledonia might be given a greater political voice, but the economic realities of that territory mean that the white Caldoches still wield real local political and economic power, and the French state has not always acted as an impartial arbitrator between the two major ethnic groups. Wallisians and Mahorais hold elective office in their territories, but real power, economic might and technical assistance all come from France. In the DOMs, economic and political power is uneasily shared among the metropolitan administrators and businesses, the local bourgeoisie, especially the *métis* elite, and antagonistic political factions which agree to be coopted into the system or at least participate from time to time in its processes. In short, 'one person, one vote' and financial transfers have not created economic and social equality in the DOM-TOMs and have only incompletely brought about the *départementalisation économique* which Valéry Giscard d'Estaing called for in the 1970s to complement the new political arrangements of 1946 and 1958.

The French system has proved itself versatile enough to accommodate remarkable differences of opinion in the DOM-TOMs: *indépendantiste* politicians hold office in many parts of the *outre-mer* and have sometimes served as favoured interlocutors of the French government. This situation also points to the internal dynamic which structures society and politics in each of the DOM-TOMs. Electoral strategies, including support for metropolitan parties, clientelism and pork-barrelling, as well as ideological swings, make it possible for individuals to achieve and maintain immense power, as the case of Aimé Césaire and, to a much lesser extent, the late Jean-Marie Tjibaou have amply proved. But each of the DOM-TOMs also has its own particularities — regional conflicts, ethnic quarrels, political faction-fighting — which make it impossible to understand the DOM-TOMs solely as extensions of metropolitan France, colonial or otherwise. Furthermore, the DOM-TOMs have proved able to bargain for greater consideration from Paris, bartering their loyalties, their strategic locations and the global advantages which they provide France for greater amounts of money, political restructuring and cultural recognition. Far from being passive observers of metropolitan machinations, the DOM-TOMs have shown themselves active participants in shaping their role inside France and in winning concessions from the *métropole*. Indeed the economic concessions have been so substantial that, in most respects, any semblance of a self-reliant economic organisation has long since disappeared. The struggle by both the *métropole* and the various DOM-TOMs to win the maximum advantage is a continuing aspect of the phenomenon of the *départements et territoires d'outre-mer*, an issue of power, of collaboration and resistance, occasionally of subterfuge, threats and near blackmail. Yet it implies a degree of mutual advantage, reciprocity and even symbiosis which the DOM-TOMs and the *métropole* derive from their continued association.

THE 'PRACTICE' OF THE DOM-TOMs

The stakes which the DOM-TOMs represent for their own populations and for France itself provide possibilities for the use and abuse of the DOM-TOMs. Perhaps the most obvious lies at the level of ideology and political philosophy. The DOM-TOMs can be seen as 'the last French colonies' or 'ces îles que l'on dit françaises' ('these so-called French islands')[7] crying out for liberation from an oppressive colonial power. Alternatively they are portrayed as extensions of France itself — showcases for French achievements, oases of prosperity and democracy surrounded by poor and unstable independent nations: they are 'windows' to other regions of the world. Moreover they are 'la chance de la France', even 'la chance de l'Europe'. General de Gaulle's exclamation to the crowds which cheered him in Martinique — about how French the local population was — and François Mitterrand's calls for decolonisation without independence are examples both of continuing political attitudes and of the appropriation of the DOM-TOMs to the uses of national political strategy. Discourse on the future of the DOM-TOMs is characterised by rhetoric and hyperbole amongst proponents of the French presence and amongst *indépendantistes*. For French politicians and strategists the DOM-TOMs are *enjeux* (stakes) and *atouts* (trump-cards), key locations in a global physical presence with opportunities for future *enrichissement* (enrichment) and *exploitation*. For *indépendantistes* they are homelands, increasingly occupied by colonialists, even in the *vieilles colonies* by *esclavagistes* (slavers), denying the local people their proper separate destiny in the modern world. Yet, for all that, contact between France and the DOM-TOMs is slight. The DOM-TOMs are barely known in the *métropole*, and rarely if ever mentioned in standard texts on the history, politics, or geography of France. Direct contacts have been episodic, now largely limited to tourism, national service and bureaucratic transfers — except at times of political crisis when the DOM-TOMs have taken on a different, but transitory, role in French affairs. At perhaps no time more than in the administration of Bernard Pons as Minister of the DOM-TOMs, in the Chirac government from 1986 to 1988, was there such an undisguised effort to use the DOM-TOMs to satisfy French ideological and electoral purposes.

Despite the overall cost of maintaining the DOM-TOMs, they sometimes bring rewards, monetary and other, to different individuals and groups. For politicians, they provide sources of votes, party membership and, occasionally, funding. Various French companies, such as the Société le Nickel, UTA and Air France, banks and other financial institutions all reap profits from their activities in the DOM-TOMs.[8] The *Békés*, Caldoches and some Polynesian *demis* have amassed wealth from their plantations, commercial and mining activities in the *outremer*. At a different level, the vast number of *fonctionnaires* in the DOM-TOMs earn their livings and owe their status to the French state, a state which rewards them with salaries considerably higher than those in the *métropole*. Thousands of migrants from the DOMs who have gone to the mother country have sought particular advantages from their move, though their ambitions have sometimes been disappointed. Legal and illegal migrants into the DOM-TOMs — Indians and Asians in the nineteenth century, the Haitians and Surinamese in the contemporary Caribbean, and the Hmong in Guyane — have hoped for better opportunities in the DOM-TOMs.

Neither loyalists nor secessionists dismiss the DOM-TOMs as useless. They are the homes of long-established populations, transformed landscapes developed and pioneered by settlers or the birthright of peoples forcibly transferred from one continent to another. They offer potential agricultural, commercial, mineral and maritime wealth, posts for French observation of world activities and the spread of French culture. *Indépendantistes* see the DOM-TOMs as regions for establishing new forms of successful political and economic independence; their opponents see the DOM-TOMs as laboratories for democracy, racial cohabitation and economic development without the dangers of independence. In different contexts they have been perceived as models of the French way of life, and beacons for 'the Pacific way', 'Antillanité' or other cultural identities. Similarly, for outside observers, the DOM-TOMs can be guarantees of French social and economic interests in particular regions (and the Third World in general), thorns in the side of regional projects, such as a 'nuclear-free and independent Pacific', or safeguards against foreign belligerence. The obstinacy and even vitriol of both defenders and opponents of French sovereignty over the DOM-TOMs testify to the importance they hold in world, regional and local affairs.

TOWARDS THE FUTURE

Indépendantistes have argued both that the DOM-TOMs should become independent because they are small territories which are not really necessary or even useful to France and, more often, that they hold great wealth which France is mismanaging and expropriating. Above all, *indépendantistes* demand sovereignty for those seen as the genuine indigenous occupants of these last outposts of empire (in the case of New Caledonia) or for the dominant population most oppressed by European overlords (as in the Antilles). Attempts have been made to calculate the cost of the DOM-TOMs to the *métropole*. However, critics of such calculations have rightly pointed out that trying to determine the cost of the DOM-TOMs is not only absurdly difficult but as illogical as trying to discover the cost of Brittany, Corsica or any other region of metropolitan France. Furthermore, when France granted citizenship to DOM-TOM residents, it took on responsibility for their welfare and the development of their regions which cannot be shunned on the basis of cost.[9]

Undoubtedly much money flows from the *métropole* into the DOM-TOMs, though the structure of consumption in these transfer economies ensures that a high proportion of it flows back and also produces other benefits for France. The DOM-TOMs provided raw materials and workers when France experienced a shortage of labour, but they have also contributed to national prestige and the enrichment of French culture. Of paramount significance remains the international dimension of their relationship to France. They give France a legitimate right to be considered a sovereign power in all the major oceans of the world; to enjoy the third-largest maritime zone in the world, to wield international influence through such projects as a military force (based on nuclear deterrence constantly tested by experimentation) and a space programme; and to promote its influence in international organisations, particularly in the European Community, by stressing the value of the DOM-TOMs for France's partners. For a country which has refused to withdraw to its European boundaries, the DOM-TOMs provide the physical and territorial basis of a global presence, enabling France to stress and to demonstrate its international status. Supporters and critics are well aware of this international 'trump' or 'joker', to use two favourite words of Bernard Pons.

Strategic interest seems particularly crucial to France's continued commitments to, and presence in, the DOM-TOMs. Most apparent in French Polynesia and Guyane, it is also important elsewhere. Indeed in France's global strategic arena the DOM-TOMs are integrated; fear of the 'domino effect' provides one reason for France's determination to remain in New Caledonia. Even Kerguelen may provide a possible fallback position for nuclear testing, should France long continue this expensive programme, and Mayotte could offer a deep-water port between the Suez and Antarctica. Consequently, France has met regional challenges to its overseas presence with blank indifference or new forms of aid delivery and technical cooperation to neighbours of the DOM-TOMs. Key recipients of French aid include Caribbean states such as Dominica and St. Lucia, Mauritius and the Seychelles, Réunion's Indian Ocean neighbours, and the states of the central Pacific, especially Fiji.[10] Through the DOM-TOMs, France has retained both a rationale for being and a means to be a world power; power and authority were not seen to be separate from physical presence and sovereignty. France has not therefore retained the DOM-TOMs for economic reasons. Pierre Messmer, 'It is not material interests which tie Réunion to the *métropole*, it is political, human, physical and spiritual unity. Réunion is France in the Indian Ocean.'[11] More accurately, the converse is true: material interests tie the DOM-TOMs to the *métropole* but political and cultural issues tie France to the DOM-TOMs. Strategic reasons have come overwhelmingly to shape the structure of France's presence in distant seas.

Much of the controversy about the DOM-TOMs centres on their future political status. Independence groups exist in almost all of the DOM-TOMs, although such groups are often divided between those who wish for an immediate and total independence, those who want to prepare for independence over a longer transition period, and those who prefer the maintenance of some constitutional links with France. However, it seems unlikely that any of the independence groups will be immediately successful. In Guyane and Réunion, they are tiny factions, and they do not exist at all in Saint-Pierre or Wallis and Futuna (or, of course, the TAAF). In Martinique and especially Guadeloupe, they are larger but very far from being the majority parties. Only in New Caledonia, and to a lesser extent French Polynesia, are there strong and adamant movements for independence, but various factors work against an accession of either of those territories to independence in the near future.[12] At the other end of the spectrum, there have been calls for the *départementalisation* of New Caledonia, Mayotte and even the TAAF.[13] Such a development also seems unlikely given the different and complex economic and social structures, plus the cost, political opposition (domestically and internationally) and the criticism that *départementalisation* would call down upon France. Even for the DOMs, few politicians continue to support an inflexible *départementalisation* of the sort envisaged in 1946.

Several imaginative proposals have been made for constitutional changes in the relationship between the DOM-TOMs and metropolitan France. Edgard Pisani, as French High Commissioner in New Caledonia in 1985, suggested 'independence in association with France' as the appropriate future for that territory, and the Institut du Pacifique has called for a 'treaty of free association' between New Caledonia and France.[14] One observer of the French *départements* of the Caribbean region has called for a federation of states under the French flag, a community which would include a European France and an Antillo-Guyanais state (itself a union of Martinique, Guadeloupe and Guyane).[15] Others have proposed the creation of three French 'regions', in the Indian Ocean, Pacific and Atlantic, which would be administered by a central coordinating authority.[16]

By contrast, other public figures, notably Aimé Césaire, have called for a moratorium on institutional change, while not abandoning their hope for eventual autonomy or independence. For radical opponents of French control, this begs the question since they believe that social and economic development can take place only in the context of independence and, as the economic structure becomes more artificial, independence becomes less likely. However, moratoria in practice have considerable support; an official moratorium was legislated for New Caledonia under the Matignon Accord, for at least a ten-year period ending in 1998, and both conservative and socialist governments have indefinitely postponed a referendum on the future of Mayotte. One of the remarkable features of the DOM-TOMs is the widespread dissatisfaction with existing statutes, apparent amongst all shades of political opinion, and the consequent failure to resolve these differences of opinion in a satisfying manner. The administrative trend, however, seems to move towards a devolution of authority to local governments in the DOM-TOMs, symbolised by the *décentralisation* laws of 1982, the statute for French Polynesia in 1984 and plans for an interim provincial federation in New Caledonia legislated in 1988. Such a devolution will not solve any of the pressing problems of the DOM-TOMs — regional disparities in development, a substantial lag behind the *métropole* in salaries and living standards, widespread unemployment and an increasingly unbalanced economy — but it may quieten dissatisfaction and allow more local control over metropolitan transfers. The policy of the current government is to maintain such decentralisation, promote economic development and secure the advancement of disadvantaged groups in the DOM-TOMs — an approach perhaps inevitably castigated by critics from different positions as either giving in to local (and sometimes minority) demands or trying to reinforce the French presence and maintain the loyalty of DOM-TOM citizens. Such differences of opinion are sure to persist.

Government policies for the DOM-TOMs also provide perspectives on the *métropole* itself. Projects for the economic development of the DOM-TOMs reflect the capacity of a France buffeted by economic difficulties, unemployment and competition in the world market and challenged with the necessity of restructuring its own economy. Better education and training, economic 'rationalisation' without the creation of even greater unemployment, the invention of new products and services which France can produce and export are all challenges to the nation as a whole which are particularly apparent in the unusual economic situations of the DOM-TOMs. Politically, the demands for greater local self-government in the DOM-TOMs echo similar demands in French regions such as Corsica and at the different levels of communal, departmental and regional government. The question of administrative decentralisation is magnified at the level of the DOM-TOMs by the problem of distance. Decentralisation and a reduction in the powers of the state are of key interest to all political parties in a state which has often been criticised for being bureaucratic, centralised, elitist and ossified. Culturally, the multi-ethnic populations of the DOM-TOMs create 'domestic' reflections on the problems of accommodation by the general French population to cultural diversity, the arrival and installation of foreign residents (especially those of different ethnic backgrounds), and the cross-fertilisation of the different cultures which coexist in France, as well as the revival of racism in France. The DOM-TOMs thus test the limits of French society and culture to allow for differences in language, mentality and race, the definition of 'Frenchness', the adaptation of non-Europeans to France and the benefits and disadvantages of *francisation*. On the international stage, the DOM-TOMs have also posed the question of what France's role in world affairs can and should be, of how it might combine national defence with international cooperation, and promote development in the Third World without implementing (or being accused of) neo-colonialism. Finally the participation of the DOM-TOMs in various regional organisations, and their exclusion from others, raises questions of whether France can convince neighbouring countries of the DOM-TOMs and political rivals that it can achieve just societies, economic prosperity and democracy. In short, the future of the DOM-TOMs is, in many respects, the future of France itself.

THE 'LAST COLONIES'?

France is not the only country which maintains constitutional links with overseas domains. The United Kingdom still has some twenty colonies, now renamed 'dependent territories', spread around the world, the Dutch administer six islands in the Caribbean, the Spanish have two enclaves in North Africa, the Portuguese control Macao, the Danish have Greenland and the Faeroe Islands, and the United States, Australia and New Zealand have territories in the Pacific; the United States also has territories in the Caribbean and Australia has islands in the Indian Ocean. Altogether over forty overseas territories are dependent on European or other developed nations.[17] Indeed in the post-war years territorial acquisitions by some large powers have continued, including the assimilation of the Baltic States into the Soviet Union and Indonesian expansionism into Irian Jaya and East Timor, whilst in Antarctica a phase of competitive and collaborative colonialism has occurred.

Administrative arrangements differ among these regions. Some are integral parts of the *métropole*, such as the Spanish territories and the American states of Alaska and Hawaii. Others are attached to the *métropole* by treaties of free association, still others are administered directly by the mother country. Levels of economic development, social structures and cultures also differ among these territories. For instance, they range from colonies of white settlement (such as the Falkland Islands and Gibraltar) to mixed-race societies (the British, American and Dutch West Indies and Bermuda) to territories in which the Europeans are a distinct minority (for instance, Hong Kong and Macao). Future plans for these territories also vary — Hong Kong and Macao will be ceded to China, the Dutch Caribbean island of Aruba is being prepared for independence, and in others, such as Bermuda and Puerto Rico, some groups seek independence while others prefer continuation of the present 'colonial' relationship; almost everywhere there are also groups which prefer a strengthening of the relationship — a clear parallel to *départementalisation*.

The apparent anomaly of vestiges of overseas empires is thus far from unique to France, nor is experimentation with different constitutional and administrative arrangements. These overseas territories, like the French ones, have also been the scene of friction and even war with neighbouring states, as in Gibraltar and the Falkland Islands. Only in France, however, have current overseas territories been invested with such ideological and political significance, in part because of their substantial population. Furthermore, France's desire to remain a global power has created a use for the DOM-TOMs not promoted for the territories of Britain, the Netherlands or Denmark. Finally, only in France have the overseas regions been so consciously grouped together as a particular unit and so closely integrated into the political economy of the *métropole*.

Nations maintain ties with independent countries, especially with their more recently independent colonies. The British Commonwealth institutionalises ties between the United Kingdom and its former colonies, just as France has signed agreements for aid, trade and military bases with its former colonies and maintains a cultural relationship with most of them through Francophonie. Both countries, as well as many other developed nations, are accused of neocolonialism with regard to the poorer nations of Africa, South America, Asia and the Pacific. Particularly during the apogee of decolonisation in the 1960s and 1970s, perhaps not coincidentally coming at a time of global economic growth, the emergence of the New Left and *tiers-mondisme*, most observers believed that independence would be the normal course of political development for colonies, and that the new states should work to create economic self-sufficiency and break as many ties as possible with their former masters and other hegemonic powers.

This proved not to be the case, especially for the small island microstates which belatedly achieved independence. Most Third World nations which suffer from limited land areas and growing population pressure on scarce resources, poor standards of living, climatic problems or lack of raw materials have become rapidly indebted to international bankers or their patrons (often the former colonial masters). Island countries have few resources, except the sun and sea which can be developed for tourist resorts, an independent status which facilitates the setting-up of offshore banking and financial tax havens, and a few fisheries, agricultural and handicraft products to trade. Such sovereign states as Kiribati and Vanuatu in the Pacific, Dominica and St Lucia in the Caribbean and the Seychelles and Maldives in the Indian Ocean are largely dependent on some combination of these activities; even more significantly, they have become more dependent over time on international migration (and remittances), often to the former colonial power, and aid from international or bilateral sources. Political independence may have been acquired, but economic and strategic independence has proved impossible to obtain, thus limiting political gains. Many island states have thus abandoned costly and disappointing attempts to achieve greater self-reliance and have reassessed development strategies to try to negotiate a more advantageous form of dependency; they use such strategies as concessionary migration and trading schemes to achieve new paths to development.[18] The smaller independent states have thus moved closer, in a rather different way, to achieving the same form of political economy as that of the DOM-TOMs; this is an increasingly negotiated form of development and dependence, as they too move from production to consumption and away from a structure of development based on local resources.

Since small, insular states (and many larger ones, especially on the African continent) cannot aspire to full economic independence, the sorts of ties that exist between the DOM-TOMs and France may seem of great benefit. The DOM-TOMs may lack independence, but they are assured of a certain level of funding and financial transfers by the *métropole*, their citizens receive pensions, family allocations and the other benefits of the welfare state, they can migrate freely to metropolitan France, they are full citizens of a European state, and their residents have access to systems of education and some hope of social mobility. Many of these benefits are unavailable to other residents of remaining 'colonies'; even the residents of the British overseas territories, with the exception of those in Gibraltar and the Falklands, have a special passport and do not enjoy the right of abode in Britain. The DOM-TOMs, and some other dependent territories, have gained a 'pseudo-welfare system' and what 'appears to be dependency with affluence, a result of massive transfusions rather than expropriation of resources.'[19] Observers of the DOM-TOMs are aware of this model: the leader of the major pro-independence party in New Caledonia has spoken about a new form of 'inter-dependence' between France and its territories, while a Guyanais observer has coined the term of *'décopendance'* to describe the special economic and political links between France and the DOMs.[20] Not surprisingly such a model may increasingly appeal to many impoverished states.

This kind of model also resembles the situation in Corsica, France's Mediterranean island region, a part of France only since 1769. Despite the efforts of Napoleon, himself a Corsican, the island remained poorly integrated into France. However, from late in the nineteenth century, it began to undergo a series of structural changes, later effectively replicated in the DOM-TOMs, that more closely linked it to France. Efforts were made to replace the Corsican language and local traditions with French culture. Migration to France began and the resultant depopulation and the increase in imported goods reduced the significance of the agricultural system. Many expatriate Corsicans found employment in the French administration, particularly as colonial bureaucrats. Tourism, most dramatically in the 1960s, transformed the economy as it was simultaneously doing in the Antilles. Frustration mounted as tourist profits drifted back to France, *pieds-noirs* settled on the most productive agricultural land after the independence of Algeria, and mainland French people took many professional jobs. Various autonomist groups opposed these developments and from 1975 onwards violence increased. The escalation of violence, later associated with the Front de Libération Nationale Corse (FLNC), was met by French attempts to pour vast sums of money into infrastructural development, the proliferation of regional organisations designed to promote other forms of economic change, and the outlawing of organisations such as the FLNC. Decentralisation of authority, and the promulgation of a new statute for Corsica, however, have emphasised a number of features similar to those which characterise the DOM-TOMs: emigration; disparities in incomes and development standards between periphery and centre; high levels of unemployment and an unbalanced economy that has become bureaucratic and increasingly artificial; imports vastly in excess of exports; minimal industrialisation; and an important role for tourism.[21]

As in New Caledonia the most prominent nationalist group, the FLNC, claims that the indigenous population has effectively become a minority in their own country; great resentment is especially reserved for French mainland public servants and the *pieds-noirs*. Political parties of quite different philosophies have pressed for greater autonomy or full independence. Under Giscard the approach to Corsica was virtually identical to policy for New Caledonia. The president refused to recognise the existence of a 'Corsican people' and, though prepared to continue heavy subsidies, rejected any constitutional changes that would give greater autonomy; French insensitivity towards the Corsican language and cultural concerns and the harassment of political militants contributed to a cycle of violence and repression. Mitterrand's Socialist government expressed sympathy for the viewpoint that 'French-Corsican relations have generally represented a quasi-colonial situation' and Corsica was given special status, with its own elected parliament, which first met in 1982. The government created a university in Corsica and also promoted study and teaching of Corsican language and culture.[22] Yet decentralisation of power was not enough

to stem minority demands for independence, and violence and bombing have continued in recent years.

Corsica, because of its isolation and cultural particularities, is an
extreme example of nationalism in metropolitan France, but is far from
the only one. France in the 1970s experienced a rise in regionalism and
micro-nationalism, especially in Brittany and also in the Basque
country and the Catalan region, Occitania, and even the Alsatian and
Flemish regions. A combination of economic, political and cultural
issues that suggested internal colonialism have occasionally led to
minority demands for independence in some of these areas; like
Corsica, the extreme peripheries of France have suffered various historical disadvantages and have either dialects or languages and customs
which emphasise uniqueness. A weak sense of territorial identity, the
lack of a tradition of independent existence (except in Corsica and, to a
lesser extent, Brittany), emigration and the transfer economy have substantially limited French micro-nationalist movements;[23] some, in any
case, limit their goals to linguistic and cultural recognition. By no
means are all autonomist or *indépendantiste*; some, in fact, trace their
origins to conservative nineteenth-century regionalism. Belief in the
unified, centralised and indissoluble state remains exceptionally
powerful in France, with predictable echoes among regional groups in
both the *métropole* and the DOM-TOMs.

THE TIES THAT BIND

The DOM-TOMs have followed a different path of evolution from the
more widely assumed trajectory of political independence and economic self-sufficiency. Links with France are an insurance against some
of the vagaries of the world market, political upheaval, invasion and
natural disasters. Even when income and other resources are maldis-
tributed and political, economic and cultural centralism is exercised in
an authoritarian and discriminatory manner, residents of the *outre-mer*
can hope for certain minimal benefits from their mother country. At a
time when the scale of international association is significantly expanding, through the transformation of Eastern Europe, the widening of the
EC, initiatives for a 'Greater Maghreb' and proposals for Pacific Rim
economic cooperation, their ties may represent a new sort of international relationship. It is unlikely that the last phases of the process of
formal decolonisation will be reversed or that any other country would
ask to become a DOM-TOM,[24] but the institutional arrangements
which the DOM-TOMs embody no longer seem so unusual as they did
during the apogee of global decolonisation. Indeed some argue that the

process of *départementalisation* represents a form of decolonisation without independence; Albert Ramassamy, the senator for Réunion, suggests that 'for the old colonies that have become *départements* integration is a means of decolonisation just as much as independence for those who have chosen that.'[25] Yet this form of 'decolonisation' has not of course been wholly successful; within the DOM-TOMs there is an inequitable distribution of resources, unemployment rates are much higher than in France and ethnic tensions overlie cultural and economic differences. Many in the DOM-TOMs are unhappy with their dependent status, and remaining a colonial possession was not an option that appealed in the Comoros, Djibouti or Vanuatu.

Granting independence to the French DOM-TOMs would be difficult, especially considering the almost certain decline in living standards which independence would bring unless France were willing to maintain its level of funding at present levels, an unlikely prospect and one that has been specifically rejected in the case of New Caledonia. The great disparities in standards of living between the DOM-TOMs and their independent neighbours result from an artificial transfer economy, but the removal of such support would cause economic havoc in territories which have moved away from reliance on their limited alternative sources of revenue. Decolonisation of the DOM-TOMs would have been easier in 1946, or even in the following two decades, when such transfers, the establishment of the social security system and the growth of the bureaucracy were not so well developed. Yet, in that era, few such tiny states had achieved independence. Changes in the last twenty years, including the advent of consumer society, have increased gaps between the DOM-TOMs and their neighbours and made acceptance of a fall in living standards less likely. The very success of France in reforming the DOM-TOMs, and the willingness to search for greater equality (or at least 'parity'[26]) between the DOM-TOMs and the *métropole*, can thus diminish the real possibilities (or desires) for separation. The current injection of money into Mayotte similarly widens the gap between it and the Comoros and works against reunification there. Through parliamentary politics, air transport, education, the media, migration and marriage, the populations of the DOM-TOMs are tied more closely, and more profoundly, to France than ever before. Likewise their regional ties are as limited as they have ever been. Yet where inequality is combined with ethnic distinctiveness and remoteness from the locus of power, demands for independence are never likely to be extinguished, as the present global resurgence in ethnic nationalist movements demonstrates. As Jean-Marie Tjibaou once claimed: 'So long as one Kanak survives a problem for France remains.'[27]

If any DOM-TOM were to become independent, logic suggests that it would be one of the *vieilles colonies* or the two largest Pacific territories. In none of them does this seem in any way imminent, and indeed the tide appears to be running against any of these achieving independence, even in substantial association with France. Moreover, even if one DOM-TOM became independent, a domino effect is not certain to follow. It is unlikely that Saint-Pierre and Miquelon, Wallis and Futuna or Mayotte would ever willingly accede to independence, though other states have had independence thrust upon them against their will. There are obvious problems for independence in the other DOM-TOMs as well. Many white New Caledonians could seek secession from an independent Kanaky, as might Saint-Barthélémy and Saint-Martin from an independent Guadeloupe; already the 'nuclear outposts' of Mururoa and Fangataufa legally belong to the *métropole* rather than to French Polynesia. Ultimately, it is improbable that France would abandon its claims on the uninhabited islands of Clipperton, the Iles Eparses and the TAAF, unless it were forced to do so. In short, it is difficult to imagine that French 'decolonisation' will ever be complete and reduce France to its hexagonal boundaries. There is too much at stake for France; the ties that bind are likely to endure.

Notes

Chapter 1 Overseas France

1. The most important general works published in recent years are G. Lasserre *et al.*, *La France d'outre-mer* (Paris, 1974); J.C. Guillebaud, *Les Confettis de l'empire* (Paris, 1976); J.E. Vié, *Faut-il abandonner les DOM?* (Paris, 1978); P. de Baleine, *Les Danseuses de la France* (Paris, 1979); 'Les Iles où l'on parle français', a special issue of *Hérodote*, Vol. 37–38 (1985); P. Vallin, *Les 'Frances' d'outre-mer* (Paris, 1987); Jean-Luc Mathieu, *Les DOM-TOM* (Paris, 1988) and his *Petite histoire de la Grande France* (Paris, 1989).

2. France first went to St Christopher (St Kitts) in the Caribbean in 1625 and only a decade later colonised Guadeloupe and Martinique.

3. 'Guyane' will be used throughout this study to distinguish French Guiana from the two Guianas colonised by the British and Dutch (now independent Guyana and Surinam, respectively).

4. The brochure is from the French travel agency Nouvelles Frontières.

5. Letter of 11 May 1987.

6. Letters of Albert Ramassamy, 16 September 1987, Paul Moreau, 24 May 1987, Marcel Henry, 11 May 1987.

7. Quoted in John Connell, *New Caledonia or Kanaky? The Political History of a French Colony* (Canberra, 1987), p. 424.

Chapter 2 The Colonial Heritage

1. The most succinct treatment is the 'Que sais-je?' volume, Xavier Yacono, *Histoire de la colonisation française* (Paris, 4th edn., 1984). On the early centuries of French expansion, see Robert and Marianne Cornevin, *La France et les Français outre-mer* (Paris, 1990). The most recent comprehensive survey is Jean Meyer, *et al.*, *Histoire*

de la France coloniale. Des Origines à 1914 (Paris, 1991) and the companion volume, Jacques Thobie, *et al., Histoire de la France coloniale. 1914–1990* (Paris, 1990). See also the 'Aventure coloniale de la France' series, of which several volumes have already appeared. The first, Jean Martin, *L'Empire renaissant, 1789–1871* (Paris, 1987), also reviews the formation of the first overseas empire.

2. The best general survey of the early history of the Antilles is Pierre Pluchon, *Histoire des Antilles et de la Guyane* (Toulouse, 1982). A particularly useful interpretation of economic and social questions is Alain-Philippe Blérald, *Histoire économique de la Guadeloupe et de la Martinique du XVIIe siècle à nos jours* (Paris, 1986), which also has a thorough bibliography.

3. On sugar, see C. Schnakenbourg, *Histoire de l'industrie sucrière en Guadeloupe (XIXe-XXe siècles)* (Paris, 1980); Jean Meyer, *L'Histoire du sucre* (Desjonquières, 1988); Sydney Mintz, *Sweetness and Power: The Place of Sugar in Modern History* (New York, 1985); and D. Watts, *The West Indies: Patterns of Development, Culture and Environmental Change since 1492* (Cambridge, UK, 1987).

4. On the Guianas, see the 'Que sais-je?' volume by Jean-Claude Giacottino, *Les Guyanes* (Paris, 1984) and Serge Mam-Lam-Fouck, *Histoire de la société guyanaise: Les Années cruciales: 1848–1946* (Paris, 1987), which includes material on the earlier period as well and a detailed bibliography.

5. New works on the Revolution in the colonies are Yves Benot, *La Révolution française et la fin des colonies* (Paris, 1988), Jean-Pierre Bondi and François Zuccarelli, *16 Pluviôse An II: Les Colonies de la Révolution* (Paris, 1989) and 'La Révolution française et les colonies', a special issue of the *Revue française d'histoire d'outremer*, 76 (1989).

6. Paul Fregosi, *Dreams of Empire: Napoleon and the First World War, 1792–1815* (London, 1989).

7. A useful comparative perspective on slavery in the Caribbean is Jean-Luc Jamard, 'Variantes, abolitions et transformées de rapports "esclavagistes". Esquisse comparative: transitions caribéennes', *Social Science Information* 26 (1987), pp. 155–90.

8. Once again, the 'Que sais-je?' volume is the best introduction, André Schérer, *La Réunion* (Paris, 1985); a fuller treatment is Marcel Leguen, *Histoire de l'Ile de la Réunion* (Paris, 1979).

9. The essential work is Charles Guyotjeannin, *Saint-Pierre et Miquelon* (Paris, 1986).

10. The literature on the 'new imperialism' is enormous. Good starting points are Yacono's book and the 'Aventure coloniale de la France' series and, comparing France with other nations, Jean-Louis Miège, *Expansion européenne et décolonisation de 1870 à nos jours* (Paris, 2nd edn., 1986).

11. On recent works, see Robert Aldrich, 'A Note on the Renewal of Colonial Studies in France', *Contemporary French Civilization*, Vol. XII, No. 2 (Summer/Fall 1988), pp. 263–8. Of particular importance for new interpretations are Jacques Thobie, *La France impériale, 1880–1914* (Paris, 1982), Jean Bouvier, René Girault and Jacques Thobie, *L'Impérialisme à la française, 1914–1960* (Paris, 1986) and Jacques Marseille, *Empire colonial et capitalisme français: Histoire d'un divorce* (Paris, 1984). On the idea of colonies, the key studies are Charles-Robert Ageron, *France coloniale ou parti colonial?* (Paris, 1973) and Raoul Girardet, *L'Idée coloniale en France de 1871 à 1962* (Paris, 1972). As relates to New Caledonia, see Robert

Aldrich, 'The Place of New Caledonia in French Historiography', in M. Spencer, A. Ward and J. Connell, *New Caledonia: Essays in Nationalism and Dependency* (St Lucia, Queensland, 1988), pp. 22–37.

12. Jacques Marseille, *L'Age d'or de la France coloniale* (Paris, 1986). Charles-Robert Ageron argues, however, that even into the 1930s, the French were not entirely converted to colonialism; see his 'La Perception de la puissance française en 1938–1939: le mythe impérial', *Revue française d'histoire d'outre-mer*, Vol. LXIX (1982), pp. 7–22. For a further contribution to the debate, see Catherine Coquery-Vidrovitch, 'Mythes et réalités de l'idée coloniale française entre les deux guerres', in Robert Aldrich (ed.), *France: Politics, Society, Culture and International Relations* (Sydney, 1990), pp. 159–97.

13. The standard work is still Raymond Betts, *Assimilation and Association in French Colonial Theory, 1890–1914* (New York, 1961).

14. See Robert Aldrich, *The French Presence in the South Pacific, 1842–1940* (London, 1990). For more detailed studies: on Tahiti, Colin Newbury, *Tahiti Nui: Change and Survival in French Polynesia, 1767–1945* (Honolulu, 1980) and Pierre-Yves Toullelan, *Tahiti colonial (1860–1914)* (Paris, 1984); on New Caledonia, Bernard Brou, *Histoire de la Nouvelle-Calédonie: les temps modernes, 1774–1925* (Nouméa, 1973) and *Espoirs et réalités: la Nouvelle-Calédonie de 1925 à 1945* (Nouméa, 1975) as well as John Connell, *From New Caledonia to Kanaky?* (Canberra, 1987); on Wallis see Alexandre Poncet, *Histoire de île Wallis: Le Protectorat français* (Paris, 1972); and on the New Hebrides, Joël Bonnemaison, *La Dernière île* (Paris, 1986).

15. See Hervé Chagnoux and Ali Haribou, *Les Comores* (Paris, 1980); Jean Martin, *Comores, quatre îles entre pirates et planteurs* (Paris, 1983); René Battistini and Pierre Vérin, *Géographie des Comores* (Paris, 1984); and Malyn Newitt, *The Comoro Islands Struggle Against Dependency in the Indian Ocean* (Boulder, 1984). The only recent book that treats Mayotte separately is Mabé Brolly and Christian Vaisse, *Mayotte* (Paris, 1989).

16. The historiographical controversy is discussed in Edouard de Lépine, *Questions sur l'histoire antillaise* (Fort-de-France, 1978).

17. See J. Petot, *L'Or de Guyane* (Paris, 1986) on the gold rush and Michel Pierre, *La Terre de grande punition* (Paris, 1982); Charles F. Gritzner, 'French Guiana Penal Colony: Its Role in Colonial Development', *Journal of Geography* 63 (1984), pp. 314–19; and Alexander Miles, *Devil's Island: Colony of the Damned* (Berkeley, 1988) on the penitentiary.

Chapter 3   Decolonisation and Institutional Change since 1940

1. Brian Weinstein, *Eboué* (New York, 1972). On Sautot, John Lawrey, *The Cross of Lorraine in the South Pacific* (Canberra, 1982) and on the EFO, Emile de Curton, *Tahiti 40* (Paris, 1973). More generally, see Paul-Marie de la Gorce, *L'Empire écartelé (1936–1945)* (Paris, 1988).

2. On the South Pacific, see Robert Aldrich, *The French and the South Pacific since 1940* (London, forthcoming), ch. 1.

3. On the French empire since the 1930s, see in particular, Xavier Yacono, *Les Etapes de la décolonisation française* (Paris, 2nd edn., 1985).

4. Quoted by Yacono, *op. cit.*, p. 56.

5. A recent comparative work is R.F. Holland, *European Decolonization, 1918–1981*

(London, 1985); for more detail see Miles Kahler, *Decolonization in Britain and France* (Princeton, 1984).

6. On Vietnam, see Daniel Hémery, *Ho Chi Minh. De l'Indochine au Vietnam* (Paris, 1990).

7. Though administration was transferred to India in 1954 and a treaty of cession was signed in 1956, the instruments of ratification were not signed until August 1962. France also negotiated the option for French subjects to retain their citizenship. Only a minority chose to do so but there are now about 15,000 Indians who are French citizens despite a most tenuous connection with France. They cannot legally hold dual citizenship and are effectively aliens within India. By contrast, they can vote in French national elections (W.F.S. Miles, 'Citizens Without Soil: The French of India (Pondicherry)', *Ethnic and Racial Studies*, 13 (1990), pp. 250–73.

8. On Tunisia and Morocco, R. Le Tourneau, *Evolution politique de l'Afrique du Nord musulman (1920–1961)* (Paris, 1962).

9. The best English-language study is Alistair Horne, *A Savage War of Peace: Algeria 1954–1962* (London, 1977).

10. 'Constitution française du 4 octobre 1958', *Documents d'études: Droit constitutionnel et institutions politiques*, No. 1.04.

11. Hervé Chagnoux and Ali Haribou, *Les Comores* (Paris, 1980).

12. On Djibouti, see the general works published since 1977 cited in Chapter 2.

13. John Beasant, *The Santo Rebellion: An Imperial Reckoning* (London, 1984), and Joël Bonnemaison, *La Dernière île* (Paris, 1986); Richard Shears, *The Coconut War* (Sydney, 1980) provides a more irreverent discussion.

14. See the chapters on France and Black Africa, France and the Third World and Francophonie in Robert Aldrich and John Connell (eds), *France in World Politics* (London, 1989).

15. On the *départementalisation*, see Victor Sablé, *La Transformation des îles d'Amérique en départements français* (Paris, 1955), and the appropriate sections of Henri Descamps, *La Politique aux Antilles françaises de 1946 à nos jours* (Paris, 1981), Henri Bangou, *Les Voies de la souveraineté: Peuplements et institutions à la Guadeloupe* (Paris, 1988) and Jean Houbert, 'Reunion II: The Politics of *Départementalisation*', *Journal of Commonwealth and Comparative Politics*, 18 (1980), pp. 325–47.

16. There was a difference between this wording in the constitution of October 1946 and the March law on *départementalisation*, which had specified that laws passed by the National Assembly would be applicable in the DOMs 'if expressly mentioned in the texts'.

17. The Constitution of 1946 did not specify whether the legislative or executive authority would make the appropriate exemptions or adaptations, but the *Conseil constitutionnel* and the *Conseil d'Etat* held that this could be done by both the government and the legislature in their respective domains.

18. The decrees making pre-1946 laws applicable had to be promulgated by 1 January 1947, but this period was extended to 31 March 1948 and, in practice, continued afterwards.

19. The essential discussions on the constitutional and institutional links between France and the *outre-mer* are the studies by Patrick Shultz in the *Juris-Classeurs*

Administratif, 'Départements d'outre-mer', Fascicule 130, No. 2, 1984, 'Collectivités territoriales d'outre-mer', Fascicule 131, No. 5, 1986, and 'Territoires d'outre-mer', Fascicule 132, No. 2, 1984. Fascicules 780, 785 and 790 contain further information. See also Jean-Claude Fortier and Christian Vitalien, 'Régions d'Outre-Mer', Fascicule 8 (1987). The *Juris-Classeurs* are periodically updated and are the authoritative reference on legal questions in France; the articles contain complete bibliographies. More generally, see the classic, but now dated, study by François Luchaire, *Droit d'outre-mer* (Paris, 1959), François Miclo, *Le Régime législatif des DOM et l'unité de la République* (Paris, 1982) and Sylvie Jacquemart, *La Question départementale outre-mer* (Paris, 1983) on the DOMs, and Pierre Lampué, 'Le Regime constitutionnel des territoires d'outre-mer', *Revue de droit public*, 50 (1984), pp. 5–20 on the TOMs and also Jean-François Auby, 'Le Statut de la France "périphérique" ', *Actualité juridique — Droit administratif* (20 June 1989), pp. 347–54. There are also especially useful articles in 'L'Administration des départements d'outre-mer', a special issue of the *Revue française d'administration publique*, 31 (1984), and the 'Dossier Collectivités locales', of the *Bulletin d'information du CENADDOM*, 76 (4e trimestre 1984). See also the special issue of the *Revue politique et parlementaire*, 924 (1986), on the different systems of the Caribbean.

20. See, for example, Michel-Henry Fabre, 'L'Unité et l'indivisibilité de la République. Réalité? Fiction?', *Revue de droit public*, 98 (1982), pp. 603–22.

21. See the discussions in Miclo, *op. cit.*, and Jacquemart, *op. cit.*

22. François Luchaire, 'La Réforme régionale dans les départements d'outre-mer', *Revue Juridique et Politique, Indépendance et Coopération* 37 (1983), pp. 567–73.

23. In the case of the Djibouti, the Giscard government decided (and the *Conseil constitutionnel* upheld the decision) to restrict the vote to French citizens resident in the territory for a minimum of three years. This was an effort to keep transient residents (including *fonctionnaires* appointed for three-year postings) from weighting the voting. The same arrangements were employed in the New Caledonian independence referendum of September 1987. The proposed referendum in New Caledonia in 1998 will limit the franchise to electors living in the territory in 1988 and their children who reach voting age by 1998.

24. The powers of the *communes* are those existing before 1982, as the measures passed in that year relating to the *communes* were not applicable in the *outre-mer*, either to DOMs or TOMs. French Polynesia, incidentally, also has a network of administrative districts between the communal and territorial level. There also exist in the DOMs the electoral districts of *cantons* and *arrondissements*, although these have no separate administration.

25. The statute is printed, with commentary, in *Ve'a Hau Fenua* (the official publication of the government of French Polynesia), No. 1, June 1985.

26. See John Connell, *New Caledonia or Independent Kanaky?* (Canberra, 1987). See also Chapter 8.

27. John Connell, 'New Caledonia: The Matignon Accord and the Colonial Future', Research Institute for Asia and the Pacific, Occasional Paper No. 5, University of Sydney (1988).

28. In addition to his section on Mayotte in the *Juris-Classeurs*, see Patrick Schultz, 'Le Statut constitutionnel et administratif de Mayotte', *Penant: Revue de droit des pays d'Afrique*, Vol. 96, No. 790–791 (1986), pp. 97–128.

29. Thierry Michalon, 'La République française, une fédération qui s'ignore?', *Revue de droit publique*, No. 98 (1982), pp. 623-88.

30. The best study of the Secrétariat d'Etat is that of Frantz Lebon, 'Le Secrétariat d'Etat aux départements et territories d'outre-mer sous la Ve République', unpublished DEA thesis (Etudes Politiques), University of Paris, 1985. There is also material in J.-E. Vié, *Faut-il abandonner les DOM?* (Paris, 1978).

31. The heads of the DOM-TOM ministry in the Fifth Republic, with the dates of their tenure, have been Jacques Soustelle (1959-60), Robert Lecourt (1960-1), Louis Jacquinot (1961-2), Jean de Broglie (1961-2), Louis Jacquinot (1962-6), Pierre Billotte (1966-8), Joël Le Theule (1968), Michel Inchauspé (1968-9), Henry Rey (1969-71), Pierre Messmer (1971-2), Xavier Deniau (1972-3), Bernard Stasi (1973-4), Joseph Comiti (1974), Olivier Stirn (1974-8), Paul Dijoud (1978-81), Henri Emmanuelli (1981-3), Georges Lemoine (1983-6), Bernard Pons (1986-8), Olivier Stirn (1988) and Louis Le Pensec (since June 1988). Le Pensec is also official spokesman for the Rocard government.

32. The DOM-TOM ministry budget in 1985 amounted to only 0.17 per cent of the civil budget of the French state, but this amount itself made up only 6.37 per cent of money allocated to the DOM-TOMs in the budgets of the various French ministries and other institutions (Lebon, *op. cit.*, p. 55.)

33. There was a *secrétaire-général* of the DOMs attached to the Ministry of the Interior from 1946 to 1958; from 1958 to 1977, the office was attached to the DOM-TOM ministry. It was then changed into the post of *directeur-général* of the DOMs, but was abolished in 1979.

Chapter 4   Population and Society

1. M.M. Horowitz, *Morne-Paysan: Peasant Village in Martinique* (New York, 1967), pp. 9-10.

2. J. Hurault, *Français et Indiens en Guyane* (Paris, 1972).

3. See John Connell, *New Caledonia or Kanaky?* (Canberra, 1987); Dorothy Shineberg, 'Un Nouveau Régard sur la démographie historique de la Nouvelle-Calédonie', *Journal de la Société des Océanistes* 39 (1983), pp. 33-43.

4. Alan Moorehead, *The Fatal Impact* (London, 1966).

5. Greg Dening, *Islands and Beaches: Discourse on a Silent Land* (Melbourne, 1980), p. 240.

6. Ben Finney, *Polynesian Peasants and Proletarians* (Cambridge, Mass., 1973), p. 18.

7. André-Louis Sanguin, 'Saint-Pierre et Miquelon, département français d'Amérique du Nord', *Norois* 110 (1981), pp. 133-243.

8. André Schérer, *La Réunion* (Paris, 1985), p. 21; Jean Benoist, *Paysans de la Réunion* (Aix-en-Provence, 1984), pp. 179-83.

9. David Watts, *The West Indies* (Cambridge, UK, 1987), pp. 319-22.

10. Horowitz, *op. cit.*, p. 11; see also Watts, *op. cit.*, pp. 348-50.

11. Horowitz, *op. cit.*, p. 13. A detailed account is given by Singaravélou, *Les Indiens de Guadeloupe* (Point-à-Pitre, 1985).

12. Bernard Dumaz, *Guadeloupe: économie agricole. Le Malaise à fleur de sable* (Paris, 1986), p. 11.

13. Alain-Philippe Blérald, *Histoire économique de la Guadeloupe et de la Martinique* (Paris, 1986).

14. Stephen Roberts, *The History of French Colonial Policy* (London, 1929), p. 501.

15. André-Louis Sanguin, 'Saint-Barthélémy, île normande des Antilles françaises', *Etudes normandes* 30 (1981), pp. 57–77.

16. Jean-Luc Bonniol, 'Contrepoint Créole', *Les Temps Modernes* 39 (1983), pp. 2048–71; see also Jean-Luc Bonniol, *Terre de Haut des Saintes: Contraintes insulaires et particularisme éthnique dans la Caraïbe*, (Paris, 1980).

17. Yves Monnier, *L'Immuable et le changeant: Etude de la partie française de Saint-Martin* (Bordeaux, 1983).

18. Serge Mam-Lam-Fouck, *Histoire de la société guyanaise* (Paris, 1987), pp. 69–70.

19. *Ibid.*, p. 78.

20. *Ibid.*, p. 164.

21. Schérer, *op. cit.*, p. 61.

22. *Ibid.*, pp. 71–4. See also Firmin Lacpatia, *Les Indiens de la Réunion* (Saint-Denis, 1982) and Dominique Durand, *Les Chinois de la Réunion* (Saint-Denis, 1981).

23. Colin Newbury, *Tahiti Nui* (Honolulu, 1980), p. 158. For Chinese migration and settlement there is one detailed account, Gérald Coppenrath, *Les Chinois de Tahiti: de l'aversion à l'assimilation, 1865–1966* (Paris, 1967).

24. Alain Saussol, *L'Héritage. Essai sur le problème foncier mélanésien en Nouvelle-Calédonie* (Paris, 1979), p. 251; see also Connell, *op. cit.*, pp. 84–105. From then onwards, 'All activities of any scale and even the occupation of land, however dispersed and exceptional, are tied to the politics of immigration', (C. Robequain, *Les Richesses de la France d'Outre-mer* (Paris, 1949), p. 41).

25. Connell, *op. cit.*, pp. 85, 91.

26. Dening, *op. cit.*, p. 266.

27. V.D. Stace, *The Pacific Islanders and Modern Commerce* (Noumea, 1954), p. 5.

28. See, for example, F. Sodter, 'Dépopulation et reprise démographique aux îles Marquises', *Bulletin de la Société des Etudes Océaniennes* 244 (1988), pp. 10–26; Bengt Danielsson, *Work and Life on Raroia* (London, 1956), pp. 113–16.

29. Quoted in Connell, *op. cit.*, p. 218.

30. Jean Chesneaux, 'Can Two Opposite Views of the Past be Turned into One of the Future?', *Pacific Islands Monthly* 52 (December 1981), p. 27.

31. To some extent this policy was effectively in operation before its more formal elaboration in the early 1970s; see Alan Ward, 'New Caledonia, 1945 to 1955: Labour Policy and Immigration', in M. Spencer, A. Ward and J. Connell (eds), *New Caledonia* (St Lucia, Qld, 1988), pp. 81–105.

32. Virginia Thompson and Richard Adloff, *The French Pacific Islands: French Polynesia and New Caledonia* (Berkeley, 1971), pp. 458–60.

33. Jean-Claude Roux, 'Migration and Change in Wallisian Society', in R.T. Shand (ed.), *The Island States of the Pacific and Indian Oceans* (Canberra, 1980), p. 174.

34. Alan Ward, 'The Independence Movement and the Plan Dijoud in New Caledonia', *Journal of Pacific History* 15 (1980), p. 198.

35. Two final 'waves' of migration to New Caledonia brought migrants from Vanuatu, initially seeing in New Caledonia 'a kind of El Dorado' and subsequently moving as 'refugees' from the failed Santo secession movement, a situation which caused some resentment amongst New Caledonian Melanesians. See Connell, *op. cit.*, pp. 224–5.

36. David Lowenthal, 'French Guiana: Myths and Realities', *Transactions of the New York Academy of Sciences* Series II, Vol. 22 (1960), pp. 528–40.

37. See, for example, Elie Castor and Georges Othily, *La Guyane: les grands problèmes, les solutions possibles* (Paris, 1984), pp. 60–89.

38. Myriam Toulemonde-Niaussat, 'Les Hmongs en Guyane', *Les Dossiers de l'outre-mer* 85 (1986), pp. 37–43.

39. R. Calmont, C. Gorgeon and J.Y. Urfie, 'Les Haïtiens en Guyane: une immigration en cours de stabilisation?', *Les Dossiers de l'outre-mer* 85 (1986), pp. 27–36.

40. Catherine Gorgeon, 'La Communauté brésilienne en Guyane: un groupe en voie d'intégration', *Les Dossiers de l'outre-mer* 85 (1986), pp. 44–9.

41. Sophie Bourgarel, 'Migrations sur le Maroni: le cas des réfugiés surinamiens en Guyane', *Cahiers d'Outre-Mer* 41 (1988), pp. 425–31.

42. Dumaz, *op. cit.*, p. 160.

43. André-Louis Sanguin, 'Saint-Martin, les mutations d'une île franco-néerlandaise des Antilles', *Cahiers d'Outre-Mer* 35 (1982), p. 131; M. Etna, 'Notes sur les problèmes démographiques de Saint-Martin', *Revue du CERC* 3 (1986), pp. 205–17.

44. Denise Daveira, 'Douze Ans d'immigration haïtienne en Guadeloupe', *Revue du CERC* 3 (1986), pp. 164–80.

45. L. Hurbon, 'Racisme et sous-produit du racisme: immigrés haitiens et dominicains en Guadeloupe', *Les Temps Modernes* 39 (1983), pp. 1988–2003.

46. Jean Koechlin and Marc Boye, 'Mayotte, bilan écologique, possibilités de développement, programme d'études', in *Nature et Hommes dans les îles tropicales* (Bordeaux, 1984), p. 157; Institut d'Emission d'Outre-Mer, *Mayotte: Exercice 1988* (Paris, 1989).

47. In recent years, however, there has been a greater diversity of migrant origins. Thus in New Caledonia in July 1989 the Service des Etrangers recorded residents from seventy-one different countries, excluding France and other DOM-TOMs, a total of more than 3200 people, *Les Nouvélles hebdo* 91 (16 November 1989), pp. 8–10.

48. P. Marshall, 'Martinique and Guadeloupe', *Latin American and Caribbean Review*, (London, 1985), p. 213.

49. M. Coutty, 'Les Nouveaux "Métros"', *Les Temps Modernes* (1983), pp. 1940–5.

50. There are numerous accounts of migration from the overseas *départements* to France; the most useful include Alain Anselin, *L'Emigration antillaise en France: Du Bantoustan au Ghetto* (Paris, 1979) and Pierre-Leval Sainte-Rose, *Le Jeune Antillais face à la migration* (Paris, 1983), and René Calmont, 'Emigration guyanaise en France', *Equinoxe* 7 (1978), pp. 38–41. An early account of mi-

gration from Réunion is Isabelle Tal, *Les Réunionnais en France* (Paris, 1976). Statistical data on the recent situation of DOM-TOM migrants in France is in INSEE, *Recensement général de la population de 1982: Les populations des DOM-TOMs en France métropolitaine* (Paris, 1985).

51. Association générale des étudiants guadeloupéens (AGEG), *L'Emigration travailleuse guadeloupéene en France* (Paris, 1979), pp. 20–1.

52. Quoted in Sainte-Rose, *op. cit.*, p. 22.

53. Quoted in Sainte-Rose, *op. cit.*, p. 23.

54. BUMIDOM also recruited some workers for New Caledonia at the time of the nickel boom, further diversifying that territory's population. See Connell, *op. cit.*, pp. 224.

55. Ivor J. Butcher and Philip E. Ogden, 'West Indians in France: Migration and Demographic Change', in P.E. Ogden (ed.), *Migrants in Modern France: Four Studies* (Queen Mary College, Department of Geography, Occasional Paper No. 23, London, 1984), p. 50.

56. AGEG, *op. cit.*, p. 13.

57. *Op. cit.*, pp. 22, 23.

58. Jean Houbert, 'Réunion II: The Politics of *Départementalisation*', *Journal of Commonwealth and Comparative Politics* 18 (1980), pp. 340–1.

59. Butcher and Ogden, *op. cit.*, p. 64.

60. Pierre-Leval Sainte-Rose, 'Le Retour du migrant à la Martinique', *Revue du CERC* 3 (1986), pp. 181–204.

61. John Connell, 'Wallis and Futuna Workers in New Caledonia and the New Hebrides', in C. Moore, J. Leckie and D. Munro (eds), *Labour in the South Pacific* (Townsville, 1991), pp. 133–9; Albert Likuvalu, 'History and Migrations in Wallis and Futuna', in N. Pollock and R. Crocombe (eds), *French Polynesia* (Suva, 1988), pp. 216–25.

62. Jean Morisset, 'La Fin de l'Amérique française et Saint-Pierre-et-Miquelon', *Hérodote* 37–38 (1985), pp. 261–8.

63. A.W. Brittain, 'Cohort Size and Migration in a West Indian Population', *International Migration Review*, 24 (1990), pp. 703–21.

64. Jean Glasscock, *The Making of an Island: Sint Maarten. Saint-Martin* (Wellesley, 1985), pp. 51–3.

65. John Connell, *New Caledonia or Kanaky?* (Canberra, 1987).

66. Michel Debré, 'La Réunion: le naufrage provoqué', *Le Figaro*, 30 May 1984.

67. Joseph-Josy Lévy, *Un Village du bout du monde: Modernisation et structures villageoises aux Antilles françaises* (Montreal, 1976), p. 109.

68. Tal, *op. cit.*, p. 39.

69. Quoted in Fred Constant, 'La Politique française de l'immigration antillaise de 1946 à 1987', *Revue européenne des migrations internationales* 3 (1987), p. 20.

70. Yves Charbit, 'Transition démographique aux Antilles françaises', *Population et Sociétés* 139 (1980).

71. Albert Lopez, 'La Santé en transition à la Réunion de 1946 à 1986', *Annales de Géographie* 546 (1989), p. 160; P. Festy, *Croissance et révolution démographique à la Réunion* (Paris, 1983).

72. Philip Ogden, 'France in the Caribbean', *Geographical Magazine* 52 (1979), p. 199.

73. Houbert, *op. cit.*, p. 339. See Alain Jourdain, 'Baisse de fecondité et planification familiale à la Réunion', *Annaire des Pays de l'Océan Indien* 7 (1980), pp. 257–86.

74. William Miles, *Elections and Ethnicity in French Martinique: A Paradox in Paradise* (New York, 1986), p. 162.

75. B. Bridier, 'Quel avenir pour le géranium et le développement agricole des Hauts de l'Ouest de la Réunion?', *L'Agronomie tropicale* 40 (1985), p. 351. This transition is discussed in greater detail in Chapter 5.

76. John Connell, *Migration, Employment and Development in the South Pacific: Country Report No. 5: French Polynesia*, (Noumea, 1985), p. 27.

77. Jean Fages, 'Migrations et urbanisation en Polynésie Française', *Cahiers d'ORSTOM* 11 (1974), pp. 243–358.

78. Horowitz, *op. cit.*, p. 80.

79. Philippe Séguin, 'La Démographie, les migrations et le développement en Nouvélle-Calédonie', unpublished conference paper, Noumea, 1982, p. 8.

80. Patrick Leigh Fermor, *The Traveller's Tree* (London, 1950), p. 219.

81. Dumaz, *op. cit.*, p. 155.

82. Peter Curson, 'The Small Urban Settlement in New Caledonia', *South Pacific Bulletin* 15 (1965), pp. 22–4.

83. Marie-José Jolivet, *La Question Créole: Essai de sociologie sur la Guyane française* (Paris, 1982), p. 13.

84. Jean-Pierre Doumenge, *Du Terroir à la ville. Les Mélanesiens et leur espace en Nouvelle-Calédonie* (Talence, 1982), p. 1.

85. Etienne Vanaa, 'Interview' in R. Crocombe and P. Hereniko (eds), *Tahiti: The Other Side* (Suva, 1985), p. 128.

86. Robert I. Levy, 'Interview' in R. Crocombe and P. Hereniko, *op. cit.*, p. 106.

87. M.H. Gire, 'Juvenile Delinquency in French Polynesia', in *Regional Seminar on Health and Social Planning and Urbanisation* (Noumea, 1970), p. 133.

88. Bengt Danielsson, 'French Polynesia: Nuclear Colony', in A. Ali and R. Crocombe (eds), *Politics in Polynesia* (Suva, 1983), p. 40.

89. Paul De Deckker, 'Mutations et développement: Wallis et Tahiti', *Civilisations* 29 (1979), p. 317.

90. Gilles Blanchet, *L'Economie de la Polynésie Française de 1960 à 1980* (Papeete, 1984).

91. Albert Flagie, 'Delinquency and Dependency in the French West Indies: The Case of Guadeloupe', University of the West Indies (Trinidad), Working Papers on Caribbean Society, Series C, No. 2, 1978. In Cayenne the Cité HLM Palétuviers shanty town is associated with Brazilian migrants, drugs and malnutrition.

92. Connell, *New Caledonia or Kanaky?* (Canberra, 1987).

93. Lévy, *op. cit.*, p. 105.

94. Saussol, *op. cit.*, p. 305.

95. H.C. Brookfield, *Colonialism, Development and Dependence. The Case of the Melanesian Islands in the South Pacific* (Cambridge, UK, 1972), p. 105.

96. Fages, *op. cit.*, p. 248.

97. Nancy Pollock, 'Takapoto: La Prospérité: Retour aux îles', *Journal de la Société des Océanistes* 60 (1978), pp. 133-5.

98. Victoria J. Lockwood, 'Development and Return Migration to Rural French Polynesia', *International Migration Review* 24 (1990), pp. 347-71.

99. P.-L. Sainte-Rose, 'Le Retour du migrant à la Martinique', *Revue du CERC* 3 (1986), pp. 181-204.

100. Jean-Claude Guillebaud, *Les Confettis de l'empire* (Paris, 1976), p. 48. Two accounts of Caldoche society are Alain Saussol, 'Trente mille "Caldoches" en Nouvelle-Calédonie', *Hérodote* 37-38 (1985), pp. 129-44, and Frédéric Bobin, 'Portraits caldoches', *Esprit* 151 (1989), pp. 14-26.

101. Quoted in Claude Gabriel and Vincent Kermel, *Nouvelle-Caledonie: La Révolte Kanake* (Paris, 1985), p. 57.

102. Quoted in J. Garofalo, 'La France lointaine des Caldoches', *Paris Match* 1858 (4 January 1985), p. 34.

103. Jean Guiart, *La Terre est le sang des morts* (Paris, 1983), p. 101.

104. Bernard Brou, *Peuplement et population de la Nouvelle-Calédonie* (Noumea, 1980), pp. 31-2.

105. Michael Spencer, *New Caledonia in Crisis* (Canberra, 1985), p. 10.

106. Quoted in Guillebaud, *op. cit.*, p. 178.

107. See Connell, *New Caledonia or Kanaky?* pp. 219-20.

108. Philippe de Baleine, *Les Danseuses de la France* (Paris, 1979), p. 80.

109. *Ibid.*, p. 186.

110. This may not always be the case. In Mayotte 'the present administration of the island shows all the rigidities and sluggishness of a departmental administration; in no way does it encourage development since the salary system encourages French bureaucrats to remain in the island for the briefest possible time' (T. Michalon, 'Mayotte et les Comores', *Le Monde Diplomatique* 369 (December 1984), p. 10).

111. Lopez, *op. cit.*, p. 155.

112. Guy Cabort-Masson, *Les Puissances d'argent en Martinique* (Fort-de-France, 1984), pp. 81, 27.

113. Jean Benoist, *Un Développement ambigu: Structure et changement de la société réunionnaise* (Saint-Denis, 1983), pp. 37-8.

114. John Connell, 'New Caledonia: The Matignon Accord and the Colonial Future', Research Institute for Asia and the Pacific, Occasional Paper No. 5 (Sydney, 1988).

115. Elise Paulin, *Etat et reproduction de la dépendance de la Martinique* (Thèse de troisième cycle, Université de Paris VIII — Saint-Denis, 1984).

116. Dumaz, *op. cit.*, p. 115.

117. Benoist, *op. cit.* pp. 26-30.

118. Newbury, *op. cit.*, pp. 290-4; see Thompson and Adloff, *op. cit.*, p. 110.

119. Horowitz, *op. cit.*, p. 14; see also Jolivet, *op. cit.* and Chapter 6.

120. C. Barat, R. Gauvin and J. Némo, 'Société et culture réunionnaises', *Les Dossiers de l'outre-mer* 85 (1986), pp. 50-79; see also Michel Giraud, *Races et classes à la Martinique: les relations sociales entre enfants de différentes couleurs à l'école* (Paris, 1979).

121. Quoted by Gary P. Freeman, 'Caribbean Migration to Britain and France: From Assimilation to Selection', *Caribbean Review* 11 (1982), p. 30.

122. Richard D. Burton, *Assimilation or Independence? Prospects for Martinique* (Montreal, 1978), p. 21.

Chapter 5   Economic Change: From Production to Consumption

1. F. Allan Hanson, *Rapan Lifeways: Society and History on a Polynesian Island* (Boston, 1970), pp. 35-9.

2. Barrie Macdonald, *Cinderellas of the Empire: Towards a History of Kiribati and Tuvalu* (Canberra, 1982). In most respects, perceptions of limited profits turned out to be quite accurate though, albeit briefly, the Japanese era in the tiny Micronesian islands did result in the transfer of profits from the Pacific to Japan (see Mark R. Peattie, *Nan'yo: The Rise and Fall of the Japanese in Micronesia 1885-1945* [Honolulu, 1988]).

3. Richard D. Burton, *Assimilation or Independence? Prospects for Martinique* (Montreal, 1978), p. 9.

4. Elise Paulin, *Etat et reproduction de la dépendance de la Martinique* (Thèse de 3e cycle, Université de Paris VIII — Saint-Denis, 1984), p. 77.

5. *Ibid.*

6. The plantation dominated life in this depressing era. Novels such as Joseph Zobel's *La Rue Cases-Nègres* (Paris, 1950), which later became a prize-winning film directed by Euzhan Palcy, examined the social problems of plantation workers. The work was translated into English as *Black Shack Alley* (London, 1980).

7. Intermittent attempts continued to be made to develop productive activities in the outlying islands of the TAAF, just as in other colonies. Symptomatic of these attempts was the development of a lobster industry employing more than one hundred people which survived in Saint-Paul from 1928 to 1931, but then collapsed after the death of numerous workers because of deficiency diseases from the lack of fresh foods. (See Roger Brunet *et al.*, *La France d'outre-mer* (Paris, 1974), pp. 153-4 and Jean-René Vanney, 'Ces Iles du bout du monde: les terres Australes françaises', *Hérodote*, 37-38 (1985), pp. 181-200.) In Saint-Pierre the soil is so impoverished, and the climate so bleak, that soil has been imported from France for domestic gardens.

8. Colin Newbury, *Tahiti Nui* (Honolulu, 1980), p. 314.

9. Jean Gottman, 'The Isles of Guadeloupe', *Geographical Review* 35 (1945), p. 202.

10. André Lucrèce, 'Notes anthropologiques sur quelques problèmes du développement en Martinique', *Carbet* 1 (1983), pp. 87-100. See Paulin, *op. cit.*, p. 107; Burton, *op. cit.*, pp. 12-15; Claude de Miras, 'L'Economie martiniquaise: croissance ou excroissance', *Revue Tiers-Monde* 29 (1988), pp. 366-7.

11. Guy Cabort-Masson, *Les Puissances d'argent en Martinique* (Fort-de-France, 1984), p. 38.

12. Alain Buffon, 'Transferts et déséquilibres de croissance: le cas de la Guadeloupe', in *Miroir de la Dépendance*, 9 April 1982, pp. 15–16.

13. Jean Houbert, 'Réunion II: The Politics of *Départementalisation*', *Journal of Commonwealth and Comparative Politics* 18 (1980), pp. 336–7.

14. Anne Elizabeth Bault, 'Le Rhum en Guyane', *Dossiers de l'outre-mer* 81 (1985), pp. 20–5; M. Tarché, 'L'Agriculture guyanaise: Bilan et perspectives', *Dossiers de l'outre-mer* 81 (1985), pp. 8–13.

15. Buffon, *op. cit.*, p. 16; Bernard Dumaz, *Guadeloupe: Economie agricole. Le Malaise à fleur de sable* (Paris, 1986), p. 95.

16. André-Louis Sanguin, 'Saint-Martin, les mutations d'une île franco-néerlandaise des Antilles', *Cahiers d'Outre-Mer* 35 (1982), p. 127.

17. André-Louis Sanguin, 'Saint-Barthélémy, île normande des Antilles françaises', *Etudes normandes* 30 (1981), p. 64.

18. André Schérer, *La Réunion* (Paris, 1985) p. 103; see also B. Bridier, 'Quel avenir pour le géranium et le développement agricole des Hauts de l'Ouest de la Réunion?', *L'Agronomie tropicale* 40 (1985), pp. 342–56; Jean-Louis Guébourg, '"Petite Ile", une commune agricole de l'île de la Réunion en mutation', *Cahiers d'Outre-Mer* 42 (1989), pp. 192–3.

19. Jean Koechlin and Marc Boye, 'Mayotte, bilan écologique, possibilités de développement, programme d'études', *Nature et Hommes dans les îles tropicales* (Bordeaux, 1984), p. 152.

20. Jean-Pierre Doumenge, *Du terroir à la ville: Les Mélanésiens et leur espace en Nouvelle-Calédonie* (Talence, 1982).

21. John Connell, *New Caledonia or Kanaky?* (Canberra, 1987), pp. 134–43, 173–93.

22. Douglas Oliver, *Two Tahitian Villages: A Study in Comparison* (Honolulu, 1981), pp. 23, 8, 27.

23. Victoria L. Joralemon, 'Development and Inequity: The Case of Tubuai, a Welfare Economy in Rural French Polynesia', *Human Organization* 45 (1986), p. 283.

24. Gilles Blanchet, *L'Economie de la Polynésie Française de 1960 à 1980* (Papeete, 1984), pp. 13–14.

25. Colin Newbury, 'Trade and Plantations in Eastern Polynesia: The Emergence of a Dependent Economy', in R.G. Ward (ed.), *Man in the Pacific Islands* (Oxford, 1972), p. 161.

26. Nancy Pollock, 'Takapoto: La Prosperité: Retour aux îles', *Journal de la Société des Océanistes* 60 (1978), pp. 133–5.

27. Buffon, *op. cit.*, p. 16. Cyclone Hugo, in September 1989, had exactly the same effect, devastating the agricultural economy, in addition to causing five deaths and extensive damage to property and infrastructure; see Pierre Pagney, 'A Propos de Hugo ... Les cyclones tropicaux, un risque majeur', *Bulletin de la Société Languedocienne de Géographie* 113 (190), pp 97–118.

28. Jean-François Dupon, 'Where the Exception Confirms the Rule: The Cyclones of 1982–1983 in French Polynesia', *Disasters* 8 (1984), pp. 34–7.

29. Roger Cans, 'French Guiana: A Grave for the Taxpayer Back Home', *Guardian Weekly*, 17 May 1987, p. 14.

30. Victoria Lockwood, 'Development, French Neocolonialism and the Structure of the Tubuai Economy', *Oceania* 58 (1988), pp. 177, 180.

31. Paulin, *op. cit.*, p. 154; see also J.C. Martin, 'Commerce extérieur et production agricole et alimentaire dans les départements d'outre-mer', *Cahiers des statistiques agricoles* 22 (1975), pp. 1–24.

32. Ben R. Finney, *Polynesian Peasants and Proletarians* (Cambridge, Mass., 1973), p. 65; see also Ben R. Finney, 'Economic Change and Dietary Consequences among the Tahitians', *Micronesica* 2 (1965), pp. 1–14.

33. Finney, *Polynesian Peasants, op. cit.*, p. 76; see also Oliver, *Two Tahitian Villages, op. cit.* A similar situation is true of Réunion; see Albert Lopez, 'La Santé en transition à la Réunion de 1946 à 1986', *Annales de Géographie* 546 (1989).

34. Bengt Danielsson, *Work and Life on Raroia* (London, 1956) p. 102; Newbury, *Tahiti Nui*, p. 147.

35. Winston Williams, 'Pearl Shell Diving in the Tuamotus', *National Geographic* 121 (April 1962), p. 516. By the late 1980s French Polynesia was reported to be importing about 80 per cent of its food. Sarah Walls, 'French "Dancing Girls" Don't Come Cheap', *Sydney Morning Herald*, 12 August 1989, p. 20.

36. The *indépendantiste* party, Libération Kanake Socialiste, went so far as to argue that this new food dependency had political implications: 'The introduction of rice, tinned beef, casseroles, etc. . . . has overturned Kanak society because these products have been introduced to create dependence as part of a politics of cultural assimilation led by the West' (quoted in Connell, *New Caledonia or Kanaky?*, p. 176).

37. Richard Price, 'The Dark Complete World of a Caribbean Store', *Review* 9 (1985), pp. 217–18, 215.

38. Connell, *op. cit.*, pp. 124–33.

39. Newbury, *Tahiti Nui*; see also François Doumenge, *L'Homme dans le Pacifique Sud* (Paris, 1966), pp. 451–65.

40. Marie-José Jolivet, *La Question Créole: Essai de sociologie sur la Guyane française* (Paris, 1982), p. 119.

41. Michel Derse, 'Les Pêches guyanaises à la conquête de nouveaux espaces, analyse des vingt dernières années', *Cahiers d'Outre-Mer* 41 (1988), pp. 357–78; Alain Merckelbagh, 'La Pêche et l'aquaculture en Guyane', *Dossiers de l'outre-mer* 81 (1985), pp. 26–31.

42. R.D. Gillett and R.E. Kearney, *An Assessment of the Skipjack and Baitfish Resources of French Polynesia*, (Noumea, 1983).

43. Cans, *op. cit.*, p. 14.

44. Connell, *op. cit.*, pp. 143–4; Jean-Marie Kohler, *Pour ou contre le pinus: Les Mélanesiens face aux projets de développement* (Noumea, 1984).

45. Buffon, *op. cit.*, p. 17.

46. Paulin, *op. cit.*

47. Cabort-Masson, *op. cit.*, p. 158.

48. Burton, *op. cit.*, p. 16.

49. Sanguin, 'Saint-Barthélemy', *op. cit.*, p. 68.

50. Auguste Armet, 'Mal-développement et dépendance sanitaire et sociale aux Antilles "Françaises"', *Carbet* 1 (1983), p. 42.

51. In Martinique alone, for example, post-war international creations included the Caisse Centrale de Coopération Economique (CCCE), the Société de Développement Régional Antilles-Guyane (SODERAG), the Société de Développement de la Martinique (SODEMA) and the Société d'Aide Technique et de Cooperation (SATEC), all of which had functions akin to those of development banks. Martinique also benefited from the European Economic Community for funding from institutions such as the Fonds Européen de Développement (FED), the Fonds Social Européen (FSE) and Fonds Européen de Développement Régional (FEDER). A similar panoply of institutions emerged in the other overseas *départements* and, to a belated but growing extent, in the territories. In the case of Guyane this is well described by Jolivet (*op. cit.*, pp. 213–15, 217–21).

52. For Saint-Pierre and Miquelon, this structure is described by Charles Guyot-jeannin, *Saint-Pierre et Miquelon* (Paris, 1986), pp. 121–2; for New Caledonia, Connell, *op. cit.*, pp. 152–3; and for French Polynesia, Barry Shineberg, 'The Image of France: Recent Developments in French Polynesia', *Journal of Pacific History* 21 (1986), p. 157. The general situation in the *départements* is described by Jean-Paul Eluther, 'L'Evolution des prestations familiales dans les DOM', *Revue Juridique et Politique, Indépendance et Coopération* 35 (1981), pp. 783–95. There are numerous accounts of the situation in the Antilles, including Buffon, *op. cit.*, Burton, *op. cit.*, Claude de Miras, *op. cit.*, pp. 365–83, and Fred Constant, 'La Politique française de l'immigration antillaise de 1946 à 1987', *Revue Européenne des Migrations Internationales* 3 (1987), p. 14.

53. Shineberg, *op. cit.*, p. 159.

54. Philippe de Baleine, *Les Danseuses de la France* (Paris, 1979); see also Houbert, *op. cit.*, pp. 342–3.

55. Houbert, *op. cit.*, p. 342; William F.S. Miles, *Elections and Ethnicity in French Martinique* (New York, 1986) p. 143.

56. De Baleine, *op. cit.*, pp. 59, 66.

57. Buffon, *op. cit.*, p. 22. This was also a function of the uneven distribution of incomes; in 1976, in Martinique, public servants represented 25 per cent of the workforce but received 55 per cent of all wages and salaries: Alain-Phillipe Blérald, 'Guadeloupe — Martinique: A System of Colonial Domination in Crisis', in F. Ambursley and R. Cohen (eds), *Crisis in the Caribbean* (Kingston, 1983), p. 155.

58. Lévy, *Un Village du bout du monde* (Montreal, 1976), p. 20.

59. Child support payments have become particularly important in places like Martinique, where there are many single mothers and more than half of all children are born out of wedlock (Miles, *op. cit.*, p. 142).

60. Lévy, *op. cit.*, p. 69.

61. Bridier, *op. cit.*, pp. 351–2.

62. Oliver, *op. cit.*, pp. 175, 28.

63. Bernard Gorsky, *Island at the End of the World* (London, 1966), p. 96.

64. Blanchet, *op. cit.*, pp. 16–17.

65. Perhaps the most bizarre provision of transport infrastructure has been in Saint-Martin where, between 1971 and 1973, France constructed Espérance airport some 12 km away from the Juliana international airport on the Dutch side. It was widely regarded as a political decision, following the 1967 rebellion in neighbouring Anguilla, with France constructing its own airport to avoid the possible necessity to seek Dutch permission to land troops on Saint-Martin (Jean Glasscock, *The Making of an Island: Sint Maarten, Saint Martin* [Wellesley, 1985], pp. 96–7). See also Yves Monnier, *L'Immuable et le Changeant* (Bordeaux, 1983); Pollock,
    op. cit.; Joralemon, *op. cit.*, p. 285.

66. Lopez, *op. cit.*

67. Connell, *op. cit.*, p. 165.

68. Miles, *op. cit.*, p. 143; Lopez, *op. cit.*

69. Lopez, *op. cit.*, p. 156.

70. This is discussed further in Connell, *op. cit.*, pp. 166–8. The clash between Melanesian and European values in education is considered in Chapter 6.

71. It should be noted, however, that Mauritius has its own university, the University of the South Pacific (in Fiji) provides facilities for islanders from most states in the Pacific, and the University of the West Indies (with four campuses) serves the Caribbean.

72. Miles, *op. cit.*, p. 152.

73. *Le Point*, 19 December 1988.

74. For example, Beverley Ormerod, 'Discourse and Dispossession: Edouard Glissant's Image of Contemporary Martinique', *Caribbean Quarterly* 27 (1981), p. 2.

75. Dan Mulville, 'Martinique', *Geographical Magazine* 36 (May 1963), p. 41.

76. Joralemon, *op. cit.*, p. 285.

77. Edouard Glissant, *Le Discours antillais*, (Paris, 19891) p. 51.

78. Tourism to Saint-Pierre and Miquelon, however, has been quite substantial. From 1972 to 1982, the average number of visitors was 11,900 and this figure rose to over 13,600 in 1984 (when the dollar had a high exchange rate) and 23,400 in 1988, in addition to one or two thousand visitors from cruise ships each year. Guyotjeannin, *Saint-Pierre et Miquelon*, p. 101; see also E. Miller, 'Saint-Pierre and Miquelon: A Place for Food Lovers and Seal Watchers', *Earthwatch News* 6 (1985), p. 2.

79. Nowhere was the growth of tourism more spectacular than in the two tiny, previously impoverished Caribbean islands of Saint-Martin and Saint-Barthélemy, where from the end of the 1960s tourism became an effective 'monoculture' as all other economic activities (except the construction industry) foundered, to the point where there is serious concern that the two islands have become 'prisoners' of the tourist industry, and of the international airline system and global economy that service them (Sanguin, 'Saint-Barthélemy', *op. cit.*; Monnier, *op. cit.*).

80. L. Turner and J. Ash, *The Golden Hordes: International Tourism and the Pleasure Periphery* (London, 1975), p. 165. Symptomatic of this trend was the purchase by Marlon Brando of a Tuamotuan island for his personal use.

81. John Connell, '"Trouble in Paradise": The Perception of New Caledonia in the Australian Press', *Australian Geographical Studies* 25 (October 1987), pp. 54–65.

82. Claude Robineau, *Du Coprah à l'atome* (Paris, 1984), pp. 458–62. This coincided with MGM's filming of 'The Mutiny of the Bounty' in French Polynesia, an extravaganza which took ten months, used 2000 extras as well as 8000 other employees, cost $US27 million and 'constituted a temporary economic boom' which stimulated metropolitan and local capitalists to invest in tourist development (C. Robineau, 'The Tahitian Economy and Tourism', in B.R. Finney and K.A. Watson (eds), *A New Kind of Sugar: Tourism in the Pacific* (Honolulu, 1977, 2nd edn.), p. 62).

83. Buffon, *op. cit.*, p. 21; see also Jean-Claude Baptistide, *Tourisme et Développement de la Guadeloupe* (Basse-Terre, 1980).

84. Robineau in Finney and Watson, *op. cit.*, p. 74; see also Y. Monnier, 'Aménagements touristiques et bouleversements écologiques dans les petites îles: l'exemple de Saint-Martin', *Iles Tropicales: Insularité, 'Insularisme'* (Bordeaux, 1987), pp. 17–34.

85. Paulin, *op. cit.*, p. 175; see also Burton, *op. cit.*, pp. 17–18. In New Caledonia and Réunion, and to a lesser extent elsewhere, there is also significant local tourism or week-end touring. The substantial transfer of funds and high wages has enabled the generation of a local leisure industry in many of the DOM-TOMs, to the extent that New Caledonia, for example, regards itself as the windsurfing capital of the world. In contrast to international tourism, local tourism is inevitably in the rural areas, in the Isle of Pines (New Caledonia) and Les Hauts (Réunion); hence it makes some contribution to the local economy. See for example, Henri Berron, 'Les Petites activités dans le développement des Hauts de la Réunion: le cas des chambres d'hôtes', *Iles Tropicales: Insularité, 'Insularisme'* (Bordeaux, 1987), pp. 295–303.

86. V. Thompson and R. Adloff, *The French Pacific Islands: French Polynesia and New Caledonia* (Berkeley, 1971), pp. 53–5.

87. Robineau, *Du Coprah à l'atome*, *op. cit.*, p. 147; Robineau, 'The Tahitian Economy and Tourism', *op. cit.*, pp. 62–3.

88. Blanchet, *op. cit.*, p. 30.

89. Danielsson, *op. cit.*

90. Robineau, *Du Coprah à l'atome*, *op. cit.*

91. *Ibid.*, pp. 62–3.

92. Greg Chamberlain, 'French Guiana', *Latin American and Caribbean Review* (London, 1985), p. 98.

93. F. Schwarzbeck, 'Recycling a Forgotten Colony: From Green Hell to Outer Space in French Guiana', *Caribbean Review* 16 (1984), pp. 22–5, 47–8.

94. M. Le Fèvre, 'Le Programme Ariane', *Dossiers de l'outre-mer* 81 (1985), pp. 49–56; Mark Wise, 'France and European Unity', in Robert Aldrich and John Connell (eds), *France in World Politics* (London, 1989), pp. 58–9.

95. Le Fèvre, *op. cit.*, p. 53.

96. Jolivet, *op. cit.*, p. 229.

97. *Ibid.*, p. 227.

98. Brunet, *op. cit.*, p. 153. See also Yves Frenot, Philippe Vernon and Alain Bellido, 'A Bibliography of Terrestrial Ecosystems on the Iles Crozet, Indian Ocean', *Polar Record* 25 (1989), pp. 121–30.

99. Two decades ago the view that nuclear testing in French Polynesia would be merely transient was not unusual: 'The utility of the islands as a base for nuclear testing is probably drawing to a close' (Thompson and Adloff, *op. cit.*, p. 87). However, testing has continued and the very few partial scientific inquiries, operating under severe constraints, have failed to produce evidence of the destruction of the atolls, though evidence of some medical problems is more convincing (Tilman Ruff, 'Fish Poisoning in the Pacific: A Link with Military Activities', Australian National University Peace Research Centre, Working Paper No. 63, Canberra, 1989.) There is widespread opposition to nuclear testing in French Polynesia and to what has been described as the 'industry of death' inflicted on the islands (see Shineberg, *op. cit.*, p. 161). Despite growing demands for some form of compensation, one member of the Territorial Assembly has recently commented: 'Everyone is against nuclear testing — but they're in favour of the centre' (*Sydney Morning Herald*, 10 October 1989).

100. Robineau, *Du Coprah à l'atome, op. cit.*, p. 356.

101. Finney, *Polynesian Peasants, op. cit.*, p. 66; see also Ben R. Finney, 'Money Work, Fast Money and Prize Money: Aspects of the Tahitian Labor Commitment', *Human Organization* 26 (1967), pp. 195-9.

102. Hanson, *op. cit.*, p. 84.

103. These statistics come from a range of sources including various census volumes, INSEE publications on the DOMs and the publications of the Departments of Statistics in New Caledonia and French Polynesia. Few formal socioeconomic statistics (other than the censuses) are available for Mayotte and Wallis and Futuna and overall the data are often not comparable, having been collected in different years, with different procedures and definitions.

104. There are, however, considerable inequalities in the structure of employment. This is particularly apparent in New Caledonia where few Melanesians and Polynesians are employed in the professions, and there has been no effective 'localisation' policy since no statutes legally differentiate Melanesians from other races, all of whom are French citizens. Apart from very obvious quantitative differences in participation in the wage labour force, there exist clear qualitative diffferences: 'Europeans are mainly in positions of responsibility, Melanesians carry out the most basic tasks; such is the product of a century of colonial history' (Doumenge, *op. cit.*, p. 382; see Connell, *New Caledonia or Kanaky?*, p. 158).

105. Miles, *op. cit.*, p. 142.

106. Bridier, *op. cit.*, pp. 149-50.

107. Lopez, *op. cit.*, p. 166.

108. Paulin, *op cit.*

109. G. Amable, 'Les Grèves à la Réunion', *L'Economie de la Réunion* 14 (1984), pp. 7-11.

110. B. Petitjean-Roget, 'Pour comprendre la situation économique des Antilles', *Les Temps Modernes* 441-2 (1983), p. 1866.

111. Yves Lacoste, 'Ces îles où l'on parle français', *Hérodote* 37-38 (1985), pp. 16-17.

112. R. Shears and I. Gidley, *The Rainbow Warrior Affair* (Sydney, 1985).

113. Karl Rensch, 'Wallis and Futuna: Total Dependency', in A. Ali and R. Crocombe (eds), *Politics in Polynesia* (Suva, 1983), pp. 4-17.

114. Miles, *op. cit.*, p. 147.

115. Armet, *op. cit.*, p. 36.

116. De Baleine, *op. cit.*, pp. 183, 44–5.

117. Cans, *op. cit.*, p. 14.

118. Recently this has proved a popular choice for the future direction of DOM-TOM economies, building on trends in both the world economy and the DOM-TOMs (see Jean-Yves Rochoux, 'Du sucre aux services ou du développpement agricole économique à la Réunion', *Iles Tropicales, Insularité, 'Insularisme'* (Bordeaux, 1987), pp. 266–70; Jean Crusol, *Changer la Martinique: Initiation à l'économie des Antilles* (Paris, 1986).

Chapter 6   Culture, Identity and National Consciousness

1. On European attitudes towards non-Europeans, see Victor Kiernan, *Lords of Human Kind* (London, 1969); William B. Cohen, *The French Encounter with Africans* (Bloomington, 1989); James Clifford, *Person and Myth: Maurice Leenhardt in the Melanesian World* (Berkeley, 1982) on New Caledonia; and Eric Vibart, *Tahiti: Naissance d'un paradis au siècle des Lumières* (Paris, 1978). On the Western discovery of African and Oceanic art, see William Rubin (ed.), *'Primitivism' in Twentieth Century Art* (New York, 1984).

2. Raymond F. Betts, *Assimilation and Association in French Colonial Theory, 1890–1914* (New York, 1961), p. 8.

3. A good example of the early political impact of religion is given in F.A. Hanson, 'Political Change in Tahiti and Samoa', *Ethnology* 12 (1973), pp. 1–13. See also Kerry R. Howe, *The Loyalty Islands: A History of Culture Contact 1840–1900* (Canberra, 1977).

4. Eboué was governor of Chad and one of the first colonial administrators to rally to the Free French in 1940; Bourguiba, Senghor and Ho became, respectively, leaders of Tunisia, Senegal and North Vietnam.

5. See Jean-Marie Kohler and Loïc J.D. Wacquant, *L'Ecole inégale: Eléments pour une sociologie de l'école en Nouvelle-Calédonie* (Noumea, 1985).

6. This is a constant critique voiced by writers on DOM-TOM culture, including all of those listed below.

7. On culture in Saint-Pierre, see Pierre Guyotjeannin, *Saint-Pierre et Miquelon* (Paris, 1986), pp. 81–8.

8. See Edith Kovats-Beaudoux, 'Les Blancs créoles: continuité ou changement?', *Les Temps Modernes* 39 (1983), pp. 1912–23, and Jean-Luc Jamard, 'Les Blancs Créoles de la Martinique: Minorité ethnique privilégiée et classe dominante?', *Social Science Information* 19 (1980), pp. 167–97.

9. Yves Monnier, *L'Immuable et le changeant. Etude de la partie française de l'île Saint-Martin* (Bordeaux, 1983).

10. See John Connell, *New Caledonia or Kanaky?* (Canberra, 1987), and K.J. Hollyman, *Mille et un mots calédoniens* (Noumea, 1983).

11. See Annick Cojean, 'Mayotte: Empire des femmes', *Le Monde*, 16 December 1988, and Michael Lambek, *Human Spirits: A Cultural Account of Trance in Mayotte* (Cambridge, UK, 1981).

12. This was especially the case in Haiti with voodoo. On these questions, see, for example, Daniel Guérin, *Les Antilles décolonisées* (Paris, 1956), Michel Leiris,

      Contacts de civilisations en Martinique et en Guadeloupe (Paris, 1955) and Maurice
      Lemoine, *Le Mal antillais* (Paris, 1982).

13. Lemoine, *op. cit.*, p. 93.

14. Marie-Denise Shelton, 'Africa Revisited: Two French West Indian Novels',
    Caribbean Review 14 (1980), pp. 33-6.

15. Léopold Sedar Senghor, *Ce que je crois* (Paris, 1988), pp. 136-7.

16. See the various writings of Césaire, Damas and Senghor as well as, on African
    history, those of Cheik Anta Diop, e.g. *Precolonial Black Africa* (Westport, Conn.
    1967).

17. Senghor, *op. cit.*

18. See, in particular, Césaire's *Cahier d'un retour au pays natal* (1939), *Discours sur le
    colonialisme* (1950) and *Culture et colonisation* (1956); on his work, A. James
    Arnold, *Modernism and Négritude: The Poetry and Poetics of Aimé Césaire*
    (Cambridge, Mass., 1981), especially Chapter 6 ('Politics and Poetics') and for a
    critical view of *négritude*, Alain Blérald, *Négritude et politique aux Antilles* (Paris,
    1981).

19. See David Caute, *Fanon* (London, 1970) as well as Fanon's own *Peau noire,
    masques blancs* (1952) and *Les Damnés de la terre* (1961).

20. Edouard Glissant, *Le Discours antillais* (Paris, 1981); see also his *Poetique de la
    Relation* (Paris, 1990). On his work, see Beverley Ormerod, 'Discourse and Dis-
    possession: Edouard Glissant's Image of Contemporary Martinique', *Caribbean
    Quarterly* 27 (1981), pp. 10-12, and *An Introduction to the French Caribbean Novel*
    (Port of Spain, 1985).

21. Among recent works of note are: Edouard Glissant, *Mahagony* (Paris, 1987),
    Daniel Maximin, *Soufrières* (Paris, 1988), Raphaël Confiant, *Le Nègre et l'amiral*
    (Paris, 1988) — the first of his novels written in French rather than Creole — and
    the works of Patrick Chamoiseau: *Chronique des Sept Misères* (Paris, 1986), *Solibo
    Magnifique* (Paris, 1987), *Martinique* (Paris, 1988), *Au Temps de l'antan* (Paris,
    1988) and *Antan d'enfance* (Paris, 1990). Significantly, all of these have been pub-
    lished in Paris.

22. Jean Bernabé, Patrick Chamoiseau and Raphaël Confiant, *Eloge de la créolité*
    (Paris, 1989).

23. *Ibid.*, 'Créolité et politique', pp. 57-9.

24. Alain-Philippe Blérald, *La Question nationale en Guadeloupe et en Martinique*
    (Paris, 1988); see also J.-P. Jardel, 'Identités et idéologies aux Antilles françaises:
    Négrisme, négritude et antillanité', *Recherches Sociologiques* 15 (1984),
    pp. 209-31.

25. Dany Bebel-Gisler, *Le Défi culturel guadeloupéen* (Paris, 1989), p. 150.

26. Lambert-Félix Prudent, 'La Langue créole aux Antilles et en Guyane', *Les Temps
    Modernes* 39 (1983), p. 2072.

27. Oral literature is discussed by Bebel-Gisler and other writers on *créolité* and is
    incorporated, in particular, into Chamoiseau's works.

28. Yves Charbit, 'Union Patterns and Family Structure in Guadeloupe and Mar-
    tinique', *International Journal of the Sociology of the Family* 10 (1980), pp. 41-55;
    Jacques André, 'Le Coq et la jarre: Le sexuel et le féminin dans les sociétés afro-
    caribéennes', *L'Homme* 25 (1985), pp. 49-75.

29. Bebel-Gisler, *op. cit.*, pp. 18–19.

30. See Simone Henry-Valmore, *Dieux en exil* (Paris, 1988).

31. Francis Affergan, 'Etudes sur quelques rapports psycho-sociaux en Martinique', *L'Homme et la Société* 39 (1976), pp. 217–43.

32. Especially those furthest removed from French norms. See, e.g., Alan B. Anderson, 'Recent Acculturation of Bush Negroes in Surinam and French Guiana', *Anthropologica* 22 (1980), pp. 61–84.

33. In addition, some communities retain particular cultural traditions, especially religion. This is particularly true of the Indians in the DOMs.

34. Raymond Massé, 'Les adventistes du Septième Jour aux Antilles françaises: anthropologie d'une espérance', *Canadian Review of Social Anthropology* 15 (1978), pp. 452–65.

35. See Nicholas Thomas, 'The Force of Ethnology: Origins and Significance of the Melanesia/Polynesia Division', *Current Anthropology* 30 (1989), pp. 27–41.

36. Howe, *op. cit.*

37. See Douglas L. Oliver, *Oceania: The Native Cultures of Australia and the Pacific Islands* (Honolulu, 1988).

38. On changes in Tahiti, see Robert Aldrich, *The French Presence in the South Pacific 1842–1940* (London, 1990), Chapter 7, and on the 'new order' in Polynesian society, the studies in notes 39 and 40.

39. Michel Panoff, *Tahiti métisse* (Paris, 1989).

40. Alan Moorehead, *The Fatal Impact* (London, 1968). For different views, see Panoff, *op. cit.*, Alain Barbadzan, *Naissance d'une tradition* (Paris, 1982), Claude Robineau, *Du Coprah à l'atome* (Paris, 1984), Jean-François Baré, *Tahiti, les temps et les pouvoirs* (Paris, 1987) and Greg Dening, *Islands and Beaches* (Honolulu, 1989).

41. See Anne Lavondès, 'Culture et identité nationale en Polynésie', *Cahiers de l'ORSTOM, Série Sciences humaines*, 21 (1985), pp. 137–50.

42. On Wallis and Futuna, see Karl Rensch, 'Wallis and Futuna: Total Dependency', in Ahmed Ali and Ron Crocombe (eds), *Politics in Polynesia* (Suva, 1983), pp. 14–17. Typical of the retention of Polynesian cultural forms is the kava drinking in ceremonies; see Richard Rossille, *Le Kava à Wallis et Futuna*, (Bordeaux, 1986).

43. On Melanesian culture, see Alban Bensa and Jean-Claude Rivierre, *Les Chemins de l'alliance* (Paris, 1982), as well as the older works by Maurice Leenhardt, such as *Do Kamo* (Paris, 1947) and by Jean Guiart, *Structure du Chefferie en Mélanésie du Sud* (Paris, 1963).

44. Leenhardt, *op. cit.*, p. 69; Bronwen Douglas, '"Written on the Ground": Spatial Symbolism, Cultural Categories and Historical Process in New Caledonia', *Journal of the Polynesian Society* 91 (1982), pp. 383–415.

45. Bronwen Douglas, 'Bouarate of Hienghene: Great Chief in New Caledonia', in D. Scarr (ed.), *More Pacific Island Portraits* (Canberra, 1979), pp. 35–57; on the Loyalty Islands, see Howe, *op. cit.*

46. Bensa and Rivierre, *op. cit.*

47. Jean-Marie Tjibaou and Philippe Missotte, *Kanaké: Mélanésien de Nouvelle-Calédonie* (Papeete, 1978); Tjibaou, 'Recherche d'identité mélanésienne et société

traditionnelle', *Journal de la Société des Océanistes* 53 (1976), pp. 281–92 and 'Etre Mélanésien aujourd'hui', *Esprit* 57 (1981), pp. 81–94; Apollinaire Anova-Ataba, *D'Ataï à l'indépendance* (Noumea, 1984); Déwé Gorodey, *Sous les Cendres des conques* (Noumea, 1985); on the *écoles populaires kanakes*, see Marie-Adèle Néchéro-Jorédié, 'A Kanak People's School', in Michael Spencer, Alan Ward and John Connell (eds), *New Caledonia* (St Lucia, Queensland, 1988), pp. 198–219. See also the various literary pieces published in the New Caledonian review *Bwenando*.

48. J.M. Kohler, P. Pillon and L. Wacquant, *Jeunesse canaque et coutume en Nouvelle-Calédonie* (Noumea, 1985).

49. Arvin Murch, *Black Frenchmen* (Cambridge, Mass., 1971).

Chapter 7   The Shape of Politics in the DOM-TOMs

1. William F.S. Miles, *Elections and Ethnicity in French Martinique: A Paradox in Paradise* (New York, 1986), p. ix; Maurice Satineau, *Contestation politique et revendication nationaliste aux Antilles françaises: Les Élections de 1981* (Paris, 1986), p. 19; Alain Miroite, *La Démocratie dans les DOM: l'exemple de la Guadeloupe* (DEA en Sciences Politiques, Université de Paris-I, 1984), p. 4. Cf. Henri Descamps, *La Politique aux Antilles françaises de 1946 à nos jours* (Paris, 1981), p. 27, who speaks of metropolitan institutions being 'parachuted' into the DOMs. Fred Constant, *La Retraite aux flambeaux: Société et politique en Martinique* (Paris, 1988), refers to the 'export' of French institutions (p. 62), which results in a 'contradiction' between Antillais conditions and European political structures. Justin Daniel, *Administration locale et clientélisme: Le Cas de la Martinique* (Thèse de Doctorat en Sciences Politiques, Université de Paris-I, 1983), pp. 180–1, says that this 'export' amounts to the imposition of the institutions of a developed country onto a developing country.

2. Constant, *op. cit.*, pp. 15–16.

3. Miles, *op. cit.*, pp. 60–1; Satineau, *op. cit.*, p. 13; Constant, *op. cit.*, p. 116.

4. The main recent works on the Antilles are those listed in note 1, above, and Henri Bangou, *Les Voies de la souveraineté* (Paris, 1988); there is also material in most of the general studies. On politics in New Caledonia, see, in particular, Myriam Dornoy, *Politics in New Caledonia* (Sydney, 1985) and John Connell, *New Caledonia or Kanaky?* (Canberra, 1987). Unfortunately, there is very little on Guyane. It should be noted that politics in Saint-Pierre and Miquelon is rather different from that in other DOM-TOMs because of the evident differences in Saint-Pierre's history and the homogeneity of the population; the TAAF, without a permanent population, has no domestic political life.

5. On abstentionism, see Descamps, *op. cit.*, pp. 63–5; Miles, *op. cit.*, pp. 67–71, 140; Satineau, *op. cit.*, pp. 52–5, 178 and 183–90.

6. Descamps estimates the 'structural' abstention of those who cannot vote because of absence, illness, etc. at 20 per cent (*op. cit.*, p. 65), while Satineau places the figures, more generally, between 20 and 25 per cent of the electorate (*op. cit.*, p. 55); elsewhere, however, Satineau says the 'incompressible' abstention rate is 5–10 per cent (*op. cit.*, p. 184).

7. See Connell, *op. cit.*

8. Satineau, *op. cit.*, pp. 30, 56, 199.

9. Satineau, *op. cit.*

10. Miles, *op. cit.*, pp. 136-8.

11. Descamps, *op. cit.*, p. 153.

12. Miles, *op. cit.*, pp. 71-2; Satineau, *op. cit.*, p. 56, says that each ballot for the Elysée is a 'plébiscite du président sortant' ('a plebiscite for the out-going president') and a reflex vote 'à sauvegarder l'acquis' ('to preserve what has been won').

13. See Miles, *op. cit.*, and Satineau, *op. cit.*

14. This was not, however, true in the TOMs where the spectre of potential independence in New Caledonia strongly influenced voting patterns.

15. On the role of the media in the Antilles, see Miles, *op. cit.*, pp. 76-80, and Satineau, *op. cit.*, p. 54; on New Caledonia, see Michael Spencer, 'It's not all Black and White', in Michael Spencer, Alan Ward and John Connell (eds), *New Caledonia* (St Lucia, Queensland, 1988), pp. 175-97.

16. Louis Doucet, *Vous avez dit Guyane?* (Paris, 1981), p. 122.

17. Satineau, *op. cit.*, p. 54.

18. On fraud, see Descamps, *op. cit.*, pp. 66-9 (including the well-known example of the Le Moule elections); Miles, *op. cit.*, pp. 75-6; Constant, *op. cit.*, p. 51 (who points to the historical antecedents of fraud in nineteenth century Martinique) and *op. cit.*, p. 127. Allegations about ballot-rigging were made in New Caledonia in 1986 and 1988.

19. On the 1960 statute, Descamps, *op. cit.*, p. 122; on French Polynesia, Virginia Thompson and Richard Adloff, *The French Pacific Islands* (Berkeley, 1971); on New Caledonia, Connell, *op. cit.*, pp. 340-9, and Helen Fraser, *New Caledonia* (Canberra, 1989).

20. On New Caledonia see Jean-Marie Kohler, 'The Churches in New Caledonia and the Colonial Order', in Spencer, Ward and Connell (eds), *op. cit.*, pp. 145-74; on Wallis and Futuna, see Jean-Claude Roux, 'Pouvoir religieux et pouvoir politique à Wallis-Futuna', *Bulletin de la Société d'Etudes Historiques de la Nouvelle-Calédonie*, 75 (1988), pp. 13-30, and Frédéric Bobin, 'Les Royaumes de Wallis et Futuna saisis par le doute', *Le Monde*, 15 April 1987.

21. A useful account of the transformations of class and their relationship to politics is Willie L. Baber, 'Political Economy and Social Change: The Bissette Affair and Local-Level Politics in Morne-Vert', *American Ethnologist*, 12 (1985), pp. 489-504.

22. Pierre-Albert Murtil, *Indépendance pour la Guyane* (Paris, 1977), p. 86; see also Chapter 5.

23. Constant, *op. cit.*, p. 136; cf. Satineau, *op. cit.*, p. 67.

24. Constant, *op. cit.*, p. 130 and, on individualism, pp. 21 and 132-3; for a different view, Bangou, *op. cit.*, pp. 97-8.

25. Satineau, *op. cit.*, p. 179. New Caledonia, however, may provide an exception. See Chapter 8.

26. Descamps, *op. cit.*, p. 17; on general questions of race, see also Bangou, *op. cit.*, p. 61 and Constant, *op. cit.*, p. 42.

27. Of course, racial questions have of late become more significant in France, particularly concerning immigration and the residence of North Africans in France, and have contributed to the growth of the Front National; see Max Silverman, '*Travailleurs immigrés* and International Relations', in Robert Aldrich and John

Connell (eds), *France in World Politics* (London, 1989), pp. 74–100. Many Antillais in France suffer from racist attacks and an Antillais, Harlem Désir, is the founder of one of the main anti-racist groups in France, SOS-Racisme. (See 'Les Noirs en France', *Le Nouvel Observateur*, 8 November 1990, pp. 4–12.)

28. There are other factors as well. Satineau, *op. cit.*, pp. 192–5, talks about the role of religion, especially fundamentalist Protestantism, in political life in the Antilles. Constant (*op. cit.*, p. 35) points to the importance of Freemasonry. It has also been suggested that the dominance of women voters, with a certain conservative orientation, is important; see Miles, *op. cit.*, pp. 72–3 and Satineau, *op. cit.*, p. 56.

29. Rodolphe Alexandre, 'Le Conseil général de Guyane (1946–1982)', *Equinoxe*, 16 (1982), pp. 19–37.

30. Constant, *op. cit.*, pp. 19, 63 and 170; cf. Miles, *op. cit.*, pp. 93–5 and 135.

31. On Césaire, see the references in Miles and Constant, as well as the works on Césaire listed in their bibliographies and Césaire's own writings. On his 1956 statement, Descamps, *op. cit.*, pp. 87–9, and on his 1981 'moratorium', Miles, *op. cit.*, pp. 84–5, Constant, *op. cit.*, p. 189 and Satineau, *op. cit.*, p. 119, who says that Césaire's moratorium 'was intended to break the traditional form of electoral debate in the Antilles, the core of which was *départementalisation* or independence'. See also Chapter 8.

32. On Galmont, see Jean-Marie Billaud's articles in *Equinoxe* 4 (1977), pp. 1–25, and 5 (1977), pp. 1–27; on his successor, see Rodolphe Alexandre, 'Justin Catayée et le Parti socialiste guyanais', *Equinoxe*, 17 (1983), pp. 28–52 and 18 (1984), pp. 1–31.

33. In the event of the death or resignation of the French President, the President of the Senate becomes President of the Republic *ad interim* and oversees the election to choose a new President.

34. Daniel, *op. cit.*, p. 442; see also, Descamps, *op. cit.*, p. 39, on the longevity of politicians.

35. On Réunionnais politicians, Marcel Leguen, *Histoire de l'Ile de Réunion* (Paris, 1979), and Debré's own memoir, *Une Politique pour la Réunion* (Paris, 1974).

36. On Pouvana'a, Danielsson, *op. cit*; on Flosse, various articles in *Pacific Islands Monthly*, and in general, William Tagupa, 'Some Aspects of Modern Politics and Personality in French Polynesia', *Journal of Pacific History* 9 (1974), pp. 10–15.

37. See Dornoy and Connell, *op. cit.*, and the articles in *Kanaky*, July 1989. The special issue of *Bwenando* (121-4, July 1989) provides a first attempt to review his work and philosophy; see also Alain Rollat, *Tjibaou le Kanak* (Lyon, 1989). After his death the organisation of the FLNKS exhibited a degree of disarray; see Chapter 8.

38. On political generations, Satineau, *op. cit.*, pp. 220 and 222–6; Descamps, *op. cit.*, pp. 10, 57.

39. Miles, *op. cit.*, p. 126. This generational conflict in Martinique was labelled a clash between the so-called *vieillards français* and the *chiffristes*.

40. On this latter point, see Satineau, *op. cit.*, pp. 198–9 and 223; on the importance of the use of language, Constant, *op. cit.*, p. 128.

41. On Indians in Guadeloupe, Satineau, *op. cit.*, p. 63; on Réunion, Leguen, *op. cit.*

42. On clientelism, Satineau, *op. cit.*, p. 173; Constant, *op. cit.*, pp. 52 and 130; Jean

Houbert, 'Réunion II: The Politics of *Départementalisation*', *Journal of Common-wealth and Comparative Politics* 18 (1980), p. 335 and Daniel, *op. cit.*, p. 326.

43. See Baber, *op. cit.*; M. Horowitz, *Morne-Paysan: Peasant Village in Martinique* (New York, 1967).

44. Constant, *op. cit.*, p. 52.

45. Daniel, *op. cit.*, pp. 139, 206-7, 306.

46. On the *bourgeoisie de couleur*, Descamps, *op. cit.*, pp. 18, 58 and 153, and Constant, p. 65.

47. Constant, *op. cit.*, pp. 82, 108.

48. Constant, *op. cit.*, p. 112.

49. Willingness by some Antillais politicians to dispense jobs and money and to form alliances has caused others to criticise them for '*alimentarisme*' and failure to attack colonialism (Satineau, *op. cit.*, p. 123; cf. Constant, *op. cit.*, p. 126, and Daniel, *op. cit.*, p. 315). Such arrangements, according to these critics, engender an abuse of the system by the populace, including office-holding, nepotism, illegitimate social service payments, a parallel economy and *débrouillardise*, taking advantage of the system in clever (and sometimes irregular) ways in order to get ahead. (Constant, *op. cit.*, pp. 82, 86; on the informal sector, see Daniel, *op. cit.*, p. 212 ff.)

50. On the wooing of DOM-TOM politicians by the metropolitan parties, Descamps, *op. cit.*, p. 12; Constant, *op. cit.*, p. 173; and Daniel, *op. cit.*, p. 300.

51. Satineau, *op. cit.*, p. 15.

52. Maurice Satineau, *Le Miroir de Nouméa* (Paris, 1987).

53. That DOM-TOM politics is reactive is suggested by Miles, *op. cit.*, p. 219. Henri Oberdoff theorises about a '*décalage*', or lag, between metropolitan and DOM-TOM politics (quoted in Miles, *op. cit.*, p. 134.) Descamps points to the way the DOM-TOMs have served as laboratories for administrative reforms before they are introduced in the *métropole* (*op. cit.*, pp. 163-4.)

54. On Guadeloupe, see Henri Bangou, *Le Parti socialiste français face à la décolonis-ation: de Jules Guesde à François Mitterrand* (Paris, 1985).

55. Alexandre (1983), 'Justin Catayée . . .', *op. cit.*

56. For the views of a pro-socialist Guyanais politician, see Elie Castor, *1981-1985: La Gauche au pouvoir, pour la Guyane: l'espoir* (Paris, 1986).

57. See Michel Capron and Jean Chesneaux, 'Objectifs communs et grande diversité des mouvements indépendantistes', *Le Monde Diplomatique*, 337 (August 1985), pp. 2-3, and the various articles in the bulletin of the Centre d'Information Guadeloupe, Guyane, Martinique. See Chapter 8.

58. On New Caledonia, Dornoy, *op. cit.*, and Connell, *op. cit.*

59. See William F.S. Miles, 'Electoral Flip-Flop in the French Caribbean: Mitterrand and Martinique', *French Politics and Society* 8 (1990), pp. 39-52.

60. Elie Castor and Georges Othily, *La Guyane: les grands problèmes, les solutions possibles* (Paris, 1984), p. 26.

Chapter 8   Towards Independence?

1. Guy Martin, 'France and Africa', in R. Aldrich and J. Connell (eds) *France in World Politics* (London, 1989), pp. 101-25; R. Aldrich and J. Connell, 'Franco-

phonie: Language, Culture or Politics', in Aldrich and Connell, *op. cit.*, pp. 170–93.

2. Alvin Murch, *Black Frenchmen: The Political Integration of the French Antilles* (Cambridge, Mass., 1971).

3. D.K. Fieldhouse, *The Colonial Empires: A Comparative Survey from the Eighteenth Century* (London, 1987), p. 411.

4. Quoted in John Beasant, *The Santo Rebellion: An Imperial Reckoning* (Melbourne, 1984), p. 150.

5. Virginia Thompson and Richard Adloff. *The French Pacific Islands: French Polynesia and New Caledonia* (Berkeley and Los Angeles, 1971); Douglas Oliver, *Two Tahitian Villages* (Laie, 1981), pp. 18, 266.

6. Bengt and Marie-Claude Danielsson, the former a veteran of the *Kon-Tiki* expedition, in their *Moruroa Mon Amour* (Melbourne, 1977) graphically argued against what they described as this 'crime against the Polynesian people and humanity at large'.

7. Quoted in Bengt Danielsson, 'French Polynesia: Nuclear Colony', in A. Ali and R. Crocombe (eds), *Politics in Polynesia* (Suva, 1983), p. 212.

8. Quoted in Thompson and Adloff, *op. cit.*, p. 326.

9. Myriam Dornoy, *Politics in New Caledonia* (Sydney, 1984); John Connell, *New Caledonia or Kanaky?* (Canberra, 1987).

10. Alan Ward, *Land and Politics in New Caledonia* (Canberra, 1982).

11. S.B. MacDonald and A.G. Gastmann, 'Mitterrand's Headache. The French Antilles in the 1980s', *Caribbean Review* 16 (1984), p. 20.

12. Dany Bébel-Gisler, 'De la Culture guadeloupéenne de l'indépendance', *Les Temps Modernes* 441–2 (1983), pp. 2004–25.

13. Camille Chauvet and Guy Cabort-Masson, *La Face cachée de la France aux Antilles* (Fort-de-France, 1980).

14. Alain Blérald, *La Question nationale en Guadeloupe et Martinique* (Paris, 1988), pp. 136–7.

15. Quoted in Richard Burton, *Assimilation or Independence? Prospects for Martinique*, (Montreal, 1978), p. 46; see also Robert Ageneau, 'Autonomie ou indépendance pour les Antilles et la Guyane', in Collectif des Chrétiens pour l'Auto-détermination des DOM-TOMs, *Quel Avenir pour les DOM?* (Paris, 1978), pp. 44–6.

16. William F.S. Miles, *Elections and Ethnicity in French Martinique: A Paradox in Paradise* (New York, 1986), p. 49.

17. Quoted in Burton, *op. cit.*, p. 47.

18. Harold Mitchell, *Caribbean Patterns: A Political and Economic Study of the Contemporary Caribbean* (London, 1972), pp. 287–8.

19. Paul Vergès, 'Le Parti Communiste Réunnionnais et l'autonomie', in Collectif des Chrétiens, *op. cit.*, pp. 68–79; Marcel Leguen, *Histoire de l'Ile de la Réunion* (Paris, 1979), p. 248; Michel Robert, *La Réunion: Combats pour l'autonomie* (Paris, 1976); and John M. Ostheimer, 'Réunion: France's Remaining Bastion', in J.M. Ostheimer (ed.), *Politics of Western Indian Ocean Islands* (New York, 1975), pp. 102–38.

20. Alain Blérald, *op. cit.*, pp. 30–1; see AGEG, *L'Emigration travailleuse guade-*

loupéenne en France (Paris, 1978), pp. 99–142, and AGEG, *Notre Combat* (Paris, 1976).

21. Miles, *op. cit.*, pp. 52–3; Ageneau, *op. cit.*, pp. 55–61; Burton, *op. cit.*; Maurice Satineau, *Contestation politique et revendication nationaliste aux Antilles françaises* (Paris, 1986), pp. 136–41.

22. Miles, *op. cit.*, p. 53; see also Blérald, *op. cit.*, p. 133, Satineau, *op. cit.*, pp. 147–9 and Ageneau, *op. cit.*, pp. 55–9.

23. Blérald, *op. cit.*, p. 132; Satineau, *op. cit.*, pp. 142, 223.

24. Anon, 'Les Occupations de terre en Guadeloupe', *Les Temps Modernes* 39 (1983), pp. 1974–87; Satineau, *op. cit.*, p. 146.

25. Jean-Claude Guillebaud, *Les Confettis de l'empire* (Paris, 1976), pp. 224–5; Pierre-Albert Murtil, *Indépendance pour la Guadeloupe* (Cayenne, 1977).

26. Jean Houbert, 'Réunion II. The Politics of *Départementalisation*', *Journal of Commonwealth and Comparative Politics* 18 (1980), pp. 345, 334.

27. Miles, *op. cit.*, pp. 94, 106.

28. Connell, *op. cit.*, pp. 262–98.

29. Marie-Adèle Néchéro-Jorédié, 'An *Ecole Populaire Kanak* (EPK): the Canala Experiment', in M. Spencer, A. Ward and J. Connell (eds), *New Caledonia* (St Lucia, Queensland, 1988), pp. 198–218.

30. John Connell, 'New Caledonia: The Evolution of Kanaky Nationalism', *Australian Outlook* 41 (1987), pp. 37–44.

31. John Connell, 'New Caledonia: The Matignon Accord and the Colonial Future', Research Institute for Asia and the Pacific, Occasional Paper No. 5, Sydney, 1988.

32. Quoted in Connell, *New Caledonia or Kanaky?*, p. 445.

33. Connell, 'New Caledonia: The Matignon Accord', p. 12.

34. *Op. cit.*, p. 13.

35. *Op. cit.*, pp. 13–14.

36. A number of books reflect on the events in Ouvea from various perspectives, including Edwy Plenel and Alain Rollat, *Mourir à Ouvea: Le Tournant Calédonien* (Paris, 1988), Gilbert Picard, *L'Affaire d'Ouvéa* (Paris, 1988), Patrick Forestier, *Les Mystères d'Ouvéa* (Paris, 1988) and Claude Gabriel and Vincent Kermel, *Les Sentiers de l'espoir* (Paris, 1988).

37. Connell, 'New Caledonia: The Matignon Accord', p. 15.

38. *Op. cit.*, pp. 17–18.

39. *Op. cit.*, pp. 19–20.

40. *Op. cit.*, pp. 20–2.

41. John Connell, 'New Caledonia', *The Contemporary Pacific* 2 (1990), pp. 361–5; Alain Rollat, *Tjibaou le Kanak* (Lyon, 1989).

42. Quoted in *Le Courrier Australien*, October 1989.

43. Quoted in *Les Nouvelles Calédoniennes*, 14 August 1985.

44. Union Populaire pour la Libération de la Guadeloupe (UPLG), *Conférence Internationale des Dernières Colonies de la France* (Pointe-à-Pitre, 1985); M. Capron and J. Chesneaux, 'Objectifs communs et grande diversité des mouvements indépen-

dantistes', *Le Monde Diplomatique* 337 (August 1985), pp. 2–3; Alain Rollat, 'Une Strategie commune', *Le Monde*, 9 April 1985. In 1971 as a precursor to this conference, representatives from each of the *vieilles colonies* attended a Convention for Autonomy held in Martinique, and denounced 'the maintenance of a system of colonial relations which departmentalization tends to perpetuate (Miles, *op. cit.,* p. 212).

45. The proceedings of a Colloque International at Lyon (November 1987) which brought together representatives from Guadeloupe, New Caledonia and Corsica is in Dominique Ghisoni, Wassissi Iopué and Camille Rabin (eds), *Ces Iles que l'on dit françaises* (Paris, 1988).

46. William Tagupa, 'Electoral Behaviour in French Polynesia, 1977–1982', *Political Science* 35 (1983), pp. 30–57.

47. Quoted in *Pacific Islands Monthly* 53 (August 1982), pp. 22–3.

48. Quoted in *Pacific Islands Monthly* 56 (May 1985), p. 53.

49. Quoted in *La Dépêche de Tahiti*, 17 December 1984.

50. For example, see Danielsson, *op. cit.,* p. 223.

51. Anon, *op. cit.,* p. 1987; UPLG, 'La Situation politique en Guadeloupe depuis le 10 Mai', *Les Temps Modernes*, 39 (1983), pp. 1961–73.

52. Quoted by Fred Constant, *La Retraite aux Flambeaux. Société et Politique en Martinique* (Paris, 1988), p. 189.

53. Constant, *op. cit.,* pp. 191–2.

54. Quoted in Constant, *op. cit.,* p. 197.

55. Constant, *op. cit.,* p. 198.

56. Miles, *op. cit.,* p. 243.

57. Satineau, *op. cit.,* p. 235.

58. MacDonald and Gastmann, *op. cit.,* p. 21; see M. Giraud and U. Santamaria, 'L'Enjeu caraïbe', *Les Temps Modernes* 441–2 (1983), pp. 1797–1814.

59. *Antilla*, 228 (12 February 1987), p. 33.

60. To others, such as the Guadeloupean pastor Pierre Fertin, this emphasis on sugarcane cultivation has become 'a liturgical obsession' (personal communication, 15 February 1987).

61. This summary is based on discussions with two prominent UPLG leaders, Eryc Edinval and Lucien Perutin, in Pointe-à-Pitre on 18 February 1987. See also UPLG, *Quelle indépendance pour la Guadeloupe?* (Pointe-à-Pitre, 1984).

62. *Antilla*, 287 (12 May 1988), p. 27.

63. UPLG, 'La Situation politique', p. 1971.

64. Guy Cabort-Masson, *Les Indépendantistes face à eux-mêmes: La Remise en question* (Fort-de-France, 1989).

65. *Le Monde*, 15 March 1988.

66. Greg Chamberlain, 'French Guiana', *Latin American and Caribbean Review* (London, 1985), p. 99.

67. P. Boggio, 'Guyane's restless Indians and fearful Creoles', *Guardian Weekly*, 21 April 1985 (*Le Monde*, 7 April 1985).

68. J.-P. Gomane, 'Perspectives de la France outre-mer', *Politique Etrangère* 50 (1985), p. 433.

69. F. Luizet, 'Que devient Mayotte?', *Le Figaro*, 12 February 1985.

70. UPLG, 'Discours du representant de UPLG', in UPLG, *Conférence Internationale*, p. 6.

71. Quoted by L. Greilsamer, 'Is Médecin the doctor Nice wants?', *Guardian Weekly*, 8 December 1985 (*Le Monde*, 6 November 1985).

72. E. Weber, *Peasants into Frenchmen: The Modernisation of Rural France, 1870–1914* (London, 1977).

73. Quoted in the *Sydney Morning Herald*, 30 July 1988.

74. Michael Keating, 'The Rise and Decline of Micronationalism in Mainland France', *Political Studies* 33 (1985), pp. 1–18.

75. Quoted in *Les Nouvelles Calédoniennes*, 16 February 1985. Of all the French political parties the Front National is the strongest adherent of this perspective. In Martinique campaigning against support for the 1988 national referendum on the future of New Caledonia, the local Front National representative argued: 'Nothing safeguards Martinique and Guadeloupe against independence. To vote yes would be to vote for eventual independence in New Caledonia and to provide for such a possibility for the whole of the DOM-TOMs on the same principles as a house of cards', (*France-Antilles*, 11 November 1988).

76. Jean-Claude Martinez, 'Conclusion', in J.-C. Martinez (ed.), *La Nouvelle-Calédonie: La Stratégie, le droit et la république* (Paris, 1985), p. 209.

77. Connell, *New Caledonia or Kanaky?*, pp. 293–4.

78. Andre-Louis Sanguin, 'Saint-Barthélémy, Ile Normande des Antilles Françaises', *Etudes normandes* 30 (1981), p. 75. See also Marie-Noëlle Hervé, 'Saint-Barthélémy, L'île enfermée', *Le Monde*, 27 June 1987.

79. Jean Glasscock, *The Making of an Island: Sint Maarten, Saint-Martin*, (Wellesley, 1985), p. 87.

80. Jean-Luc Bonniol, 'Contrepoint Creole', *Les Temps Modernes* 39 (1983), p. 2069.

81. John Teariki, in *Pacific Islands Monthly* 54 (January 1984), p. 41.

82. Stephen Henningham, 'Keeping the Tricolor Flying: the French Pacific into the 1990s', *The Contemporary Pacific* 1 (1989), p. 106; cf. Connell, 'New Caledonia: The Matignon Accord', p. 19.

83. Quoted in *Pacific Islands Monthly* 54 (January 1984), p. 41. A survey in Martinique and Guadeloupe in the late 1970s suggested that the main reasons for popular opposition to independence are the belief that the islands lack adequate resources for self-reliance and the fear of losing employment opportunities in Paris (see Claudie Beauvue-Fougeyrollas, *Les Femmes antillaises*, Paris, 1979).

84. Quoted in Satineau, *op. cit.*, p. 143.

85. Burton, *op. cit.*, p. 62

86. Conseil National des Comités Populaires, 'Contribution', in UPLG, *Conférence Internationale*, pp. 58–65.

87. Quoted in Edouard Glissant, 'Une Société morbide et ses pulsions', *Le Monde Diplomatique* 279 (June 1977), p. 17.

88. Quoted in Guillebaud, *op. cit.*, p. 59.

89. William F.S. Miles, 'Mitterrand in the Caribbean: Socialism (?) Comes to Martinique', *Journal of Interamerican Studies* 27 (1985), p. 65.

90. See F. Schwarzbeck, 'Recycling a Forgotten Colony: From Green Hell to Outer Space in French Guiana', *Caribbean Review* 16 (1984), p. 47; Gomane, *op. cit.*, p. 199.

91. Burton, *op. cit.*, p. 56.

92. John Connell, 'Melanesian Nationalism: A Comparative Perspective on Decolonisation in New Caledonia', in M. Spencer, A. Ward and J. Connell (eds), *New Caledonia: Essays in Nationalism and Dependency* (St Lucia, Queensland, 1988), pp. 230-53.

93. Miles, *Elections and Ethnicity*, p. 214.

94. Albert Ramassamy, *La Réunion, décolonisation et integration* (Saint-Denis, 1987), p. 8. See also A.W. Murch, 'Political Integration — an Alternative to Independence in the French Antilles', *American Sociological Review* 33 (1968), pp. 544-62.

95. Serge Mam-Lam-Fouck, *Histoire de la société guyanaise* (Paris, 1987), pp. 224-7.

96. See H. Brunschwig, *Mythes et réalités de l'impérialisme colonial français, 1871-1914* (Paris, 1950) and R. Girardet, *L'Idée coloniale en France* (Paris, 1972).

97. Quoted in *France-Antilles*, 26 June 1987.

Chapter 9   The DOM-TOMs and the Wider World

1. For an overview, *Les Dossiers de l'Outre-Mer*, 83 (1986), on 'Complémentarités Métropole-Outre-Mer'.

2. Paul Vallin, *Les 'Frances' d'outre-mer* (Paris, 1987), pp. 22, 86.

3. Letter of 24 May 1987.

4. Letter of 11 May 1987.

5. Letter of 16 September 1987.

6. Letter of 19 November 1987.

7. Letter of 11 May 1987.

8. Jean-Emile Vié, *Faut-il abandonner les DOM?* (Paris, 1978), p. 135.

9. Robert Aldrich and John Connell, 'Beyond the Hexagon', in Robert Aldrich and John Connell (eds), *France in World Politics* (London, 1989), pp. 1-15. See, too, the standard history of French foreign policy, Alfred Grosser, *Affaires extérieures: La Politique de la France 1944-1984* (Paris, 1984).

10. Quoted in Philippe Leymarie, *Océan Indien* (Paris, 1981), p. 233.

11. Guyotjeannin, *Saint-Pierre et Miquelon* (Paris, 1986). p.122.

12. François Gèze *et al.*, *L'Etat du Monde* (Paris, 1983).

13. Stuart Inder, 'Vacant Possessions', *Pacific Islands Monthly*, February 1989, p. 50.

14. *Le Monde*, 29 May 1987; 14, 19, 21 April 1988.

15. Bengt and Marie-Thérèse Danielsson, *Poisoned Reign* (Harmondsworth, 2nd edn., 1986) and Stewart Firth, *Nuclear Playground* (Sydney, 1987), Chapter 10.

16. Robert Aldrich and John Connell, 'Francophonie: Language, Culture or Politics?', in Aldrich and Connell (eds), *op. cit.*, pp. 195–221, and the most recent full-scale
    study, Michel Tétu, *La Francophonie: histoire, problématiques, perspectives* (Paris, 1988).

17. Jean Houbert, 'Décolonisation et dépendance: Maurice et la Réunion', *Annuaire des Pays de l'Océan Indien* 8 (1981), p. 121.

18. See Robert Aldrich, *France and the South Pacific since 1940* (London, forthcoming).

19. See Chapter 6.

20. François Ravault, 'Le Français dans une société pluri-culturelle: l'exemple de la Polynésie', *Anthropologie et Sociétés* 6 (1982), pp. 89–105; Stephen J. Schooling, *A Sociolinguistic Survey of New Caledonia* (Noumea, 1982).

21. Quoted in *Le Nouvel Observateur*, 23 November 1989, p. 70.

22. J.C. Roux, 'Présence et originalité du fait francophone en Melanésie du Sud', *Bulletin de la Société d'études historiques de la Nouvelle-Calédonie*, 65 (1985), p. 27.

23. *Sydney Morning Herald*, 8 December 1986; *Le Monde*, 29 May, 11 June, 2 September 1987; 15 March, 14, 21 April, 8 May 1988.

24. The other overseas territories in the Caribbean are Puerto Rico and the American Virgin Islands (the United States); Aruba and the Netherlands Antilles (Bonaire, Curaçao, Saba, Sint-Eustatius and the Dutch part of Saint-Martin) (Netherlands); the British Virgin Islands, Anguilla, Montserrat, the Turks and Caicos Islands and the Cayman Islands (United Kingdom). Bermuda in the Western Atlantic is also still a British possession.

25. On geopolitics in the Caribbean, see J. Heine and L. Manigat (eds), *The Caribbean and World Politics* (New York, 1988).

26. William F.S. Miles, 'Mitterrand in the Caribbean: Socialism (?) Comes to Martinique', *Journal of Interamerican Studies* 27 (1985), p. 70.

27. Louis Dupont, *Les Départements français d'Amérique* (Paris, 1988).

28. There have been reports that several political groups in Dominica, faced with independence from Great Britain, considered the possibility of asking to become a French *département*.

29. Anthony Payne, *The International Crisis in the Caribbean* (London, 1984), p. 101.

30. On developments in neighbouring islands, see Catherine A. Sunshine, *The Caribbean: Survival, Struggle and Sovereignty* (Boston, 1985).

31. Centre National d'Etudes Spatiales, 'Les Activités spatiales en France' and other documentation from the CNES.

32. Auguste Toussaint, *Histoire de l'Ocean Indien* (Paris, 1981).

33. British forces, however, remained in Oman until 1975 because of internal troubles there, and also in the Seychelles until the independence of that country.

34. Independence for Mauritius did not meet with the unanimous approval of the colony's population. The Creole minority were particularly concerned over future domination by the Indian majority. The Creoles who form almost all of the

population of the Mauritian dependency of Rodrigues considered secession and supposedly made contacts with the French in Réunion to discuss the possibility of Rodrigues being reintegrated into the French *outre-mer*. See Jean Houbert, 'Décolonisation et dépendance', pp. 103-23.

35. See Simon Winchester, *Outposts* (London, 1985), Chapter 2, 'British Indian Ocean Territory and Diego Garcia', and André Oraison, 'Les Avatars du B.I.O.T.: Le Processus de l'implantation militaire américaine à Diego Garcia', *Annuaire des Pays de l'Océan Indien*, 6 (1979), pp. 172-209.

36. The main works on the geopolitics — and other aspects — of the contemporary Indian Ocean are Philippe Leymarie, *Océan Indien*, and Jean-Pierre Campredon and Jean-Jacques Schweitzer, *France, Océan Indien, Mer Rouge* (Paris, 1986). See also Alain Lamballe, 'La France et l'Océan Indien', *Civilisations* 30 (1980), pp. 102-9; Jean-Pierre Gomane, 'France in the Indian Ocean', in L.W. Bowman and I. Clarke (eds), *The Indian Ocean in Global Politics* (Boulder, 1981), and Jean Houbert, 'France in the Indian Ocean: Decolonizing without Disengaging', *The Round Table* 198 (1986), pp. 146-66. On the role of Réunion, see Centre des Hautes Etudes sur l'Afrique et l'Asie Modernes, *La Réunion dans l'Océan Indien* (Paris, 1986) and Emile Martinez, *Le Departement français de la Réunion et la coopération internationale dans l'Océan Indien* (Paris, 1988).

37. In addition to the works cited above, see H. Labrousse, 'L'Europe et l'Océan Indien: perspectives géopolitiques et stratégiques', *Annuaire des Pays de l'Océan Indien* 7 (1980), pp. 17-34.

38. Jean-Noël Pouliquen, 'Pour qui garder les îles Kerguelen?', *Défense nationale* 44 (1988), pp. 33-8.

39. Jacques Moine, 'Océan Indien et progressisme', *L'Afrique et l'Asie modernes* 4 (1979), pp. 3-23.

40. Gomane, *op. cit.*, pp. 193-4, Campredon and Schweitzer, *op. cit.*, pp. 130-209, 218.

41. Martinez, *op. cit.*, p. 51.

42. See Martinez, Gomane, and Campredon and Schweitzer.

43. Andrew Oraison and François Miclo, 'A qui appartient le récif de Tromelin?', *Annuaire des Pays de l'Océan Indien* 3 (1976), pp. 269-89.

44. See A. Oraison and F. Miclo, 'Les Iles Tromelin, Glorieuses, Jean de Nova, Europa et Bassas da India (Des curiosités juridiques)', *Penant*, 743 (1984), pp. 136-70.

45. Campredon and Schweitzer, *op. cit.*, p. 22; Martinez, *op. cit.*, p. 45.

46. *L'Express*, 4 August 1989, pp. 32-4.

47. Martinez, *op. cit.*, pp. 40-1.

48. Quoted in *Le Monde*, 22 November 1985.

49. On Djibouti, see Campredon and Schweitzer, *op. cit.*, pp. 289-333.

50. Houbert, 'France in the Indian Ocean', p. 155.

51. Approximately 15,000 French nationals live in the old French *comptoirs de l'Inde* (in addition to many other French residents of India), 17,000 live in Madagascar, 300 in Mauritius, 1000 in the Comoros, 200 in the Seychelles, plus others in the Gulf and African states. Campredon and Schweitzer, *op. cit.*, p. 139.

52. Houbert, *op. cit.*, p. 153; Gomane, *op. cit.*, pp. 199-200; Lamballe, *op. cit.*,

pp. 105-6; Leymarie, *op. cit.*, pp. 85-109; Campredon and Schweitzer, *op. cit.*, pp. 15-16.

53. Houbert, *op. cit.*, p. 153; Gomane, *op. cit.*, p. 200.

54. On Soviet actions, see Leymarie, *op. cit.*, pp. 132-52.

55. Gomane, *op. cit.*, p. 197.

56. Quoted in *Le Monde*, 24 December 1987.

57. Lamballe, *op. cit.*, p. 107.

58. General Roux, in 1975, was reported as saying that one reason for the presence of the French Indian Ocean forces was to 'maintenir le sentiment national, s'opposer à toute tentative de séparatisme' (quoted in Leymarie, *op. cit.*, p. 229).

59. Quoted in Leymarie, *ibid.*, p. 193.

60. *Ibid.*, p. 209.

61. Martijn Wilder, *Antarctica: An Economic History of the Last Continent* (Sydney, 1991).

62. Alain Auger, 'L'Intérêt économique et stratégique des "Terres australes et antarctiques françaises"', in Institut du Pacifique, *L'Antarctique* (Paris, 1985), pp. 13-64. See also Jean Robert, *L'Antarctique et la Terre Adélie* (Aix-en-Provence, 1990).

63. Keith Suter, 'Kerguelen: A French Mystery', *Newsletter of the Antarctic Society of Australia*, No. 16 (March 1989), pp. 5-10. Suter argues, first, that although French officials say such a transfer would prove too costly, 'French governments have consistently been willing to pay high costs for their nuclear programs.' Secondly, although Paris formally denies such a plan, 'to a cynic on French political practice (such as myself) an official denial is tantamount to an affirmation.' Other reasons he cites include a random personal observation by a French consul in Melbourne, regional opposition to French testing in the Pacific, French sensitivity about foreign inspections of Kerguelen and the sinking of a trawler (the *Southern Raider*) illegally fishing in the waters of Kerguelen in 1986.

64. Institut du Pacifique, *op. cit.*, and 'L'Antarctique', *Problèmes politiques et sociaux*, La Documentation française, publication No. 540 (1986).

65. Paul-Emile Victor, 'L'Enjeu antarctique et la Terre Adélie', Institut du Pacifique, *op. cit.*, p. 82.

66. Victor, pp. 91-100; Cousteau, quoted in the *Courrier Australien*, April 1989.

67. F. Baumel, 'La France et les enjeux du Pacifique', *Revue des deux mondes* 25 (1984), pp. 48-58. The major statement is in Institut du Pacifique, *Le Pacifique, 'nouveau centre du monde'* (Paris, 2nd edn., 1986); for a critique, see Robert Aldrich, 'Rediscovering the Pacific: A Critique of French Geopolitical Analysis', *Journal de la Société des Océanistes* 87 (1989), pp. 57-71.

68. John Beasant, *The Santo Rebellion: An Imperial Reckoning* (Sydney, 1985). On the recent history of the region, see Ron Crocombe, *The South Pacific* (Auckland, 1983).

69. All of these developments are covered in *Pacific Islands Monthly* and *Islands Business*, the major news magazines of the South Pacific, and also in *Pacific Defence Reporter*.

70. The most recent general works are those of Robert Aldrich, 'France in the South

Pacific', in John Ravenhill (ed.), *No Longer an American Lake? Alliance Problems in the South Pacific* (Berkeley, 1989), pp. 76–105, Phillip Methven, 'In Deference to De Gaulle: The French Approach to Security in the South Pacific', *Contemporary Southeast Asia* 10 (1989), pp. 385–410, and Stephen Bates, *The South Pacific Island Countries and France: A Study in Inter-state Relations* (Canberra, 1990).

71. A general French criticism of France's Pacific policy is Jean Chesneaux, *Transpacifiques* (Paris, 1987).

72. See, for example, Richard Shears and Isobelle Gidley, *The Rainbow Warrior Affair* (Sydney, 1985).

73. Roland Paringaux, 'La France mal-aimée du Pacifique', *Le Monde*, 3 April 1986.

74. Norman MacQueen, 'Sharpening the Spearhead: Subregionalism in Melanesia', *Pacific Studies* 12 (1989), pp. 33–52.

75. See, for example, Rocard's comments in the *Sydney Morning Herald*, 21 August 1989.

76. The essential works on French geopolitics and strategy in the South Pacific are the special issues of *Politique Etrangère*, 'La France et le Pacifique Sud', 52 (1987), and the special issue of the *Journal de la Société des Océanistes*, 'Géopolitique et stratégie dans le Pacifique', 87 (1989).

77. The main political study of the French nuclear testing — and a bitter denunciation of French policy — is Bengt and Marie-Thérèse Danielsson, *Poisoned Reign* (2nd edn, Harmondsworth, 1986).

78. Aldrich, in Ravenhill, *op. cit.* Cf. Danielsson, *op. cit.* and Henri Fages, 'Un intérêt majeur de la France en Océanie: le CEP', *Journal de la Société des Océanistes* 87 (1989), pp. 11–20; and Helen Fraser, *New Caledonia: Anti-Colonialism in a Pacific Territory* (Canberra, 1988).

79. Pierre Messmer, in 1986, stated that 'Wallis and Futuna are in a strategic position in the centre of the South Pacific and this will become increasingly important in the future.' Quoted in *Les Nouvelles calédoniennes*, 14 October 1986. The possibilities of using Clipperton as a military base are discussed in J.-P. Gomane, 'Perspectives de la France outre-mer', *Politique Etrangère* 50 (1985), pp. 419–35, and Philippe Leymarie, 'Les Enjeux stratégiques de la crise néo-Calédonienne', *Le Monde Diplomatique* 372 (March 1985), pp. 12–13.

80. See Guy Ladreit de Lacharrière, 'Le Droit de la mer dans le Pacifique-Sud', in Institut du Pacifique, *Pacifique Sud et Océanie* (Paris, 1984), pp. 154–61.

81. Much of this section is based on the presentations at a colloquium on 'La Vocation océanique de l'outre-mer français', organised by the Institut Français de la Mer, Paris, 16 June 1987, an unpublished paper distributed at the colloquium, Olivier Sevaistre and Alain Auger, 'Bilan et perspectives de l'outre-mer français', and the dossier on the French DOM-TOMs in *La Nouvelle Revue Maritime* 404 (1987).

82. J. Martray, 'L'Enjeu maritime des territoires français du Pacifique', in J.-C. Martinez (ed.), *La Nouvelle-Calédonie: La Stratégie, le Droit et la République* (Paris, 1985), pp. 161–6.

83. Bernard Pons, Minister of the DOM-TOMs, in *La Nouvelle Revue Maritime*, *op. cit.*, p. 8.

84. The annual report of IFREMER documents the organisation's scientific activities. Various other French organisations, such as ORSTOM, are also involved in maritime research in the DOM-TOMs.

85. Jon van Dyke and Robert A. Brooks, 'Uninhabited Islands and the Ocean's Resources: The Clipperton Island Case', in Thomas A. Chingan (ed.), *Law of the Sea: State Practice in Zones of Special Jurisdiction* (Washington, 1982), pp. 351-92.

86. Their concerns were apparently unfounded since in neither case were the leases extended for more than one year. See, for example, David Doulman, 'The Kiribati-Soviet Union Fishing Agreement', *Pacific Viewpoint* 28 (1987), pp. 20-39.

87. Excerpts from the Treaty of Rome and other relevant documents are reprinted as appendices in Victor Sablé, *La Politique de coopération régionale entre les DOM-TOM et les Etats ACP (Rapport au Premier Ministre)* (Paris, 1986) and in Ernest Moutoussamy, *Un Danger pour les DOM: L'Intégration au marché unique européen de 1992* (Paris, 1988).

88. Four Frenchmen from the *outre-mer* have been elected to seats in the European Parliament: two are the Martiniquais Jean Crusol (on the Socialist list) and the Réunionnais Paul Vergès (on the Communist list). From the Pacific territories, Gaston Flosse (French Polynesia) and Dick Ukeiwe (New Caledonia) have been elected on the RPR list.

89. Greenland, formally part of the EC, has now withdrawn from full membership.

90. Bernard Pons, 'Discours d'ouverture du Ministre des Départements et Territoires d'Outre-Mer à la Commission des Communautés Européennes', 2 June 1987.

91. Moutoussamy, *op. cit.*, pp. 7, 11, 20; see also William F.S. Miles, 'Electoral Flip-Flop in the French Caribbean: Mitterrand and Martinique', *French Politics and Society* 8 (1990), pp. 50-1.

92. Moutoussamy, *op. cit.*, pp. 48, 33.

93. See the reports, e.g. in *France-Antilles*, in January 1989. See also Yves Roland-Gosselin, 'POSEIDOM: Helping the French Overseas Departments to Cope with 1992', *The Courier* 116 (1989), pp. 52-5.

94. Sablé, *op. cit.*, pp. 25-8.

95. See Sablé for details. Sablé writes only about the DOMs, but many of his points are also applicable to the TOMs.

96. At a colloquium held by the Institut Français de la Mer, June 1987.

97. Jean-Pierre Gomane, 'Perspectives de la France outre-mer', *Politique Etrangère* 50 (1985), p. 419.

98. Jean-Claude Roux, 'Nouvelle-Calédonie: Un Noeud stratégique et une chance nationale', in J.-C. Martinez (ed.), *op. cit.*, pp. 167-76.

99. Quoted in *Pacific Islands Monthly* 52 (April 1981).

100. Raoul Girardet, *L'Idée coloniale en France* (Paris, 1972).

Chapter 10 The Ties that Bind

1. R.F. Holland, *European Decolonization, 1918-1981* (London, 1985), p. xii.

2. Jean-Claude Guillebaud, *Les Confettis de l'empire* (Paris, 1976), pp. 17–18.

3. Melanesians did not, however, gain the vote until the late 1950s.

4. The acquittal in Noumea in October 1987 of those charged with the ambush and murder of nine Melanesians at Hienghène, New Caledonia, by a jury that included no Melanesians has been seen as an example (see *Le Monde*, 9 August 1989).

5. Jean-Luc Mathieu, *Les DOM-TOM* (Paris, 1988), pp. 12, 46.

6. For Martinique, this is well summarised in graphic terms by Auguste Armet, 'Mal-développement et dépendance sanitaire et sociale aux Antilles "Françaises"', *Carbet*, 1 (1983).

7. Dominique Ghisoni, Wassissi Iopué and Camille Rabin (eds), *Ces Iles que l'on dit françaises* (Paris, 1988).

8. Although the level of such profits is uncertain. For example, the Indosuez bank has sold its branches in New Caledonia and French Polynesia to the Australian bank Westpac. (See *Le Courrier Australien*, November 1989).

9. Anon, 'Le prix d'un TOM', *La Nouvelle Revue Maritime*, No. 404 (1987), p. 3. As in the former Indian possessions there are, however, cases where citizenship has been retained but France provides little development aid.

10. See Stephen Henningham, 'French Spending in the South Pacific', *Pacific Economic Bulletin* 4 (1989), pp. 30–8.

11. See Chapter 8.

12. On possible *départementalisation* of the TAAF, see Alain Auger, 'L'Intérêt économique et stratégique des "Terres australes et antarctiques françaises"', in Institut du Pacifique, *L'Antarctique* (Paris, 1985), pp. 13–64.

13. On Pisani, see chapter 6; Institut du Pacifique, *Le Pacifique, 'nouveau centre du monde'* (Paris, 1986).

14. Guy Numa, *Avenir des Antilles-Guyane: Des Solutions existent* (Paris, 1986).

15. Paul Vallin, *Les 'Frances' d'outre-mer* (Paris, 1987).

16. The present authors are now preparing a full-scale comparative study of *The Last Colonies: Overseas Empires in the Contemporary World*; see also Aldrich and Connell, 'Europe's Overseas Territories: Vestiges of Colonialism or Windows on the World?', in H. Hintjens and M. Newitt (eds), *The Importance of Being Small: Micro Islands in the International System* (London, in press).

17. In addition, France has special relations with the sovereign states of Andorra and Monaco. The French President and the Spanish bishop of Urgel are co-heads of the State of Andorra. A French *fonctionnaire* is the Ministre d'Etat, the head of the administration, of Monaco. Furthermore, France is responsible for the defence of Monaco, and the Prince of Monaco, through a 1918 treaty, promises 'to exercise his right to sovereignty in perfect conformity with the political, military, naval and economic interests of France'. (*Juris-Classeurs, Principauté de Monaco*, 091 (1919), Fascicule 1). On Andorra, see André-Louis Sanguin, 'L'Andorre, micro-état pyrénéen: quelques aspects de géographie politique', *Revue géographique des Pyrénées et du Sud-Ouest* 49 (1978), pp. 455–74.

18. John Connell, *Sovereignty and Survival: Island Microstates in the Third World* (Sydney, 1988).

19. James G. Peoples, *Islands in Trust* (Boulder, Col., 1985).

20. François Burck, leader of the Union Calédonienne, quoted in *Le Courrier australien*, October 1989.

21. J.-M. Bohuon, 'Réflexions sur l'évolution des départements d'Outre-Mer', *Equinoxe*, 25 (1988), pp. 76–88.

22. See Eleonore Kofman, 'Dependent Development in Corsica', in R. Hudson and J. Lewis (eds), *Uneven Development in Southern Europe* (London, 1985), pp. 263–83 and Robert Ramsay, *The Corsican Time-Bomb* (Manchester, 1983). See also the special issue of *Peuples méditerranéens, Corse: Ile paradoxe*, No. 38–39 (1987); P. Hainsworth and J. Loughlin, 'Le Problème corse', *Contemporary French Civilization* 8 (1984), pp. 349–67; and Gilles Sénécal, 'L'Enigme corse: nationalisme périphérique et administration socialiste (mai 1981-mars 1986)', *Canadian Review of Studies in Nationalism* 15 (1988), pp. 121–9.

23. See Michael Keating, 'The Rise and Decline of Micro-Nationalism in Mainland France', *Political Studies*, 33 (1985), pp. 1–18.

24. There are nonetheless some comments on the virtues of *départementalisation*. Michael Manley, the Prime Minister of Jamaica, has recently observed: 'In the Caribbean we are accelerating the integration process because we will not survive as a set of disparate mini-states, unless we want to become a department of France.' (Altaf Gauhar, 'Manley Rides the New Wave', *South*, 105 (1989), p. 11).

25. Albert Ramassamy, *La Réunion, décolonisation et intégration*, (Saint-Denis, 1987), p. 8.

26. 'Parité' was the word used by Bernard Pons in the National Assembly in 1986, when he discussed social welfare payments and minimum wages in the DOM-TOMs and, in his argument, the impossibility of aligning these with metropolitan norms. Aimé Césaire, in his inimitable style, replied: 'Liberté, égalité, parité? — Chiche!' ('Liberty, equality, parity? How dare you!').

27. Quoted in John Connell, *New Caledonia or Kanaky?* (Canberra, 1987), p. 445.

Bibliographical Essay

IN THIS BIBLIOGRAPHY, preference is given to English-language sources, followed by standard and recent French accounts. Further detailed references are found in the notes to individual chapters.

There is much literature on the history of French expansion. Raymond Betts, *Tricouleur: The French Overseas Empire* (London, 1978) provides a useful introduction in English, as do the sections on France in D.K. Fieldhouse, *The Colonial Empires* (second edition, London, 1982). A standard French-language text on colonialism and imperialism is Jean-Louis Miège, *Expansion européenne et décolonisation de 1870 à nos jours* (Paris, 1986). The most recent study is Jean Meyer, *et al.*, *Histoire de la France coloniale. Des Origines à 1914* (Paris, 1991) and the companion volume, Jacques Thobie, *et al.*, *Histoire de la France coloniale. 1914–1990* (Paris, 1990). There are also two series on France overseas under the general editorship of Bernard Lauzanne; one series is organised chronologically, and the first volume is Jean Martin, *L'Empire renaissant, 1789–1871* (Paris, 1987); the second series is organised thematically. For other references to recent publications, see Robert Aldrich, 'A Note on the Renewal of Colonial Studies in France', *Contemporary French Civilization* 12 (1988): 263–8. As for decolonisation, see, in particular, Miles Kahler, *Decolonization in Britain and France* (Princeton, 1984).

The best-known work on the DOM-TOMs is J.-C. Guillebaud, *Les Confettis de l'empire* (Paris, 1976), a good journalistic account, although

increasingly dated. Even older is the illustrated volume by G. Lasserre
et al., *La France d'outre-mer* (Paris, 1974). J.-E. Vié, *Faut-il abandonner
les DOM?* (Paris, 1978) is a work by a former official in the DOM-TOM
ministry; both it, and P. de Baleine, *Les Danseuses de la France* (Paris,
1979) are critical of French policy. Sylvie Jacquemart, *La Question
départementale outre-mer* (Paris, 1983), discusses administrative questions. 'Les Iles où l'on parle français', a special issue of the geographical
journal *Hérodote* 37–38 (1985) covers the DOM-TOMs and other Francophone islands. Jean-Luc Mathieu, *Les DOM-TOM* (Paris, 1988) is
the most recent full-length, but rather technocratic, study. Mathieu has
also published a briefer and more historical study, *Petite histoire de la
Grande France* (Paris, 1989). More polemical are P. Vallin, *Les
'Frances' d'outre-mer* (Paris, 1987), a defence of the DOM-TOMs, and
the anti-colonialist collection edited by Dominique Ghisoni, Wassissi
Iopué and Camille Rabin, *Ces Iles que l'on dit françaises* (Paris, 1988).
Also critical is the work by a *député* from Guadeloupe, Ernest Moutoussamy, *Les DOM-TOM: Enjeu géopolitique, économique et stratégique*
(Paris, 1988). For up-to-date information on legal and institutional
questions, consult the authoritative *Juris Classeurs*, and for background, François Luchaire, *Droit d'outre-mer* (Paris, 1959) and François Miclo, *Le Régime législatif des DOM et l'unité de la République*
(Paris, 1982).

Material on the DOMs is scarce in English. William Miles, *Elections
and Ethnicity in French Martinique: A Paradox in Paradise* (New York,
1986), is one of the few academic studies, while Alexander Miles,
Devil's Island: Colony of the Damned (Berkeley, 1988), gives a readable
general account of Guyane. Not surprisingly, material in French is
easier to find. Two older books have become classics: Michel Leiris,
Contacts de civilisations en Martinique et en Guadeloupe (Paris, 1955)
and Daniel Guérin, *Les Antilles décolonisées* (Paris, 1956). On the
French West Indies in general, a useful compendium is a special issue,
'Antilles', of *Les Temps Modernes* 39 (1983). Three works by Alain-
Philippe Blérald, *Négritude et politique aux Antilles* (Paris, 1981), *Histoire économique de la Guadeloupe et de la Martinique du XVIIe siècle à
nos jours* (Paris, 1986), and *La Question nationale en Guadeloupe et en
Martinique* (Paris, 1988), are fine examinations of cultural, economic
and political questions, respectively. An important recent work with
quite a different interpretation is that of Fred Constant, *La Retraite aux
flambeaux: Société et politique en Martinique* (Paris, 1988). See also
Henri Descamps, *La Politique aux Antilles françaises de 1946 à nos jours*
(Paris, 1981) and Maurice Satineau, *Contestation politique et revendication nationaliste aux Antilles françaises: Les Elections de 1981* (Paris,
1986). On Guadeloupe, recent publications include Henri Bangou, *Les*

Voies de la souveraineté. Peuplement et institutions à la Guadeloupe (Paris, 1988) and Dany Bebel-Gisler, *Le Défi culturel guadeloupéen* (Paris, 1989). The best studies of Guyane are those of Serge Mam-Lam-Fouck, *Histoire de la société guyanaise: Les Années cruciales: 1848–1946* (Paris, 1987), although it does not cover the years after the Second World War, and Marie-José Jolivet, *La Question créole: Essai de sociologie sur la Guyane française* (Paris, 1982). Concerning cultural questions in the Creole DOMs: many of the works of Aimé Césaire and Frantz Fanon, two seminal figures, have been translated. Edouard Glissant, *Le Discours antillais* (Paris, 1981) is an important analysis and a more recent manifesto is Jean Bernabé, Patrick Chamoiseau and Raphaël Confiant, *Eloge de la créolité* (Paris, 1989).

There exists no full-length study in English of the other DOM, Réunion, or the two *collectivités territoriales*, Mayotte and Saint-Pierre and Miquelon. In French, see Marcel Leguen, *Histoire de l'Ile de la Réunion* (Paris, 1979); André Schérer, *La Réunion* (Paris, 1985), as well as the *Annuaire des Pays de l'Océan Indien*; Charles Guyotjeannin, *Saint-Pierre et Miquelon* (Paris, 1986); and Mabé Brolly and Christian Vaisse, *Mayotte* (Paris, 1989). As for the TAAF, see Institut du Pacifique, *L'Antarctique* (Paris, 1985) and Jean Robert, *L'Antarctique et la Terre Adélie* (Aix-en-Provence, 1990).

The Pacific TOMs are rather better served by English-language publications. In general, see Robert Aldrich, *The French Presence in the South Pacific, 1842–1940* (London, 1990), for the historical background. An older but still useful overview is Virginia Thompson and Richard Adloff, *The French Pacific Islands: French Polynesia and New Caledonia* (Berkeley, 1971). On the history of Tahiti, there is Colin Newbury, *Tahiti Nui: Change and Survival in French Polynesia 1767–1945* (Honolulu, 1980) and, for a highly critical view of French activities in French Polynesia in the past few decades, Bengt and Marie-Thérèse Danielsson, *Poisoned Reign* (second edition, Harmondsworth, 1986). On New Caledonia, many works in both English and French have been published since the political controversies of the 1980s; in English, see in particular John Connell, *From New Caledonia to Kanaky? The Political Economy of a French Colony* (Canberra, 1987), Myriam Dornoy, *Politics in New Caledonia* (Sydney, 1984), and Michael Spencer, Alan Ward, and John Connell (eds), *New Caledonia: Essays in Nationalism and Dependency* (St Lucia, Queensland, 1988). There is no full-length study of Wallis and Futuna in English; in French the standard but dated work is Alexandre Poncet, *Histoire de l'île Wallis* (Paris, 1971). As for other French sources, Michel Panoff, *Tahiti métisse* (Paris, 1990) supplies a good introduction to that island, and Pierre-Yves Toullelan, *Tahiti colonial (1860–1914)* (Paris, 1984) gives detailed historical background. On economic questions, an essential work is Gilles Blanchet, *L'Economie de la Polynésie française de 1960 à 1980* (Paris, 1985). The most thorough recent French study of New Caledonia is Alban Bensa, *Nouvelle-Calédonie: Un Paradis dans la tourmente* (Paris, 1990). See also the special issue, 'Nouvelle-Calédonie: Pour l'indépendance', of *Les Temps Modernes* 41 (1985) which provides references to more detailed works. For a more traditional viewpoint, there is Bernard Brou, *Trente ans d'histoire de la Nouvelle-Calédonie, 1945-1977* (Noumea, n.d.).

Various books place the French DOM-TOMs in their regional context and look particularly at French strategic and international interests. For instance, concerning the French presence in the Indian Ocean, see Philippe Leymarie, *Océan Indien: Le Nouveau Coeur du monde* (Paris, 1981); CHEAM, *La Réunion dans l'Océan Indien* (Paris, 1986) and Jean-Pierre Campredon and Jean-Jacques Schweitzer, *France, Océan Indien, Mer Rouge* (Paris, 1986). On the Antilles, see Louis Dupont, *Les Départements français d'Amérique* (Paris, 1988). And on the Pacific, Institut du Pacifique, *Le Pacifique, 'nouveau centre du monde'* (second edition, Paris, 1986); Jean Chesneaux, *Transpacifiques* (Paris, 1987); the special issue, 'La France et le Pacifique Sud', of *Politique Etrangère* 52 (1987); and 'La France et le Pacifique', a special issue of the *Revue française d'histoire d'outre-mer* 76 (1989). More generally, on French foreign policy, see Robert Aldrich and John Connell (eds), *France in World Politics* (London, 1989) and Alfred Grosser, *Affaires extérieures: La Politique de la France, 1944-1984* (Paris, 1984).

More specific information on the DOM-TOMs abounds, often in official publications or somewhat obscure periodicals. The French economic and demographic bureau, Institut National de la Statistique et des Etudes Economiques (INSEE), publishes much statistical information on the population and economies of the DOM-TOMs, and the departmental and territorial bureaus also have numerous publications; the Institut d'Emission d'Outre-Mer, the finance authority for the DOM-TOMs, produces annual reports on each of the *départements* and territories. The Centre National de Documentation des Départements d'Outre-Mer (CENADDOM) issues studies of the DOMs, as well as the journal *Les Dossiers de l'outre-mer*. Public and private organisations in the DOM-TOMs also publish journals; for instance, there is the *Bulletin de la Société d'études historiques de la Nouvelle-Calédonie* and, for French Polynesia, the *Etudes Océaniennes*; also covering the Pacific is the *Journal de la Société des Océanistes*. Political groups throughout the DOM-TOMs publish many pamphlets and other materials, most of which are unfortunately ephemeral. Some social science journals, such as *Equinoxe* in Guyane and *Carbet* in Martinique, have had an erratic publication history, but they contain interesting and useful articles. Much material on the DOM-TOMs is also published by the Institut Français de la Recherche Scientifique pour le Développement en Co-opération (still known by its former acronym, ORSTOM), the French publishing houses L'Harmattan and Editions Caribéennes and the French universities in the Antilles-Guyane, Réunion and the Pacific.

Current affairs are covered by the metropolitan newspapers, such as *Le Monde*, as well as such DOM-TOM newspapers as *France-Antilles*, *La Dépêche de Tahiti*, *Les Nouvelles-Calédoniennes*, the *Journal de la Réunion* and the *Journal de Mayotte*. There are also other periodicals, for instance, a monthly magazine in Mayotte, *Jana na Léo*, and the irregular newspaper of the Union Calédonienne in New Caledonia, *L'Avenir*. In addition, support groups for political movements in the DOM-TOMs issue newsletters in Paris, for example, the monthly *Kanaky* and the bulletin of the Centre d'Information Guadeloupe-Guyane-Martinique.

Finally, there are several specialised bibliographical aids, although not all the DOM-TOMs are covered. On the Pacific, Indian and southern Indian Ocean regions, a good reference book is François Doumenge, Alain Huetz de Lemps and Odile Chapuis, *Contribution française à la connaissance géographique des 'Mers du Sud'* (Talence, 1988); on the Antilles, there is the printed directory of the Bibliothèque Schoelcher, the *Catalogue du Fonds Local, 1883–1985* (Fort-de-France, 1987).

Glossary

Administrateur supérieur. The chief resident administrator in Wallis and Futuna and the head of the TAAF.

AEF. Afrique Equatoriale Française, the French colonial possessions in central Africa before 1960.

Ancien Régime. The period in French history preceding the Revolution of 1789.

Anciennes colonies. See *Vieilles colonies.*

Antillanité. Cultural identity of the Antillais, usually considered a mixture of African, European, and Caribbean values and traditions. *Antillanité* is often associated with the writer Edouard Glissant.

Antilles. West Indies.

AOF. Afrique Occidentale Française, the French possessions in west Africa before 1960.

Assemblée territoriale. Elected assembly in the French TOMs.

Assimilation. Policy current in the nineteenth century of a close attachment between the colonies and the *métropole*, implying administration of the colonies directly from Paris, a monopoly on trade and other economic activities by the *métropole* and a cultural integration of the colonies into the 'mother country'.

Association. Policy which replaced that of *assimilation* in the 1890s and allowed greater possibilities for political, economic and cultural autonomy between the colonies and France (with the maintenance, however, of central administration) and parallel development of colonies without full integration into the French system.

Bagne. The penitentiary in Guyane or New Caledonia; thus, *bagnards*: transported prisoners.

Béké. White residents of the *vieilles colonies*. The term is used exclusively for descendants of the old sugar planters and other early settlers, and usually refers to the prosperous white elite of Martinique, but also to that of Guadeloupe and Réunion.

Bonis. Groups of escaped slaves who settled in the Amazonian jungle of Guyane and often reverted to African traditions and ways of living.

Brousse. The countryside ('bush') of New Caledonia.

Caldoches. The long-term white settlers of New Caledonia, both the residents of Nouméa and the rural white population (*broussards*; see *Brousse*).

Cantonnement. In New Caledonia, the policy, begun in 1868, of confining Melanesians to *réserves* and expropriating their lands for European use.

Capitation. A head-tax levied on residents of some French colonies.

CEP. Centre d'Expérimentation du Pacifique, the nuclear testing facility in Mururoa and Fangataufa atolls in French Polynesia.

Circonscriptions. Electoral districts.

Code de l'indigénat. A code regulating native populations in some French colonies, such as New Caledonia, where it was instituted in the late 1800s. It allowed indigenous residents to be punished (by fines, labour or detention) for a wide variety of offences through administrative rather than judicial processes.

Code noir. Code, promulgated in 1685, which regulated the treatment of slaves in the French plantation colonies.

Collaborateurs. French people who collaborated with the Germans during the Nazi occupation of France in the Second World War, or, more broadly, those who supported the Vichy government of Marshal Pétain or the Axis powers.

Collectivité territoriale. The official legal status of Saint-Pierre and Miquelon, and Wallis and Futuna; in the former case, the status is similar to that of a DOM, while in the latter it more closely resembles a TOM.

Communes. French municipalities, each of which has an elected mayor and *conseil municipal*.

Comptoirs. The five small outposts of the French empire in India, that were given back to India in 1954.

Conseil constitutionnel. Government organ which assures the validity of elections and referenda and guarantees the constitutionality of French legislation.

Conseil d'Etat. French administrative body composed of experts which gives advice to the government on proposed legislation; the supreme administrative body in France.

Conseil économique et social. Local and national consultative committees on economic and social questions with some members elected and others appointed to represent various interests.

Conseil général. The elected council of each French *département*.

Conseil régional. The elected council of each French *région*.

Conseils de gouvernement. Consultative assemblies in French colonies or, in the case of French Polynesia, the executive of the *assemblée territoriale* according to the legislation of 1984.

Creole. The coloured population of the West Indies and the Indian Ocean, generally of mixed African and European ancestry. Creole is also the French-based language spoken as a vernacular by this population. More generally, Creole is the body of customs, traditions, clothing, music and food associated with this population. The word is also sometimes applied to the native European population of the *vieilles colonies*, especially as in '*blancs créoles*'.

Créolité. The culture of those islands colonised by France as plantation colonies (the French West Indies, Haiti, St Lucia, Dominica, Réunion, Mauritius and the Seychelles), often promoted as the authentic culture of these islands. The concept is also sometimes applied to other areas with mixed races and cultures (Brazil, other Caribbean islands, etc.).

Décentralisation. The project, implemented by legislation in 1982, which sought to decentralise French administration. For example, it gave greater powers to the *conseils généraux* and their presidents.

Demis. In French Polynesia, the population with mixed Polynesian and European or Chinese ancestry.

Départementalisation. The process which in 1946 made the *vieilles colonies* full-fledged *départements* of France.

Départements. One of the 110 administrative divisions of France, including the overseas *départements*. Each elects a *conseil général*, presided over by an elected president. The French state is represented in each *département* by a *préfet*.

Départements d'outre-mer (DOM). The overseas *départements* of Martinique, Guadeloupe, Guyane and Réunion, whose legal and political structure is, in principle, the same as in the metropolitan *départements*.

Député. A member of the lower house of the French Parliament, the Chambre des Députés (or Assemblée Nationale), elected by universal suffrage for terms of five years.

DOM. See *Départements d'outre-mer.*

EC. European Community.

EFO. Etablissements Français d'Océanie, which were Tahiti and the surrounding islands (the Leeward and Windward Islands of the Society Islands), plus the archipelagos of the Australs, Marquesas, Gambiers and Tuamotus. Renamed French Polynesia in 1957.

Elysée. Colloquial expression for the French presidency, from the name of the president's residence, the Elysée Palace.

Engagés. Indentured labourers recruited to work in the colonies, both Europeans and non-Europeans, especially Africans and Asians.

Exclusif. In theory, the proper relationship between France and its colonies in the *ancien régime,* in which the *métropole* maintained a total monopoly over trade with, export to and import from its colonies.

Fifth Republic. French political regime since 1958.

FLNKS. The Front de Libération Nationale Kanake et Socialiste, the pro-independence coalition in New Caledonia.

Fonctionnaires. Employees in the French administration, including government bureaucrats but also teachers and others who are part of the French civil service. Together they are the *fonctionnariat.*

Fourth Republic. French political regime from 1946 to 1958.

Francisation. Gallicisation, the process of 'Frenchifying' non-Frenchmen and women in language, culture and behaviour.

Francophonie. The concept used to organise the world's French speakers and, usually, the countries in which they live into a cultural unity with political overtones.

Front National. Reactionary and racist French political party of the extreme right, led by Jean-Marie Le Pen.

Gendarme. National French law enforcement officer.

Haut-Commissaire. High Commissioner; the chief French administrator in New Caledonia and French Polynesia (formerly called a 'governor').

Hexagone. The colloquial term for France, derived from the geographical shape of the European territory.

Indépendantiste. A supporter or promoter of independence for one or several of the DOM-TOMs.

Intendants. Regional officials, appointed by Paris, in the colonies of the *ancien régime.*

Kanaks. Melanesians who seek independence or support *indépendantistes.* More generally, the word is often used as synonymous with Melanesians.

Légion: Légionnaires. The French Foreign Legion and its members. The Legion was set up in 1831; in the DOM-TOMs detachments of the Legion are currently posted in French Polynesia, Guyane and Mayotte.

Loi-cadre. Type of French law which sets out in general terms a major change in legislation or regulation, such as the 1956 *loi-cadre* concerning the DOM-TOMs.

Marrons. Slaves who illegally fled from plantations and took refuge in mountainous regions or, in Guyane, in the jungle, or escaped overseas.

Matignon. Colloquial expression for the French prime minister and his staff, from the name of his residence, the Matignon Palace.

Matignon Accord. The agreement signed in June 1988 between the two dominant political groups in New Caledonia, the RPCR and the FLNKS, and the French government, on the future economic and political status of New Caledonia.

Métis. People of mixed racial background. In the French West Indies, usually those of African and European parentage; in Réunion, those with European, African, Malagasy or Indian ancestry; in Oceania, those of mixed Polynesian or Melanesian and European (or, sometimes, Asian) blood. *Métissé* is the adjective.

Métropole. France, the mother country, or more generally, any colonising power in relation to its overseas possessions. *Métropolitains*: people of metropolitan origin who may live overseas.

Mulâtres. Mixed-race residents of the West Indies and Réunion.

Négritude. Cultural movement which rediscovered and emphasised the significance of the African heritage of blacks in Europe and the colonies, and sought a new black identity and pride. The movement began in the 1930s and is associated with such writers as Aimé Césaire, Léopold Sedar Senghor and Léon-Gontran Damas.

Octroi de mer. A tax collected on all goods entering a colony, irrespective of their origin. Similar taxes were already collected in the *ancien régime*, but the *octroi de mer* was institutionalised in the nineteenth century. It continues to be collected in the DOMs and provides the main source of finance for municipal budgets.

Ordonnateur. A colonial official, second in the administrative hierarchy to the *intendant* or governor, responsible for the economic affairs and accounts of the colony.

Outre-mer. Overseas; in this instance, the French overseas areas.

Pacte colonial. Exclusive political and economic relationship between France and its colonies, especially during the *ancien régime*.

Parti colonial. Legislative group (and their supporters outside the parliament) which in the late nineteenth century promoted French expansion and the development of colonies.

PCF. Parti Communiste Français, the French Communist Party, currently led by Georges Marchais.

Petits blancs. Less prosperous white settlers in the French colonies, such as those who lived in the New Caledonian *brousse* or the *Hauts* of Réunion. Most are farmers or pastoralists, and many have been in the colonies for several generations.

Pieds-noirs. Former long-term European settlers in French Algeria.

Préfet. Prefect, the representative of the French state in each *département*. The prefects of the DOMs are charged with extra duties in addition to those exercised by prefects in the *métropole*.

PS. Parti Socialiste, the French Socialist Party associated with President François Mitterrand.

Rayonnement. The spread and promotion of the French way of life, French culture and French influence.

Région. One of 25 French administrative divisions, which group together several neighbouring *départements*. In the DOM-TOMs, however, the *régions* of Martinique, Guadeloupe, Guyane and Réunion each have only one *département*.

Réserves. Reservations in which Melanesians in New Caledonia were confined from the late nineteenth century to the Second World War.

Résistants. Those who continued resistance to the Germans after the fall of France in 1940 and refused to support the Vichy regime. The *Résistants* fought the occupiers and the Vichy regime inside France and allied with the Free French under the leadership of General de Gaulle outside France in the campaign for the liberation of the nation.

RPCR. Rassemblement pour la Calédonie dans la République, main conservative and anti-independence party in New Caledonia, currently led by Jacques Lafleur.

RPR. Rassemblement pour la République, French political party, conservative in ideology and seeing itself as the successor to Gaullism, currently led by former prime minister Jacques Chirac.

Rue Oudinot. The seat in Paris of the French colonial Ministry, later the Ministry (or Secretariat of State) of the DOM-TOMs; thus, these institutions.

Second Empire. French political regime, under Napoleon III, from 1852 to 1870.

Sénat. Upper house of the French parliament, composed of 318 members elected by universal adult suffrage for terms of nine years.

TAAF. Terres Australes et Antarctiques Françaises, including the islands of the Southern Ocean (Kerguelen, Crozet, Saint-Paul and Amsterdam) and Terre Adélie, the French region of Antarctica.

Territoires d'outre-mer (TOM). At present, French Polynesia, Wallis and Futuna and New Caledonia. According to the constitutions of

1946 and 1958, the TOMs are overseas territories in the French Republic, but have greater autonomy than do the DOMs.

Third Republic. French political regime from 1871 to 1940.

Tiers-mondisme. 'Third-World-ism', interest in and promotion of the Third World.

TOM. See *Territoires d'outre-mer.*

UDF. Union pour la Démocratie Française, centrist coalition of French political parties, whose members include former president Valéry Giscard d'Estaing and former prime minister Raymond Barre.

Vieilles colonies. Colonies which France took over in the 1600s which became *départements d'outre-mer* in 1946, Martinique, Guadeloupe, Guyane and Réunion. Also called *anciennes colonies.*

Index